# ULTIMATE AMBIGUITIES

# Ultimate Ambiguities
*Investigating Death and Liminality*

Edited by
Peter Berger and Justin Kroesen

berghahn
NEW YORK · OXFORD
www.berghahnbooks.com

Published by

*Berghahn Books*

www.berghahnbooks.com

**Library of Congress Cataloging-in-Publication Data**

Ultimate ambiguities : investigating death and liminality / edited by Peter Berger
and Justin Kroesen.
     pages cm
   Includes bibliographical references and index.
   ISBN 978-1-78238-609-4 (hardback : alk. paper) —
   ISBN ISBN 978-1-78238-610-0 (ebook)
   1.  Death--Social aspects--Case studies. 2.  Death--Religious aspects--Case studies.
3.  Funeral rites and ceremonies--Case studies. 4.  Liminality--Case studies.  I. Berger,
Peter, 1969- II. Kroesen, J. E. A. (Justin E. A.), 1975
   BD444.U478 2015
   306.9--dc23

                                                                                            2015007887

**British Library Cataloguing in Publication Data**

A catalogue record for this book is available from the British Library

Printed in the United States on acid-free paper

ISBN 978-1-78238-609-4 (hardback)
ISBN 978-1-78238-610-0 (ebook)

*In memory of Georg Schütte: friend, flatmate, anthropologist, dancer*

# Contents

# Part III. Imageries

# List of Illustrations

## Figures

## Tables

# Preface

Death provides the paradigm of liminality. This is evident from the fact that, frequently, periods of transition are symbolically associated with death. Yet, the many volumes on death in the social sciences and humanities do not deal specifically with liminality. The present volume investigates these ultimate ambiguities, assuming that, because of the disintegrating forces of liminality, they can pose a threat to social relationships but are nevertheless crucial periods of creativity, change, and emergent aspects of social and religious life.

The book explores ultimate ambiguities from an interdisciplinary perspective—mainly from social anthropology and religious studies—and presents a global range of historical and contemporary cases outlining emotional, cognitive, social, and political implications of death and liminality. What are the consequences of Christianization and Hindu fundamentalism for the Sora, a highland community of Middle India, whose practice of communicating over years with their departed via female shamans has now drastically been altered? How did family members of assassinated and disappeared victims of previous state terror in Argentina mourn their dead and what were the political consequences? How did ideas on death mark the changes in European history? What does a premortem liminal period mean in the case of Islamic fundamentalist suicide bombers?

Besides presenting specific cases, the volume also engages in debating death and liminality theoretically, drawing on contributions of writers such as Hertz, Turner, Durkheim, Ariès, and Elias.

We want to thank the Berghahn Books staff for their support and efficient work during all stages of the publication process.

*Peter Berger*
*Justin Kroesen*
Groningen, the Netherlands, August 2015

# Introduction

*Peter Berger*

> "I had lost my father. But at the same time, I had also found him. As
> long as I kept these pictures before my eyes, as long as I continued
> to study them with my complete attention, it was as though he were
> still alive, even in death. Or if not alive, at least not dead. Or rather,
> somehow suspended, locked in a universe that had nothing to do
> with death, in which death could never make an entrance."
> —Paul Auster, *The Invention of Solitude*

"Sure as death." This idiom refers to the quality of inevitability of a
certain phenomenon. In this sense, certainly, death is a sure thing.
However, beside the fact that as humans we all share the condition of a
limited lifespan, beyond the datum of inescapable annihilation at some
point in our lives, death remains distressingly ambiguous: "uncertainty
. . . surrounds death" (Bloch and Parry 1982: 17). We do not know when we
will die, or how, or where, let alone are we able to be sure of what follows
death or what the exact status of a deceased person is. This ambivalence is
brought out clearly in the scene referred to in the above quote from Paul
Auster's *The Invention of Solitude* (1982: 14). A son (the author himself) is
contemplating old photographs of his recently deceased father. Life and
death seem intertwined, but oddly so, not in any way one could be sure of.
Auster suggests different renditions of this entanglement of life and death
and the "or," and "or rather" indicate the irreducible uncertainty of the
situation. The ambiguities surrounding death are ultimate in two senses:
they refer to the end of a lifetime and they are so elementary. This volume
deals with various manifestations of such ultimate ambiguities.

Paradoxically perhaps, the elementary aspect of ambiguity can also be
framed as being its vital aspect. The fundamental ambiguities concerning death—and, as such, life—are not only extremely generative of ideas,
practices, and social relationships, but also of paradoxes and contradic-
tions. Hence, many scholars have claimed that death has been pivotal in

producing human cultural and religious forms. Bronislaw Malinowski ([1948] 1974: 47), for example, claimed that "[o]f all sources of religion, the supreme and final crisis of life—death—is of the greatest importance." Moreover, not only is death considered to be crucial in generating religion; religion is also said to be *about* death, and death rituals are understood to be *about* society and culture. Regarding the former claim, Edmund Leach (1976: 71) argued that the "central doctrine of all religion is the denial that death implies the automatic annihilation of the individual self." In connection to the cultural meanings of death, Richard Huntington and Peter Metcalf (1979: 2) wrote that, in all societies, "the issue of death throws into relief the most important cultural values by which people live their lives and evaluate their experiences." The contributions collected in this volume all testify to this communicative and creative power of death, in particular with reference to its inherent ambiguities.

As its main characteristic, the notion of ambiguity evokes the concept of liminality. Actors, objects, spaces, and times may have a quality of indeterminacy, or, as Victor Turner (1967) described it, a quality of being "betwixt and between." Not only does death share this quality of in-betweenness and ambiguity, but it can also be said to be paradigmatic of liminality. This is also shown in the fact that symbolisms of liminality very often draw on the imagery of death. Many anthropologists have described how novices have to "die" in order to be "reborn" in a new form of social existence. As such, it is astonishing that no anthropological study I know of deals with liminality explicitly in the context of death. The excellent contributions of Bloch and Parry (1980) or Humphreys and King (1981), for instance, do not consider the aspect of liminality in any specific way.

Though the situations and qualities of liminality are discussed in every chapter of this volume, it is not Turner's concept of liminality that is necessarily at stake. When thinking about liminality, Turner's work is obviously highly relevant, and several contributions explicitly deal with his work; however, this volume should not be misunderstood as a collection of test cases of his ideas. As is well known, Robert Hertz ([1907] 1960) was the first to deal extensively with the "intermediary" period found in death rituals that also involve a "secondary burial." He stressed that death should be understood as a process (rather than as an event) in the course of which the collective representation of death changes in connection with societal dynamics. In particular, he drew attention to the correspondence between the changing status of the soul, the body of the deceased, and the survivors. In connection to their intermediary status, Hertz (e.g., [1907] 1960: 36f) clearly formulated the prevalent qualities of marginality, impurity, anxiety, restlessness, and confusion typical of liminality. As many contributions to this volume show, Hertz's ideas still prove to be fertile ground in attempts at understanding death as a social and intellectual phenomenon.

Turner, strangely, does not refer to Hertz's crucial contribution in his key works on liminality; instead he makes the work of Arnold van Gennep ([1909] 1960) his main starting point. The latter's threefold scheme of rites of passage—the phases of separation, transition, and incorporation—has become commonplace in the humanities and social sciences. With reference to funerals, van Gennep makes some relevant general observations. While the rites of transition are often of very long "duration and complexity" (1960: 146), the rituals of incorporation are even more significant. Apparently, humans are very concerned about the final status and place of the dead, and, if these are not properly buried, the spirits of the dead remain liminal and are usually considered to be vengeful and dangerous (160). From the perspective of the living, death rituals are considered as a—at times, heavy—duty, but also as a fundamental right. The deprivation of this right by those in power has led to resistance in antiquity as well as in recent history. The famous case of Sophocles shows how unacceptable Creon's verdict not to bury Polyneices was to Antigone, who challenged the king's authority in order to pay her last respects to her brother. Creon's twofold outrage—to disregard what is sacred to the gods and to kill Polyneices a second time—had drastic divine consequences (see also Bremmer in this volume). Another example of the intolerability of enduring the uncertainty and liminality of the dead, or presumed dead, is provided by Argentina's recent history as discussed by Ton Robben (this volume). The military government obviously underestimated the potential and determination of the Mothers of the Plaza de Mayo, who were bereft of their sons and of any knowledge of their whereabouts, another unbearable form of ultimate ambiguity.

The concept of liminality, as developed by Turner on the basis of van Gennep's work, has been applied to all kinds of contexts in very diverse disciplinary frameworks. Being so widely employed has not always contributed to the sharpness and, hence, the usefulness of liminality as an analytical tool. Of course, Turner himself contributed to the dilution of the concept as he applied it to various situations himself and created a cousin of liminality, namely, the "liminoid" that "*resembles* without being identical with the 'liminal'" (Turner 1982: 32, emphasis in the original). While the liminal, Turner says, refers to ritual contexts in so-called tribal societies, with a stress on collectivity, seriousness, and obligation (also the disorder and license being prescribed), he describes as liminoid genres of modern art, literature, and science that emphasize individuality, play, and optionality (1982: 42f, 53f). What both have in common is their potential to challenge and temporarily set aside normative structures.

In my view, Turner's most important ideas concerning liminality are contained in his early writings, especially in "Betwixt and Between: The Liminal Period in *Rites de Passage*" (1967). During the liminal period in rites of passage, transitional beings are both not yet and no longer classified, and from this ambiguity springs its creative impact, liminality being "a realm of pure possibility whence novel configurations of ideas and relations may arise" (1967: 97). Thus, on the one hand, society and the "factors of existence" (1967: 106) are made the object of reflection, and imagination is let loose so that there is a chance of new ideas emerging. On the other hand, neophytes undergoing the ritual experience new forms of relationships among themselves, a community of equal individuals outside the normative social structure, something Turner later came to call "communitas" (1969: ch. 3). However, this potentiality is limited and restricted, and usually the status quo of society is reconfirmed and its key values reemphasized. After all, the function of the ritual process was to bring about a transformation in the status of particular persons and reconstitute society in so doing. This is the functional aspect of Turner's early contributions. As I read Turner, both aspects of liminality—the ideational and the social—are, or can be, connected to a third element of liminality: the sacred and secret objects he calls "*sacra*, the heart of the liminal matter" (1967: 102). These objects can be employed in various ways. They are exhibited to the neophytes, can entail normative views and instructions about society and the cosmos, and may invite speculative thinking about the world. What Turner holds for liminal situations in general is also true for the sacra: they are simple in form or structure but culturally complex and rich in interpretative potential. Considering the functional side of Turner's approach above, it is obvious that this part of his ideas reflects his cultural side and his stress on (the production of) meaning. When dealing with death, Turner's ideas offer a significant stimulus. Obviously, the "factors of existence" are never more at stake than in the contexts of death, and the corpse itself may assume the function of *sacra*. Death offers a creative space for rethinking life and reformulating social relationships because of its inherent ambiguity.

The volume is divided into three sections that deal with different dimensions of ultimate ambiguities. The first section is concerned with the description and analysis of contemporary ritual practices in liminal situations; the second section approaches ultimate ambiguities from a more theoretical angle, critically discussing analytical concepts, while mental and material images and imageries are the topic of the third section.

Empirically observed ritual practices and related ideas about death and liminality are at the heart of the first three contributions to the first section. They all deal with examples from the Indian context, especially

Indian tribal (Adivasi) communities that are otherwise hardly the focus of attention when ideas and practices concerning death in South Asia are being discussed. **Erik de Maaker** takes us to a contemporary highland society in the Northeast of the subcontinent, a community called Garo. His contribution is inspired by the work of Robert Hertz in that it analyzes the relationships between corpse, soul (ghost), and the living. De Maaker particularly focuses on the ambivalent status of various materializations of the dead prominent in the ritual process, most notably the corpse. He explores the nature of vitality that is significantly related to the corpse as the source of impurity (*marang*). But also other objects related to death are ambivalent as they have been made by the living and/or reside with them, yet are associated with the deceased. The most conspicuous of these objects is the effigy that is created on the second day of the mortuary ritual and set up in the yard of the deceased's house (as with the Kyrgyz yurt described by Hardenberg in this volume, close to but not in the house). This effigy not only symbolizes the deceased but it actually "re-presents" him or her. Some Garo hold that the ghost actually animates the effigy, and it is treated accordingly, especially being fed. With the effigy, the Garo turn death as an abrupt and dangerous event into a controlled ritual process. The effigy is subject to slow, gradual, and public decay, without, however, the dangerous pollution pertaining to the corpse. In the long ritual process of death, the living not only reorganize and renew their social relationships; ultimate ambiguities also provide the space for their reinterpretation.

While material objects play a significant role in the gradual process of transforming a dead person among the Garo, it is the communicative dimension that is stressed in the case of the Sora of Middle India. As **Piers Vitebsky** describes, the Sora regularly communicate with their dead via shamans; indeed, in their case, the realms of the living and of the dead seem to be mutually constitutive. Moreover, the ideas of the Sora concerning the dead also include a complex theory of suffering as a person joins a certain category of spirits after death and inflicts his or her own experience of suffering and death on kinsmen. In this way, the dead remind the living of their continuing relationship by making them ill and eventually causing their death. The dialogues with the dead, among many other things, create a space in which the deceased person can eventually be transformed from a virulent member of a category of illness into a benign ancestor that passes on his or her name to a child. In this way the living try to cope with the event and pain of death, and as the dead are transformed, so are the memories of them, from a painful and fearful memory to one unconnected to suffering. Vitebsky conceptualizes the dialogues as a shared experience and as a perpetual communitas of death and living.

but recognizes the messy nature of liminality and communitas, lacking clear-cut boundaries between "structure" and "antistructure."

**Peter Berger** compares the ideas and practices surrounding death in a tribal highland society of Middle India called Gadaba with those of high-caste Hindus. In both contexts, the dead are fed and, in the ritual process, become food as well. Beyond such similarities, fundamental differences are apparent too. The rituals of the Gadaba pivot around reciprocal exchange, assimilation, and replacement of the dead, while in the Hindu case such symmetrical transactions are out of the question. Here, impurity, inauspiciousness, and sin have to be transferred from the deceased to his or her son and to Brahman ritual specialists—such transactions precluding reciprocation. Not being a mere ritual detail, this difference between uni-laterality and symmetry points to quite different worldviews. For Hindus, death and rebirth is thoroughly "ethicized," as Gananath Obeyesekere (1980) has called it, and behavior during lifetime and the time of death directly affects the status of the next rebirth. In contrast, such moral considerations of merit and demerit are irrelevant in the Gadaba case. Their death rituals concern society and those affinal and agnatic relationships ensuring its continuation. Hindu death rituals are more ambivalent, as Nina Mirnig (in this volume) also points out. On the one hand, the transformation of the ghost into an ancestor is important, but a matter of the family and not of the community, as with the Gadaba. On the other hand, the value of liberation, a vital part of Hindu cosmology for centuries, permeates their view of death.

While the first three contributions of this section are based on ethnographic descriptions, the material of analysis, as well as the context of the described practices, are very different in the case presented by **Pieter Nanninga**. The deaths of suicide bombers deviate from the usual fate Muslims expect after death as well as from the common ritual process. So-called martyrs are said to enter heaven straightaway, and often there is no body that can be buried, as in the previous Argentinian example. Focusing on the well-documented suicide attacks of 9/11, Nanninga shows how the ritual process fits quite well with the general tripartite structure of rites of passage. Suicide bombers are separated socially, spatially, and mentally from society, and could be said to be reintegrated by the new genre of martyrdom videos. Significantly, however, liminality precedes and does not follow death. Premortem liminality is highly regulated, and everyday activities are strongly ritualized, orienting the attackers mentally towards the otherworldly realm and sacralizing their violent plans.

Violence is also an important dimension of **Ton Robben's** contribution to the second section of the volume, which discusses analytical concepts related to ultimate ambiguities. Among all contributions, the latter expression is perhaps most suitable with reference to the dramatic case presented and analyzed by Robben as he deals with the liminal processes that abducted persons and their relatives went through during and after the military regime in Argentina. In fact, liminality is multiplied and intensified in these cases, which is why Robben speaks of the "biliminality" of the disappeared and their searching kin. As noted before, the uncertainty of the fate of their abducted children was unbearable for the parents, who were not intimidated by the despotic violence and therefore inactive, as the regime had first assumed they would be, but began a relentless search for the disappeared that was then recognized by those in power as potentially politically disruptive. Robben shows that the liminal statuses of searcher and searched were interdynamic and at the same time had an impact on the changing political situation as they were shaped by it. After the new democratic government was elected in 1983, a collective death ritual was held that was supposed to provide closure. But while in a legal sense ambivalence was resolved for the disappeared, in the personal sphere this closure was often difficult to achieve, and politically it was even unwanted by many of the Mothers of the Plaza de Mayo.

In his analysis of Kyrgyz death rituals, **Roland Hardenberg** approaches the notion of liminality by focusing on three dimensions he suggests can be distinguished in specific ethnographic contexts: the emotional, the cognitive, and the social dimensions. In his case at hand, the emotional aspect is highly elaborated, as especially (but, significantly, not only) female relatives of the deceased are expected to mourn the dead for 40 days in a yurt that has especially been set up for this occasion. Hardenberg argues that it is through these intense, standardized, and prolonged mourning activities that a transformation of grief into a memory of the deceased is achieved. Regarding the cognitive dimension, the author contends that far from being a matter of antistructure, liminal time and space in Kyrgyz death rituals are highly structured, so much so that he speaks of "hyperstructure." The third, the social dimension, pivots mainly around sacrifice and commensality. While death breaks up relationships, as Hertz has noted, social relations are reconstituted through repeated situations of hospitality and food sharing.

In relation to the topic of this volume—death and liminality—**Peter Berger** discusses the analytical potential of a much-neglected concept: Durkheim's notion of collective effervescence. Much like Turner with his concept of liminality, Durkheim was concerned with understanding the emergent aspects of social life (beside the problem of continuity), and he regarded those assemblies that generate intense emotions, which in turn may trigger novel social and ideational forms, as crucial in this regard.

Partly building on the critical contributions of Lukes and Baumann, Berger argues that the social outcomes of effervescence are often too narrowly connected to uniformity of ideas and the production of social cohesion, while the effects of such experiences based on joined action are diverse and unpredictable. After a critical discussion of Tim Olaveson's comparison of effervescence and communitas, Berger suggests analytically distinguishing three types of effervescence: systemic, negative, and evenemential. This latter form is also a recognition of a blind spot in the anthropology of death, namely that, since Hertz's contribution, which stressed the processual aspect of death, anthropologists have tended to ignore death as an event. The three types of effervescence are discussed in relation to death as part of ritually structured life cycles and "dead-body politics" (Verdery 1999) in the public domain of bureaucratic societies.

The third and final section of this volume considers images and imageries of death and liminality, including ideas of the soul and its relation to the body, as well as its fate in the afterlife and material, musical, and textual representations thereof.

In ascetic terms, the ultimate experience and condition is certainly liberation, and one would perhaps expect little ambiguity about the ritual status of a person once liberation is thought to have been achieved. Yet, as **Nina Mirnig** argues, Shaiva tantric death rites revolve around a tension between worldly and transcendental orientation. In an attempt to be more attractive to mainstream Brahmanical society, which stresses the male role of householder when alive and of ancestor when dead, medieval Shaiva specialists accommodated their ritual practice, which led to several paradoxes that are still traceable in contemporary Hinduism. Originally for the Shaiva ascetics, liberation was already granted during one's lifetime by way of initiation but fully manifested itself only on the death of the person. From this perspective, postmortem rituals that deal with the transformation of a ghost into an ancestor were not only unnecessary but also contradicted the main value of liberation. However, a curious combination of both paths—communal and ascetic—was constructed, with one liminal period ending with death (when liberation was fully realized and, indeed, a second liberation ritual was included) and a second one beginning with death (the ritual transformation into an ancestor). In this situation, the author argues, it is difficult to say where a "ritual of passage" begins or ends.

**Justin Kroesen** and **Jan Luth** are concerned with a central ambiguity in the Christian theology of death. The question of the whereabouts of body and soul between the moment of death of a person and the Last Judgment has never been fully resolved by theologians. From the sixth century onwards, the idea of a personal judgment immediately after death became common, and the concept of the soul in Purgatory served as an image of its liminal status. Later in Protestant popular belief, the idea of death as sleep became very prominent, a feature the authors show with reference to the tombs designed by the seventeenth century Flemish-Dutch artist Rombout Verhulst and the music of Johann Sebastian Bach a century later. The works of Verhulst and Bach show that popular imagination developed largely independently from doctrinal views, such as Luther's and Calvin's divergent opinions of the nature of the sleep, and that representations of sleep and rest left room for different interpretations—for example, with regard to the relationship between body and soul. The occasion of a second general judgment after the individual first one appears to be unnecessarily redundant and is reminiscent of the double liberation discussed in Nina Mirnig's contribution. Both are examples of how cultural imagination and practice are necessarily entangled in inconsistencies and paradoxes in their attempt to come to terms with the ultimate ambiguity of death.

On the basis of textual and iconographic evidence, **Jan Bremmer** is concerned with the representations and practices of death in Archaic Greece (800–500 B.C.E.). He starts by noticing that the idea of *psyche* is not connected to emotional states, as we might assume from the common usage of the term nowadays, but is perceived as a vital aspect of a human being and, moreover, the basis of consciousness. It is the *psyche* that goes to the underworld, but only if the death rituals have been appropriately performed. As mentioned earlier in this introduction, the right to a proper burial (for the deceased) and the obligation (for the living) to perform death rituals are strongly evident in the Greek material. The three parts of death rituals—preparation of the corpse, procession, and cremation—show that death rituals, at least of the upper echelons of society, were highly public events. Moreover, not only were the rituals concerned with the transformation and passage of the deceased, the latter being de-individualized in the process, but they were also a demonstration of life—not a denigration of the here and now, but a celebration of society.

**Yme Kuiper's** contribution revisits the general theme we encountered before, the fear of loss and the attempt to preserve in the face of death and decay, and returns to the biographical dimension with which this introduction started. Also, it once more testifies to the vital, generative side of ultimate ambiguities as death and decay are transformed into a memorial novel. In his analysis of the context and content of Giuseppe Tomasi di Lampedusa's *The Leopard*, Kuiper shows how death, destruction, and degeneration are dealt with on different intersecting levels. The prince of Lampedusa only turned into a novelist shortly before his death and partly in order to come to terms with the destruction of his palace in 1943, the end of Sicilian nobility and his own life. Kuiper uses Edward Said's notion of "late style" — which resembles in significant ways the notion of liminality as it is outside time, creative, and concerned with the unconventional and abnormal — to conceptualize Lampedusa's transformation. The author transposes and relates his own experiences to his protagonist, his great-grandfather Don Fabrizio, Prince of Salina, and his historical context, the process of national unification after the conquest of Sicily in 1860 by Giuseppe Garibaldi. While Don Fabrizio experienced the beginning of the gradual decay of the Sicilian aristocracy, his alter ego Lampedusa perceived this process as being consummated during his lifetime and with his death.

**Peter Berger** (PhD Berlin 2004) is associate professor of Indian religions and the anthropology of religion at the Faculty of Theology and Religious Studies of the University of Groningen. He was a visiting professor at the University of Zürich in 2012 and visiting fellow at the Centre for Advanced Studies at the University of Munich in 2015. His books include *Feeding, Sharing and Devouring: Ritual and Society in Highland Odisha* (de Gruyter 2015), and he coedited *The Modern Anthropology of India* (Routledge 2013), *The Anthropology of Values* (Pearson 2010), and *Fieldwork: Social Realities in Anthropological Perspective* (Weissensee 2009).

# References

Auster, Paul. 1982. *The Invention of Solitude*. London: Faber & Faber.
Bloch, Maurice, and Jonathan Parry, eds. 1982. *Death and the Regeneration of Life*. Cambridge: Cambridge University Press.
Hertz, Robert. (1907) 1960. *Death and the Right Hand*. Aberdeen: Cohen & West.
Humphreys, S.C., and Helen King, eds. 1981. *Mortality and Immortality: The Anthropology and Archaeology of Death*. London: Academic Press.
Huntington, Richard, and Peter Metcalf. 1979. *Celebrations of Death: The Anthropology of Mortuary Ritual*. Cambridge: Cambridge University Press.
Leach, Edmund. 1976. *Culture and Communication: The Logic by which Symbols Are Connected*. Cambridge: Cambridge University Press.
Malinowski, Bronislaw. (1948) 1974. "Magic, Science and Religion." In *Magic, Science and Religion and Other Essays*. London: Souvenir Press, 17–92.
Obeyesekere, Gananath. 1980. "The Rebirth Eschatology and Its Transformations: A Contribution to the Sociology of Early Buddhism." In *Karma and Rebirth in Classical Indian Traditions*, ed. Wendy D. O'Flaherty. Berkeley: University of California Press, 137–64.
Turner, Victor W. 1967. "Betwixt and Between: The Liminal Period in *Rites de Passage*." In *The Forest of Symbols*. Ithaca: Cornell University Press, 93–111.
———. 1969. *The Ritual Process: Structure and Anti-Structure*. Chicago: Aldine.

————. 1982. *From Ritual to Theatre: The Human Seriousness of Play*. New York: PAJ.

van Gennep, Arnold. (1909, in French) 1960. *The Rites of Passage*, trans. Monika B. Vizedom and Gabrielle L. Caffee. Chicago: University of Chicago Press.

Verdery, Katherine. 1999. *The Political Lives of Dead Bodies: Reburial and Postsocialist Change*. New York: Columbia University Press.

*Part I*

# Rituals

*Figure 1.1.* The effigy of a man named Chengan, a few months after his death (photo Erik de Maaker).

*Chapter One*

# Ambiguous Mortal Remains, Substitute Bodies, and other Materializations of the Dead among the Garo of Northeast India

*Erik de Maaker*

When the news spread that Bansing had died, people reacted in a reserved manner. Bansing lived in a small village in the West Garo Hills of India, where it is customary, when a death occurs, for relatives and friends to go to the house of the deceased and pay their respects. Depending on their relationship to the one who died, they take on particular roles in relation to the funeral. When Bansing died, I was residing in another part of the same village. When I came to know of his death, I asked people there if they would go over to the house of the deceased. In reply to my question, a man said, "No one will attend his funeral; there will be no one there. It's not good." A women who had seen Bansing after his death explained the situation: "His entire face is swollen, and his stomach is bloated." This unusual condition scared people.

In a Garo cultural context, death always creates pollution (*marang*), which can be a cause of further deaths. Curious to know as to whether people would truly avoid the funeral, I went over to the house of Bansing. To my surprise, I encountered quite a few people there. The gazebo at the center of the courtyard was filled with men, albeit their mood somewhat subdued and not their usual joyful selves. Even though Bansing's death was frightening, the need to comply with the obligation to attend had taken precedence. But as if to keep their distance from the deceased, none of them touched the vessel of rice beer that had been provided by the household of the deceased.

Accompanied by a friend, I entered the house in which Bansing's dead body was kept in state. Around the corpse, a couple of women were holding a wake, as is customary. When I asked if I could take a picture of Bansing's dead body, my friend indicated that that was not possible. She did not want to explain herself, but I gathered that she considered it unwise to preserve an image of someone who had died a threatening death, as if the *marang* created by it might become part of the picture as well. At the time, no one was willing to talk about the cause of Bansing's death. But many months later, when it had become something of the past, people explained to me that the bloatedness of the corpse had told them that he had died of black fever (*kala azar*), a disease much feared since it is almost always lethal for the one who contracts it.

Bansing's death was experienced as exceptionally problematic, but even in more innocent cases, as when people die of old age, death brings about *marang*. This is particularly due to the corpse, its decay, and the resulting stench and secretions. To contain this *marang* as much as possible, people want to fairly rapidly dispose of a dead body, and do so within one, or at the most two, days after death has occurred.

In a Garo cultural context *marang* is an important concept. It is associated with death, as well as with blood and violence in general. It is dangerous, yet also conditional to social life. Childbirth involves blood and afterbirth, which are *marang*. Violent conflicts, and the weapons that people use to fight them, are also *marang*. Even the blazing fire that is used to clear the new swiddens is *marang*, as it can enclose people and kill them in an instant. Since *marang* is always dangerous, the containment and, if possible, purging of *marang* is a central cultural concern.

Yet, people's relationship to a corpse is ambiguous. Even though the corpse is firmly associated with *marang*, it is not only an object of fear, but also the previous embodiment and "likeness" of a person who died. For the survivors, it continues to maintain a very strong connection to the deceased person. Consequently, preceding the disposal of the corpse, the deceased is still so closely associated with his or her earlier existence as a living being that he or she continues to have a kind of social presence. So, a corpse is mourned over and cared for because of its close association to the deceased person, while it is simultaneously feared for its *marang*.

The corpse is also liminal, as it is in transition from its earlier state as a living body towards decay and disintegration. In order to control this transformative process as much as possible, people arrange for disposal through burial (common) or cremation (only rarely). The treatment encompasses several phases by which a corpse is step by step removed from its earlier existence as a social person. With this treatment, people set the pace: they temporalize, which gives them some sort of control over an otherwise dangerous process.

The liminality of the corpse, its "in betweenness" (van Gennep [1909] 1960) has consequences for other constituents of the mortuary process. In his well-known examination of secondary burials among the Berawan of Borneo (now Kalimantan), Hertz ([1907] 1960: 45) pointed out "correspondences" between the "trajectories" of the corpse, the deceased, and the survivors. Each of these transforms in the course of a funeral, and the weeks, months, and years that follow after. As already mentioned, the corpse is disengaged from its earlier role as a living person, and disposed of. The deceased, as a spiritual presence (such as a soul), gradually gains distance from the living, to settle in an afterworld. The mourners adjust their relationship with the diseased, eventually allowing them to redefine their social networks, ideally in such a way that they compensate for the loss they faced. Hertz noted that the various trajectories were not only connected, but also mutually interdependent, most specifically in that the transformation of the corpse, notably its decay and decomposition, defines the speed and degree at which the survivors can resume everyday social relationships.

In the introduction to this volume, Berger points at the significant connection between the ambiguity of death and its "vital aspect," the generative and creative potential of death. Death is often associated with fecundity and rebirth, but can also trigger "collective effervescence" among people. The latter notion was first introduced by Durkheim, who regarded mourning a collective rite that can bring about a state of heightened consciousness in those who engage in it ([1912] 2008: 276). In his discussion of effervescence, Berger (ch. 7 in this volume) notes that some mortuary rituals aim to overcome and avoid such situations, while other control effervescence by integrating it systematically in the ritual process. Rather than completely suppressing the vital aspect of funerals, they translate the threat posed by death and the vulnerabilities it reveals into rituals that facilitate the "regeneration" of society (Bloch and Parry 1982). This revitalization, Bloch and Parry maintain, tends to be aimed at the resource that "is *culturally conceived* to be the most essential to the reproduction of the social order" (7, emphasis in the original). In this chapter, I explore the nature of the vitality of Garo mortuary rituals, and the ways in which vitality is dealt with. More specifically, I trace the temporalization of the mortuary process, as well as the impact it has on mortal remains, substitute bodies, and other materializations of the dead. I argue that the ritualization imposed does not only result in a controlled and gradual change of the presence of the dead. It also provides people with the possibility of engaging the dead, which has very real consequences for the social networks that they themselves create.

## Death and the Continuation of Marriages

The Garo are the majority community in the Garo Hills of India, the westernmost extension of a hilly range crammed between the Brahmaputra valley (to the north), and the plains of Bangladesh (in the south). From colonial days onwards, the Garo classify as a tribal community. In India, "tribe" is generally associated with (among others) an acephalous, kin-oriented social organization and a subsistence-oriented mode of production. Most communities categorized as tribal in fact comply with such characteristics only to a certain degree, if they do so at all. More in general, the term "tribe" is applied—somewhat arbitrarily—to communities that are considered marginal to mainstream Hindu- and Muslim-dominated society (Béteille 1998).

Nowadays, the majority of the Garo are Christians, which is a relatively recent phenomenon (De Maaker 2013). Until the 1970s, most Garos appear to have been Songsareks, practitioners of the traditional Garo religion (Burling [1963]1997: 336). Songsareks now constitute a substantial minority among the Garo, albeit notably in certain clusters of villages in the western and southeastern part of the Garo Hills. The data analyzed in this chapter, some of which has also been included in my earlier work (De Maaker 2006), derives from one of the Songsarek majority areas in rural West Garo Hills. These were collected during field visits conducted between 1997 and 2014, including an intensive two-year fieldwork period between 1999 and 2001. The area had (and has) a sizeable Christian minority, and all kin groups included both Christians and Songsareks, so death rites performed for deceased practitioners of the traditional religion always involved Christian participants as well. The only way in which Christians would distinguish themselves there was through disengagement with aspects of the rituals explicitly referring to the Songsarek deities.

According to the Songsareks, the world is populated by numerous deities (*mitde*), of which only a few are known to men. These *mitde*s are of a predatory nature, as it is their inclination to suck "life fluid" from people, animals, and plants. People thus find themselves in an essentially hostile environment, and require the protection of some of these deities in order to survive. This propitiation is the responsibility of entire villages, but essential offerings can only be made by (or on behalf of) the village head (*nokma*). Engaging the deities expresses and solidifies people's claim to land surrounding their village, also vis-à-vis possible claims made by adjacent villages.

The position of the village head does not only depend upon his role as a prime sacrificer. Equally significant, he is considered the eldest kin of all the village's residents. Garo trace matrilineal kinship, and descent is reckoned from grandmother, to mother, to daughter. Generally, residence is matrilocal: couples live in the village of birth of the wife. The wife of the village head is considered a direct descendant of the wife of the first headman and is, as such, the one who has taken her place. This combination of descent and replacement is a general principle and results in extensive classificatory kinship. In addition to real kin (by birth), every Garo has many classificatory mothers, grandmothers, fathers, sisters, brothers, and so on. It is not uncommon for people to have classificatory grandparents who are younger than they are themselves. The double principles of descent and replacement-linked-to-residence give rise to "houses" (*nok*) (as in the "House of Windsor"), units of relatedness, rights, and property that are sustained through time. Similar to the house societies of Southeast Asia (Waterson 1990; Carsten and Hugh-Jones 1995: 3), Garo houses provide shape to house-oriented villages. Garo villages consist of clusters of houses, inhabited by women who trace kin ties to one another.

As a rule, men marry into villages other than their own. These marriages imply alliance relationships between husband-givers and husband-takers, which are notably in the case of prestigious houses (such as those of village heads) continued over many generations. The alliance relationships are maintained between localized matrilineal kin groups and allow men from one village to marry into another one. Villages, matrilineages, collectively hold onto land that is transferred in the female line. Marriage alliances should be continued upon death; at least that is the commitment that comes with a marriage for the larger constituent kin groups to which the partners belong. Close relatives of a person who has died should replace him or her with someone to take his or her place. This ensures continuation of the marriage alliance, and thus sustenance of a house and all that belongs to it. Marriage alliances are important, particularly for those houses that hold title to land.

Funerals are essential for the continuation of marriage alliances, since the replacement of deceased husbands and wives is ideally negotiated before the disposal of the corpse. The obligation to replace a deceased person, and thus honor the commitment that comes with a marriage alliance, is then fulfilled at a time that the deceased still has some sort of a social presence among the living. The dead are thus of great relevance to the relationships that people trace and to the kind of entitlement and claims that these relationships bring forth.

## Transformations of the Soul

People consider life and death as distinct states of being that are closely connected. Everyone who is alive has a *janggi*, a soul. Such a *janggi* can't be seen, and is without substance. Yet, it manifests itself in wind, as a breeze. It is this breeze that enables and requires people who are alive to breathe. In breathing, the taking in and blowing out of air, and the concomitant movement of the chest, the presence of the *janggi* shows.

*Janggis* are presumed to exist preceding the birth of a child. *Janggis* are believed to be free floating and longing to embody a child that has not yet been born. Initially, when inside the womb, a fetus is thought to be without a *janggi*. Upon connection to the fetus, the *janggi* makes the fetus move. In other words, once a mother-to-be feels that the fetus in her belly moves, she knows that it has obtained a *janggi*. The *janggi* remains permanently connected to the body, even though during life it can temporarily move out of the body, resulting in out-of-body experiences. Death occurs when there is an irreversible separation between the *janggi* and the body, which implies that the person stops breathing. This separation transforms the *janggi* into a *mi'mang*, a ghost (Christians are, according to the official religious tenets, not supposed to go along with this, since these state that, upon death, the *janggi* goes to heaven).

A *mi'mang* maintains a strong association with the corpse and whatever remains of it after burial or cremation. All material objects relating to the deceased are in one way or another believed to be imbued by its *mi'mang*. The *mi'mang* tends to manifest itself as the person it was during life, in the dreams of close relatives of the deceased person, notably in the days and weeks soon after death.

The *mi'mang* is of an ambiguous nature. On the one hand, it is the closest people can get to someone who died, a loved one who is missed but cannot be interacted with any longer. On the other hand, a *mi'mang* belongs to the realm of the dead and poses danger to the living.

The afterworld, usually referred to as Balpakram (also a place within the geographical confines of the Garo Hills), is imagined as the realm of *mi'mangs*. People presume that existence there in many ways resembles life on earth. But relocation to Balpakram does not restrict their presence in a variety of objects among the living as well. Similar to the Songsarek deities, *mi'mangs* are also believed to be omnipresent.

Songsareks seldom attribute death to natural causes such as old age. Rather, death is believed to occur due to people being bitten by a deity or an animal. A person who has been bitten becomes weak (*jomoa*). This attracts *mi'mangs*, who try to abduct the ill person's *janggi* to the afterworld. *Mi'mangs* can bite as well. Such biting results in further weakening. If the *mi'mangs* succeed in their attempt at abduction, the *janggi* leaves (*janggi chota*). This causes the person's breathing to stop and results in his or her death. People who had been severely ill told me that among the *mi'mangs* that tried to abduct them were deceased relatives. People presume that these deceased relatives want to continue the relationships that they have maintained during earlier life and thus take their husband, wife, child, brother, or sister along with them to the afterworld. Since *mi'mangs* can inflict death, people are scared of all of them, even of their own deceased relatives. Nevertheless, once a person has died, the *mi'mangs* who have killed him or her are supposed to guide the deceased to the afterworld. This ambiguity finds expression during a funeral. At that time, food is provided to the *mi'mangs* who are expected to collect and guide the deceased to the afterworld. With the removal of the corpse from the house, these *mi'mangs* are chased away.

## The Mortal Remains: Transformation, Disposal, and Abandonment

As mentioned in the introduction, the corpse is approached with ambivalence. It represents *marang* but is also closely associated with the person who the deceased used to be. The deceased person needs to be honored and prepared for his or her relocation in the afterworld, which aligns with the preparations of the corpse for disposal. The treatment of the corpse and the subsequent handling of its remains are believed to influence the fate of the *mi'mang*.

The *mi'mang* is also associated with the personal belongings of the deceased person, particularly those that have been close to his or her body and have his or her sweat, such as clothing and bedding. People also use the close association of the corpse to the *mi'mang* to associate certain objects with it. As the corpse is laid out, they place coins and heirloom jewelry on it that will become important gift items later on in the mortuary ritual.

Mortuary rituals are preferably conducted from the house in which someone lived. In the house, close relatives of the deceased person undress the corpse and place the bare dead body on a sleeping mat and some blankets or bed sheets. It is covered with several layers of large cloth. Only the head, hands, and feet are exposed. This arranging in state confirms the transition of the deceased from a person who used to be alive into a corpse that is about to be disposed of.

A wake is held around the corpse for a period of a half to one and a half days. The corpse is normally disposed of on the second day of the mortuary ritual. The removal from the house, followed by either burial or cremation, is said to initiate the journey of the *mi'mang* of the deceased to the afterworld. This is normally done at dusk, which is believed to be the time of day that suits *mi'mang*s best. The disposal is thought of as beneficial for the *mi'mang*, since it liberates him from being too closely connected to the living. At the same time, it is an act of violence. After all, the removal from the house ends his or her physical presence in the house he or she once lived in.

The removal of the corpse from the house is ritually marked in a variety of ways, in which affection with and connection to the deceased are expressed, as well as the need for separation. First, a mother of the deceased person pours some "water for *mi'mang*" (*chimi'mang*) into the mouth of the deceased. Someone told me, "This water is given to the *mi'mang* since the road to the afterworld is long and hot. Unless water is offered, its throat will get dry." That woman then ties a sling over her left shoulder—a gift for her from the household in which the death has occurred. People told me that a sling, tied over the left shoulder, allows the *mi'mang* of the deceased person to be carried in it (in everyday life, a sling is tied over the right shoulder), thus providing that woman with the capacity to carry the *mi'mang* of the deceased home. She then bathes the corpse. The bath is the last treatment given to the corpse before it is taken out of the house.

It is men's work to shroud the corpse and take it out of the house. Two men carry the shrouded body to the front door and over the threshold into the courtyard. This passage is again ritually marked. When the corpse passes through the door, a woman smashes an earthenware rice cooking pot on the floor of the rear of the main room, and exclaims something like "My child was born to live, born for a place! Oi Challang! Oi!" With the breaking of the pot, and the exclamation that accompanies it, people express grief about the death that has occurred. "Challang" is a mythical ancestor, invincible, and reference is made to his name to indicate that the death that has occurred does not pose a threat to the continuity of the matrilineage. The breaking of the pot also indicates separation, the end of sharing meals with the deceased. Even stronger, it also shows that the deceased is no longer welcome to have food inside the house, and indeed, from then on, he or she is only being fed in the courtyard.

During the past couple decades, burial has become the dominant mode of disposal. Burials are conducted in a dedicated plot of forest. At the burial ground (*gopram*), graves are hard to locate, since they are not marked and become quickly overgrown with weeds and shrubs. Graveyards are perceived as places where "everywhere corpses could be buried" as someone remarked, and men who dig a grave sometimes chance upon the skeletal remains of an earlier burial. The mortal remains continue to be associated with the dead in general, but do not serve as places to commemorate them. Graveyards are places were *mi'mang*s are believed to manifest themselves, particularly at night. *Mi'mang*s can show themselves either as the people they used to be, or as skeletons, and people therefore treat graveyards as secluded areas. Any sort of cultivation is prohibited at a graveyard, as is the harvesting of fruit-bearing trees, hunting, and the logging of wood or bamboo. At graveyards, the location of mortal remains, people primarily fear the dead.

Previously, most corpses were cremated, and cremation still figures in relation to dead who are attributed a high social status, but also those who have died in a way that is considered dangerous for the survivors. Over the last couple of decades this has changed, and nowadays most of the dead are buried. People claim that this is motivated by a burial requiring considerably less work than a cremation. It is likely that this changeover has been inspired by Christian practices, which have become widespread throughout the Garo area. In South Asia, Christians always bury their dead. In a way, Christian practices prove to Garo people that a burial suffices, in most cases, to contain the "death pollution" (*marang*) of the corpse. Nevertheless, people continue to regard cremation as "true custom" (*niam chongmot*). Cremation, the rapid destruction of the corpse, radically controls the putrefaction that the corpse is subject to, and is considered very effective in containing the *marang* that it is associated with. It is also regarded the most respectful treatment towards the deceased person. People of high repute, such as a village headman or his wife, are likely to be cremated, particularly if they themselves have insisted that their corpse be treated as such. In being more traditional and more thorough, it is believed to be more satisfactory for their *mi'mang* than a burial.

A pyre, lit in the evening, burns for many hours. By the next morning, when it has turned into a heap of smoldering ashes, people collect some of the bones. Later that day, they bury these in the courtyard. Funeral pyres are made in the forest, and people abandon the rest of the remains. In the wet season, shrubs and bamboo quickly cover a former cremation ground. The place is avoided for one or two years, but in the long run no restrictions apply to its usage, and it has no relevance for remembering the deceased.

The few pieces of bone that have been collected from the pyre are buried in the courtyard in front of the house in which the deceased person lived. The woman who has collected the bones wraps these in a piece of white cloth, and puts them into a hole that has been dug. The hole is sealed with a flat stone, and covered with earth. A repository (*delang*) is subsequently constructed over the buried bones.

The repository is a rectangular box about five feet long, two feet wide, and three feet high. Rice on the ear, which people who attended the mortuary ritual brought for the deceased, is put into the repository. Unginned cotton that was also presented to the deceased is put in one or two baskets that are kept on or next to it. I was told more than once that the rice and cotton are seed grains to be used by the dead person in the afterworld. Other gifts that people have made to the *mi'mang* are also kept in, or tied to, the repository, and thus brought within the vicinity of the bones. Among these are usually more than a dozen dried gourds, which are said to enable the *mi'mang* to draw drinking water in the afterworld. The transition of the *mi'mang* to the afterworld thus comes coupled with the idea that the survivors should enable it to start a new life there. A funeral is a rite of separation, but it is also a new beginning. Death is closely associated with the regeneration of life, as Bloch and Parry (1982: 9) have shown. Here, this is evident in the seeds that are provided to the deceased and the gourds meant for drawing water.

When a corpse is buried, there are no bones to be brought back to the village, but that does not keep people from making a repository that is dedicated to the deceased person. At the repository, daily food offerings are made to the deceased. A woman explained to me that *mi'mang*s are fussy about food: "What is given in the evening should be thrown away in the morning. What is given in the morning should be thrown away in the evening. . . . Just like a human, it won't eat food when it is given fresh food on top of rotten rice." If the *mi'mang* of a deceased person has consumed the food provided, the constitution of that food is believed to change—the actual food remains; *mi'mang*s don't physically eat. But food that has been "consumed" by a *mi'mang* turns brown and attains a bad smell.

A repository is kept for about two weeks, and then it is burned. Ideally, a repository should be kept until the first new moon that follows the death. In practice, the repositories of common people are destroyed after ten to fourteen days, irrespective of the position of the moon. Its destruction again induces an important transformation of the ties between the deceased and the people who he or she earlier lived among. The burning of the repository concludes the period immediately following death, throughout which people have cared for the deceased person on a daily basis. When I was walking towards a village in which later that afternoon a repository would be burned, a man asked me, "Are you going to attend the discarding of her *mi'mang*?" (*mi'mang galgenma*). The burning of the repository brings the separation of the deceased from the living significantly further.

After the burning of the repository, the buried pieces of bone in the earth underneath (if present) cease to act as a reference to the deceased.

People know that certain places in a courtyard "have bones" (*greng donga*), but they forget about their precise location. From time to time, houses are rebuilt, which usually entails being shifted to a different location. Eventually, a courtyard is abandoned and becomes jungle again. Initially, such an old ward is referred to as an "old village" (*songgitcham*), and left untouched. But after one or two generations, the land can again be put to any use, even to make swiddens or plantations. The mortal remains, and the places where bones are buried, thus completely stop being connected to the deceased.

## A New Embodiment for the Deceased Person

The remnants of the corpse quickly lose their significance, certainly as objects of remembrance of the dead. Instead, after the funeral, a substitute body is created for the diseased. This is an effigy (*kima*), made of wood or bamboo, that comes to be regarded as a new embodiment of the deceased person. The effigy is placed in the courtyard, a few yards to the left of the house of the dead man or woman, facing it. People emphasize that the effigy is made "to the likeness of a person" (*mande dakgipa*). Or, as someone put it, "Its flesh [body] is made to resemble that of the deceased person."[1] A man who is skilled at woodwork uses a chopper to cut a head in one of its ends. With black paint, consisting of blood from a cow slaughtered at the funeral mixed with soot or with crushed carbon from an old battery, he paints eyes, ears, and a mouth. He also draws a necklace on the effigy and places numerous dots all over its face.

It is not just in its features that the effigy is made to relate to the deceased person, but also by dressing it in the best of his or her clothes. It is adorned with cheap, nonheirloom jewelry. The clothes and jewelry have usually been kept on the dead body while it was laying in state. The earrings that are used for the effigy were left on the ears of the deceased until the corpse was about to be shrouded. Women who qualify as mothers to the deceased person dress the effigy, together with the man who has done the wood carving. They make the effigy of a man wear a shirt and a jacket. An effigy of a woman is dressed in festive, bright, contrasting colors. Each effigy is made to wear a turban, which is adorned with a plume of cock's tail feathers. The dress, and particularly the cock's tail feathers, make it appear as if the effigy is ready for the grand annual postharvest celebration (*Wangala*), which is the only occasion for which people dress up like this. The dead are not presented as poor and needy, but in their best clothes, as respected, affluent, and proud. Being poor and needy makes one vulnerable, which is considered dangerous and undesirable for the living as well as for the dead. An umbrella is placed above the effigy, providing it with protection against sunshine and rain. Small personal possessions of the deceased person, such as slippers, a comb, and a toothbrush, are put on the effigy as well. The sling bag of a dead man is hung onto it, with whatever betel nuts, tobacco, and money it contains. Arms are only made for the effigies of men, and if a man had a walking stick, it is put under one of the arms.

Many people believe that the association between the effigy and the deceased person is so strong that his or her *mi'mang* is able to animate it. I met people who claimed that—either in real life or in dreams—they had seen effigies "move around" or even "dancing in the courtyard at night." These kind of stories can scare people a great deal. Referring to such a belief, an elderly women expressed dislike that the effigy made for a young woman was given a basket to wear. She said, "It makes her effigy restless, always wanting to go here and there. It charges it with an urge to work." The strong identification of an effigy with a dead person is reflected in *niam* (customary law), equating it in certain respects to a living person. To take something away from an effigy is an offence, as serious as stealing from someone. To hack at an effigy with a chopper or a sword is equated to an attempt at murder. Effigies are attributed senses, comparable to people. They need to be dressed (in the best possible way) and can be hurt. Yet, if they manifest themselves beyond their everyday ordinary stationary selves and come alive, they are feared like the walking dead.

The effigy allows for the presence of the deceased person close to the house in which he or she lived, yet not inside that house. Here, the use of clothes and other personal possessions of the deceased on the effigy is of relevance. These belong to the *mi'mang* and cannot remain inside the house in which the deceased lived. The clothes, bedding, and other personal belongings (such as sandals, comb, and toothbrush) of a dead man or woman cannot be used by other people. Apart from the clothes that are used to dress the effigy of the deceased person, the remaining personal belongings are cremated with the corpse, left on the grave, or thrown into the forest. It is believed that a *mi'mang* attacks anyone who dares to take from it.

The surrogate body, which an effigy is, is subsequently subjected to a delayed, slow process of decay and gradually loses its identification with the deceased person for whom it was made. Nothing that drops from an effigy is ever put back onto it. In the courtyard, the effigy is exposed to heat, wind, rain, and sunshine, and to insects such as termites. The clothes wear, tear, and eventually fall off. As the wood rots, the features of the face are the first to disappear. Six to ten years after its creation, an effigy has completely vanished. As a surrogate body, the effigy lacks blood. Consequently, perhaps, its decay does not involve the *marang* that is such a central concern with the decay of a physical body.

As long as an effigy stands, it enables the household that has planted it to make offerings to the dead person represented by it. Every year, households should offer some of their new swidden maize to the dead. Maize is the first crop to be harvested. A man said, "We cannot eat the new maize until some of it has been given to the *mi'mangs*." The presence of an effigy allows a household to make incidental offerings of rice beer to the dead as well. Once, a woman offered some rice beer to her son. She told me, "I give it, thinking he [the *mi'mang* of her son] may want to come to his mother." As long as an effigy stands, a household can make offerings to the dead that it represents. Once the poles have vanished, such offerings can only be made at less dedicated locations, if they are made at all.

An effigy can last for months or even years, but it is never more than a temporary representation. Initially, it is explicitly identified with the deceased for whom it has been made. As it degrades, this association becomes less obvious, and people may forget what dead person it is associated with. The protracted decay of the effigy allows for a gradual diminishing of the social presence of the deceased among the living. In their choice of materials, and the effigy's exposure to the elements, people set the time for this slow decay and thus for the duration of the continued presence of the deceased in the courtyard where he/she once lived.

## The End of Cooking

Feeding is an important social act. As long as someone who has died is fed, he or she is remembered. Feeding a deceased person implies that he or she has a presence among the living. As long as the corpse is around, the deceased is given food inside the house. After the corpse has been removed from the house, the deceased is fed at the repository, in the courtyard, and then occasionally at its effigy.

People start providing cooked food to the *mi'mang* soon after the corpse has been laid out. Only married women who classify as kin of the deceased can cook "food for *mi'mang*" (*mimi'mang*). In preparation, they bring some swidden rice and an egg. A woman argued that "*Mi'mangs* do not like the curry made with dried fish that people eat. They like egg. For them, egg resembles beef." Each of the women cooks her *mimi'mang* in turn, at the fireplace in the main room of the house. This fireplace is normally never used for the preparation of food. The food is cooked in an old earthenware pot, with "water for *mi'mang*." This is water kept in a gourd that is black with soot. "*Mi'mangs* don't like things clean, but old and dirty," a woman said. Once cooked, the food is wrapped in leaves. The leaves are folded in such a way that the top of the packet remains open, with the halved egg clearly displayed on top of the rice. "That way, the *mi'mang*s know it is meant for them," I was told. Food packaged for consumption by people requires the leaves to be folded very differently, so *mimi'mang* is always clearly distinguishable. The packages with *mimi'mang* are placed on either side of the head. In addition, women bring biscuits, areca nuts, bananas, and folded leaves with flattened rice (*rongchu*), as food for the deceased person. Once the corpse has been taken out of the house, all this food is discarded in the forest. People eat none of it.

Throughout the first days or weeks following a death, people of the household in mourning provide daily food offerings at the repository. There, they should again offer cooked rice with egg, preferably at dawn and dusk. Ideally, this should be food cooked especially for the *mi'mang* in the courtyard. Prosperous households can afford the two daily food offerings, but for the poorer ones, these are a real burden. Rather than cooking food twice a day especially for the *mi'mang*, they may offer once a day a little of the food that has been cooked for the people of the household.

When the repository is taken apart and burned, a mother of the deceased person cooks rice with egg for the last time. She does so in the courtyard, using the cooking pot and other utensils that have been set aside for this ever since the death occurred. The food is offered at the spot where the bones of the deceased are buried or could have been buried. Once the food has been cooked, the pot and the gourd are broken. The stones that were used to support the pot are thrown into the forest. None of the utensils should be put to further use. With the breaking of the pot and discarding of the utensils, people from the household in which the deceased person lived state that no more cooked food can be prepared for the particular *mi'mang*. The deceased stops being a recipient of hot food. This signals it becoming one step less of a social entity. From then on, the deceased is only incidentally offered rice beer, tea, or bananas at its effigy. Thus places at which the deceased is fed, the frequency at which food is offered, and the nature of the food provided all serve to phase the gradual decline of the social presence of the deceased person, thereby defining the temporality of the mortuary process.

## Ambiguous Gifts

During a funeral, a variety of objects are made to associate with the *mi'mang* of the deceased person. These include slings, coins, and heirlooms. These objects are distributed during the mortuary ritual by representatives of the household of the deceased person to his or her matrilineal relatives.

Such gifts are generically referred to as *ma'gual* (De Maaker 2012). They are associated with the corpse, yet do not imbibe its *marang*.

The least significant among these are the coins. When the corpse has been laid out, people place one rupee coins on it. Some of these are put in the hands, others on the chest, the thighs, the throat, the mouth, or at the center of the forehead. Old people sometimes collect such coins in the years preceding their death. One day, a woman asked me to change two ten rupee notes into coins "for when I die, as 'hand-held money' (*jakgipani tangka*)," she said. Women who attend the mortuary ritual can bring coins as well. The number of coins displayed indicates the prestige of a deceased person. Children or poor persons' corpses have one or two coins, but those of people with a high status can easily have thirty to forty coins. When the corpse is about to be taken from the house, the coins are distributed among female matrilineal kin of the deceased person.

Likewise, slings, in which babies and infants are carried, are also placed on the dead body. A sling symbolizes the capacity of women to give birth and to rear and nurture children. A sling is only given to a woman who classifies as a mother to the deceased person. The widower or widow, or someone else who is very near to the one who died, gives slings to women who engage in the wake. A woman who receives a sling is identified as a close female matrilineal relative of the dead person. With a sling or coin, people substantiate their relationship to the deceased. This connection emphasizes the importance of the kinship tie that they are tracing to the close relatives of the one who died.

When the corpse is put in state, heirloom jewelry is placed on top of it, or near it. Heirloom weapons are kept close to it or against the rear wall of the main room. According to ethnographic sources, in the past gongs were made to associate with the corpse as well. Enothsing Sangma (1984) writes that the body of a rich old man was laid out "over a bed of gongs." All these heirloom objects are assets of the household of the deceased. It may involve necklaces that are made with multiple strings of metal rings (*sillitting*), chains made with coins of twenty-five paisa (*suki mipal*) or fifty paisa (*repa mipal*), and necklaces woven of silver wire (*kakam* or *kunal*). Waist belts (*senki ripok*) are only displayed when a woman has died, since they are not worn by men, but most of the jewelry can equally be used at the death of a man or a woman. The number and kind of heirlooms that are displayed depends on the prosperity of the household and on the importance that is attributed to the deceased person. Individual pieces of jewelry can vary in value from a hundred to a couple of thousand rupees.

Heirlooms are presumed to be very old. According to oral histories, the heirlooms derive from Tibet, where Garos would initially come from. This does not imply that all of them are physically equally enduring, and people mentioned that, until recently, gongs, heirloom jewelry, and weapons had been made by Bengalis from the nearby plains. Most heirlooms degrade, or have parts that degrade, due to the extreme heat and humidity that characterizes the wet season in the Garo Hills. The stone, bone, or silver parts of heirloom jewelry are lasting, but the cotton strings with which they are threaded decay. Swords and spears rust, since they are made of iron. Shields of wood or bamboo sooner or later rot. Of all heirlooms, brass gongs are the most enduring. Such gongs are attributed great ancestry, suggesting that they have been transferred at mortuary rituals since time immemorial.

A woman said, at the death of a man whom she regarded as her younger brother, "It is like bone of my younger brother" (*angni angjongni greng*). The gong, she said, would help her to remember him. People thus maintain that the heirlooms represent the bones (*greng*) of the deceased at whose mortuary ritual they are offered. The heirlooms are the most important *ma'gual*. When faced with a death, a household can offer the heirlooms that it has obtained as *ma'gual* to others. But an heirloom should never be offered as *ma'gual* to the people from whom it has been received as *ma'gual*.

People do not remember the history of an heirloom, and the successive transfer of heirlooms as *ma'gual* renders anonymous the deceased with whom a particular heirloom was previously associated. Consequently, the transfer of an heirloom at successive mortuary rituals associates it with an ever growing number of dead. Apart from the most recently deceased, all these are anonymous.

Their association with the dead renders these objects valuable. It also compels people to live up to the obligations that acceptance of such a gift implies. If people do not act as expected, they not only fail in their relationship to their relatives, but also in their commitment to the deceased. The physical association of the deceased with these gifts emphasizes the importance of compliance with these commitments.

## Conclusions

The dead are ambiguous, at once dangerous and beneficial. The danger they pose emanates from a corpse being a source of *marang*. *Marang* can cause further deaths. The dead are also dangerous, since many people assume that dying results from being abducted by them, implying that the dead are instrumental in the occurrence of deaths. Yet, the dead are also beneficial and supportive, especially as they are central to social relationships. Objects that become associated with the dead, by placing them on or in the vicinity of the dead body, gain additional value from this attribution. The transfer of these objects, without exception, involves the tracing or confirmation of kin relationships. Relationships that are highlighted in such a way do not only involve the living but encompass the dead as well.

Death itself, as a stage, is inherently unstable and liminal. The transition from life to death, that is, to die, is for the person concerned no doubt a watershed event. Yet, from the perspective of the survivors, it presents itself also as a change in phase of existence, since for them there is a certain continuity between the qualities of a person who is alive and those that characterize him or her immediately after death.

Initially, someone who has died is closely associated with the living person he or she used to be, but this association gradually wanes. In the first hours and days following death, a recently deceased person is still vividly present in people's memories, and emotionally related to. These associations, combined with ideas of what the deceased has transformed into, shape a continued social presence of the one who died. The deceased can be remembered, for instance, as a father or a friend, and is thus associated with his or her earlier human roles. But a deceased person will also be remembered for the fields he has cultivated or the gardens he or she owned, since usage rights are transferred to the heirs. Over time, the dead gradually lose this close association with the living beings they used to be. Rights and belongings are taken over by the living, and memories fade. The social presence of the deceased person wanes, eventually to a point where it can effectively cease to exist.

People attempt to deal with the ambiguity and liminality of the dead by phasing the death ritual and thus attempting to control its temporality. Throughout life, the unity between the components of a person (such as body and soul, but also reputation and rights) remains unquestioned. Death implies a process of disintegration in which the relationship between these various components is only gradually loosened. The disintegration of the deceased is spread out over various phases of the mortuary process, as shown in Table 1.1, which distinguishes four (unequal) periods of time. The first and the second phase each refer to a single day. The third phase encompasses several years; the last phase can even stretch over several decades. From the first day of the mortuary ritual onwards, people act in ways that are conducive to the guidance of the soul of the deceased to the afterworld. The dissolution of the deceased as a social person is induced by the treatment that people give to the corpse (undressing, bathing, laying out in state, disposal). Each of these actions transforms the body of what used to be a living person into a corpse ready for disposal.

On the first day, the corpse is bathed and laid out inside the house. People use the corpse to provide gifts to the deceased: cooked food and

**Table 1.1.** The disintegration and transformation of a deceased person

| Phase | First day of the mortuary ritual | Second day of the mortuary ritual | The first couple of years after death | After a couple of decades |
|---|---|---|---|---|
| Material presence | | | | |
| Corpse | The cremation or burial controls the putrefaction that the corpse is subject to. | Following a cremation, some bones are taken back to the village and buried there. The rest of the remains are abandoned. | The place where the bones are buried in the courtyard will be remembered vaguely. | The bones are forgotten. |
| Effigy | | An effigy (*kima*) is created as a new embodiment of the deceased person. | The effigy slowly decays. | The effigy has disappeared. |
| Heirlooms | Heirlooms (and money) equaling the bones of the dead person are offered to maternal relatives. | Heirlooms (and money) equaling the bones of the dead person are offered to maternal relatives | People who have obtained heirlooms (and money) as gifts use these in relation to other dead. | Anonymously, a dead man or woman continues to be represented by the heirlooms (and money) that have been offered as *ma'gual* at the time of his or her death. |
| Providing food to the deceased | Food is cooked for the deceased inside the house. | People create a repository at the spot where the bones are buried, or could have been buried. At the repository, daily food offerings are made. After two to four weeks, the repository is burned. | People offer each year, as long as an effigy is in front of their house, some of their first crops. Incidental offerings of food and rice beer are also made. | The deceased is no longer fed. |

goods required on the way to and in the afterworld. Heirloom objects are placed with the corpse to associate them with the deceased. These can act as his or her representations until long after the disposal. Some of these objects are relatively short-lived and abandoned or destroyed within days or weeks after the funeral. Others are attributed importance over a long period of time. The association of some of these objects with the person who died even translates to people considering these objects as owned by the deceased. This renders them "social" (Kopytoff 1986: 64), and even attributes them with a biography and a history (Hoskins 1998: 7).

On the second day of the mortuary ritual, the corpse and all personal belongings of the deceased are removed from the house in which the deceased has lived. With the burial or cremation, the mortal remains lose much of their importance. In the courtyard in front of the house in which the deceased person lived, a repository is erected. This comes to hold food and other gifts for the deceased, and should safeguard his or her good standing in the afterworld. Also, an effigy is created, which ensures a prolonged and public presence of the deceased among the living and allows them to make occasional offerings.

People who belong to other houses, also those located in other villages, can engage the *mi'mang* as well. Claiming a relationship to the dead contributes to the prestige of a person or the household he or she belongs to. It can also substantiate claims towards land and the resources affiliated with that. In the weeks, months, and years that follow, annual food offerings can still be made to the deceased. While the effigy slowly decays, people continue to remember the deceased in stories and through photographs.

Finally, in the last phase, individual traits of the deceased person can no longer be remembered, except perhaps for his or her name. The extent to which a deceased person is remembered in genealogy depends on the importance attributed to his or her house. Once a person's name has been forgotten, his or her social image ceases to exist altogether. In heirloom objects (notably brass gongs) that are associated with the corpse and that have been used as gifts at the time of the mortuary ritual, the deceased continues to have an anonymous presence.

The Garo Songsarek mortuary process, as it extends over time, can thus serve to control the *marang* brought about by death, as well as its other dangerous aspects, while it channels the presences of the dead towards the reassessment, continuation, and redefinition of social relationships. The vitality of the Garo dead is not so much about generative powers attributed to them, but about people's ability to tap into the relationships and claims that become manifest through them. That is, for them, the "culturally most essential" resource, as mentioned in the introduction to this chapter, that a death ritual regenerates.

People attribute to the dead the authority to constitute essential social relationships. Daniel de Coppet (1981) went as far as arguing, for the 'Aré'Aré of Melanesia, that the dead have a "life-giving" capacity. He (ibid.: 176) concluded that "society builds up its own character of permanence through the repeated dissolution *into* the ritual and exchange process of the main elements composing each individual." Such a dissolution of the dead is effectuated among the Garo by means of a prolonged mortuary process, for which people set the time. But more than that, the extended presence of the dead serves not merely to regenerate social relationships; it allows for their reinterpretation. The Garo attribute authority to their dead, primarily through the association with memorial objects, but use that authority to strategically articulate and redefine the ties that define their social belonging, which includes their claims to residence and land.

**Erik de Maaker** (PhD Leiden 2006) is assistant professor at the Institute for Cultural Anthropology and Development Sociology of Leiden University in the Netherlands. He specializes in the anthropology of religion, the anthropology and sociology of South Asia, and visual anthropology. Most of his work is on changing notions of relatedness and belonging among the upland communities of South Asia's eastern borderlands. For an overview of his publications see http://leidenuniv.academia.edu/ErikdeMaaker.

## Note

1.   For a child, a very simple effigy is made using bamboo poles. These poles are then dressed with the clothes of the deceased child.

## References

Béteille, Andre. 1998. "The Idea of Indigenous People." *Current Anthropology* 39, no. 2: 187-192.

Bloch, Maurice, and Jonathan Parry. 1982. "Introduction: Death and the Regeneration of Life." In *Death and the Regeneration of Life*, ed. Maurice Bloch and Jonathan Parry, 1–44. Cambridge: Cambridge University Press.

Burling, Robbins. (1963) 1997. *Rengsanggri: Family and Kinship in a Garo Village.* Reprint, with an additional chapter, Philadelphia: University of Philadelphia Press.

Carsten, Janet, and Stephen Hugh-Jones. 1995, eds. *About the House: Lévi-Strauss and Beyond.* Cambridge: Cambridge University Press.

Coppet, Daniel de. 1981. "The Life-Giving Death." In *Mortality and Immortality: The Anthropology and Archeology of Death*, ed. S.C. Humphreys and Helen King, 175–204. London: Academic Press.

De Maaker, Erik. 2006. "Negotiating Life: Garo Death Rituals and the Transformation of Society." PhD diss., Leiden University.

———. 2012. "Negotiations at Death: Assessing Gifts, Mothers and Marriages." In *Negotiating Rites*, ed. Ute Hüsken and Frank Neubert, 43–55. Oxford: Oxford University Press.

———. 2013 "Have the Mitdes Gone Silent? Conversion, Rhetoric, and the Continuing Importance of the Lower Deities in Northeast India." In *Asia in the Making of Christianity: Conversion, Agency, and Indigeneity, 1600s to the Present*, ed. Richard F. Young and Jonathan A. Seitz, 135–162. Leiden: Brill.

Durkheim, Emile. (1912) 2008. *Elementary Forms of Religious Life*, trans. C. Cosman. Oxford: Oxford University Press.

Hertz, Robert. (1907) 1960. *Death and the Right Hand*. Aberdeen: Cohen & West.

Hoskins, Janet. 1998. *Biographical Objects: How Things Tell the Stories of People's Lives*. New York: Routledge.

Kopytoff, Igor. 1986. "The Cultural Biography of Things: Commoditization as a Process." In *The Social Life of Things: Commodities in Cultural Perspective*, ed. Arjun Appadurai, 64–91. Cambridge: Cambridge University Press.

Sangma, E.C. 1984. "Traditional Garo Religion in its Social Matrix." PhD diss., Guwahati University.

van Gennep, Arnold. (1909, in French) 1960. *The Rites of Passage*, trans. Monika B. Vizedom and Gabrielle L. Caffee. Chicago: University of Chicago Press.

Waterson, Roxana. 1990. *The Living House: An Anthropology of Architecture in South-East Asia*. Singapore and Oxford: Oxford University Press.

*Figure 2.1.* A Sora shaman (center) in trance speaks with the voice of a recently deceased child. The child's mother embraces her child through the shaman's body (photo Piers Vitebsky).

*Chapter Two*

# Structures and Processes of Liminality
## The Shape of Mourning among the Sora of Tribal India

*Piers Vitebsky*

A key aspect of liminality in "rites of passage" (van Gennep [1909] 1960) is a sense of unstructure or antistructure, during a period when human actors step outside the sense of structure that gives form to our anthropological notions of society. While on the way between a point of separation and another point of reintegration, actors pass "through a cultural realm which has few or none of the attributes of the past or coming state" (Turner 1969: 94). Instead, they enter a state which Turner calls "communitas," and which is characterized by "homogeneity and comradeship" (95).

Van Gennep and Turner focus on moments of transition with quite a short time span, such as the actions surrounding sacrifice or initiation. In these, an individual or a group goes through a transformation that is clearly defined; if a group, all members go through it at the same time. This is a key feature of Turner's understanding of communitas in particular, derived as it is from his ethnographic examples of cohorts of initiands in Zambia. Between them, van Gennep and Turner develop a model which clearly marks the dynamic contours of the opening and closing phases of separation and reintegration, and also makes the in-between phase of liminality relatively easy to identify since the opening and closing phases mark them off so distinctly from something else that we might call nonliminal or ordinary life.

But the important central stage itself is more complex and mysterious than the stages on either side. Turner seems to grant liminality a certain

degree of structure, as indeed it must have if it is also to function as process. But even so, this is not only distinct from the structure of ordinary
life, but also somehow less structured. It is partly this that gives the state
of communitas its extreme sense of undifferentiation. Between them,
liminality and communitas serve as an ontological compost heap from
which new life emerges after a process that is necessarily obscure and
even immune from ordinary analysis.

However, the study of a different ethnographic example will show
how death in particular can complicate the basic contours of this model.
It will extend our understanding of liminality as a process—of the meta-
bolic process of the compost heap, so to speak. An examination of the
Sora of tribal India will show how liminality can contain within itself a
great complexity, with an elaborate logical structure of its own. The state
of liminality has to do some hard work, and it amplifies Turner's sense of
a structure within a structure. This structure involves a transformation
that is at the same time cosmological, ontological, social, and emotional.
If the moment of separation at death is at least fairly clear, Sora cosmology makes it difficult to say where the liminal state ends and what
constitutes a reintegration: at what point, and into what state? What is a
Sora person when alive, and what are they being separated from when
they die, and what are they later reintegrated to? When, if ever, does the
liminal phase ever stop? This uncertainly has a knock-on effect on our
understanding of communitas: the liminality of the Sora dead spills over
onto the living as the dead draw them into their own state of postmortem communitas.[1]

The Sora of Orissa number several hundred thousand (which by
Indian standards makes them a small minority group) and are part
of a wider belt of so-called megalithic cultures of India and southeast
Asia (Fürer-Haimendorf 1943; Rousseleau 2012; Berger, in this volume).
They speak a language of the Austroasiatic family, which is related to
Cambodian and to the languages of the Orang Asli of Malaya and of the
hill tribes of Vietnam (Condominas [1975] 1994). Apart from the anoma-
lous Khmer empire, the speakers of these languages consistently lie at
the jungly margins of the great empires and mainstream civilizations
of Asian history (see Scott 2009). In India, they are generally considered more ancient and more aboriginal than the much larger Aryan and
Dravidian populations of the subcontinent. Though this picture is disputed for political as well as scholarly reasons, it is clear that their non-
literate cultures lie well outside the Hindu mainstream (see also Berger,
in this volume; Pfeffer 2001; for a detailed account of Sora cosmology, see
Vitebsky 1993, which contains detailed background and analysis of the
cases cited in the present chapter).[2]

A living Sora has a *puradan* (soul). After death this briefly becomes a *kulman* (ghost). This stage is brief and undeveloped because a *kulman* is inarticulate, and, as we shall see, the entire Sora interaction between living and dead depends on verbal articulacy on both sides. So a *kulman* is immediately converted by rituals into a *sonum*. The concept of *sonum* is complex. It corresponds broadly to the term "spirit" in Christian and post-Christian European languages, but functions in a particular way in a cosmology where the liminal state of the dead is particularly elaborated and prolonged.[3]

Each dead person has two contrasting aspects, or kinds of *sonum*-hood. As a named individual, he or she is an ancestor-*sonum* (*idai*) in a particular patrilineage; but the same dead person is also absorbed into one of a range of collective categories that unite all those who died of a particular cause. Thus—to take examples where the link between symptom and category is most obvious—people killed by leopards become part of the collectivity called leopard-*sonum*, and people who die of leprosy become part of leprosy-*sonum*. We might call these collective categories event *sonums* or experience *sonums*. They cross-cut lineage membership in a way which subverts the unity of the lineage: one man may die of leprosy and his brother be killed by a leopard, so they end up separated into different collectivities based on the form of their death. These experience *sonums* are spread around the landscape, located for example in prominent rocks. It will take several years, and several stages of their funeral rites, to lead these brothers away from their death sites and reunite them in the underworld with the ancestors of their own lineage.

All illnesses and deaths are caused by dead people who have themselves suffered from similar symptoms. The experience *sonums* in effect represent modalities of suffering. The trigger for the attack involves a combination of opportunity (such as walking past their site on the landscape) plus a relationship of kinship or other close involvement. The dead person repeats in you the same symptoms from which he or she died: a dead leper gives you leprosy; a dead leopard-victim kills you by sending a leopard. Once you are dead, you will join your attacker in whichever experience-*sonum* corresponds to the symptoms you now both share.

But this suffering is not just an existential property of human mortality. The essence of this theory of suffering is that its specific forms are transmissible from one sufferer to the next. Each person's life will contain numerous episodes of illness, with various symptoms. Every time you fall ill (or suffer a leopard attack), a divination will reveal that this is because of a relationship between you and a dead person whom you knew when that person was alive. Most illnesses do not result in death, so your life will contain constant reminders of relationships with numerous other people whom you have known and who are now dead. For example, open ulcers may be a reminder from a leprosy victim, while a clawing or biting sensation may have been sent by a leopard victim. You will then make offerings in order to prevent these from escalating into something more serious. The cure consists of offering the dead person the soul of a sacrificial animal as a substitute for your own soul. If the substitute is accepted, you recover. But sooner or later, everyone develops a condition from which they do not recover, and embarks on the journey into postmortem existence.

A dead person is perpetuated among the living, within time. But this perpetuation can take a negative or a positive form, and the entire system is concerned with regulating and controlling this balance. This perpetuation is seen in terms of a gradual progression between the two idioms of experience-membership and ancestorhood. In the early stages after death, the death-experience fills the entire scope of a person's being and leaves room for nothing else: inflicting illness is the only way he has to perpetuate himself (since the most important shamans are female, I generally refer to unspecified shamans as "she" and patients as "he").[4] But from the very first stage of the sequence of funeral rites, the ancestors (as impersonated by the shaman's assistants) work hard to rescue him from his position as a prisoner of a fatal experience (in the late 1970s, I became one of these shaman's assistants for the lineage that included Jamano, below). Now there begins a struggle to hold him to a new state, that of an ancestor. He "reverts" (*gorod*) spontaneously to cause illness in others; rites of healing for the patient send him back. As he is persuaded by the living during dialogues, the impulse to revert gradually weakens and eventually fades away altogether. The dead person finally evolves into a pure ancestor who perpetuates himself in a more welcome idiom, by giving his name back to a new baby in his lineage and protecting that baby from attacks by other *sonums*.

The reason the living know about all this is that the dead explain the process themselves in exhaustive detail, whether at each stage of their own funeral or on the many occasions when they attack a living patient with illness. A key property of the liminal state of the dead is the ability to talk about it in a very articulate way. The dead send messages about where they are and how they are, and this opens up a space for discussion and negotiation. A dead person's state of liminality can last over years of discussion. This dialogue reveals a process of transition, in which each stage is also a significant state. In every Sora village, almost every day, there will be a group of people clustered around a shaman in a trance, negotiating with a succession of dead people who speak through her mouth. I have followed living and dead speakers since the 1970s as they persuade, cajole, tease, remind, and deceive in their attempts to uncover—and change—each other's state of mind. The dead talk in exactly the same way as living people, and I shall suggest later that this shared discourse is an indicator of a broad and loose sense of communitas which includes not only the dead but also the living.

A person who feels sick goes to a shaman for a divination, and couches his suffering in a grammatical form that emphasizes the patient's own sense of victimhood. This is the closest that Sora can get to the passive voice: "They are grabbing me, they are eating me (*jumtingji, nyamtingji*)." The goal of the divination is to find out who is doing this and why. Divination is thus a technique for revealing the attacker, whose identity is hidden in this agency-masking grammatical construction. It becomes possible to say not only that the patient is being attacked, but also by whom. It is this which exteriorizes what we might call the patient's inner feelings and makes them part of the "objective" world outside. In the course of the dialogue, various dead people turn up. Most of them deny that they are the cause, until one arrives who claims responsibility and begins to negotiate terms.

Sooner or later, a negotiation fails, and the patient dies. The sense of grammatical passivity is carried over into his newfound state. The morning after death, the deceased is summoned for an inquest ("Tell us which *sonum* took you"). Though he may still be confused by the shock of his own death, he is now in a position to help the living to interpret the cause. In August 1979, the old man Jamano died coughing blood. The following morning, members of his extensive lineage crowded into his house to squat around the shaman and interrogate the dead man (condensed from Vitebsky 1993: 110–16). As the old man's *sonum* started to speak through her mouth, his son urged him vehemently: "One moment you were walking around, the next you were dead. Don't hesitate, don't be afraid—speak out!" "You died alone, no wife, no daughter-in-law, no daughter with you," added Jamano's widow, "you were all on your own. Tell us how you died, how you perished!"

Through the hubbub of voices, Jamano could be heard saying, "Then I vomited, I vomited twice there. I vomited on the ground beneath the verandah: 'Hey children, my heart is tearing, it's sprouting out of my chest! . . . Ow, they're prodding my anus like a buffalo, ow, my body is racked, ow, it's tearing apart,' I said."

The son interrupted, "Was it earth-*sonum*, was it *simu-sonum*? Was it our father's people? Our mother's people?" He suddenly flared up, "Or did someone instigate it with sorcery? You speak out and I'll go and find him and slurp up all his blood!"

The dead Jamano himself started to speak again: "I was sitting on the veranda; it was only later that I went inside. I cried, 'Help me, Mandebo; help me, Sunamo; help me, children; save me, protect me!'"

He was interrupted by a chorus of pitying noises, with many voices talking at once: "We couldn't hear, we were all in our separate houses." "They pounced and beat him up without warning." "Why didn't you put up a fight, why did you offer yourself to them?" "Who was the main one to grab your hair, to get on top of you?" "Did they drag you off as you hugged the main pillar of the house?" "Which way did they take you after they wrenched you off the pillar?" There was a sudden attentive hush as Jamano went on, "It was Momo who first dragged me off."

With this crucial moment of revelation, Jamano was starting to lead the survivors towards a verdict on the circumstances of his death. The symptoms had already pointed towards a category called "*ratud,*" a *sonum* which attacks travelers walking along paths with the symptoms of violent sickness and sudden collapse. Momo was a recent victim of *ratud,* which, it was now emerging, has also taken Jamano as a new victim. As a new recruit, Momo had acted as the "front-person" (*abmang-mar*) for all the other *ratud* people, who were the "shadow people behind his back" (*lub-dung-maranji*). Starting from this link, the discussion would move forward over many weeks and months to rake over big questions of lineage, inheritance, love, and sorcery—it turned out that Momo's attack was incited by the sorcery of Jamano's brother—as befitted a grand elder with a lifetime's accumulation of descendants, allies, and enemies. But one key goal of the inquest was to establish that Jamano was now likely to affect the living as the most recent and most virulent agent of *ratud* sickness.

Some weeks later, Jamano received the next stage of his funeral sequence as a memorial stone was planted (Vitebsky 1993) and a number of buffalos, given by various kinsmen, were sacrificed. This was followed over the next three years by several further stages of his funeral. At each phase of the funeral, a group of shaman's assistants, men of his own patrilineage and sometimes the anthropologist, impersonated his ancestors as they struggled to rescue him from *ratud-sonum.* This transformation was cosmological, as we moved him from one location on the landscape to another, but it also served as a map of a transformation that was ultimately ontological, as we turned him from one kind of *sonum* into another. The ancestors will rescue him from wherever he is in a range of experience *sonums,* as they chant:

| | |
|---|---|
| whether [he is] in sorcery-house | whether in *kurab*-house |
| whether in sun-house | whether in moon-house |
| whether in *manne*-house | whether in *simu*-house |
| whether in bone-scrunching house | whether in bone-grinding house |
| whether in eat-up-victim | whether in drink-up-victim |
| whether in police-station house | whether in arrest-victim house . . . |

This cosmological and ontological transformation has a goal or end-state which is deeply social. The lineage ancestors lead him from the antisociety of his fellow experience-victims into their own company. It is this which undoes the destructive impact of death itself. If this state can be achieved and held stable, it seems—at least for the moment—that it will be the ultimate destination of the entire process of postmortem liminality. Their invocation thus continues:

| | |
|---|---|
| our born child | our hatched child |
| our young child | our baby child |
| our grandchild | our child |
| joining | merging |
| into our company | into our group |
| into our binding | into our bundle |
| let us comfort | let us escort |
| into our food hand-out | into our food share-out |
| the protruding-fanged *sonum* | the curving-fanged *sonum* |
| has snatched and eaten up | has snatched and drunk up |
| our born child | our hatched child |
| let us hold our axes | let us grab our axes |
| let us brandish our swords | let us brandish our knives |
| let us speak like an advocate | let us speak for the defense |
| let us be forceful-mouthed | let us be forceful-toothed |
| let us lead him towards us | let us bring him by the arm towards us |
| come brothers | come lineage-members . . . |

At first sight, we could say that this is the stage that corresponds to van Gennep's reintegration and thus to the end of the phase of liminality. However, the Sora seem to be saying that it is not so simple to undo or limit the impact of a death. In the first place, this transformation is not immediately successful. This is known because the dead person is still being diagnosed, like Momo, as the cause of illness in others. This is the reason why illnesses and deaths continue to occur: there are always recently dead people who are not fully transformed and who thus keep on recruiting new victims.

The formal funeral sequence takes three years (interestingly, the same period that it takes to wean and name a baby—dying and becoming a person are both gradual and comparable processes). The chants imply that this should be sufficient to convert the person definitively into an ancestor. But, actually, the dead person may continue long after this to revert from the state of ancestorhood back to the experience-*sonum* that caused his death.

Why is the transformation so hard to sustain? A person who has recently died is unstable cosmologically, ontologically, and socially—but also emotionally. There is a direct correlation, not only between an incompletely transformed person and his tendency to attack, but also with the impact of his appearance in the dramatic scenario of a trance. A recently dead person will turn up and speak in direct response to the presence of a mourner whom he has the power to distress. The bereaved person may greet the deceased and even passionately embrace the shaman through whom the *sonum* speaks; but often he or she will weep silently on the outskirts of the group and it is left to a more confident and collected interlocutor to speak with the *sonum* on the main mourner's behalf.

Here is a little girl who died recently through the agency of leprosy-*sonum*. The child addresses her mother, but the mother is too distressed to speak, and the child is answered by an aunt. As with Momo above, the full explanation of her death requires the combination of an experience *sonum* that corresponds to her symptoms, plus the involvement of a previous victim as the front-person. As well as expressing pity for the dead child, the conversation also dwells explicitly on the risk that she may pass her illness on to the living:

| | |
|---|---|
| Dead girl: | (arriving from the Underworld, faintly) "Mother, where are my gold nose-rings?" |
| Living aunt: | "They must have burned up in the pyre, darling; we looked but couldn't find them." |
| Girl: | (petulantly) "Why don't you show me my nose-rings?" |
| Aunt: | "They were so tiny. If I'd found them, of course I'd show them to you. Oh my love, my darling, don't cause your own illness in others. Can you say that your mother and father didn't do enough sacrifices for you? They didn't turn their backs or refuse to help you, did they? Think of all those pigs they offered, all those chickens, goats, buffalos, my lovely child." |
| Girl: | (addressing her silent mother, and crying) "Mother, you were horrid to me, you scolded me, you called me Scar-Girl, you called me Leper-Girl, you said, 'You're a big girl now, why should I feed you when you sit around doing nothing?'" |
| Aunt: | "She didn't mean it, she couldn't help saying it. You were growing up and there were such a lot of chores to do." |
| Girl: | (sulkily) "I want my necklaces." (unreasonable childish tone) "Why can't I have my nose-rings? I have to go digging, shoveling, and leveling fields in the underworld, all without my nose-rings. I came out in scars all over, my fingers started dropping off. That illness was passed on to me; that's how I got ill." |
| Aunt: | "But don't you pass it on, don't you give it to your mother and little sisters!" |

| Girl: | "If I grab them I grab them, if I touch them I touch them, if I pass it on I pass it on: that's how it goes." |
| Aunt: | "Your cough, your choking, your scars, your wounds, don't pass them on!" |
| Girl: | (calling back as she returns to the underworld) "My Mummy doesn't care enough about me!" |

This dialogue (and many like it) points to a further dimension of the transformation song performed in the persona of the ancestors. It reveals starkly that in rescuing the dead person from his or her death-experience, the living are also protecting themselves. The sacrifices that the girl's family made to try to save her while she was alive are important, and it will now be the turn of the girl herself to demand sacrifices every time she makes another person ill. But sacrifice is only one part of the process, and a relatively mechanical part at that. The key technique is dialogue itself, and particularly its function of negotiation and persuasion. We see how in the little girl's early, unbearably painful appearances, the shaman reproduces her speech habits and tone of voice with uncanny realism. The girl responds to the mood of her mother and aunt by accusing them in words that echo what we might call their own self-reproach: "if only we'd known how ill you were, if only we'd been kinder." This distress among the living is matched by the girl's inclination to pass on her illness to her family, causing further deaths. She is begged not to perpetuate her own suffering onto others. But this is not because she is a nasty person (indeed, the shaman makes her seem sweet and vulnerable). Rather, her dangerous state is an unavoidable counterpart to her pitifulness. As the girl herself says, this is just what recently dead people do: it is a property of *sonums* at an early stage of their liminal state.

This state may last far longer than the three years of the sequence of funeral rites. A dead person may attack the living ten or twenty years later, if not as a front-person then certainly as one of the crowd of hangers-on behind him or her. This tendency corresponds not so much to time alone, as to shifts in emotional attitudes which come about broadly through the passage of time. People who have died some years ago may still some-times be dangerous and demanding (remember the word *gorod*, mean-ing "revert"), but they are gradually less likely to be diagnosed as a main troublemaker.

These qualities diminish according to how far the dead have lost their power to distress. The appearance of the recently deceased little girl plumbs emotional depths and raises topics which still evoke anxiety, guilt, and confusion. By contrast, older *sonums* are often greeted with facetious or abusive banter. This style is especially well developed among older women (in-marrying wives and daughters-in-law who were obliged to be more polite when they were younger—significantly, this is the main demographic category who provide the shamans). Here is an elderly woman talking to her husband, who has been dead for some years. The dead husband has turned up for a drink and a smoke (both ingested through the mouth of the shaman while she is in a liminal state of her own):

| | |
|---|---|
| Dead husband: | "It's me—I've just been babysitting in the underworld." |
| Living wife: | "Call yourself a babysitter, and you've left the baby for leopards to snatch while you come and talk to us!" |
| Dead husband: | "Now I've gone to live with my son-in-law down below." |
| Living wife: | "Big deal! You didn't do any work while you were alive, why would you go to the trouble of building your own house down there? Did Raduno or Indaro ever see you doing any work up here? It took enough of their money to do sacrifices for you when you were alive. So now you're a babysitter down below?" |
| Dead husband: | (ungraciously) "How do I know whose money you did it with, or how well you did it? It didn't save me anyway, did it?" |

Here, we see the process of transformation halfway completed. The tone of the conversation between husband and wife is specific enough to give an insight into what their married life was probably like (I did not know the family when the husband was alive). The scenario of living with his daughter and son-in-law in the underworld, looking after their baby and then neglecting it while he comes up to earth to talk to his wife, plays amusingly with the framework of Sora cosmology and uses it for social and legal ends. There are still matters of inheritance under dispute: in fact, their dead daughter has remarried in the underworld as part of a strategy to influence the outcome of a property dispute among the living (Vitebsky 1993: ch. 8). However, there is no sense that the husband is still dangerous, or that he and his wife still have unfinished emotional business. Not all conversations at this stage are flippant or abusive in tone. They can also be affectionate; but an important characteristic of this phase is that it has passed beyond the domain of aggression, fear, and weeping.

This husband is well on the way to becoming a pure ancestor. Someone who has been dead for an even longer time will eventually have no close personal emotional involvement with the living at all and will no longer attack as an agent of his original death-experience. Indeed, as my collections of genealogies make clear, the circumstances of his death are no longer even remembered. Such old ancestors are barely distinguishable in personality and show a uniformity in the tone and content of their conversation. These *sonums* turn up to receive what is theirs by right. They provide the rationale for many aspects of kinship and inheritance among the living, and thereby guarantee the integrity and continuity of the lineage. They take a swig of palm wine and a puff of tobacco and are dismissed quickly ("Why are you cadging from me? . . . Why don't you keep those other *sonums* off our back? . . . Have your drink and piss off!"). This rudeness itself is a sign that their transformation into ancestorhood is complete.

This shift makes sense only because of the real presence of the feelings of fear and aggression in the early stages. The cruel realism of early postmortem dialogues, such as that with the little girl, allows her eventual rescue to be more than just a rescue. It is a transformation on a theological scale which amounts to a redemption from the event and the pain of death itself.[5]

This is the ultimate function of the process which takes place within the liminal state. In repeated dialogues over months and years, the living will gradually persuade the girl to acknowledge that her family did their best to save her. She will allow the living to coax her away from the bad company of other leprosy victims and into the good company of her ancestors. The little girl will turn into an ancestor-*sonum* herself, and her influence on her family will become increasingly benign. The process of mourning will finally be completed when she gives her name to a new baby in the lineage. The vocabulary that describes the process of giving one's name to a descendant does not use the transitive verbs of eating and aggression, with their polarity between active and passive, in which the dying person shifts his perspective from being the victim of someone else's aggressive action to being the perpetrator of his own, from being "grabbed," "seized" or "eaten up" to doing the "grabbing," "seizing" or "eating." Instead, renaming uses intransitive forms which emphasize mutual identification and set up a different kind of analogy with a living person. Here, there is a transmission without aggression, and the repetition is not one of action but of being, not of a form of suffering but of social identity.

The idiom of eating, too, is reversed, as the old ancestors nourish their descendants by passing something of their soul-force into their crops and thus into every mouthful they consume. The naming ceremony repeats the tunes and drumming of the funeral, but with a striking emotional transformation: at the center of the dancers there are no weeping mourners. This redemption operates on every level at once, transforming the dead person's cosmological position and her ontological state, as she moves from worse locations to better ones across the earth, sky, and underworld, and her social relationship with her family and lineage. As ambivalences and resentments are resolved, she will be liberated from the pain of her death.

But it is not only the dead person who is transformed. The dead person's emotional distress is shared with the living mourners. Through the process of transforming the deceased, the living are likewise freed from

grief and guilt. Thus, their redemption operates in parallel, and the resolution works both for the dead and for the living at the same time. The
technique of dialogue enables the living and the dead to heal themselves
and each other at the same time.

The fact that both living and dead are involved together in this process
of redemption raises complex questions about the Sora sense of communitas. During dialogues, a group of persons bring themselves into a relationship with the dead person that amounts to a kind of shared consciousness.
This consciousness encompasses a mixture of feelings. Thinking about the
deceased is focused through an awareness of his suffering, a suffering that
continues into the present. On the one hand, the living share the dead's
suffering out of compassion (*abasuyim*). But at the same time, they fear
(*batong*) the dead person whom they love, since he will later become an
aggressor himself and repeat the form of his death on them. Often, those
whom you loved the most while they were alive are the ones you fear the
most once they are dead, and an attack may be motivated equally by the
dead person's anger or by his attachment: "I miss you so much I don't
want to be alone without you—come and join me!"

When Jamano is dragged into the collectivity of *ratud-sonum* victims,
his shared state of communitas with them seems clear. But what of his son
and the other mourners, who love him yet fear being drawn into the same
state by that love itself? The deceased is not in this alone, and not even just
in the company of his fellow victims. All those who gather round to interrogate him, and maybe also others beyond, are his potential victims, and
some of them will inevitably become his actual victims.

Let us look more closely at a living person's susceptibility to attacks from
the dead. Their influence is mutual, as living and dead mold each other's
state of mind. A *sonum*'s effect on you depends on that *sonum*'s own state
of mind, but it also equally reflects how you feel about that dead person.

Although the formal funeral sequence lasts for three years, it can take a
generation or more for a dead person to become a pure ancestor, free from
any taint of his or her death experience. Each *sonum*, at any given moment,
has its own cosmological location and its own relationship to each of its
mourners. The dead communicate with us by a combination of making
us ill and then talking about what they are doing to us and why. They are
reminding us of their existence and forcing us to think of them. So instead
of rituals of curing or healing, I am inclined to call these responses rituals
of acknowledgement. The dead person is reminding you of their contribution to making up your cumulative biography and personhood.

Just as the state of the dead changes over time, so does the way we think
and feel about them. The oldest *sonums* who speak are almost devoid of
personality and leave their living interlocutors indifferent, while others,

like the little girl, have great emotional power over those whom they address and cause them extreme distress. By analyzing the emotional tone of each encounter between dead *sonum* and living mourner, we have seen a close correlation between unsettled moods in a dead person and a tendency to revert readily to his experience mode, that is, a direct correspondence between a dead person's cosmological status and his state of mind.

But we are now in a position to understand a further correspondence, that between the dead person's state and the susceptibility of the living mourner. In the Sora view of the world, it is the dead who initiate each encounter, as well as set the emotional tone. The living are caught on the back foot each time and have to respond defensively in order to change the terms of the encounter.[6]

Some dead people are harder to redeem than others, and here, too, the cause is said to lie with the dead person herself, who is still unhappily trapped in the circumstances of her own death, and even with further social dynamics in the wider society of the dead. Here is a young wife speaking a few months after she suddenly collapsed and died while walking back from her father's village (condensed from Vitebsky 1993: 173–75). This death, like Jamano's, was diagnosed as caused by *ratud-sonum*. The main target of her emotional impact is her young husband, but in the present example the role of talking to her is taken by the husband's mother:

| | |
|---|---|
| Dead woman: | (faintly) "I got eaten up, I got drunk up, mothers—" |
| Mother-in-law: | "Ah, my dear, it was so sudden, just like that, you . . ." (continues inaudibly) |
| Dead woman: | "After I came and joined your family, mothers—" |
| Mother-in-law: | "Yes, 'this is my house, this is my home' you said. Have a drink before you go!" |
| Dead woman: | (small, shaken voice) "O dear, really I got eaten up, I got drunk up." |
| Mother-in-law: | "Didn't we do all your sacrifices? If only you'd been ill first [we could have done something—but your death was so sudden]. Didn't we do all your sacrifices, yet—" |
| Dead woman: | "My soul had already been absorbed (*jakîd*) into *ratud-sonum*." (calling out) "'Help me, fathers, help me!' I cried, 'aunts, uncles, mother-in-law, father-in-law!'" |
| Mother-in-law: | "How could we see you?" |
| Dead woman: | (tearful) "'Where's my husband, where's my husband, I want to be with him, I want to speak to him!' is all I cried." (quiet again) "They ate me up fresh-and-alive (*rongtapada*)." |
| Mother-in-law: | "You can't say we didn't plant a memorial stone for you or do your sacrifices, can you?" (vehement torrent) "Leave abandon that house that home, that place that location, |

that seat that site, leave it abandon it. . . . Say you're going to your in-laws, and go to Bat's Nest, Bodigan, Jelabbab, Kupa" (places where her in-laws' lineage reassemble in the underworld).

Dead woman:   "Yes, my father-in-law's ancestors have rescued me."

Mother-in-law:   "Then make the change—will you stay like that in Eating-up-House Drinking-up-House?"

Dead woman:   "My father-in-law says, 'Let's go and live together over there'" (in the underworld).

Mother-in-law:   "Well, if they've redeemed you, if they've rescued you—"

Dead woman:   "Yes, they have. But the *ratud*-people won't release me, they won't let me go!"

Mother-in-law:   "'Let me go!' you should say, 'I've got my in-laws, I've got my brothers-in-law, I've got my new kinsmen, I've got my sisters-in-law,' you should say!"

The mother-in-law here is the same woman who was talking to her dead husband in the previous dialogue. But here there is none of her abusive banter or witty sarcasm. The rate at which the dead person moves away from her original death-experience is related not simply to the evolution of her own state, but also to the evolution of the feelings that the *sonum* and all her various mourners have for each other. It is also related to the wider social dynamics that encompass the dead and the living. This young woman's death was shocking for many reasons apart from its suddenness. She had married for love, in defiance of her father's family. The *ratud*-people who had killed her were associated with her own family ancestors, and her defiance of their disapproval is reflected in the dialogue's strong emphasis on the transferal of her loyalty to her husband's family.[7] The rescuing that any dead person will receive from a group of ancestors is here very pointedly pitched against the rival claims of the lineage into which she was born and from which she has walked away. At another moment, she revealed that the real target of the *sonum*'s attack was her baby son, and that she had died while bending over to protect that baby. The unweaned baby was now alive but motherless and very vulnerable. But if the son survived, this would affirm the validity of her love-marriage and console her widowed husband. At another moment, the dead woman encouraged her husband to marry her younger sister as a replacement mother for the child, and this did indeed happen.

A *sonum* is a relational concept in several senses that all reinforce each other. It is related to you through kinship or friendship; it can be a cause of events in your life, including the bodily states that amount to your medical history; it can reduce you to tears; and it can cause your death and force you to share the pain of its owner's death. This dead woman remained unhappy, unresolved, and dangerous until her younger sister, now married to the same man, gave birth to a daughter. The dead woman came and gave the baby her own name, thereby also becoming the new baby's protector.[8]

If we shift our focus from the feelings of the dead to those of the living, we can also see that the reason why the redemption of the deceased can be a slow and painful process is that the living person is also unable to free himself from his memory of the dead person's suffering. By this interpretation, an illness then appears as a resurgence of this old memory. Rites of healing (or acknowledgement) use dialogue to take this old, painful memory and convert it into a more benign form, the memory of the person free of suffering and seen only as an ancestor. Whenever we remember the pain and the specific form of his death, we make ourselves vulnerable to the experience-*sonum* aspect of his being; by transforming this memory, we become open to his protective ancestral function. The *sonum*'s new state can take over only gradually because the memory persists of what things were like before the transformation. Reversions (*gorod*) then appear as throwbacks or recrudescences of these old memories, so that it requires frequent confirmation of our newer feelings to repress them.

We can translate the word "*sonum*" as "a Memory," with a capital *M*, as distinct from the ordinary use of the word "memory" as a function of the mind. This translation can be read back into Sora phrasing to yield propositions such as "All illnesses and deaths are caused by Memories" or "When a shaman goes into trance she leads the Memories one by one to speak with their rememberers." It is through this play between their interior and exterior properties that Memories are able to be both deeply intimate and publicly negotiable in the shouting match of dialogue. A *sonum* is my Memory of a person whom I loved (or didn't, as the case may be); it is also someone who can turn in conversation to address any one of a dozen assembled rememberers in a manner specific to each of them and at the same time common to all. Unlike a "Western" memory, which is located in the mind of its rememberer, a *sonum* has the locus of its existence outside the minds of any of the people whom it affects, and instead resides in a feature of the public landscape where everyone walks and works.[9]

In terms of the liminality model, the stages of separation and reintegration seem clear enough at first sight. A person is separated at the moment of death from his lineage. He is reintegrated, albeit gradually and tentatively at first, when his redemption finally becomes irreversible and he becomes fully reunited with his ancestors. The liminal stage in between is represented by his association with his fellow victims of whatever form of death (*ratud*, leopard, leprosy, etc.) has taken him. The young mother's renaming of her sister's new baby gives a particularly clear moment of reintegration or resolution.

But the end of the phase of liminality is not always so clear, as a cast of thousands, living and dead, keep shifting and changing position. Our gloss of a *sonum* as a Memory reminds us that the *sonum*'s ultimate destination is not just a reintegration. It is also a gradual decline and dissolution—a process of being forgotten (for a detailed discussion of remembering and forgetting, see Vitebsky 1993: chs. 8 and 9). The person dissolves after death into his various constituents, in which his death-experience and ancestor aspects are dispersed and reintegrated along with various aspects of his property and inheritance. One by one, the qualities or attributes of the deceased fall away from him and are returned to the living, who then have less and less reason to talk with him in detail or with emotional intensity. The last constituent to be returned is the person's name, which returns to one child among his descendants. The quick return of the young mother's name was only one way: an old man like Jamano, with numerous descendants branching into sublineages, will wait for several generations before his name is preempted by one branch to the exclusion of others.

In addition, there remains a final, vestigial residue of the deceased that continues its trajectory ever onwards, away from the awareness of the living. This is what we might call his subjective consciousness or core personhood. Eventually, this attenuated Memory dies a second death in the underworld, at which point it becomes a butterfly beyond the reach of any communication with the living—an entity with which we cannot communicate because it has no attributes of personhood, and is thus (like the early *kulman* ghost) verbally inarticulate. In a sure sign that this is also a very structural process, this occurs around the time when the deceased is passing out of living memory, around the time that there is no one left alive to remember him. We can say that a butterfly is a Memory without rememberers.

Does this second death, this total forgetting, occur in the deepest recesses of liminality? Or is it this, rather than the transformation into a safe ancestor, that represents the final stage of the dead person's reintegration? Perhaps reintegration can never be complete because the entire cosmology is a compensation and consolation for a loss that cannot be undone. The communitas of the dead is likewise not so clear-cut. The living are themselves all at various stages on the way to joining the dead, and the communitas of the dead constantly reaches out in an attempt to draw them in. The living cannot avoid sharing in this communitas a little bit all the time, with each episode of illness, each dialogue, each expression of sympathy or anxiety. But they use dialogue to avoid, for as long as possible, being engulfed in this communitas, until they too finally succumb to one among the many modes of death.

So Sora communitas, too, is both structured and yet without clear borders. Each person goes through the process of dying at different moments and at different rates. In addition, the dead interact with the living and even have a social life of their own in the underworld. All of this affects the trajectory of transformation among both the dead and the living and seems to be almost the opposite of Turner's model of a homogenized antistructure or nonstructure. It could even be said that the state of being dead has a more elaborate logic or structure than the state of being alive. It mirrors and even regulates the entire dynamic of lineages, marriage, inheritance disputes, and jealousies in the world of the living. Momo's attack on Jamano was triggered by a living man's sorcery; the dead wife intervened from the underworld to urge her living sister to marry her surviving husband; and the old man babysitting in the underworld was trying to influence the outcome of an inheritance dispute above ground.

Sora cosmology emphasizes postmortem liminality not so much as a state but as a process, and one that is never separate from the ongoing concerns of the living. It is because this process of transformation is so elaborate, even structured, that it needs a long time span to work itself through. The technique of dialogue clarifies this process and makes it manifest, but also enables it to take place. It does all this in a particular way, by bringing both dead and living into a state of very close and articulate communication and communion, precipitated by the empathy of shared symptoms. This entire society lives in a fluctuating field of perpetual communitas between the living and the dead. Within this field, the events or episodes of illness, death, and dialogue form nodes or points of concentration, in which each person's involvement in this communitas rises and falls, surges and recedes, according to daily illnesses or other moments of intensified engagement with the dead. In order to stay alive for as long as possible, the living must repeatedly separate themselves from their unavoidable engagement with the communitas of the dead.

**Piers Vitebsky** studied ancient languages before becoming an anthropologist, specializing in indigenous peoples of India and Siberia. He is head of anthropology and Russian northern studies at the Scott Polar Research Institute in the University of Cambridge. His books include *The Reindeer People: Living with Animals and Spirits in Siberia* (Houghton Mifflin 2005), *Dialogues with the Dead: The Discussion of Mortality among the Sora of Eastern India* (Cambridge University Press 1993), and *Shamanism: Voyages of the Soul from Siberia to the Amazon* (University of Oklahoma Press 2001). His book *Loving and Forgetting: Changing Forms of Loss and Redemption in Tribal India* will be published by the University of Chicago Press in 2016.

# Notes

1.  I have carried out research among the Sora since 1975 and during this period have been indebted to very many people who are listed elsewhere, mainly in Vitebsky 1993. I am grateful to Peter Berger, Bruce Kapferer, Judith Pettigrew, Anastasia Piliavsky, and Sally Wolfe for comments on the present chapter, and to the University of Tromsø (Norway) for a professorship, which funded my most recent fieldwork. Thanks, too, to my mother, who first taught me about gardening and compost heaps.
2.  "Tribe" is a conventional if controversial term which has a particular meaning in the Indian context (Dumont 1959; Ghurye 1943; Guha 1999; Prasad 2003).
3.  For ease of exposition I have used the ethnographic present. This represents the situation in the 1970s, when I first started living with the Sora. In recent years, most young Soras have become Baptists, a doctrine which leaves the liminal state of the dead unknowable. I have started to explore the implications of this drastic change in Vitebsky 2008 and 2013, and will analyze it in detail in *Loving and Forgetting: Changing Forms of Loss and Redemption in Tribal India*, in press.
4.  The separation, liminal state, and reintegration of the shaman, who enters a trance, descends to the underworld, and takes care to return alive, is another matter which cannot be dealt with here (see Vitebsky 1993 and in press).
5.  In the course of preparing my next book (Vitebsky in press) on the shift to Christianity, the new focus on ideas of redemption has forced me to reassess the old Sora religion as a theology.
6.  While holding many of the emotional variables constant, this inverts the secular model of bereavement in psychotherapy and psychoanalysis, whereby the dead exist only in the memory or mind of the mourner (Freud [1917] 1957; Vitebsky 1993: ch. 10).
7.  A married woman receives a funeral from both her natal lineage and the lineage into which she has married, becoming an ancestor to both. But a sign of a strong, long-lasting marriage is that she gradually shifts her allegiance away from the former and towards the latter, especially if she has borne male children. The decisive evidence for her ultimate loyalty is the emergence of her name among the descendants of her husband, rather than of her brothers.
8.  This happened soon after the working of this system finally became clear to me, and it was the first time that I successfully and confidently predicted where a disputed name would reappear.
9.  This is the opposite of Freud's ([1917] 1957) model of bereavement. The emotional processes he describes are strikingly similar to those of the Sora, with the crucial difference that, for Freud, the dead person no longer exists in objective or public reality, but only in a private world that the patient shares only with the analyst (see Vitebsky 1993: ch. 10).

# References

Condominas, Georges. (1975, in French) 1994. *We Have Eaten the Forest: The Story of a Montagnard Village in the Central Highlands of Vietnam*. New York: Kodansha.

Dumont, Louis. 1959. "Possession and Priesthood." *Contributions to Indian Sociology* 3: 55–74.

Freud, Sigmund. (1917, in German) 1957. "Mourning and Melancholia." In *The Standard Edition of the Complete Psychological Works of Sigmund Freud*, Vol. 14, transl. James Strachey, 239–58. London: Hogarth Press.

Fürer-Haimendorf, Christoph von. 1943. "Megalithic Ritual among the Gadabas and Bondos of Orissa." *Journal and Proceedings of the Royal Asiatic Society of Bengal* 9: 149–78.

Ghurye, G.S. 1943. *The Aboriginals — "So Called" — and Their Future*. Poona: Ghokhale Institute of Politics and Economics.

Guha, Ramachandra. 1999. *Savaging the Civilised: Verrier Elwin, his Tribals, and India*. New Delhi: Oxford University Press.

Pfeffer, Georg. 2001. "A Ritual of Revival among the Gadaba of Koraput." In *Jagannath Revisited: Studying Society, Religion and the State in Orissa*, ed. Hermann Kulke and Burkhard Schnepel, 99–123. New Delhi: Manohar.

Prasad, Archana. 2003. *Against Ecological Romanticism: Verrier Elwin and the Making of an Anti-Modern Tribal Identity*. New Delhi: Three Essays Collective.

Rousseleau, Raphael. 2012. "Megalithic Landscapes, Cultures and Identity in Northeast India." In *Nature, Environment and Society: Conservation, Governance and Transformation in India*, ed. Nicolas Lainé and Tanka B. Subba. New Delhi: Orient Longman, 17–35.

Scott, James C. 2009. *The Art of Not Being Governed: An Anarchist History of Upland Southeast Asia*. New Haven: Yale University Press.

Turner, Victor W. 1969. *The Ritual Process: Structure and Anti-Structure*. Chicago: Aldine.

van Gennep, Arnold. (1909, in French) 1960. *The Rites of Passage*, trans. Monika B. Vizedom and Gabrielle L. Caffee. Chicago: University of Chicago Press.

Vitebsky, Piers. 1993. *Dialogues with the Dead: The Discussion of Mortality among the Sora of Eastern India*. Cambridge: Cambridge University Press and Delhi: Foundation Books.

————. 2008. "Loving and Forgetting: Moments of Inarticulacy in Tribal India." *Journal of the Royal Anthropological Institute* 14: 243–61.

————. 2013. "Stones, Shamans and Pastors: Pagan and Baptist Temporalities of Death in Tribal India." In *Taming Time, Timing Death: Social Technologies and Ritual*, ed. Dorthe R. Christensen and Rane Willerslev, 119–36. Farnham: Ashgate.

————. In press. *Loving and Forgetting: Changing Forms of Loss and Redemption in Tribal India*. Chicago: University of Chicago Press.

*Figure 3.1.* An old Gadaba woman is mourning and saying farewell to a dead relative (in the body of a water buffalo) who is about to ultimately leave the village (Odisha, India) (photo Peter Berger).

*Chapter Three*

# Liminal Bodies, Liminal Food
## Hindu and Tribal Death Rituals Compared

*Peter Berger*

In the anthropology of India, a curious shift in focus is discernible that coincides more or less with the independence of the county. Before 1947, most anthropologists were concerned with tribal societies; afterwards, when many more professional anthropologists started to do research in India, attention shifted to caste and Hinduism (see Berger 2012). Accordingly, while the ethnographies on caste society have contributed significantly to general anthropological debates, most notably in terms of the themes of social stratification and hierarchy, the anthropology of Indian tribal society has scarcely been recognized in the discipline as a whole.[1]

Tribal societies are found mostly in hill regions in India—for example, in the Northeast of the country, the Nilgiri hills in the extreme South, or the huge region between the two rivers Ganges and Godavari known as Middle India. To a greater or lesser extent, these highland societies have had contact with the population of the plains, which was and is still predominantly Hindu. Throughout Indian history, and certainly not today, we hardly come across any tribal communities living in complete "splendid isolation," as in other parts of the world. As a result, we encounter a much more complex situation where, throughout the centuries, different societal and religious systems interact with one another—either rarely or frequently, superficially or intensively, as the case may be. This situation may be one of the reasons why scholars have not always found it easy to

---

clearly distinguish tribes from castes, and some questioned the usefulness of these categories altogether.

Early on, Louis Dumont and David Pocock (Dumont [1957] 1970: 3) described the tribal societies merely as "people who have lost contact" with Hindu civilization, and Dumont did not concern himself any further with these highlanders in his immensely influential work on India. On the basis of his ethnographic experience with the Kond, Frederik Bailey (1961) suggested a continuum approach, an ideal type of caste and tribe at either end, and the empirical cases somewhere in-between, closer to one or the other of the poles. While some other authors have argued against such an approach, stating that tribal and Hindu (caste) configurations display principally different sets of social structures and values (Parkin 1992; Pfeffer 1982, 1997; see also Hardenberg 2010), anthropologists of the post-colonial discourse have held that caste and tribe are rather to be understood as products of British colonial administrative and ethnographic efforts (Dirks 2001; van Schendel and Bal 2002).

Certainly caste and tribe as administrative categories are a colonial heritage. In the context of "protective discrimination," the Indian government is still reserving seats in the parliaments and posts in the administration, among other things, for those communities that every decade anew are scheduled as "caste" ("Scheduled Caste," SC), "tribe" ("Scheduled Tribe," ST), or "Other Backward Classes" (OBC), regularly leading to conflicts. However, the generally arbitrary administrative classification—in one census a community may figure as ST, and then as OBC ten years later—is not really a proper guide for an anthropologist aiming at investigating and understanding social life and cultural patterns of any such community. These classifications, and the political scenarios they give rise to, can themselves be the object of anthropological enquiry, but they certainly do not help much in an attempt to understand what a tribe or caste is, or what it means to be a member of such a community. If we want to understand Indian society and culture—highland or lowland—as lived and conceptualized, a (historically conscious) careful empirical investigation and comparative analysis is a promising way to do that. When dealing with India, especially with Hinduism, the rich textual traditions and sources obviously have to be taken into account as well. On such a basis, cultural differences can be outlined, independent of administrative classifications.

I do share the view, pointed out in the introduction to this volume, that ideas and practices surrounding death manifest key ideas and structures of the society concerned. Hence, I think it is worthwhile to compare Hindu and tribal death rituals in order to understand cultural differences and similarities, and I will present such a comparison here.[2] My own ethnographic research focused on a highland community of southern Orissa[3] called Gadaba.[4] Before I started my research, not much was known about the Gadaba, but the last stage of their death rituals had attracted the attention of several scholars and was well documented (Fürer-Haimendorf 1943; Izikowitz 1969; Pfeffer 1991, 2001). In a sense, this death ritual served as a starting point for my analysis of the ritual system as a whole (Berger 2007a). In highland Orissa, with poor medical facilities and cerebral malaria being endemic, death is part of everyday life, and I witnessed many deaths and documented all stages in detail. Although I have attended Hindu death rituals (high caste as well as low caste), I never documented them systematically, and my description of Hindu ideas and practices of death are based on the rich indological and anthropological literature. Some preliminary remarks are necessary before I commence with a description and analysis of the cases.

Is the Gadaba material representative of tribal India? In a sense the ritual process following death in a Gadaba community is unique, and the final phase of death mentioned above even identifies the Gadaba as a particular ethnic group in the region. However, there are many family resemblances found in death rituals throughout Middle India, and the features that I will emphasize in my analysis of Gadaba death rituals are also valid for many of the other communities (see, for example, Behera 2010; Demmer 2007; Elwin 1945, 1950; Fürer-Haimendorf 1953; Parkin 1992; Pfeffer 2006; Reichel 2009; Vitebsky 1993).

Are Hindu death rituals sufficiently homogenous? Obviously, we can choose whether we want to stress idiosyncrasies or want to discern general common patterns. This also holds for the question about whether there is such a thing as Hinduism at all, or whether we should speak rather of Hindu religions. At least some authors (Fuller 1992; Michaels 1998) hold that it is justified to speak of Hinduism as a coherent religious system, and, by the same token, many scholars have argued with reference to Hindu death rituals that—notwithstanding regional differences and variations among high and low castes—the core of the ritual process is the same (Kaushik 1976: 267; Knipe 1977: 111; Nicholas 1982: 374; see also Inden and Nicholas 1977: xii, 37; Knipe 2007: 62).

In what follows, I will first present an outline of Gadaba death rituals and also briefly sketch the social structure of this highland society. This will be followed by a description of the ritual process following the death of a Hindu. The consecutive comparison will show that in both ritual processes, a stress on food and bodies is discernible. The deceased is fed and provided with a new body in both cases. Moreover, the dead also become food. Despite these similarities, I shall argue that the ritual processes display fundamental differences. I will in particular focus on the nature of the ritual transactions and the values they imply.

## Gadaba Death Rituals

As elsewhere in Middle India, Gadaba society is structured along "horizontal" lines (Pfeffer 1997). What this means is that patrilineal descent defines membership in local groups, but genealogical reckoning (the vertical dimension) is otherwise irrelevant, and local groups oppose each other in various contexts. Exchange relationships of different kinds are crucial in this pattern, and death rituals are first of all rituals of exchange, as will be seen (see also De Maaker, in this volume).

The Gutob-speaking Gadaba I am mainly concerned with here number approximately fifteen thousand individuals who live in compact villages on a plateau about nine hundred meters above sea level in the Koraput district in the state of Orissa. They are cultivators who grow wet rice in extended and terraced river beds, and mainly millet on the dry slopes surrounding their villages. Several communities of cultivators like the Gadaba live on the plateau in their own villages, while noncultivating communities, such as those of gardeners, blacksmiths, or petty traders and musicians, are dispersed over the area and are found in smaller or larger numbers in nearly all the villages of cultivators. In Gadaba villages, these service communities are known as "late-comers," as opposed to the Gadaba, who are "earth-people." Since the former are largely irrelevant in terms of the performance of death rituals, I will not be concerned with them any further here (see Berger 2002).

As far as the social structure is concerned, Gadaba society as a whole is divided into four clan categories of cobra, tiger, sun, and monkey, which empirically take shape in villages. Thus we find villages where one or the other category dominates and is considered as its founder ("earth-people"). All people belonging to a certain descent category regard its other members, irrespective of residence, as "brothers" or "sisters," and members of all other categories as potential marriage partners. Thus, we find a simple but fundamental and all-encompassing opposition between "brothers" (*bai*) and "others" (*bondu*), or, in anthropological jargon, between agnates and affines.

Life-cycle rituals are basically the same for men and women. Individuals pass through a sequence of ritual processes that gradually transform them from the presocial status of "navel" or "flower" to a full-fledged social and ritual being. The culmination of this process is marriage, not death. Two social relationships are especially important in the ritual production of a social person. The first concerns the above-mentioned category of brothers, the second, marriageable others. Both kinds of relationships—agnatic brothers or affinal others—are involved in alimentary exchanges in different life-cycle rituals. In particular, it is through feeding of a special kind of sacrificial food (*tsoru*) that individuals are transformed into social and ritual persons (Berger 2007b). Accordingly, the crucial agnatic relationship is literally called that of "sacrificial-food-brother" (*tsorubai*). This kind of relationship exists between two local groups—for example, between villages—which are connected in this way through the generations. In the context of life-cycle rituals, food-brothers are called on to cook and serve sacrificial food. Not only during rites of transition but also during times of crisis, when the cosmological order or tradition (*niam*) is temporarily in danger, food-brothers are called upon to sacrifice, cook, and feed, as it is said, in order to "restore order" (*niam korbar*). Such services are always reciprocated on another occasion.

The second important affinal relationship in life-cycle rituals is that of the maternal uncle or *mamu*. Marriage relationships, too, are collective, symmetrical, and permanent. That means that a local group of, for example, Cobras of a particular locality would regularly give away their sisters and daughters to another village, who can be anything except Cobra, with, for instance, Tiger being acceptable. The significant symmetrical aspect lies in the fact that the Tiger group also gives their own sisters away to the Cobra; the transactions thus go both ways. Women that are given away for marriage are considered as "milk-gifts" and their brothers as givers of the milk. A man will always have a special responsibility towards his sister's children—that is, to the offspring of his milk-gift. Like the food-brothers, the maternal uncle cooks and feeds sacrificial food during life-cycle rituals. Although the food prepared and fed is materially the same, as it consists of rice, blood, and meat, it is the social quality of those who prepare the food that makes it fundamentally different. Those who cook and feed also transmit a social quality along with the food. Thus agnatic and affinal sacrificial food is very different, and each contributes in its own way towards making the receiving person grow ritually.

The Gadaba generally conceive of death as a violent event, in which a person is subject to an attack of aggressive "consumption."[5] The "life-force" of humans may be consumed by demons, for example. However, there are also other agents who kill people, such as malevolent ghosts or sorcerers in the neighborhood. However, the fact that a death is violent does not necessarily make it a bad death. Bad deaths are spatially liminal. To die on a path between villages, for example, or to die in the forest outside of any settlement, is dreaded. The ghosts of such persons are dangerous and likely to cause more death. The cosmological order (*niam*) is threatened, and the food-brothers are called upon to sacrifice in the name of society as a whole in order to restore the sacred order. In such cases, twelve animals must be sacrificed (twelve suggesting the social whole). In what follows, I will focus on a normal death, which requires fewer sacrifices and preferably takes place in the house of the dying person.

Among the Gadaba, death is dealt with in four consecutive steps spanning a period of about one generation. I will briefly point out their essential features with reference to the focus at hand—that is, bodies and food—and will also indicate those moments qualifying as effervescent situations (see ch. 7 in this volume). When a person dies, the life-force (*jibon*) leaves the body and is believed to roam around freely. For a while, the life-force is thought of as being attached to the social quality of the deceased person. This social quality is called *duma*. While the life-force is beyond human influence, the *duma* is at the center of all ritual practices that I will describe in the following paragraphs. Immediately after death, while life-force and *duma* are still joined, the threat of further deaths or misfortune is greatest. As noted above, depending on the circumstances, the *duma* may be vengeful, and he or she has to be appeased through ritual action, most crucially by being fed.

The corpse is cremated as quickly as possible, preferably on the day the person has died. On this day, the food-brothers of the local group and the maternal uncle of the deceased are informed because they are the ones who have to perform the most important ritual functions.[6] The body is cremated, and then the *duma* receives sacrificial food for the first time. Also, while still at the cremation site, the food-brothers take an axe belonging to the deceased, detach the axe head, and reattach it top-down. This moment is the beginning of the period of impurity, which affects all brothers of the village—that is, all of the people sharing the same descent category.

Mourning is exclusively the work of women. During several transitory moments in the ritual process, women wail in a highly standardized way. However, the intensity of the expression differs according to kinship distance. Generally, women put their hands on their heads and start wailing loudly and melodically, alternately raising and lowering their voices. Close female kin (sisters, widows, daughters, mothers) usually perform acts of self-mutilation, tearing their hair, beating their chests, and scratching their cheeks until they bleed. When women of another village visit the house of a deceased person, they start wailing as they enter the yard, whereas they may have been engaged in cheerful conversation only seconds before. Typical moments of female expression of grief are when the corpse is brought out of the house to be washed in the yard, when it is taken away to the cremation ground, and on the cremation ground itself. While girls learn this behavior at a very early age, there is no such standardized way for men to show their grief. I have seen men who had just lost close relatives being held by others in order not to become violent; twice I have seen men turning somersaults out of desperation. The stylized public female expression of grief is thus in stark contrast with the complete lack of a stylized form among men. It is not that men are not allowed to show grief publicly, but that they do not have a prescribed way to come to terms with their overwhelming emotions.

The period of impurity only lasts until the third day, when the axe of the deceased is returned to its normal form. On that day, the food-brothers and the maternal uncle of the deceased again go to the cremation ground to feed the *duma*. In addition, in the house of the deceased, the *duma* is provided with liquor by his maternal uncle and told to leave the living in peace. Even during this first phase of liminality, when death pollution is prevalent, restrictions on the living related to impurity are minimal. The widow or the widower is not allowed to cook, change clothes, or to wash for these three days, and then life generally returns to normal. As will be seen, this contrasts with the stress on pollution in Hindu death rituals.

Even though the phase of impurity has ended, the *duma* is still considered to be restless. A gust of wind or a rustle in a tree are considered to be evidence of its activity and presence. Moreover, the villagers may still become possessed by the *duma*, who has not yet joined the "community of the dead" (*duma kul*). Therefore, two more ritual steps are required before the final status of the deceased is achieved.

Usually some months after death, a major ritual is performed, which is more or less the same as the previous one, since it involves the feeding of the *duma* by the food-brothers and the *mamu*. However, it takes place on a much larger scale. Not only is the whole village of the deceased involved, but affines from other villages also visit the house of the deceased. Again, females will show their grief at various moments, as described above. The affines bring cattle as a typical gift.[7] Some of the cattle are slaughtered, and the pieces of raw meat distributed among representatives of the different local groups. One cow is also sacrificed for the deceased, who is fed by all the households of the village, both on the cremation ground and in his or her house. This ritual serves to finally detach the *duma* from the sphere of the living and to join it with the community of the dead. The *duma* is now quiet but not yet transformed into an ancestor (*anibai*). The transformation is finally completed in a ritual performance called *go'ter*, which, because of its spectacular features, drew the attention of earlier ethnographers, as I mentioned above.

The ritual takes place roughly about once a generation in any particular locality and is performed by a local group of brothers—for example, by all the agnates of a village or a segment thereof. It is thus a collective endeavor and involves the *duma* of all persons who have died since the last such occasion. All these *duma*, perhaps ten, possibly more than one hundred, are revived and reembodied in the process of the ritual, with the sons of the deceased calling out their names and thereby reawakening them during a sacrifice. Each *duma* is then transformed into the body of a living water buffalo, a feat performed by feeding the animal. Once this has been done, the buffalo is perceived as a truly liminal living *duma*, and mourned and fed by the women for several days.

How is the final transformation brought about, and by whom? The above-mentioned food-brothers and the maternal uncle of the various deceased persons are also involved in the ritual. It is, however, a specific type of agnatic relationship, which I here refer to as that of "stone-brothers" (*panjabai*, meaning unclear), which is most prominent during the last stage of death rituals. Like the food-brothers, two local groups are permanently connected as stone-brothers, and their services, again, are reciprocal. However, unlike the other relationships mentioned above, stone-brothers only appear during the last stage of the death ritual. There is no other context in which stone-brothers are called upon, but they are necessary in order to accomplish the final transformation. In their role as stone-brothers, they first replace the dead with memorial stones in and around the village of the deceased, and later take the buffalo-ghosts to their villages to be slaughtered and eaten; thus they replace and assimilate the dead by consuming them. The evening before the final day of the ritual, the stone-brothers appear in the hosts' village, where all the buffaloes are then tethered to the central memorial platform. They do not just walk into the village but conquer the place, arriving after dusk in group formation, beating drums, whistling, and swinging long sticks. While most of these men then dance around the buffaloes, beating them on their backs, and grabbing and consuming the rice and beer that the women intended to feed the buffaloes with, some erect a pair of memorial stones next to others from previous occasions.

On the morning of the final day, the buffaloes are dressed according to the sex of the deceased and decorated with his or her personal belongings: metal plates, slippers, or a school book. Then the dead finally leave the village—another intense emotional moment marked by female mourning—and the buffaloes are tied to an external stone platform in the dry fields. There they remain close to the memorial stones for most of the day.

The climax of the ritual consists of the advent of affinal buffaloes, "affinal buffaloes" being usually an oxymoron locally as buffaloes are commonly given and taken by agnates only. This sequence is maybe the most remarkable phase in the whole ritual process, and it presents several conspicuous features. Generally, affines only exchange cattle and sisters, as I have already pointed out. On this special occasion, affines of the deceased may bring buffaloes that also contain the ghosts of the respective persons.[8] Once such a buffalo has approached the area where the other buffaloes are tethered, a crowd of men chase after the animal and slice open the animal's belly to tear out the intestines. Whether eaten or buried in the fields, the intestines are believed to enhance fecundity.

When this spectacle—observed by hundreds of people—is over, the stone-brothers hastily take the hosts' buffaloes to their villages. The buffaloes may not be put to work in the fields but instead will be slaughtered and eaten during the weeks to come. What remains in the hosts' village are the memorial stones representing the permanent ancestors who have replaced the liminal dead. In the ritual process, the dead also lose their individual identity. Several sets of stones now embody a whole generation of ancestors. This is visible most prominently at the center of each village. Opposite the shrine of the local earth deity is a stone platform, the assembly place of the village. Ideally, every generation of the village since its foundation is represented by a pair of stones, one upright and the other flat, placed in the context of the final death rituals.

In this way, Gadaba transform their dead through symmetric transactions of food and bodies between local groups. What happens to the life-force of the individual deceased? Some weeks after death, the life-force detaches itself from the *duma*. At some point, the life-force then attaches itself to an embryonic body in the womb of a pregnant woman and is reborn. While not always, frequently the life-force reappears in the alternate generation, that is, a grandfather is reborn in the generation of his grandson (see Parkin 1992). The life-forces of those persons who died a spatially liminal death will not reincarnate. But a human being cannot be reborn as anything other than human. This contrasts with Hindu ideas concerning death and rebirth, to which I now turn.

## Hindu Death Rituals

Cremation is referred to as the "final rite" or "last sacrifice" (*antyesti;*[9] Pandey 1976: 253; Parry 1994: 178) because it concludes a series of life-cycle rituals called *samskara,*[10] meaning completing, purifying, or refining, which already signifies the progression involved in life-cycle rituals. In the Hindu[11] view, birth is a messy business and, above all, is ritually impure because all kinds of bodily fluids are involved. Hence, all individuals are born as Shudras, the lowest and most impure of the traditional social categories.[12] It is only through the transformations due to *samskaras*—or perfections—performed according to the code of conduct (*dharma*) defined by caste and gender that an individual can fully develop his or her moral and religious potential. At the end of a long and virtuous life, death should be a controlled affair; a voluntary relinquishment of life. This is the Hindu idea of a good death. Having sacrificed to the gods as a house-holder throughout life, the corpse of a man becomes the last oblation to Agni, the god of fire. The correct performance of these rites determines the status of the deceased in the following life. As chief mourner, the eldest son carries the burden of fulfilling these rites for his parents. "Bad deaths" are those where the "deceased has revealed no intention of sacrificing his body (e.g., the victim of violence or accident), or of renouncing its desires (e.g., suicide)" (Parry 1994: 163). Few male Brahmans pass through all four of the traditional life-stages, the last two being dedicated to ascetic values and liberation, the stage of the forest dweller, and, finally, of the renouncer. Parry (1994: 189) significantly describes cremation as "last-ditch renunciation." What only few actually perform in life (renunciation) can be achieved at death.

As in the example of the Gadaba, the elements of food and body are cru-cial in Hindu death rituals, irrespective of gender, caste status, or region. Food and body are key factors in kinship, or, more generally, in belong-ing. What makes people kin is the fact that they "share a body," which is the literal meaning of *sapinda*, a kinship unit including males who share the body of an ancestral male from seven generations back (Inden and Nicholas 1977: 13f; Knipe 1977: 118).[13] Kinship is best sustained by sharing food, which is one reason why food is a precarious element for Hindus.[14] It affects the state of being, both individually and with regard to the group. Bodies are at the same time a material and a moral phenomenon, with a simple soul-body dichotomy not applying here. Hindus distinguish between a gross body (*sthula sarira*), constituted through nourishment and containing the five elements (*mahabutas*),[15] and a subtle body (*lingasarira* or *suksmasarira*), associated with the mind and consciousness. The subtle body is modified through the actions (*karma*) of the individual, determin-ing his or her rebirth (cf. Holdrege 1998: 346f; Inden and Nicholas 1977: 63; Michaels 1998: 155).

During the process of death, the gross body is destroyed and is offered up in the cremation fire. While the corpse burns in the flames, the eldest son of the deceased, the chief mourner and sacrificer (Knipe 1977: 114), must perform the rite of breaking his father's (or mother's) skull with a bamboo pole, thereby releasing the subtle soul-body, which is considered to be the size of a thumb and is referred to as "ghost" (*preta*). Whereas the corpse was a pure offering before the cremation (Stevenson [1920] 1971: 145), after the cracking of the skull, the family is considered to be ritually polluted for the following ten days.

Specific ritual details and ideas necessarily vary from caste to caste and in different regions. Whether the rites following the tenth day are accompanied by Vedic *mantras*, for example, depends on caste status. An essential and general feature, however, is the offering of rice balls called *pinda dan*, literally the "gift of the body." They are offered in three sets of sixteen balls, ideally over a period of a year. The name of these three sets again indicates the progression involved in the rites: they are called the "impure sixteen," the "middle sixteen," and the "highest sixteen" (Parry 1994).

The first six balls are offered to unspecified ghosts and to Agni during the cremation. A further ten balls are given as offerings to the departed but, more importantly, also constitute a new body for the ghost, who is not able to receive food while in the form of the thumb-sized soul-body. During the first ten days, one rice ball should be given every day, each constituting a particular organ of the new body (Knipe 1977; Parry 1994: 196). The tenth ball constitutes hunger and thirst, or the digestive system. The ten days symbolize ten lunar months, which refers to the period of gestation. Thus death is also conceived of as a rebirth. On the tenth day, the chief mourner usually makes an offering of all ten balls, immersing them in a river. The newly constructed body has the length of a forearm and is also referred to as the "suffering body" (*yatana sarira*), because it can now suffer hunger and thirst and has to be provided with food in the following period.

During the first ten days, the ghost, the chief mourner, and the funeral priest who guides the former's performance are closely associated and even identified. They all share the most extreme pollution, and the funeral priest as well as the son frequently eat on behalf of the deceased. In eating the food for the ghost (including the second set of rice balls), the son and especially the priest must digest the sins (*pap*) accumulated by the deceased during his life. Frequently, the priest complains about this heavy responsibility and later receives a significant gift for compensation. On the tenth day after cremation, the chief mourner is tonsured and shaved by the barber, who receives utensils, bedding, and clothes for his service. The most intense period of impurity is then over, but the son cannot commence worshipping the gods until the last set of rice balls has been offered.

With his new body, the ghost now experiences severe hunger and has to be fed further. The middle set of sixteen rice balls given on the eleventh day serves this purpose. Again, the chief mourner and the funeral priest eat for the deceased. After this, the funeral priest leaves, receiving a religious gift (*sajja dan*) of a year's supply of grain. The idea is that he continues to eat for the dead on the latter's journey, but this gift also contains part of the deceased, namely his sins. Hence, receiving this ambivalent gift is not only a right but part of his duty. The ghost now embarks on its year-long journey to the abode of the ancestors, with the third set of sixteen rice balls sustaining him on his way.

The funeral rituals end with the crucial ritual sequence called "making the body" (*sapindikarana*), which ultimately achieves the transformation of the ghost into an ancestor (*pitr*) (see Mirnig in this volume). The ritual should be performed on the anniversary of the death, after the journey of the ghost has been completed, but it is usually carried out on the twelfth day, each day representing one month. The intense pollution and period of inauspiciousness have now passed. Therefore, the ritual can take place inside the house and is led by a pure priest of the family (*purohit*), rather than the relatively impure funeral priest.

At the beginning of the ritual, five Brahmans (often substituted by a certain kind of grass) are fed, who represent different lineal positions in the agnatic *sapinda* group of the deceased, that is, the direct ascending line of males. One represents the ghost, and another three his lineal male ancestors, the deceased's father, grandfather, and great-grandfather, who are remembered individually. The fifth Brahman represents the category of divine ancestors (*vishvadevas*) who reside in heaven.

Four more rice balls are then made and identified with the dead, as had previously been the case with the Brahmans.[16] One elongated ball represents the ghost, while the three round balls next to it symbolize his three lineal ascendants. The chief mourner breathes life into the rice balls, which are then believed to be the real bodies of the ghost and his ancestors (Parry 1994: 205). In the next step, called "mixing with the ancestors" (*pitr miloni*), the chief mourner cuts the long ball into three pieces and then first merges each part with one of the three ancestral balls before joining them all together. With this act of joining the bodies, the ghost is included in the category of ancestors, which comprises three generations. Accordingly, the ancestor at the other end (i.e., great-great-grandfather) is pushed out of the ancestral category to become an anonymous divine ancestor in heaven. This means that one's destiny not only depends on one's own funeral and one's own son, but also on the funerals that will follow, performed by the grandson and great-grandsons. This is why it is so crucial that the agnatic line is continued, as it guarantees each individual's successful progression to future forms of existence.

Having guided these last rites, the house priest also receives a religious gift of a year's supply of grain. Like the funeral priest preceding him, he should eat on behalf of the dead for one year. The reintegration and change of status of the deceased's son is marked by the tying of a turban. He is now the new head of the household and as such continues to worship the gods. Finally, a feast is held for the Brahmans. Although the period of inauspiciousness and pollution is over, the occasion is still full of ambivalence, as the invited Brahmans not only eat on behalf of the dead but also ingest certain undesired aspects of the deceased.

## Comparison

Not only are the deceased and his lineal ascendants brought to life in the *sapindikarana* ritual by breathing onto the rice-bodies, but the chief mourner also consumes these bodies by smelling them. The themes of revival and consumption of the dead are thus clearly present in Hindu death rituals, even if less explicitly and in a more spiritualized way than among the Gadaba. Parry mentions the belief that this consumption of the rice-bodies will lead to male offspring—that is, a son for the chief mourner: "[T]hough the notion is clearly inconsistent with karma theory, the idea is that the great-grandfather will come back as his own great-grandson" (Parry 1994: 205). The consumption of ancestral bodies thus facilitates agnatic continuity. At first sight, this seems to closely resemble the Gadaba case, as ascendants are consumed by male agnates of the succeeding generation. However, the Gadaba do not believe that consuming the dead leads to agnatic procreation. Moreover, and perhaps more significantly, while the son consumes his father (and other ascendants) in the Hindu case, the consumption of the dead always necessitates exchange among the Gadaba: exophagy instead of endophagy. The dead are consumed by agnates and clan-brothers, but from a different location, not by their sons. The reciprocal consumption of the dead between different local groups among the Gadaba results in a different pattern that stresses the identification of alternate generations. A person is consumed only indirectly by his grandson, the same person ideally also in possession of the former's life-force (for details, see Berger 2007a: 327f). Having mentioned the significance of exchange in Gadaba death rituals in contrast to the Hindu case, let me now further compare the two ritual processes.

The similarities between Hindu and Gadaba death rituals are obvious. In both cases the corpse is cremated and a new body (or several) provided. The deceased is fed while in this liminal state, but this new body is also eaten. However, there are also crucial differences, not so much concerning specific elements, such as the fact that the new body of the deceased consists of rice balls in one case and water buffaloes in the other. This is, of course, not an insignificant difference; however, the structural differences provide us with a deeper insight into the values that are expressed in each case and the social relationships that are represented and regenerated in the ritual process.

Another difference I want to highlight refers to the actors involved in the ritual practices and exchanges. In the case of the Gadaba, members of the immediate family of the deceased have no significant ritual function. The transformation of the dead is brought about through feeding and eating processes in which collective relationships are crucial. The food-brothers, the stone-brothers, and also the maternal uncle represent local groups that are permanently connected as agnates or affines with the group of the deceased.

In the Hindu case described, the most significant ritual actors are a pure and an impure Brahman priest, the barber, and the eldest son of the deceased. With regard to the first three, we can note that they denote service relationships between castes, a ritual division of labor. In rural areas, such service relationships are usually hereditary, and the families of the patron and client are permanently related. The Brahman priest will serve various high castes, but not the lowest, because of their low ritual purity. Even the barbers will not serve members of all castes, while the Dalit, members of the lowest castes, have to replicate this pattern of relationships among themselves (Moffatt 1979). The important point here is that the family of the deceased relies on members of other castes who have specialized occupations for the performance of life-cycle rituals.

Because ritual purity is a key value which structures relationships in caste society, such services can never be reciprocated. If a funeral priest conducts the rites for someone, this person (or anyone of his family) will not perform the death rituals for a member of the priest's family. Moreover, within one caste such services are also not reciprocal. The Gadaba, by contrast, do not depend on any other community in order to get their dead transformed into ancestors. The value of ritual purity is not the driving idea in their society, and thus different local groups of the same community, who are equal in status and functionally equivalent, can perform each other's death rituals; they even eat each other's dead.

This difference between asymmetrical and symmetrical social and ritual relationships is not only related to specialized occupations concerned with purity and contamination, or their absence, but also points to another, though related, aspect—the ideas of sin, merit, and liberation, and their expression in gift-giving. The rice balls offered in the context of Hindu death rites are called *pinda dan*, thus "the gift of the body." *Dan* is a very specific type of religious gift since it transfers demerit or sin. Therefore, it is a major duty of the son as chief mourner and the priests to eat *on behalf of* the deceased in order to "digest" the sins the latter has accumulated during his lifetime. The funeral priest often complains about his onerous and taxing duty. In theory, he should pass the unwanted aspects on to other Brahmins by distributing what he receives from the family of the deceased. The chief mourner will be purified by his own son after his death. The concept of *dan* precludes any reciprocity. The gift is only effective if the donor gives it without the expectation of any return. Only the so-called unseen fruits of this gift may be harvested—that is, the positive effects of this gift in a future form of existence. However, already the thought of such later gains is detrimental for the efficacy of the gift (Parry 1986).

This notion of unilateral religious gift-giving is absent among the Gadaba, as well as among many other Indian tribal societies. Accordingly, the mode of eating on behalf of the deceased is not found. You may share your food with the dead, feed them, or eat them, but you do not eat on their behalf. What reigns here is a sociology rather than a soteriology of exchange (see Trautmann, quoted in Parry 1986: 462). As has been described above, in the Gadaba case and in tribal Indian religions in general, rebirth is not "ethicized," to use Obeyesekere's (1980: 146) expression: "The otherworld [poorly conceptualized and largely insignificant among the Gadaba] is for saint and sinner alike. There is no notion of ethical compensation or reward, that is, sin and merit." Among the Gadaba, individuals do not throughout life accumulate merit or sin that is of any relevance in another form of existence. A Gadaba man of my acquaintance killed his father, who happened to be the village headman, and then followed him into office. Most people of the village would have considered him to be a morally corrupt person. However, all of his good or bad actions have no soteriological relevance, since rebirth among the Gadaba is not ethicized as it is in the case of Hindus. Given that he does not die a bad death, he will be reborn as a human being in the alternate generation, like anyone else. Moreover, as long as they receive their sacrifices, the gods are indifferent to how humans treat one another. Transgressions of the divine order always have immediate and automatic consequences but no karmic impact.

The reciprocal exchanges during death rituals (and in other contexts) in the case of the Gadaba thus serve other purposes and express other values. Whereas in the Hindu case the main referent of the death ritual is the individual who works toward a better rebirth (and perhaps liberation) and the continuity of the family, in the tribal case it is the community and, at least among the Gadaba, society conceived of as a whole. This whole consists of the complementary agnates and affines, and is above all an idea (called *baro bai tero gadi*, "twelve brothers, thirteen seats"). The ritual process also enacts this complementarity. Both agnatic and affinal relationships nourish and thus transform the deceased. However, their contributions and exchanges also express different values. Agnates or clan brothers take away the liminal deceased, replacing the buffaloes with memorial stones, thus contributing to the continuity of the local brotherhood. The affines, in their turn, contribute fertility, not in the usual form of a "milk-gift," but in the form of an affinal buffalo that is ritually slaughtered in the fields. In both cases, though, the referent is society.

Nina Miring (in this volume) has shown how medieval Shaiva ascetics with a strong otherworldly orientation tried to accommodate their rituals to the Brahmanical mainstream, those householders with social duties and a this-worldly focus. The dialogue between Brahmanical values and practices (sacrifice, ritual status, Vedic knowledge, *dharma*) and the ascetic perspective (renunciation and liberation, *moksha*) went on for many centuries from the sixth century B.C.E. onward; the four life-stages mentioned above are an attempt by the Brahmanical side to incorporate ascetic ideas that today belong to the core of Hindu values. Contemporary death rituals still reflect this century-old tension and ambivalence between society and liberation. The different bodies involved also show this ambivalence or the twofold orientation of Hindu death rituals. The "subtle body" is subject to retribution and reward, and the sacrificed "gross body" also has soteriological implications. The body constructed from rice balls in the *sapindikarana* ceremony—divided up, mixed, and consumed—focuses on ancestorhood, however. As in the Gadaba case, bodies are provided, but, unlike the tribal scenario where the ancestors are represented permanently in the midst of each village, these bodies have a fleeting existence. Even the status of an ancestor is temporary, since through the ritual actions of one's descendants one is ultimately pushed out of ancestorhood and into heaven. As Parry (1994: 209) noted, "[t]he eschatological picture is confusing, even contradictory" in Hindu religion, and when rebirth is taking place in the ritual process is also a matter of debate (see also Knipe 1977: 121f).

Both the Hindu and tribal death rituals that have been discussed here show that the ritual process as a whole cannot be neatly described in the tripartite scheme of separation, liminality, and reintegration. Surely, carrying a body to the cremation ground is an act of separation, and planting a memorial stone representing the ancestors signifies and actually brings about reintegration. However, in the Gadaba case, separation is enacted again and again. The body is removed from the house on the first day; the *duma* is then fed in order to leave human society on the third day, and then once again after many months. Finally, the buffaloes representing the *duma* are led out of the village and given away. These are repeated acts of separation, and liminality is also not an easily demarcated phase (see also Mirnig, in this volume). On the one hand, there are nested periods of liminality: three days of pollution encompassed by a period when the ghost is believed to be around and active, again encompassed by a period when the *duma* is considered to be still lingering but largely harmless, etc. The same is true of the Hindu rites. There is not just one period of liminality but several entailing different implications (with reference to pollution, danger, closeness). For the living, as Turner (1985: 209) himself acknowledged in a posthumously published contribution, it is more a matter of moving repeatedly in and out of liminality and back into ordinary life than of going though one liminal period.

For the Gadaba, moving in and out of liminality in the process of transforming their dead also means coming together repeatedly in effervescent assemblies of different kinds (see ch. 7 in this volume). In Pickering's (1984) classification, these assemblies are re-creative, no new ideas emerge but the community is morally strengthened, and the different agnatic and affinal relationships are acted out and reproduced. Collective mourning and grief is one aspect of these assemblies and is the responsibility of women. The other scenes of ritually integrated and structured, thus systemic, effervescence are not directed towards suffering and death but are a feast of life and society. This includes the aggressive approach of the buffalo-takers (the stone-brothers) and of the affines masquerading as agnates by bringing their own buffalo. What I have not described above but which can briefly be mentioned here is a mud-fight between the hosts and their affines (guests) during the final death ritual, the day after the buffaloes have been given away, which transforms into an affectionate reciprocal bathing of each other. In these different contexts, emotions are aroused and relationships challenged and confirmed at the same time.

Brahmanical Hinduism, with its stress on overcoming bodily needs and desires, avoiding pollution, spiritual refinement, and transcendental orientation, does not seem prone to effervescent assemblies but rather stresses control. This negative effervescence can be discerned in the death rituals too. Wailing of women is allowed and obligatory but it is restricted, too (Pandey 1976: 255). For example, it is restricted to the yard of the deceased's house (Conzelmann 1996: 363; Michaels 1998: 153; Stevenson [1920] 1971: 145). Effervescent scenarios in connection with death have been documented by anthropologists, mostly among low castes or Dalit communities (Parry 1994: 152–58; Randeria 1999: 92f). However, this seems to be the exception rather than the rule and does not represent the Brahmanical Hinduism I have been mainly concerned with here. The fates of the embodiments of the deceased—erected and immersed—bring out the difference well. Gadaba let their brothers erect the permanent representation of their ancestors in the middle of their village, on top of which they play cards and settle disputes. Hindus, on the other hand, immerse the constructed liminal body of the deceased in the river, to be carried away and, hopefully, liberated.

**Peter Berger** (PhD Berlin 2004) is associate professor of Indian religions and the anthropology of religion at the Faculty of Theology and Religious Studies of the University of Groningen. He was a visiting professor at the University of Zürich in 2012 and visiting fellow at the Centre for Advanced Studies at the University of Munich in 2015. His books include *Feeding, Sharing and Devouring: Ritual and Society in Highland Odisha* (De Gruyter 2015) and he coedited *The Modern Anthropology of India* (Routledge 2013), *The Anthropology of Values* (Pearson 2010) and *Fieldwork: Social Realities in Anthropological Perspective* (Weissensee 2009).

## Notes

1.  See Weisgrau (2013), Skoda and Otten (2013) for recent discussions of tribes in India, especially with reference to Rajasthan and Orissa respectively.
2.  Needless to say, this attempt I present here cannot be comprehensive. Moreover, a thorough comparison would not only focus on death rituals but would take relationships between different rituals (e.g., birth, marriage, death) into account, as rituals are not isolated events but constitute systems.
3.  This state of the Indian Union was renamed Odisha in 2011. As this contribution refers to the situation before that date, I still refer to Orissa here.
4.  Fieldwork was done for twenty-two months between 1999 and 2003.
5.  I have dealt with Gadaba death rituals in various papers that are different in the scope of rituals they consider. I have described and analyzed the last death ritual called *go'ter* in detail (Berger 2010), have written on the whole process of death rituals (Berger 2001), contextualized these death rituals in the life cycle (Berger 2007b), and tried to understand the ritual system as a whole (relating life-cycle, annual cycle, and healing rituals) in my book (Berger 2007a), which will be published in English translation in the near future. In a sense, this contribution is the logical consequence of progressively widening the scope, since it compares the tribal with Hindu death rituals.
6.  If the maternal uncle is dead, his descendants or any senior affine will perform the rituals. This points to the fact that a relationship between groups is at stake.
7.  It was still quite common to sacrifice cattle during death rituals when I started my research in 1999, although young men already then voiced their opinion that sacrificing cattle during life-cycle rituals (not the annual rituals) should stop. During my last research period in 2010, it became evident that cattle are no longer sacrificed unless the deceased has died a "bad death." To cease sacrificing cattle for those deities demanding it in the annual round of village rituals is, however, out of the question. These sacrifices have to take place, I have been told, even if nobody eats beef any more.
8.  A dead person may thus be "alive" in several animals at the same time, in the ones provided by his or her brothers and the ones brought by the affines.
9.  I do not use diacritics in this paper.
10. In relation to Hindu death rituals, I have used various sources, mainly Conzelmann 1996; Kaushik 1976; Knipe 1977, 2007; Michaels 1998; Nicholas 1982; Nicholas and Inden 1977; Parry 1994; Stevenson (1920) 1971.
11. As stated in the introduction, many scholars think that significant patterns of death rituals are shared by high as well as low castes. However, the description of ritual practices and ideas presented here refer instead to the Brahmanical—or, at any rate, high caste—view of the matter. "Hindu" thus refers to this context.

12. Normative Brahmanical ritual and religion is male focused, and it is said that women retain the ritual status of a Shudra throughout life and that only high-caste males receive the full *samskaras*, are initiated, become householders, and finally, ideally, renounce life.
13. Alternatively, Dumont (1983: 11f) states that from the perspective of a male Ego, the three ascending and three descending generations are regarded as *sapinda* relatives, thus seven, counting the generation of Ego. The rule is that a person is *sapinda* to those to whom he must offer *pinda* and to those who must offer *pinda* to him after his death.
14. For an overview of the rich literature on food in Hinduism, see Berger 2011.
15. Fire, water, air, earth, ether (Marriott 1989: 14f).
16. Thus fifty-two balls are offered in total (3 x 16 + 4).

# References

Bailey, Frederick G. 1961. "'Tribe' and 'Caste' in India." *Contributions to Indian Sociology* 5: 7–19.

Behera, Deepak K. 2010. "Death and Death Rites: The Practice of Double Burial among the Kunhu-Speaking People of Northwest Orissa." In *The Anthropology of Values: Essays in Honour of Georg Pfeffer*, ed. Peter Berger, Roland Hardenberg, Ellen Kattner, and Michael Prager, 294–316. New Delhi: Pearson Education.

Berger, Peter. 2001. "Feeding the Dead: Rituals of Transformation among the Gadaba of Koraput." *Adivasi* 41: 35–50.

———. 2002. "The Gadaba and the 'non-ST' Desia of Koraput." In *Contemporary Society: Tribal Studies, Vol. 5*, ed. Georg Pfeffer and Deepak K. Behera, 57–90. New Delhi: Concept.

———. 2007a. *Füttern, Speisen und Verschlingen. Ritual und Gesellschaft im Hochland von Orissa, Indien*. Berlin: Lit.

———. 2007b. "Sacrificial Food, the Person and the Gadaba Ritual System." In *Periphery and Centre: Studies in Orissan History, Religion and Anthropology*, ed. Georg Pfeffer, 199–221. New Delhi: Manohar.

———. 2010. "'Who Are You, Brother and Sister?' The Theme of 'Own' and 'Other' in the *Go'ter* Ritual of the Gadaba." In *The Anthropology of Values: Essays in Honour of Georg Pfeffer*, ed. Peter Berger, Roland Hardenberg, Ellen Kattner, and Michael Prager, 260–87. New Delhi: Pearson Education.

———. 2011. "Food." In *Brill's Encyclopedia of Hinduism, Vol. 3*, ed. Knut A. Jacobsen (Editor-in-Chief), Helene Basu, Angelika Malinar, and Vasudha Narayanan, 68–75. Leiden: Brill.

———. 2012. "Theory and Ethnography in the Modern Anthropology of India." *HAU: Journal of Ethnographic Theory* 2, no. 2: 325–57.

Conzelmann, Elisabeth. 1996. *Heirat, Gabe, Status: Kaste und Gesellschaft in Mandi*. Berlin: Arabisches Buch.

Demmer, Ulrich. 2007. "Memory, Performance and the Regeneration of Society among the Koya." In *Time in India: Concepts and Practices*, ed. Angelika Malinar, 185–201. New Delhi: Manohar.

Dirks, Nicholas B. 2001. *Castes of Mind: Colonialism and the Making of Modern India*. Princeton: Princeton University Press.

Dumont, Louis. (1957) 1970. *Religion, Politics and History in India: Collected Papers in Indian Sociology*. The Hague: Mouton.

———. 1983. "The Debt to Ancestors and the Category of *Sapinda*," in *Debts and Debtors*, ed. Charles Malamoud, 1–20. New Delhi: Vikas Publishing House.

Elwin, Verrier. 1945. "Funeral Customs in Bastar State." *Man in India* 25, no. 2: 87–133.

———. 1950. *Bondo Highlander*. Bombay: Oxford University Press.

Fuller, Christopher. 1992. *The Camphor Flame: Popular Hinduism and Society in India*. Princeton: Princeton University Press.

Fürer-Haimendorf, Christoph von. 1943. "Megalithic Ritual among the Gadabas and Bondos of Orissa." *Journal and Proceedings of the Royal Anthropological Society of Bengal* 9: 149–78.

———. 1953. "The After-Life in Indian Tribal Belief." *Journal of the Royal Anthropological Institute of Great Britain and Ireland* 83, no. 1: 37–49.

Hardenberg, Roland. 2010. "A Reconsideration of Hinduization and the Caste-Tribe Continuum Model. In *The Anthropology of Values: Essays in Honour of Georg Pfeffer*, ed. Peter Berger, Roland Hardenberg, Ellen Kattner, and Michael Prager, 89-103. New Delhi: Pearson Education.

Holdrege, Barbara A. 1998. "Body Connections: Hindu Discourses of the Body and the Study of Religion." *International Journal of Hindu Studies* 2, no. 3: 341–86.

Inden, Ronald B., and Ralph W. Nicholas. 1977. *Kinship in Bengali Culture*. Chicago: University of Chicago Press.

Izikowitz, Karl G. 1969. "The Gotr Ceremony of the Boro Gadaba." In *Primitive Views of the World*, ed. Stanley Diamond, 129–50. New York: Columbia University Press.

Kaushik, Meena. 1976. "The Symbolic Representation of Death." *Contributions to Indian Sociology* 10, no. 2: 265–92.

Knipe, David M. 1977. "Sapindikarana: The Hindu Rite of Entry into Heaven." In *Religious Encounters with Death: Insights from the History and Anthropology of Religions*, ed. Frank E. Reynolds and Earle H. Waugh, 111–24. University Park: Pennsylvania State University Press.

———. 2007. "Zur Rolle des »provisorischen Körpers« für den Verstorbenen in hinduistischen Bestattungen." In *Der Abschied von den Toten: Trauerrituale im Kulturvergleich*, ed. Jan Assmann, Franz Maciejewski, and Axel Michaels, 62–81. Göttingen: Wallstein.

Marriott, McKim. 1989. "Constructing an Indian Ethnosociology." *Contributions to Indian Sociology (NS)* 23, no. 1: 1–39.

Michaels, Axel. 1998. *Der Hinduismus: Geschichte und Gegenwart*. Munich: Beck.

Moffatt, Michael. 1979. *An Untouchable Community in South India: Structure and Consensus*. Princeton: Princeton University Press.

Nicholas, Ralph W. 1982. "*Sraddha*, Impurity, and Relations between the Living and the Dead." In *Way of Life: King, Householder, Renouncer. Essays in Honour of Louis Dumont*, ed. T.N. Madan, 367–79. New Delhi: Vikas.

Obeyesekere, Gananath. 1980. "The Rebirth Eschatology and Its Transformations: A Contribution to the Sociology of Early Buddhism." In *Karma and Rebirth in Classical Indian Traditions*, ed. Wendy D. O'Flaherty, 137–64. Berkeley: University of California Press.

Pandey, Rajbali B. *Hindu Samskaras: Socio-Religious Study of the Hindu Sacraments.* New Delhi: Motilal Banarsidass.

Parkin, Robert. 1992. *The Munda of Central India: An Account of their Social Organization.* Oxford: Oxford University Press.

Parry, Jonathan P. 1986. "The Gift, the Indian Gift and the 'Indian Gift.'" *Man* 21, no. 3: 453–73.

———. 1994. *Death in Banaras.* Cambridge: Cambridge University Press.

Pfeffer, Georg. 1982. *Status and Affinity in Middle India.* Wiesbaden: Franz Steiner Verlag.

———. 1991. "Der intra-agnatische 'Seelentausch' der Gadaba beim großen Lineageritual." In *Beiträge zur Ethnologie Mittel- und Süd-Indiens,* ed. Matthias S. Laubscher, 59–92. Munich: Anacon.

———. 1997. "The Scheduled Tribes of Middle India as a Unit: Problems of Internal and External Comparison." In *Contemporary Society. Tribal Studies I: Structure and Process,* ed. Georg Pfeffer and Deepak K. Behera. New Delhi: Concept, 3–27.

———. 2001. "A Ritual of Revival among the Gadaba of Koraput." In *Jagannath Revisited: Studying Society, Religion and the State in Orissa,* ed. Hermann Kulke and Burkhard Schnepel, 99–123. New Delhi: Manohar,

———. 2006. "Gesellschaftsformen verkörpern: Vom Umgang der und mit Toten." In *Verklärte Körper: Ästhetiken der Transfiguration,* Nicola Suthor, and Erika Fischer-Lichte, 49–67. Munich: Wilhelm Fink Verlag.

Pickering, William S.F. 1984. *Durkheim's Sociology of Religion: Themes and Theories.* London: Routledge & Kegan Paul.

Randeria, Shalini. 1999. "Mourning, Mortuary Exchange and Memorialization: The Creation of Local Communities among Dalits in Gujarat." In *Ways of Dying: Death and Its Meanings in South Asia,* ed. Elisabeth Schömbucher and Claus P. Zoller, 88–111. New Delhi: Manohar.

Reichel, Eva. 2009. *Notions of Life in Death and Dying: The Dead in Tribal Middle India.* New Delhi: Manohar.

Skoda, Uwe, and Tina Otten. 2013. "Odisha: Rajas and Prajas in a Multi-Segmented Society." In *The Modern Anthropology of India: Ethnography, Themes and Theory,* ed. Peter Berger and Frank Heidemann, 208–26. London: Routledge.

Stevenson, Sinclair. (1920) 1971. *The Rites of the Twice-Born.* New Delhi: Oriental Books.

Turner, Victor W. 1985. "Liminality, Kabbalah, and the Media." *Religion* 15: 205–17.

van Schendel, Willem, and Ellen Bal. 2002. "Beyond the 'Tribal' Mind-Set: Studying Non-Bengali Peoples in Bangladesh and West Bengal." In *Contemporary Society: Tribal Studies,* Vol. 5, ed. Georg Pfeffer and Deepak K. Behera, 121–38. New Delhi: Concept.

Vitebsky, Piers. 1993. *Dialogues with the Dead: The Discussion of Mortality among the Sora of Eastern India.* Cambridge: Cambridge University Press.

Weisgrau, Maxine. 2013. "Rajasthan: Anthropological Perspectives on Tribal Identity." In *The Modern Anthropology of India: Ethnography, Themes and Theory,* ed. Peter Berger and Frank Heidemann, 242–59. London: Routledge.

*Figure 4.1.* "Living martyr" Ahmad al-Haznawi, one of the 9/11 bombers, presenting his last will (Still from al-Sahab, *The Wills of the Martyrs of the Raids on New York and Washington* [2002] 1:00:17).

*Chapter Four*

# The Liminality of "Living Martyrdom"
## Suicide Bombers' Preparations for Paradise

*Pieter Nanninga*

In April 1996, a twenty-seven-year-old Egyptian wrote down his last will. In great detail, he indicated what should be done after his death. His body should be washed by a good Muslim, and he should be given new clothes, consisting of three white pieces. He wanted to be buried on his right side, with his head towards Mecca, and the men attending his funeral should mention God's name, pray, recite the Quran, and ask for God's mercy. Women should not visit his grave, he wrote, and the practice to memorialize the dead every forty days should not be performed, since he considered this to be non-Islamic. According to Islamic tradition, he asked two men to act as witnesses and signed the will as Mohammed al-Amir 'Awad al-Sayyid.[1]

About five and a half years later, the author of this will crashed an airplane into the North Tower of the World Trade Center in New York, killing himself and hundreds of others on the day that came to be known as 9/11. That early Tuesday morning, Mohammed Atta, as we have come to know him, must have been aware that the instructions for his funeral, which he had written down so thoroughly several years before, would never be executed. Nevertheless, he was convinced that he would enter paradise immediately after the plane hit the tower.

This case raises significant questions about the beliefs and practices surrounding the death of suicide bombers.[2] Unlike other deceased, suicide bombers are usually not buried by their relatives and friends. The body is often missing or not handed over by the authorities, which makes the

---

Notes for this chapter begin on page 94.

performance of death rituals impossible and precludes the performance
of the rites of passage that are deemed appropriate in their society. What
does this divergent ritual process mean for the beliefs surrounding the
death of suicide bombers? How is their transition from earthly life to the
hereafter imagined, and to what extent are the imaginaries expressed in
and produced by any rites of passage? And what role do the debates about
suicide bombers' status as martyrs play in this respect? In this chapter, I
will address these questions by examining the beliefs and practices surrounding the death of suicide bombers. In particular, I will analyze the
ritual structure of the execution of a suicide attack and its aftermath, and
explore whether Arnold van Gennep's model of the structure of rites of
passage is fruitful for better comprehending this contested form of violence. According to van Gennep ([1909] 1960), the rituals marking a person's transition from one status to another, i.e., rites of passage, contain
three stages: separation, liminality, and reincorporation, marking the
removal from the old social position, a transitional stage, and the attainment of a new position, respectively. Is this three-stage model as universal as van Gennep suggested, and can it be helpful for understanding the
remarkable status transition of suicide bombers?[3]

Although the existing literature on suicide attacks has provided important insights into the organizations and individuals behind this form of
violence (Bloom 2005; Hafez 2007; Khosrokhavar 2002; Moghadam 2008;
Pape 2005), the perceptions of the suicide bomber's transition from this life
to the next, and the ritual practices related to this transition, have never
been thoroughly studied. This chapter aims at filling this gap by analyzing suicide attacks that have been executed by jihadist organizations, and
by al-Qaeda in particular.[4] These attacks are relatively well documented,
which is especially true for the 9/11 attacks, from which I will draw my
main examples. Furthermore, jihadist media releases, such as the martyrdom videos produced by al-Qaeda's media group al-Sahab (the Clouds),
provide unique insights into the execution of suicide attacks. Based on
these sources, I will first examine authoritative traditions about martyrdom and jihadists' appropriation thereof, after which I will explore in
more detail jihadist suicide bombers' last period on earth and their departure from earthly life.[5]

## Early Islamic Martyrdom Traditions

According to early Islamic traditions, people do not enter paradise or hell
immediately after the moment of death. Until the Day of Resurrection
(*yawm al-qiyama*), they have to spend their time in the grave, which is

referred to as *barzakh*, meaning "obstacle," "barrier," or "separation." During this period, they are questioned by two angels, the so-called first judgment, after which they are allowed a glimpse of their future place in either paradise or hell. Then, the believers are left alone, while unbelievers are subjected to a so-called punishment of the grave (*'adhab al-qabr*; Wensinck 2010: 186). The period in the grave ends with the Resurrection, when all people are gathered in order to be judged on the Day of Judgment (*yawm al-din*; or the Hour, *al-sa'a*). When translated into van Gennep's terms, we can clearly recognize the three phases of the ritual process in this case: first, a separation from earthly life, then a liminal phase between this life and the next—the period spent in the grave—and finally a reaggregation after the Resurrection.

In the case of martyrs (*shuhada'*, singular *shahid*), however, this process is different. Martyrs seem to omit a liminal phase, because various traditions indicate that their souls enter paradise immediately after the moment of death. Repeatedly, the Quran states that those who are killed "in the cause of God," that is, martyrs, are not dead, but alive with their Lord and brought into the Gardens (2:154, 3:169, 9:111, and 47:4–6). Some hadiths emphasize the same point by narrating that the Prophet Muhammad assured a martyr's family members that their son had already met God (*Sahih al-Bukhari* 4.52.64 and 4.52.299). On another occasion, the Prophet said that a martyr is spared from the trial of the grave, because "the sword over his head was enough as a trial" (*Kanz al-'Ummal* Vol. 4, 596). According to other traditions, the Prophet explained the situation of martyrs in paradise by saying: "The souls of the martyrs live in the bodies of green birds who have their nests in chandeliers hung from the throne of the Almighty. They eat the fruits of paradise from wherever they like and then nestle in these chandeliers" (*Sunan Abu Dawud* 14.2514; *Sahih Muslim* 20.33.4651).

So according to these early Islamic traditions, the process characterizing a martyr's passage to the afterlife deviates from people who died a natural death. This divergence is also expressed in the rituals that are prescribed to accompany the transition. Muslims who died in a natural way should be washed several times and then covered by two or three sheets or dressed in clean clothes. Furthermore, after the example of the Prophet, funeral prayers should be offered at their graves. These rituals were absent in the case of martyrs. After the battle of Uhud, the Prophet ordered not to wash the martyrs, but to bury them in their bloodstained clothes as a sign of their purity (*Sahih al-Bukhari* 2.23.427/430/431/436 and 5.59.405; *Sunan Abu Dawud* 20.3129; Malik, *al-Muwatta* 21.16.37). Also, although some texts disagree, other traditions mention that the Prophet was not in the habit of performing funeral prayers at their graves (*Sahih al Bukhari*

2.23.427/428/431, 4.56.795, 5.59.374/405/411, and 8.76.434/590; *Sunan Abu Dawud* 14.3129; *Sahih Muslim* 30.9.5688). The early Islamic traditions thus point to a close relationship between the beliefs and practices surrounding a martyr's death. Ideas about the purity of the martyr's blood, the absence of the punishment of the grave, and the immediate entrance into paradise are reflected in the lack of ritual washing, clothing, and praying. Together with the liminal phase, the rites of passage accompanying the death of other Muslims seem to be absent in the case of martyrs.

## Jihadist Martyrdom Traditions

The classical traditions outlined above are still considered authoritative today, as becomes evident from jihadist discourses surrounding martyrdom. This can be illustrated by looking at one of the most celebrated series of jihadist martyrdom videos: al-Sahab's series *Winds of Paradise*.[6] The videos of this series, the first of which was released in 2007, all focus on several jihadists who died in operations in Afghanistan and Pakistan. In the videos, these men are shown presenting their last will and eulogized by means of biographies, operational footages, Quran recitations, and *nashids* (a cappella vocal songs). Before the videos focus on the individual jihadists, however, they contain a standardized introduction, in which martyrdom in general is the central theme.

The introduction of the *Winds in Paradise* videos (0:00–4:06) starts with a brief opening formula, which is followed by a recitation of one of the traditional martyrdom verses from the Quran (9:111), indicating that those who are slain while fighting in God's path will enter paradise.[7] Then, a brief clip of Osama bin Laden is shown, in which he recounts a hadith indicating that the Prophet himself wished to become a martyr.[8] Subsequently, the voice is heard of one of the most revered contemporary jihadist martyrs, the Palestinian 'Abdullah 'Azzam, who also emphasizes the importance of martyrdom. During his statement, the names of the martyrs featured in the video appear on screen in a paradise-like setting with green hills, colored flowers, and blossoming trees. While the names are shown one by one, a *nashid* fades in with these words:

> Does my death not come only once in my life?
> So why not make its ending my martyrdom
> When the soul of the martyr rises and approaches
> And God raises it up to a lofty status
> In bodies of birds circling in paradise
> And singing above the palaces and warbling

Seven [rewards] are won by the martyr to honor him
If you have a heart, then tell me what they are
1) The sin is forgiven with the first drop [of blood]
2) And I see my high place and abode
3) And I am secure from the horror and torment of the grave: How delightful!
4) And saved from the Resurrection
5) And crowned with the crowns of dignity
6) And given intercession for relatives, both near and distant
7) And the *houris* await my arrival longingly

By means of the *nashid*, the introduction of the videos thus refers to classical martyrdom traditions such as the green birds in paradise and the seven rewards for martyrdom, among which are immediate forgiveness of sins, being spared from the punishment of the grave, and saved from the Judgment. According to the message of these videos, those who died while fighting for God were instantly transferred to paradise.

Here too, the beliefs are reflected in the practices surrounding the death of a martyr, as rites of passage seem to be absent in the case of jihadists who were killed in battle. Although the introduction of the *Winds of Paradise* videos does not touch on this point, the rest of the videos show several pictures and footages of corpses covered with blood, thus indicating that a ritual cleansing was not performed. The blood should be considered a sign of the martyrs' purity, the above-mentioned *nashid* suggested, and the bloodstained clothes in which the martyrs are buried thus express their purity and, accordingly, their immediate transition to paradise.

Jihadists do not only connect these traditional beliefs and practices to classical categories of martyrdom such as "battlefield martyrs" (see Cook 2007), but also to the rather recent practice of suicide attacks. Since the introduction of this form of violence in Lebanon in the early 1980s, it has been highly controversial in the Islamic world—not least because of the strong prohibition against suicide (*intihar*) in early Islamic texts (e.g., Q. 4:29). Yet, according to jihadists, these operations should not be regarded as suicide, but as "martyrdom operations" (*al-'amaliyyat al-istishhadiyya*) which are carried out by "martyrdom seekers" (*istishhadiyun*) rather than "suicide bombers."

Accordingly, the *Winds of Paradise* series portrays suicide bombers in the same way as the fighters who were killed by their enemies. The first part of the series features seven martyrs, three of whom died in a martyrdom operation. The scenes about these men too, are accompanied by the recurring *nashid* that says, "I am in the gardens of eternity; I have become a new creation in the gardens." Just as the other martyrs, martyrdom seekers are believed to arrive in paradise immediately after the moment of death, and just as in the case of other martyrs, death rituals are absent. Not only are these rituals often impossible to execute because there is no corpse to wash, bury, or pray for, they are also considered unnecessary because of the martyrs' inherent purity.

Hence, jihadists have appropriated early Islamic martyrdom traditions, which express as well as shape the view that those who died in their jihad should be considered martyrs—even if they killed themselves amidst their enemies. A liminal phase after death is absent, as are the accompanying death rituals.

Yet, if we concentrate on the case of suicide bombers, we should also note that whereas the period after death might be less relevant for our purpose, it is the period *before* death that has a special character. Obviously, suicide bombers know in advance when approximately they are going to die, which gives the period before their attack a particularly ambiguous nature. During this period, they distance themselves from earthly life while preparing for death. They are in a transitional state and, as Victor Turner (1967: 93–101) would phrase it more than half a century after van Gennep had coined the term "liminality," they are "betwixt and between" life and death. For that reason, we will now focus on the period before the execution of a suicide attack in order to see whether van Gennep's model of ritual structure might deepen our understanding of the phenomenon. We will do so by following the three stages of rites of passage as described by van Gennep.

Before turning to suicide bombers' separation from their old positions, however, I need to make a brief remark on my use of van Gennep's ideas. In *The Rites of Passage* ([1909] 1960: 4–11), the French ethnographer attempted to contribute to a classification of rituals by singling out a "special category" of ritual patterns: rites of passage. By doing so, he shifted the emphasis in the study of rituals from isolated rites to the sequence of rites in their social setting. Implicit in this attempt to establish a classification of rituals is the assumption that rituals are a separate category of action that is distinguishable from other forms of social action. However, instead of singling out rituals (or rites of passage) as an a priori category of action, I would agree with Catherine Bell (1992: 74 and 88–93) that it is more fruitful to ask how and why people privilege some actions above others by *ritualizing* them. In other words, rather than exploring whether suicide attacks are rites of passage, I find it more useful to investigate how and why they, as a social practice, are ritualized—that is, strategically distinguished from other practices. So although I make use of van Gennep's ideas about what he himself considered the main interest of *The Rites of Passage*, namely, the structural process of the rites (see [1909] 1960: 191), my approach to the rites themselves diverges on important points.

## Separation

Although suicide bombers do not share a common profile and are motivated by a wide range of factors (Moghadam 2008: 27–29; Pape 2005: 199–
216), most of them are young and male. Robert A. Pape's (2005: 207–11)
data about more than 450 suicide bombers until the end of 2003 indicate
that their average age is 22.7 years and that 85 percent of them is male,
a percentage that is even higher for Muslim bombers. In their societies,
these men often occupy a position between childhood and maturity: they
are independent from their families but have not yet established a family
of their own (Juergensmeyer 2003: 173–74 and 193–94; Kramer 1991:
38–40). In other words, they are in a life stage in which they are expected
to undergo another rite of passage—marriage—which might explain the
extensive use of symbols of marriage in relation to martyrdom and suicide
attacks in several cultures (see, e.g., Oliver and Steinberg 2005: 76; Gaur
2007). Instead of marrying, however, most jihadist suicide bombers leave
their families in the period before the attack. Many of them distance themselves from their relatives and friends, give up their roles in society and
even leave their home countries to go to other places to join the jihad (Roy
2004: 302–4). According to Marc Sageman's (2004: 92) extensive database,
an overwhelming majority of jihadists join the jihad in a country where
they have not grown up (see also Hegghammer 2010).

In their new societies, the suicide bombers do not integrate, but rather
establish their own communities—for example, in the Afghan training
camps or in small, isolated groups or "cells" in European cities. The 9/11
bombers are a telling example in this respect (see McDermott 2005). All of
them had left their home countries and, except for one, all had lost contact
with their families. They all visited a training camp in Afghanistan, and
some of them were members of the so-called Hamburg cell that cut itself
off from German society. The same pattern is discernible in other cases.
Estimates about suicide bombers in Iraq and Afghanistan indicate that the
large majority are non-Iraqi and non-Afghan, respectively, which shows
that most suicide bombers first separated themselves from their original
surroundings and societies (Marzaban 2006; O'Hanlon and Campbell
2008).

This pattern could be described as the beginning of the process of
separation—the first phase in van Gennep's model of the ritual process.
Gradually, the future bombers distance themselves from their old roles
and statuses, which is also illustrated by the fact that they call themselves
*muhajirun* or "emigrants," a term referring to the Muslims who joined
the Prophet on his migration (*hijra*) from Mecca to Medina in the year
622. Another indication of the process of separation is that these migrants

usually adopt a new name once they have joined the jihad: a *nom de guerre* or *kunya,* which often refers to one of the companions of the Prophet. The nineteen 9/11 hijackers, for example, all received a *kunya* during their visits to the Afghan training camps (Fouda and Fielding 2003: 110–12), which symbolized the abandonment of their old positions and their obtainment of a new status.

The process of separation does not stop there. After suicide bombers have volunteered and/or are selected to execute an attack, they are also separated from their peers—often physically, but at least symbolically. This was the case with the 9/11 bombers, as Bin Laden himself indicated in a documentary by al-Sahab about the 9/11 attacks, *Knowledge is for Acting Upon* (2006: 1:50–6:20). In a scene showing Bin Laden speaking in front of a group of men in one of the training camps, the al-Qaeda leader emphasizes the special qualities suicide bombers must have. The trainees' character, attitude, and achievements were reported by the instructors to Bin Laden himself, he indicates, after which he personally selected the candidates for "martyrdom operations." Then, the chosen ones were separated from the other mujahidun and moved to special camps or houses, where they received a specialized training. In the case of the 9/11 bombers, the video tells, this training was given by Abu Turab al-Urduni, the son-in-law of Ayman al-Zawahiri. Altogether, Bin Laden's statements, the narrations by a voice-over, and plenty of clips of mujahidun training in one of the camps clearly illustrate the distinct status of the future suicide bombers within the al-Qaeda training camps.

The process of separation from old social positions and cultural roles is not merely physical. Future suicide bombers also mentally separate themselves from earthly life in the period before their death. This becomes evident from the last wills of the future bombers, in which they often recount how they started to downplay earthly life. To take the example of the 9/11 bombers again, the martyrdom video featuring hijacker 'Abd al-'Aziz al-'Umari not only portrays the Saudi as a "free and independent scholar" who gave up his sedentary life in order to fight for God's cause, but also as someone who sought God's rewards instead of worldly gain. Al-'Umari himself explicitly declares that he started to resist those who "love this life" and see the world as their paradise (al-Sahab 2002b: 24:16–25:05). One of the other Saudi bombers, Ahmad al-Haznawi, expressed himself in comparable terms (al-Sahab 2002a: 40:39–41:30), saying, "Divorce yourself from this world and renounce it, because, by God, it is not as valuable as you think. It is merely a fleeting enjoyment. Sitting and enjoying its delights does not distance you from death. . . . So choose for yourself the type of death you wish to die. Do you wish to die on your bed like a camel dies?[9] Or do you want to die as a martyr, strong in your faith, after you have answered the call of war and hastened to God's pleasure?" The clearest example of this mental separation from earthly life is probably provided in a narration about a third Saudi 9/11 bomber, Sa'id al-Gahmdi, about whom is said, "His body was on earth, but his heart was with the green birds beneath the throne of the Most Merciful" (al-Sahab 2002b: 7:06–7:18).

Suicide bombers thus gradually separate themselves from the world both physically and mentally. Once detached from the world, they have lost their old social positions, while they have not obtained their new status as martyrs yet. This ambiguous position is marked by a new name, which symbolizes this "in-betweenness": from the moment of their selection they are called "living martyrs" (*al-shahid al-hayy*). As far as I know, this term, which was already employed by Lebanese organizations for their suicide bombers in the 1980s, was used for the first time in the case of Talha ibn 'Ubaydallah, one of the first converts to Islam. This man had personally shielded the Prophet during the battle of Uhud, which had caused him serious wounds and had left two of his fingers paralyzed. For his bravery, the Prophet promised him paradise and rewarded him with the status of a martyr. From that moment on, he would be called a "living martyr," an ambiguous position he would occupy for more than thirty years.

Like Talha ibn 'Ubaydallah, the men selected for a suicide mission are, in their view, assured of paradise, while still dwelling on earth.[10] As living martyrs, they fall outside the existing structures and, in Turner's terms, "slip through the network of classification that normally locate status and positions" (1969: 95). They occupy a liminal position, which, as in many other cases, is strongly ritualized.

## Liminality

After their selection for a suicide attack, the future bombers undergo, if possible, a rigid program of physical and military training. In al-Qaeda's camps in Afghanistan, several courses were offered at different levels, consisting of strict programs that included physical exercises and training with different kinds of weapons and explosives, but also lessons on subjects such as geography, military strategy, and intelligence gathering (Bergen 2006: 101–3 and 410–13). Besides these more practical lessons, the mujahidun received religious training and participated in various rituals and, what Catherine Bell calls, "ritual-like activities": common activities that are ritualized to greater or lesser degrees (1997: 138–69). In addition to the five daily prayers, meetings were held in which the

Quran was studied and early Islamic traditions—about, for example, the battles of the Prophet—were read together. The trainees received lessons on authoritative predecessors, such as Ibn Taymiyya and 'Abdullah 'Azzam, and listened to sermons, poetry, and speeches by jihadist leaders visiting the camps. Furthermore, videos featuring statements by jihadist leaders or farewell messages by suicide bombers were watched together. Comparable practices are carried out by jihadists in other regions—for instance, in training camps in Iraq, Somalia, Syria, and Yemen—as well as in small-scale house meetings in Western cities.

In addition to these general activities, practices more specifically related to suicide attacks are performed some time before the attack, the most important of which is probably the writing and recording of a last will. This practice has been connected to suicide attacks since the rise of the phenomenon in the early 1980s in Lebanon, where the living martyrs had to write down a brief testament and read it out in front of a camera. Nowadays, these testaments are much longer—the reading sometimes lasts for about half an hour—and the recordings are incorporated in extensive, professionalized martyrdom videos, such as the ones by al-Sahab. The recording of these messages still represents an important moment for the future bombers, as it is their final message to the world. In the testaments, the young men justify their decision to perform a suicide attack, say farewell to their family and friends, and encourage their fellow jihadists. They thus publicly confirm their decision to abandon earthly life and underline their separation from their social position and roles by literally saying farewell. Furthermore, paradise is a frequent topic in these wills, so they also emphasize their future status as martyrs in the Gardens. For example, the earlier mentioned al-'Umari ends his will by saying to his parents, "Be patient and expectant and know that if God accepts me as a martyr and permits me to intercede, you shall be the ones for whom I will intercede. And if God, in His generosity and grace, favors me and allows me into the Garden, we shall meet there, God willing" (al-Sahab 2002b: 42:34–42:48). Accordingly, the statements made in videos like these express the ambiguous position of the living martyrs, who have abandoned their old positions, but have not yet achieved their new status yet.

The ritualized character of the period before the execution of a suicide attack increases in the days before the attack. Although the information about this period is often scarce, some unique insights are provided by a handwritten document that was found after the 9/11 attacks in the luggage of Mohammed Atta, which never made it onto the plane (Kippenberg and Seidensticker 2003). The four-page document, which was most probably written by al-'Umari, contains instructions for the hijackers regarding the last night and morning before the attack. Rather than focusing on practical issues, the instructions pay attention to the mental preparation of the bombers. In these preparations, rituals and ritual-like activities play a fundamental role. The hijackers are often instructed to say prayers and make supplications, to recite specific verses from the Quran, to renew their intention (*niyya*), and to remember God. Along these lines, the execution of the 9/11 attacks was strongly ritualized, making it an act of worship for the participants rather than a military operation. For our purpose, it is particularly interesting to note that the ritual practices executed during these last hours illustrate the ambiguous state of the perpetrators.

One of the most striking elements of the document is its emphasis on purity (Kippenberg 2011: 174–77). Several times, the men are instructed to perform ritual ablutions and to "purify the heart." These purification rituals can be seen as a symbol for the separation from this world (cf. van Gennep [1909] 1960: 20). The document states, for instance, "Purify your soul from all unclean things. Completely forget something called 'this world.'" Purification and separation from the world are explicitly related in this passage, and the former can be considered a symbol for the latter: the purification removes the last reminders of this polluted world. In an equally illustrative passage, the hijackers are instructed not to leave the apartment unless they have performed ablutions, expressing the idea that the hijackers are beacons of purity in a polluted world. At the same time, the rituals of purification also points at the hijackers' future status as martyrs, who, as we noted before, are considered inherently pure. From this perspective, the ritual ablutions can be considered as the bombers' preparation for achieving their new status as martyrs. Hence, the purification rituals express both the separation from the polluted world and the preparation for the bombers' pure status after death, thus illustrating the liminal status of the living martyrs.

Besides instructing the hijackers to perform dozens of rituals, the document ritualizes all kinds of mundane actions that the hijackers had to perform. All actions that had to be taken during the last day, from preparing the knives until entering the airplane, are connected with prayers, Quran verses, or stories about the Prophet and his companions. For instance, it says, "As you set foot onto T. [*tayyara*, airplane], make your prayers and supplications. Remember that this is a raid (*ghazwa*) for the sake of God," and "Tighten your clothes, since this is the way of the pious generations after the Prophet. They would tighten their clothes before battle." But not only minor actions are ritualized; the same is true for the possible killing of passengers should they resist, about which the document says, "If you slaughter, do not cause discomfort of those you are killing, because this is one of the practices of the Prophet." Here, the killing of a passenger is compared with the ritual slaughter (*dhabiha*) of a sacrificial animal.

As these passages show, the actions are not only ritualized, they are also constantly related to the Prophet Muhammad and his companions. The nineteen men are repeatedly compared to the warriors and martyrs of the first generations, thus expressing the idea that they were reenacting a raid (*ghazwa*) of the Prophet. This is particularly clear in the last passage of the text, which says, "If you see the enemy as strong, remember the confederates [that had formed a coalition to fight the Prophet]. They were 10,000. Remember how God gave victory to his faithful servants. God said: *When the faithful saw the confederates, they said: 'This is what God and the Prophet promised, they said the truth.'*" This passage (Q. 33:22) refers to the Battle of the Trench, where, according to tradition, 3,000 Muslims successfully defended Medina against an overwhelming majority of 10,000 enemies. Just like these Muslims, the hijackers are presented as a minority that will triumph in the end.

In short, after having separated themselves physically as well as mentally from their old positions in society, future suicide bombers can be conceived as occupying a liminal position between earthly life and the hereafter. This ambiguous state is expressed in several rituals and ritual-like activities, such as the recording of a testament and the performance of ablutions. But these rituals and ritual-like practices are not merely expressions of the living martyr's liminal status; they also play a role in the construction thereof. The ritualized preparations for a suicide attack shape the idea that the participants, as the true followers of the Prophet, are only one step away from entering paradise as martyrs and will be victorious at last, either in this life or in the next.

## Reincorporation

What about the third stage of van Gennep's model? In the first sections, we already noticed that rituals after death are absent in the case of martyrs. Are suicide bombers not reincorporated in their communities in a new status?

Usually, jihadist suicide bombers have lost contact with their families and friends a long time before their death. Their relationship with the bombers has vanished, and therefore they often do not have a strong desire to remember the deceased. This is different for the suicide bombers' fellow jihadists, however, who remain close to the bombers until briefly before their death. Yet they usually do not receive the bodies of the suicide bombers and therefore cannot bury them or visit their graves, which makes it impossible to remember the dead in the usual way. As Bin Laden remarked about the 9/11 bombers in the introduction of the video

*The Nineteen Martyrs*: "The context does not permit us to remember these men as they deserve to be remembered" (3:15–3:21). However, he subsequently indicates that the video itself should be considered an attempt to remember the nineteen men and their merits, thus pointing to the role of these videos in the commemoration of the deceased. Whereas graves and monuments are absent, the martyrdom videos are the closest jihadists get to creating a "place" of remembrance. Like the posters, photos, and graffiti commemorating the Palestinians who died in the conflict with Israel (Oliver and Steinberg 2005), jihadist videos make suicide bombers reenter the jihadist community in a new status.

As martyrs, they are an important part of the jihadist community. Accounts of their lives and deaths circulate widely, both orally, on paper, and on audio- and videocassettes. Stories about miraculous dreams before their death, about God's help with the execution of an attack, and about the smell of their corpses afterwards are common knowledge among jihadists and are seen as proof that they are fighting for the good cause. Moreover, the martyrs are believed to be in the highest paradise (*al-firdaws*), close to God, where they are allowed to intercede for people on earth (see, e.g., *Sunan Abu Dawud* 14.2516). So although the jihadists' relationship with the suicide bombers has changed, they are reincorporated in the jihadist community after death. Jihadists see their martyrs, together with other legendary Muslim fighters, as members of the small group of true believers who have fought evil throughout history. As the Saudi 9/11 bomber al-Haznawi said in his last will, "America should know that the *umma*'s wombs are still producing the likes of Khalid ibn al-Walid, Salah al-Din al-Ayyubi, Sheikh 'Abdullah 'Azzam and other men who sacrificed much for the sake of God" (al-Sahab 2002a: 58:19–58:46). In al-Haznawi's view, the successful early-Islamic commander Khalid ibn al-Walid, the legendary Saladin, the celebrated jihadist martyr 'Azzam, and contemporary jihadists like himself are all part of the same group: the nonhistorical community of the few faithful, which was once led by the Prophet and of which they are the representatives in this era. And just as their predecessors, jihadists are willing to follow the path towards death and join their brothers in paradise. As a man called Hafiz 'Usman said in his last will several years after 9/11, "In the end, I pray to God that He blesses me with martyrdom. . . . May God join me with the brothers who were martyred in the events of 11 September, and bless me with the company of the holy Prophet and all those who have been martyred up to this day" (al-Sahab 2007: 1.15:54–1.16:28). In his view, martyrs such as Atta, al-Haznawi, and al-'Umari had preceded him to paradise, which gave him the strength to execute his suicide attack on the American consulate in Karachi.

## Conclusion

Once Mohammed Atta and his men had hijacked American Airlines Flight 11 and approached the city of New York, the Egyptian knew that he would die in an act of violence that is highly controversial in the Muslim world and rejected by the large majority of Muslim scholars. How, then, did he become convinced that paradise was only minutes away? This chapter has explored the ritualized execution of suicide attacks by using van Gennep's model of rites of passage in order to elucidate cases like this one.

Although suicide attacks are a relatively novel practice, we have seen that jihadists perceive them as a continuation of the activities of the Prophet and his companions. Several authoritative traditions are selected, reinterpreted, and manipulated, and together these beliefs and practices inform the way in which suicide attacks are carried out. The result is a complex process during which young men transform from ordinary believers in a given society to suicide bombers or, in their terms, to martyrs in paradise. The structure of this process can be clarified by employing van Gennep's three-stage model. First, the future suicide bombers gradually separate themselves from their old positions and roles in society. They start to renounce their old lives, abandon their old positions both physically and mentally, and finally underline their separation by adopting a new name. Subsequently, they enter a stage that could be conceptualized as liminal. The living martyrs know that they will die soon but have not achieved their new status yet, and therefore occupy an ambiguous position between life and death. Finally, after their attack, suicide bombers reenter the jihadist community in their new status as martyrs, becoming exemplary members of the group of the few faithful that has fought evil throughout history.

Van Gennep's model thus provides useful tools to analytically distinguish different stages in the complicated transformative process of suicide bombers, namely separation, liminality, and reincorporation. But we should also acknowledge that the tripartite structure should be employed as a dynamic model that pays attention to the particularities of each case in its specific situation. For example, we have seen that, whereas Muslims normally enter a liminal phase after death, this process is divergent in the case of suicide bombers, where the period before death can be seen as liminal. Moreover, the different phases of the transformative process of suicide bombers are not as linear and successive as van Gennep suggested, but overlap and are sometimes even hardly distinguishable. Whereas we have separated the three stages for analytical purposes, the process is in fact much more diffuse and diverges in each case. So although van

Gennep's ideas have assisted the exploration of suicide bombers' last period on earth, his suggestion of a universally valid and rather static model of rites of passage should be taken with a certain caution.

Furthermore, our exploration leads us to question van Gennep's approach to rites of passage as a sui generis category of action. Van Gennep's model has been useful for drawing our attention to the importance of the ritual process that accompanies the transformation of the suicide bomber—a theme which has hitherto been largely neglected in research on suicide attacks. At the same time, it has proven to be more fruitful to focus on the practice of ritualization rather than the category of rituals as such. From this perspective, suicide attacks appear to be profoundly ritualized practices. Hence, they are strategically distinguished from other actions and privileged above ordinary acts of violence. Rituals establish authority and inscribe power on its participants—actors as well as audiences. The ritualization of suicide attacks therefore facilitates both the actors and the audience to view the perpetrators as martyrs and their actions as martyrdom operations rather than suicide or terrorism. Moreover, it empowers the participants and incites them to action. It offers the future bombers a new community and makes them feel proud and significant as members thereof. It gives them the power to execute their mission and ensures them of the status of martyrdom and all corresponding rewards.

To return to Mohammed Atta once more, on that morning in September 2001, he knew that he would die without receiving the death rites he once deemed appropriate. Yet in the months, days, and hours before his death, he and his aides had already performed these death rituals. His ritualized preparation for death strengthened his conviction that what he was doing was the right thing to do, and it reinforced his belief that he was only moments away from paradise when he approached New York on that Tuesday morning.

**Pieter Nanninga** (PhD Groningen 2014) is assistant professor of Middle Eastern studies at the Faculty of Arts of the University of Groningen. He studied history and religious studies and spent several months in Cairo and Damascus to study the Arabic language. In 2014, he earned his PhD with his thesis "Jihadism and Suicide Attacks: Al-Qaeda, al-Sahab and the Meanings of Martyrdom." His current research focuses on jihadist violence in Syria and Iraq and on the representations thereof in jihadist media releases.

# Notes

1.  A translation of the will was first published in *Der Spiegel*. See http://www.spiegel.
    de/spiegel/print/d-20240157.html. For an English version, see http://www.abc.net.
    au/4corners/atta/resources/documents/will1.htm (last accessed 1 September 2011).
2.  This chapter prefers the terms "suicide attacks" and "suicide bombers" above alterna-
    tives such as "human bombs" and "homicide bombings" because they are far more
    widely established in scholarly discourse. However, it is important to note that these
    terms are highly controversial, not least because of their association with suicide, which
    is misleading for two reasons: (1) the perpetrators of the attacks consider their actions
    to be "martyrdom operations" instead of suicide, and (2) scholars have convincingly
    argued that the motivations of suicide bombers diverge from ordinary suicides on sig-
    nificant points (see Moghadam 2008: 27–29; Pape 2005: 171–216).
3.  Van Gennep ([1909] 1960: 11) acknowledged that variations could exist between differ-
    ent rites of passage in different contexts and that he could not "achieve as rigid a clas-
    sification as the botanists have, for example." Yet, concerning the three-stage model, he
    also claimed that rites of passage show a "wide degree of general similarity" over the
    world because "man's life resembles nature" (3, 190). It was this suggestion of universal
    validity of the model that was mostly criticized in the decades after the publication of
    *The Rites of Passage*. Some critics, for instance, argued that women's experiences differed
    significantly from rites of passage involving men (see Bynum 1984; Lincoln 1981), indi-
    cating that van Gennep's model of ritual structure failed to see the complexity of the
    rituals involved.
4.  For the purpose of this chapter, the term "jihadism" refers to the loosely organized and
    dynamic movement that has developed out of the jihad against the Soviet Union in
    Afghanistan in the 1980s, which considers the jihad an individual duty for each Muslim
    and wages this jihad against both the so-called "far enemy" (the United States and its
    allies) as well as the "near enemy" (the "apostate" Muslim regimes). "Al-Qaeda," one
    of jihadism's most notorious exponents, is used here to refer only to the organization
    around the late Osama bin Laden and Ayman al-Zawahiri, which is sometimes dubbed
    "al-Qaeda Central," for the post-9/11 period. The term as employed here thus excludes
    what might be dubbed franchises, such as al-Qaeda in the Land of the Two Rivers (Iraq)
    and al-Qaeda on the Arabian Peninsula. Another consequence of this particular focus is
    that female bombers are excluded from the analysis, since jihadist suicide attacks are,
    almost without exception, executed by males.
5.  The videos mentioned in this chapter are in the possession of the author.
6.  Al-Sahab released its first video in 2001. After this release about the suicide attack on
    the American naval destroyer USS Cole in the port of Aden in October 2000, dozens
    of others have followed at an increasing speed. Although most of the videos com-
    prise short statements and operational footage, al-Sahab has also produced dozens of
    extensive martyrdom videos. These documentary-like videos feature suicide bomb-
    ers from various regions. Among them are six of the September 11 hijackers and two
    of the London bombers, but also several men who carried out attacks in Afghanistan,
    Pakistan, and Saudi Arabia. Moreover, some videos focused on several so-called mar-
    tyrs, such as the series *Winds of Paradise*.
7.  The entire verse reads, "God has bought from the believers their lives and their wealth,
    so that the Garden will be theirs—they fight in the way of God, slay and are slain. It is
    a true promise which is binding on Him in the Torah, the Gospel and the Quran. And
    who fulfils his promise better than God? Rejoice then at the bargain you have made, for
    that is the supreme triumph" (Q. 9:111).

8.  Bin Laden refers to *Sahih al-Bukhari* 4.52.54, saying, "The seal of the prophets and messengers [Mohammed] wished for this status. So be aware and wise: what is this status that the best of mankind wished for himself? He wished to be a martyr. He himself said, 'By Him in whose hands Mohammed's soul is, I would love to attack and be killed, then attack again and be killed, then attack again and be killed.' So this long life is summarized by him upon whom revelation is sent down by the Lord of the heavens and earth. This noble Prophet, to whom revelation was sent down, summarizes this life with these words. He himself wished for this status. So happy is the one who is chosen by God as a martyr."

9.  This expression refers to Khalid ibn al-Walid, who is considered one of the most successful commanders of the early Islamic armies and is said to have won over one hundred battles. Traditions narrate how he had striven for martyrdom all his life, but died with his famous last words: "I fought in so many battles seeking martyrdom, and yet here I am, dying on my bed like an old camel dies."

10. Talha ibn 'Ubaydallah is one of the ten companions who were promised paradise by the Prophet during their lifetime: *al-'ashara al-mubasharin bi-l-janna* ("the ten promised paradise"). The fact that Mohammed Atta's *kunya*, 'Abd al-Rahman al-Masri (al-Masri meaning "the Egyptian"), refers to another member of this select group, 'Abd al-Rahman bin 'Awf, is hardly a coincidence.

# References

Bell, Catherine. 1992. *Ritual Theory, Ritual Practice*. New York: Oxford University Press.

———. 1997. *Ritual: Perspectives and Dimensions*. New York: Oxford University Press.

Bergen, Peter L. 2006. *The Osama bin Laden I Know*. New York: Free Press.

Bloom, Mia M. 2005. *Dying to Kill: The Allure of Suicide Terror*. New York: Columbia University Press.

Bynum, Caroline W. 1984. "Women's Stories, Women's Symbols: A Critique of Victor Turner's Theory of Liminality." In *Anthropology and the Study of Religion*, ed. Robert L. Moore and Frank E. Reynolds, 105–25. Chicago: Center for the Scientific Study of Religion.

Cook, David. 2007. *Martyrdom in Islam*. New York: Cambridge University Press.

Fouda, Yosri, and Nick Fielding. 2003. *Masterminds of Terror: The Truth behind the Most Devastating Terrorist Attack the World Has Ever Seen*. New York: Arcade Publishing.

Hafez, Mohammed M. 2007. *Suicide Bombers in Iraq: The Strategy and Ideology of Martyrdom*. Washington, DC: United States Institute of Peace Press.

Gaur, Ishwar D. 2007. "Martyr as Bridegroom: A Folk Representation of Bhagat Singh." *Journal of Punjab Studies* 14, no. 1: 55–67.

Hegghammer, Thomas. 2010. "The Rise of Muslim Foreign Fighters: Islam and the Globalization of Jihad." *International Security* 35, no. 3: 53–94.

Juergensmeyer, Mark. 2003. *Terror in the Mind of God: The Global Rise of Religious Violence*. Berkeley: University of California Press.

Khosrokhavar, Farhad. 2002. *Les Nouveaux Martyrs d'Allah*. Paris: Flammarion.

Kippenberg, Hans G. 2011. *Violence as Worship: Religious Wars in the Age of Globalization*, trans. Brian McNeil. Stanford: Stanford University Press.

Kippenberg, Hans G., and Tilman Seidensticker, eds. *Terror im Dienste Gottes. Die "Geistliche Anleitung" der Attentäter des 11 September 2001*. Frankfurt am Main: Campus.

Kramer, Martin. 1991. "Sacrifice and Fratricide in Shiite Lebanon." In *Violence and the Sacred in the Modern World*, ed. Mark Juergensmeyer, 30–47. Special issue of *Terrorism and Political Violence* 3, no. 3. London: Frank Cass.

Lincoln, Bruce. 1981. *Emerging from the Chrysalis: Studies in the Rituals of Women's Initiation*. Cambridge, MA: Harvard University Press.

Marzban, Omid. 2006. "The Foreign Makeup of Afghan Suicide Bombers." *Terrorism Focus* 3, no. 7. See http://www.jamestown.org (last accessed October 2011).

McDermott, Terry. 2005. *Perfect Soldiers. The Hijackers: Who They Were, Why They Did It*. New York: Harper Collins.

Moghadam, Assaf. 2008. *The Globalization of Martyrdom: Al-Qaeda, Salafi Jihad, and the Diffusion of Suicide Attacks*. Baltimore: Johns Hopkins University Press.

O'Hanlon, Michael E., and Jason A. Campbell. 2008. "Iraq Index: Tracking Variables of Reconstruction and Security in Post-Saddam Iraq." See http://www.brookings.edu (last accessed October 2011).

Oliver, Anne Marie, and Paul F. Steinberg. 2005. *The Road to Martyrs' Square: A Journey into the World of the Suicide Bomber*. New York: Oxford University Press.

Pape, Robert A. 2005. *Dying to Win: The Strategic Logic of Suicide Terrorism*. New York: Random House.

Roy, Olivier. 2004. *Globalised Islam: The Search for a New Ummah*. London: Hurst.

Sageman, Marc. 2004. *Understanding Terror Networks*. Philadelphia: University of Pennsylvania Press.

Turner, Victor W. 1967. *The Forest of Symbols: Aspects of Ndembu Ritual*. Ithaca: Cornell University Press.

———. 1969. *The Ritual Process: Structure and Anti-Structure*. London: Routledge & Kegan Paul.

van Gennep, Arnold. (1909, in French) 1960. *The Rites of Passage*, trans. Monika B. Vizedom and Gabrielle L. Caffee. London: Routledge & Kegan Paul.

Wensinck, A.J., and A.S. Tritton. 2010. "'Adhāb al-Kabr." In *Encyclopaedia of Islam, second edition*, Vol. 1, ed. P. Bearman et al. Leiden: Brill.

# Videos

Al-Sahab. 2002a. *The Wills of the Martyrs of the Raids on New York and Washington*.

Al-Sahab. 2002b. *The Nineteen Martyrs*.

Al-Sahab. 2006. *Knowledge is for Acting Upon* 2.

Al-Sahab. 2007. *The Will of the Martyr Hafiz 'Usman*.

Al-Sahab. 2007–11. *Winds of Paradise*. 5 Vols.

*Part II*

# Concepts

***Figure 5.1.*** The mothers of the disappeared walking in a demonstration on the Plaza de Mayo, Buenos Aires (photo Antonius Robben)

*Chapter Five*

# Disappearance and Liminality
## Argentina's Mourning of State Terror

*Antonius C.G.M. Robben*

Pablo Fernández Meijide was seventeen years old when he was abducted from his home in Buenos Aires on 23 October 1976, in the presence of his parents, younger brother, and older sister. Five armed men, identifying themselves as members of the Federal Police, entered their apartment at two o'clock in the morning to take Pablo for a routine security check. He could be picked up the next morning at eight at Police Station 19, the anxious parents were told. Graciela and Enrique Fernández Meijide went there at the appointed hour, but the attending policeman denied having him in custody. A search for Pablo began, a habeas corpus request was submitted to the courts, and prominent members of the military and Roman Catholic Church were approached. Meanwhile, Pablo's mother tried to remain in contact with her son: "Sometimes I seemed to hear Pablo's voice. I lived as if hallucinating. When I was not doing something, some formal procedure or task for Pablo, I maintained even more this mental contact with him and I talked to him in thought. I told him 'Hold on, Pablo . . . stay alive, Pablo.' . . . [I would] 'talk' to him to tell him 'this is going to end, Pablo. You are young, this is going to pass'" (Ulla and Echave 1986: 37, 31).

Fourteen years later, Graciela Fernández Meijide told me how, over time, she had pieced together the trajectory of her son's disappearance. Pablo had entered high school in Vicente López in 1976 and become the boyfriend of María Zimmermann, who had been a member of the forbidden Guevarist Youth, which operated under the wings of the People's Revolutionary Army guerrilla organization. Around midnight of 22 October, María, her sister Leonora, and a former comrade were abducted by the First Army Corps. Graciela said, "I suppose that they asked María who was her boyfriend. I suppose that they asked for permission for a free zone to enter the capital because, if they had received a direct order to abduct Pablo, then they would have come in ten minutes. . . . They must have gone to the police station, must have asked for permission, and then arrived at our house" (interview on 20 April 1990). Pablo had not been politically active, but his circle of friends had turned him into a target. In 1984, Pablo's mother was told by a disappeared person who had escaped from the Campo de Mayo clandestine detention center that her son had been held there.

Graciela Fernández Meijide seldom dreamt about her son, but said that when she did, "I dreamt that he was alive, that he told me that he was going to return from 'that,' that which was nameless. This is why I believe that in the deepest part of oneself the disappeared person never dies, although rationally I think the opposite" (Ulla and Echave 1986: 40). Graciela continued her conversations and dreams with her son, tried to embrace him in her sleep, but he always gestured that he could not stay. In her late seventies, Graciela Fernández Meijide was finishing a book manuscript narrating a life searching for Pablo when she dreamt again about her son, but now she could caress his cheek as he cried. "I didn't awake sad but with a moving tenderness, and immediately thought that writing this book had allowed me to bid farewell to my son" (Fernández Meijide 2009: 309). The dream ended a thirty-two-year-long liminal period that began with the bewildering abduction of her son Pablo and concluded with her acceptance of his death.

A liminal period that spans more than thirty years is hardly what Arnold van Gennep and Victor Turner had in mind when they developed the concept. Van Gennep ([1909] 1960: 189–90) did mention rare initiation rites that lasted several decades, but he confined liminality exclusively to transition rites involving the crossing of temporal thresholds "of summer and winter, of a season or a year, of a month or a night; the thresholds of birth, adolescence, maturity, and old age; the threshold of death and that of afterlife." Turner ([1968] 1995: 145) did speak of permanent liminality as a state in which people realize an existential communitas at "the fringes and interstices of the social structure," instead of only temporarily experiencing communitas as an unstructured mode of bare sociality, but he expressed a preference for "well-developed liminal periods" ([1967] 1970: 95).

Turner's (1974) extension of liminality to social drama, in which the liminal phase consists of a crisis at the heart of society rather than seclusion at a marginal place, brings us closer to the liminal state of Graciela Fernández Meijide and her disappeared son, Pablo. This approach has been successfully used to analyze political kidnappings, such as the 1978 abduction and assassination of Italian Prime Minister Aldo Moro by the Red Brigades. David Kertzer (1988: 137) writes, "Political kidnapping dramas typically follow the classic structure of rites of passage. The victim is first separated from the normal social structure, through capture at gunpoint and removal from normal society. He is then placed in a liminal position, lacking his former roles and deprived of normal stimuli. During this period he suffers both physical and social degradation" (see also Wagner-Pacifici 1986). Pablo Fernández Meijide's abduction can easily be analyzed in this way by positioning his predicament in the social drama of an ideological conflict between the Argentine military and the revolutionary insurgency, but I believe that such an approach would individualize the massive disappearances that occurred in Argentine society, ritualize state terrorism, isolate the liminal personae from the wider sociopolitical context, and ignore the interactive dynamic between the liminality of relatives and disappeared kin. Instead, I prefer to use the term liminality as a condition of social indefinition in which social categories and statuses are held in abeyance and social classifications are challenged. My sense of the liminal has an affinity with anthropological thinking about conditions that challenge cultural classifications through interstitial "matter out of place" (Douglas 1966: 48; Sahlins 1976). Liminality produces ambiguous dead and ambiguous living who do not fit in the sociopolitical classifications at hand, as happened to the Argentine disappeared and their relatives. Such liminality has also been analyzed among Hutu refugees living in Tanzania (Malkki 1995), American chronic pain sufferers (Jackson 2005), and the massacred Vietnamese civilians of My Lai, whose ghosts could not find rest and whose surviving relatives struggled against the Vietnamese state to create memorials and ritual abodes to commemorate them (Kwon 2006: 89–94).

This chapter wishes to demonstrate that Argentina's disappeared and their searching relatives have been occupying interdynamic liminal statuses that changed with and influenced the sociopolitical context of Argentine society. In certain ways, this process resembles the extended dialogues between the living and the dead among the Sora of India because postmortem liminality contains so much structural adjustment that it needs such a long time span in order for this process to work itself through. According to Piers Vitebsky, this entire society lives in an all-encompassing state of perpetual liminality, a vast field of shared consciousness (after Vitebsky, in this volume). In Argentina, the prolonged liminality of ten to thirty thousand disappeared and manifold emotionally affected relatives was regarded as politically disruptive by the authorities. Repeated efforts were undertaken by the Argentine state to resolve the undefined statuses of the disappeared and their relatives, but these attempts ran aground on the public opposition from human rights organizations and the refusal of the Argentine military to clarify the disappearances. Still, the searching relatives developed ways of coping that shed new light on a current debate in bereavement studies and provide additional proof to classic insights about mourning and liminality in the anthropology of death.

The dominant view in bereavement studies is that mourners need to work through their losses for their emotional wellbeing. Strongly influenced by Freud ([1917] 1968), the ruling idea is that normal mourning requires grief work to unravel the emotional attachment between the living and the dead. The inability to accept the death of a loved one is therefore characterized as pathological mourning. Recent studies challenge this approach. Social psychologists have shown that bereaved individuals may also refashion the affective tie with the deceased as part of a functioning life (Klass, Silverman, and Nickman 1996; Kwilecki 2011; Stroebe and Schut 2001). Numerous past and present anthropological and sociological studies confirm that people may incorporate the dead actively in the flow of life through narration, remembrance, and ongoing conversation (Francis, Kellaher and Neophytou 2005; Green 2008; Hallam and Hockey 2001; Hertz [1907] 1960; Miller and Parrott 2009; Valentine 2006; van Gennep [1909] 1960; Walter 1996). In Argentina, searching relatives developed innovative ways to incorporate their relation with the disappeared in their lives and adjust these ways to changing personal and political circumstances.

I will start with a brief description of disappearance as a repressive means employed by the Argentine military, explain the search for and interaction with the disappeared by their relatives, and discuss the Argentine navy's spiritual reeducation program for disappeared captives. Next, I will analyze how the change from dictatorship to democracy modified the liminal status of the disappeared and their searching relatives through the findings of a truth commission. Finally, the contested exhumation of the disappeared will be analyzed together with strategies to transform liminality into spiritual rebirth and political memorialization.

## The Biliminality of the Disappeared and Searching Kin

The first premeditated disappearances in Argentina's modern history took place in 1946, when five men with socialist sympathies were abducted, disappeared, and tortured by the police of the city of La Plata on the suspicion of having placed bombs against the Peronist government. They were transferred from police station to police station to mislead their searching relatives. For example, the twenty-four-year-old law student José María Rosales was abducted and subsequently tortured with an electric prod to extract a confession. He declared later in court that he was moved from La Plata to the town of Avellaneda, stripped of his clothing, hooded, tied by hands and feet, and tortured until he confessed to acts he had not committed (Lamas 1956: 49–50). The disappeared student was forced into a condition of liminality that only ended when his abductors decided when he would reappear in the everyday world, either dead or alive.

The five disappeared from La Plata reappeared after several days, but two unionists who were abducted in 1962 were never found again. The disappearance of political opponents occurred regularly during the 1971–73 military rule of Lieutenant-General Lanusse, became a technique of systematic repression in February 1975 during the counterinsurgency campaign against Marxist insurgents in Tucumán province, and was instituted nationwide after the March 1976 coup d'état (Robben 2005a: 263–64). Civilians and guerrilla insurgents disappeared by the ten thousands. Thousands were released after the military decided that they did not pose a threat, while others were secretly assassinated and their bodies cremated, buried, or thrown in the Atlantic Ocean. The disappeared and their relatives were suspended in liminality as the search continued indefinitely and the military denied any involvement (Robben 2011). Tellingly, junta leader Videla disparagingly called the searching mothers protesting at the Plaza de Mayo "crazy women" because they were cultural transgressors who straddled the domestic and public domain with their politicized motherhood (Robben 2005a: 304–5). The stigmatizing qualification served furthermore to reduce a political condition to a psychological dysfunction.

Matilde Mellibovsky, whose daughter Graciela remains disappeared, described how, as if through a fog, an invisible but evolving relation emerged between her and her daughter's liminal status: "[A]n unknown, uncultivated relation in which the disappeared agonizes in impotence; convinced that his life will be completely erased from the face of the earth, *that no one will ever more know about him*. In the same manner, the mother lives the agony of uncertainty, and cannot avoid that her thought accompanies the disappeared at all times. In darkness, in hunger, in illness, in torture, in the cry for his mother, in dirt and in abuse. In death, in the rotting of that so loved matter, and in the decay of his bones" (Mellibovsky 1990: 47, emphasis in original).

The relation between the disappeared and their relatives became thus compounded by a second liminality, with complex psychological, social, and political consequences. The biliminality of the disappeared consisted, on the one hand, of being neither dead nor alive, and, on the other hand, of being banished from civil society when alive or being deprived from a passage to the hereafter when dead. The first liminality concerns their status as human beings, while the second liminality refers to them as social beings who are members of family and community, with complex social relations, social practices, and secular and sacred rituals of participation and departure. The searching kin were also suspended in biliminality as blood or conjugal relatives attached to the disappeared loved ones through primary relations and as fellow-members of community and society. They occupied one liminal status as either bereaved relatives when the disappeared were dead or as anguished searching relatives when they were still alive. The second liminal status consisted of their inability either to socialize with their abducted family members or bury the missing dead with the proper mortuary rituals.

The liminal status of the disappeared was acknowledged by their captors, who regarded their captives as socially dead. In fact, the Argentine military used the term "transfer" (*traslado*) as a euphemism for death. It is the same term used in Argentine cemeteries to indicate the transfer of human remains from one grave or cemetery to another. Perpetrators who were preparing inmates for a transfer were called Peter (Pedro) "after the saint who has the keys to heaven" (Feitlowitz 1998: 52). The disappeared were structurally and socially dead when they arrived in the secret detention centers because they had been removed from civil society and could be assassinated at will. One disappeared survivor observed how captives feared death in liminality—"that particular death which is dying without disappearing, or disappearing without dying. A death in which the person dying had no part whatever: like dying without a struggle, as though dying [while] being already dead, or like never dying at all" (CONADEP [1984] 1986: 167). This fear of death during liminality was the anxiety of falling forever in the social interstices as neither dead nor alive, as neither mourned nor mournable.

## Disappearance and Reeducation

Argentina's disappeared can be classified into six different groups: (1) people who were abducted for a few days or weeks, and then released for posing no threat; (2) people who disappeared and were assassinated; (3) persons who were disappeared, and later reappeared as legalized political prisoners; (4) disappeared persons who escaped; (5) babies and infants who were disappeared, given away, and remain unaware of their origins; (6) people who disappeared, were reeducated, and then finally allowed to return to society. The overwhelming majority of the disappeared fit in the first three groups. The first group runs in the thousands or ten thousands. The second group consists of around ten thousand documented disappeared, according to Argentine forensic anthropologists, but most human rights groups maintain that thirty thousand people were disappeared

(Brysk 1994; CONADEP [1984] 1986: 447). The third group consists of more than ten thousand detainees (Guembe 2006: 28). The fourth group is not larger than a dozen persons, whereas the last two groups run into the hundreds each. All six groups occupied liminality during the disappearance, but the last group deserves special attention because the liminal status of its members resembles best the liminality of a rite of passage.

The Navy Mechanics School or ESMA (Escuela de Mecánica de la Armada) in Buenos Aires was one of the largest clandestine detention centers during the dictatorship and specialized in the capture of members of the Montoneros guerrilla organization. It was located in the Officers' Mess. Thousands of disappeared captives were held there, of whom around two hundred were released, and about fifty inmates went through a full-fledged rehabilitation program to transform subversives into citizens (Robben 2005a: 250–55).

Captives at the ESMA had commonly been abducted by its task group, which was operative between March 1976 and December 1978. The group was subdivided into a logistics subgroup that took care of the infrastructure (cars, weapons, food, building), an intelligence subgroup that provided information about the human targets and interrogated the disappeared, and an operational subgroup that abducted and guarded the captives (Robben 2005a: 197). The typical captive was beaten up during his or her capture, hooded, and moved to the ESMA clandestine detention center by car. Blindfolded and stripped naked, the inmate was immediately subjected to lengthy torture and interrogation in the building's basement. After this dehumanization process, the captive was taken to a tiny windowless cabin in the building's attic. The inhuman conditions—blindfolded, naked, shackled, with little food—made captives feel utterly abandoned by the world and lose faith in their fellow human beings. The prolonged isolation was part of a desocialization process that deeply injured their sociality and, by extension, crippled their political engagement. The ex-disappeared Graciela Daleo observed that her captors wanted her to abandon all feelings of social solidarity and become a complete individualist. She was told repeatedly, "It's an individual process here, you have nothing to do with the rest; everything has to do with you" (Daleo 1985: 429).

Every Thursday afternoon, a committee of at least five people would discuss the status reports of the inmates and decide who was fit to live and who would die. Unrecoverable captives were moved from the attic to a smaller attic that housed the building's water tank to await their fate. The condemned were taken on their final day from the small attic to the basement, given a sedative, and taken to the airport. They were stripped of their clothing during the flight, given another sedative, and dropped one by one through the plane's hatch above the Atlantic Ocean. The emotional reactions of the surviving disappeared were closely watched on these days. Sorrow betrayed an affective attachment, signifying incomplete desocialization. Once the captive was considered to have been broken completely, the recuperation process began after the committee's positive judgment.

Recoverable captives were granted small privileges. The blindfold and shackles were removed, clothes were returned, and they were eventually allowed, or rather forced, to work. The assigned tasks drew on their professional skills, so there were carpenters, plumbers, typists, photographers, documentalists, translators, and even speechwriters who secretly worked for the political campaign of Admiral Massera, who was a junta member between 1976 and 1978. These disappeared were restored to their old professional identities but imbued with the values of Christian civilization, loyalty to the Argentine state, and respect for its authorities. If they worked and behaved in a satisfactory manner, then they would be allowed to spend a night at home, only to return to the clandestine detention center in the morning. Such privileges were not a secure sign of eventual freedom, because about 30 percent of the group of fifty was nevertheless assassinated.

A decisive step in the social rebirth of a recoverable captive was the order to write a self-critical life history. Miriam Lewin had been abducted by the Argentine Air Force on 17 May 1977 for being a member of the forbidden Peronist student organization JUP (Juventud Universitaria Peronista), linked to the Montoneros. She tried to commit suicide, but her captors removed the cyanide capsule from her mouth. She was taken to a clandestine detention center along Virrey Cevallos Street in Buenos Aires, tortured repeatedly, and in late 1977 asked to reflect on her past. She complied: "I wrote a manuscript in which I revalued my life in a straightforward manner, and I showed remorse for having tried to commit suicide" (Lewin 1985: 413). Her captors were so impressed that she was ordered to read her statement before a group of officers. A few weeks later, she received the good news: "You're reborn, kid. What you wrote fell really well, so that we have decided to save your life" (Lewin 1985: 413). In another assessment, Miriam Lewin was asked what she thought about family, whether she believed in God, and in which historical era she would have liked to live. Lewin's reflections served to ascertain whether or not she had acquired the necessary Western and Christian values during her liminal period in disappearance. She passed the test and was asked where she would like to go. She requested to be sent to relatives in the United States, but they took her to the ESMA clandestine detention center instead.

Miriam Lewin arrived at the ESMA in March 1978 and had to translate articles from *The New York Times* and *Le Monde* into Spanish. The naval officers liked her progress and allowed her to make one telephone call a month to her parents, then two calls, and finally she could briefly visit her family in the presence of an officer. The final phase of the ESMA rehabilitation program consisted of a slow renewal of contact with the outside world—a hesitant step away from the surveillance of the captors. This meant that the captive was no longer disappeared, at least not for his or her relatives, because he or she was not granted a legal status as a political prisoner. By late 1978, Miriam Lewin could spend the weekend at home. She was threatened that if she fled, then the price would be paid by her relatives and her comrades at the ESMA. She was released on 10 January 1979 but forced to work at the press office of retired Admiral Massera (Lewin 1985: 416-17).). She worked there till mid-1979 and was then given a job at the Ministry of Social Welfare. Miriam Lewin left Argentina for the United States in April 1981 (Actis et al. 2001: 236–42).

The violent separation from society through abduction, the dehumanization, desocialization, and reeducation during disappearance in liminality, the absolute submission and obedience to the captors, and the slow reincorporation into society as abiding citizens carry the unmistaken characteristics of a rite of passage. Reappearance, however, did not end the coercive supervision. Naval officers sometimes called their former captives, asking if they were doing well, and gave intimidating advice about how to run their lives.

Relatives searching for the disappeared were unaware of these secret rehabilitation programs. The military government had set up an official Resocialization Institute in June 1977 for the treatment of remorseful insurgents who had surrendered voluntarily, but it seems to have served more as a form of deception than as a genuine effort at rehabilitation (*La Nación*, 1 and 6 December 1977). Searching parents, nevertheless, clung to the hope that their son or daughter would be alive and eventually be incorporated into this program.

## Contact between the Disappeared and Relatives

Five days after the abduction of her daughter Graciela, the telephone rang in the home of Matilde Saidler de Mellibovsky. She recounts the conversation: "'Aunt! Aunt!' she said, 'It's me, Graciela!' 'No, my dear,' I said, 'it isn't your aunt, it's your mother, where are you? Where are you, my dear?' Then her voice changed: 'I'm very far away, I think I'm very far away.' I understood that it was going to be a very short phone call and I asked: 'When am I going to see you? Am I going to see you again?' And she said: 'No, no, mother, never again.' I don't know which words came next, but she said with great emotion: 'Mother, I love you, I love you.' And I had the strength to tell her: 'And I adore you and am with you, wherever you are, I'm with you.' And they cut the communication" (Mellibovsky 1990: 242).

Lilia and Lucas Orfanó had raised their two sons, Daniel and Guillermo, in the best tradition of Argentine political activism, and they had become members of the Montoneros guerrilla organization. Daniel was abducted on 30 July 1976, and five days later his parents' home was raided by an army task force. Lilia and Lucas were hooded, beaten, and abducted to the federal police headquarters—so Lilia Orfanó told me in November 1989. When they were registered by the policeman on duty, he remarked, "The family united." Apparently, their son Daniel was also held captive there. The couple was taken blindfolded to a large place with many other captives. Some were occasionally taken away for torture. Lilia told me, "At one time we heard screams that were the screams of my son, and Lucas says to me, 'That's Dani who's screaming!' and I go crazy. I call one of the guards and tell him, 'Sir, the one who is screaming is my son!' And he asks, 'What's your son's name?' 'Pantaleón Daniel Orfanó.' He leaves, returns, and says, 'No, it isn't your son.' It was a lie, it was my son, I'm certain it was my son" (interview on 12 November 1989). Lilia and Lucas Orfanó were held captive for fifteen days, poorly fed but not tortured physically, and then released. They began a search for their son Daniel and discovered through a court notice that he had been found dead but that the body would not be released. Their youngest son Guillermo was abducted on 2 December 1976 and remains disappeared.

These two examples demonstrate that abduction did not necessarily break all contacts with the disappeared. Some parents heard about their children when held for questioning, while others received letters, notes, telephone calls, and even the infants of their disappeared sons and daughters. Most parents searched for ways to reestablish contact with their disappeared children. Just as the bereaved organize a mortuary ritual to reconstruct the torn social fabric after a person has died, as has been argued by Durkheim ([1912] 1995) and Hertz ([1907] 1960), so Argentines searching for their loved ones renewed their social networks, not to mend a permanent tear but to restore it. They spoke with their friends and comrades and approached neighbors and employers to discover if they had seen their disappeared kin, knew if they were in hiding, had been detained, or had fled abroad.

When the Argentine military decided to unleash their terror campaign, they expected that the disappearances would instill so much fear in the relatives, the revolutionary organizations, and Argentine society that any political opposition would be immobilized. To the military's surprise, however, parents, spouses, and siblings began to search in hospitals, police stations, military bases, mental institutions, morgues, and cemeteries soon after their loved ones had disappeared. Resignation to death and abandoning the search were unacceptable because that was experienced as killing the disappeared by assigning them the status of deceased without any physical proof. Furthermore, the hope that the disappeared were still alive was confirmed by the reappearance of small numbers of abducted captives after months or even years in secret detention.

The tireless search of parents was driven by bonds of attachment and feelings of basic trust forged during infancy. Children develop an inner reliance that their caretakers will provide a nurturing environment and shield them from harm. This bond makes parents want to protect their children even when they have grown into adulthood. Here lies the deeper psychological cause of the anguish among parents about the unbearable liminal status of their disappeared loved ones, and of the anxiety that this undefined status might never be resolved. Basic trust was the principal driving force behind the courageous defiance of military repression and the unending search for their loved ones by thousands of mothers and fathers (Robben 2000a). Julio Morresi called an acquaintance from the police when his son Norberto did not return home on 23 April 1976. The retired inspector made inquiries at several hospitals and police stations but to no avail. Months later, Norberto's father had a fruitless meeting with an army colonel through the help of a retired lieutenant he knew from the Huracán soccer club, and even visited what might have been a clandestine detention center or way station for the disappeared where he believed his son to be held captive. Graciela and Enrique Fernández Meijide also mobilized their social and family relations to discover the whereabouts of their son Pablo. They asked military chaplain Grasselli to use his contacts with the armed forces to inquire about Pablo, and met First Army Corps commander General Suárez Mason, in whose jurisdiction their son had been abducted (Fernández Meijide 2009: 26).

When everyday social networks failed to yield any information, the searching relatives took recourse to the supernatural through the type of conversations referred to by Graciela Fernández Meijide in this chapter's introduction. Hebe Pastor de Bonafini, the president of the Mothers of the Plaza de Mayo, also tried to lessen her son's suffering by establishing mental contact: "I think and think, 'Where are you, my son? Are you in some place, maybe closer than I can imagine? . . . What are you thinking, my dear, you who always thought so much? Who now occupies your thoughts? . . . Close your eyes, like I am doing now and think of me. I'm certain that in this way everything is going to pass very soon'" (Sánchez 1985: 106–7). Estela Puccio Borrás held inner dialogues with her daughter

Adriana, who disappeared in June 1976: "Are you afraid, my little one? Are you tired? Are you awake or sleeping? Did they hurt you? Did they cut your hair?" (Puccio Borrás 1983: 92). She frequently heard her daughter say in her dreams "Come mother, stay here with me," and five years after her disappearance, as Estela was passing a sleepless night in Spain, she heard her daughter say, "Stay there [in Buenos Aires], mother, don't suffer for me anymore, think about the others and those who remain," and finally she felt that God said, "Don't suffer more, your daughter is happy" (Puccio Borrás 1983: 103, 106).

The multiple attempts at contact with the disappeared continued throughout the years of military rule but were hoped to come to fruition when the Argentine military was defeated at the Falklands (Malvinas) War in June 1982, making way for a transitional military government that called for free elections in October 1983. The expectation was great that the democratic government would free disappeared captives and ascertain the fate of all others, thus ending the biliminality of the disappeared and their relatives.

## The Truth Commission's Secular Funeral Rite

The uncertain fate of the disappeared was foremost on the political agenda of the democratic government that assumed power in December 1983. The exhumation of several mass graves in 1982 had given ominous forebodings of what had happened to the disappeared but many people believed that some were still being held alive by the military. Newly elect president Raúl Alfonsín instituted the National Commission on Disappeared Persons, or CONADEP, to resolve the issue of the disappeared and, in effect, end their biliminal status.

Conflicting feelings of trust and abandonment were aroused among the searching relatives when the truth commission declared in September 1984 that the disappeared should be considered dead even though they could not be located. The liminal status of the disappeared and their kin revealed its distinct emotional, cognitive, and social dimensions (see Hardenberg, in this volume). Cognitively, the disappeared were transformed from people missing yet alive into deceased yet unaccounted for. The CONADEP enacted a secular death ritual that reduced the biliminality of the disappeared and their searching kin to a liminal status by removing the disappeared's uncertain fate. The disappeared were now pronounced dead, and the searching relatives became bereaved relatives. Still, the deceased disappeared and their living family members each retained one liminal status. The dead still had to be buried and their souls had to depart for the hereafter, while the mourning relatives had not yet administered the proper mortuary rituals.

In a concerted effort to provide legal clarity, Argentine human rights lawyers lobbied to establish a forcibly disappeared person as a new legal persona situated between the living and the dead, to save them from their status as "liminal personae," who, according to Turner ([1968] 1995: 95) "are necessarily ambiguous, since this condition and these persons elude or slip through the network of classifications that normally locate states and positions in cultural space. Liminal entities are neither here nor there; they are betwixt and between the positions assigned and arrayed by law, custom, convention, and ceremonial." The creation of the disappeared as a legal category introduced the disappeared into a classificatory order that neutralized their disturbing liminal status, allowed relatives to solve legal issues such as property titles without the need for a death certificate, and made the disappearance an ongoing crime and thus without a statute of limitation.

Emotionally, the liminal status placed before parents and other kin an agonizing dilemma: maintaining hope that the disappeared were still alive implied that the search would continue indefinitely, while accepting their death would lead to an interminable search for the remains. Relatives coped in several ways. Some continued to believe that the disappeared were alive somewhere but had lost their true identity through amnesia provoked by torture. One Catholic mother compared her interminable wait for a sign of life to hell, but she did not imagine hell as a place with spiked beds but "with easy chairs on which one sits comfortably awaiting the mailman . . . who will bring news that will never arrive" (Mellibovsky 1990: 251). I saw many examples of this eternal wait when I visited the parental homes of the disappeared: bedrooms were left untouched, bed sheets were changed every week, and, in one home, the favorite pudding of a disappeared was prepared every few days for his unexpected arrival. Other relatives reconciled themselves with the inevitable and tried to resume the thread of life. Clearly, the status change caused by the presumption of death might make cognitive sense but was emotionally unacceptable for certain relatives.

These emotional reactions were an aspect of personal grief work, but liminality has also a social dimension. There were parents who turned their disappeared children's predicament into political activism and regarded the search for the skeletal remains as a permanent denouncement of the regime's human rights violations and the perpetrators' impunity. The refusal of the Argentine military to disclose the destination of the remains of more than ten thousand documented disappeared, or even thirty thousand disappeared as most human rights organizations have maintained, obstructed a ritual closure.

In his ethnography of the Sora of India, Vitebsky (1993: 14) has shown how the dead made use of shamans in trance to create a shared consciousness with the living and engage them in frequent dialogues during a redemption process that is lengthy, slow, and painful because "the living person is unable to free himself from the memory of what things were like before this transformation [from being alive to being dead]." The Mothers of the Plaza de Mayo went through a comparable process, not through mutually constitutive conversations with the disappeared, but by trying to divine their political ideals and course of action. They explained Argentina's political crises through the interpretive framework attributed to their children, and began fighting for a better Argentina according to what they believed to be a solution authentic to their children's revolutionary ideals.

The truth commission and the state failed to conclude Argentina's transitional phase from dictatorship to democracy when relatives could not perform the culturally prescribed burial rites, the disappearances were not recompensed through criminal convictions, and the armed forces refused to take responsibility. These three issues preoccupied the Argentine state and society for decades to come, as affected relatives and human rights organizations continued to exert moral and political pressure on successive governments.

Even though the truth commission did not locate the disappeared, its painful conclusion about their death caused a search for the human remains in order to bury them properly and complete a process of mourning that for many people had begun hesitantly but could not be followed through because of the absence of a corpse. The search for a disappeared child thus became the search for missing remains motivated by the same basic trust that had generated the tireless journeys through Argentina's institutions and military installations after the abductions. If parents harbored any guilt feelings about having been unable to protect their children from capture and to comfort them in the hour of death, then the only remaining obligation was to give them a proper burial.

## Reburial and Memorialization

The search for the skeletal remains of the disappeared began during the transitional military government when relatives of the disappeared union leader Miguel Angel Sosa were tipped off that he had been buried secretly at the cemetery of Grand Bourg near Buenos Aires. A judge ordered, in late October 1982, Argentina's first exhumation of a mass grave, which turned out to contain nearly four hundred unidentified bodies (Cohen Salama 1992: 60–62; Anonymous 1982: 11). These early exhumations were frustrating for the relatives because they were carried out without the proper forensic techniques and often failed to yield positive identifications.

Many exhumations were ordered by the courts and the CONADEP truth commission when the Alfonsín government assumed power in December 1983. The CONADEP and the Grandmothers of the Plaza de Mayo did much to improve the forensic quality by inviting foreign expertise. Exhumations were no longer a haphazard digging for anonymous remains and a painful confrontation with unknown disappeared but became a reliable means to identify the assassinated civilians, determine the cause of death, and establish pregnancies carried to completion.

One would expect all human rights organizations to support the exhumations wholeheartedly because the forensic examinations ended their liminality. Identities were restored, sacrificial political lives were revealed, judicial proof of state terrorism was gathered, and the assassinated disappeared were finally given a dignified reburial. The surprise was great when one large faction of the Mothers of the Plaza de Mayo began opposing the exhumations in late 1984, causing the group to split in 1986 into the Mothers of the Plaza de Mayo Association (Asociación Madres de Plaza de Mayo) and the much smaller Mothers of the Plaza de Mayo Founding Line (Asociación Madres de Plaza de Mayo Línea Fundadora). The majority faction feared that the reburials would lead to a national process of forgetting and a political demobilization of the human rights movement. The exhumations were condemned as a government scheme to have them accept the presumption of death of the disappeared, loosen the affective ties between surviving relatives and reburied disappeared, set a grief work in motion that would depoliticize all searching mothers and relatives, and create a reconciliatory attitude towards the past. The Mothers therefore refused any kind of economic compensation as hush money, rejected symbolic reparation as memorialization, and denied psychotherapy to induce personal mourning. Instead, they preferred counseling to cope with the emotional price of opposing the exhumations, continued their weekly protest as an active remembrance of their disappeared children, and propagated a political message of social justice (Robben 2000b: 103–7).

The resistance to ending the disappeared's liminal status through exhumations was also given a legal rationale by 1986. The exhumation turned a disappeared into an assassinated person, and a successful identification produced a *corpus delicti* or the material proof of a homicide. The twenty-year statute of limitations on homicides in Argentina implied that the perpetrators might never be convicted if the Alfonsín government went ahead with its plan to prosecute only the highest-ranking commanders. Hence, the liminality of the disappeared was maintained to prevent impunity until the political climate would become favorable to the sentencing of all perpetrators (Gorini 2008: 302–5). As had been anticipated by the Mothers, President Alfonsín passed two sweeping amnesty laws through Congress in 1986 and 1987, and his successor, President Carlos Menem, decreed two general pardons in 1989 and 1990 that freed hundreds of indicted and dozens of convicted perpetrators, including Lieutenant-General Videla and Admiral Massera, who had been given life sentences in 1985. The Mothers of the Plaza de Mayo Association proved to have been visionary with its counterintuitive rejection of the exhumations in the mid-1980s; more than twenty years later, nearly two hundred persons have been convicted, and eight hundred and twenty were on trial by March 2011 after the derogation of the amnesty laws in 2005 and the presidential pardons in 2007 by the Argentine Supreme Court (Dandan 2011).

The disappeared could not, however, remain in limbo forever because that would condemn them to the social indefinition inflicted by the military. The largest of the two Mothers of the Plaza de Mayo organizations responded by incorporating the spiritual relation with the disappeared into their political lives. They began to acknowledge publicly that their children had been revolutionaries, and embraced their political ideals. As Hebe Pastor de Bonafini remarked in 1988, "A step which cost the Mothers much was to realize that their children were political militants, revolutionary activists; the general discourse was at the beginning that my child hadn't done anything, and that they had taken him or her away because he or she was a teacher, an artist or a lawyer" (Diago 1988: 122). The political consciousness raising caused by her two disappeared sons made Pastor de Bonafini conclude that "my children have given birth to me" (Sánchez 1985: 74). This spiritual rebirth signifies an end to the liminal status of these searching Mothers in a social sense—but not necessarily in its emotional sense and for which they received counseling—and made the skeletal remains lose their significance. As Pastor de Bonafini remarked, "They have interred their bodies it doesn't matter where, but their spirit, their solidarity, and their love for the people can never be buried and forgotten" (Madres 1989 58: 11). The Mothers ended the liminal status of the disappeared by incorporating their revolutionary ideas, while most other relatives continued their joint liminality through the search for the remains.

These searching relatives, including the smaller Mothers of the Plaza de Mayo Founding Line, admitted that reburials provided a ritual closure but denied that their political fire would extinguish. Reburials were political acts that motivated the bereaved to fight for the prosecution of the perpetrators and remain actively engaged in the human rights struggle.

Furthermore, the ritual closure and personal mourning did not sever the spiritual bond with the deceased, as classic bereavement theory has argued, but changed with the passage of time and the dynamic political context. The evolving relation between Julio Morresi and his disappeared son Norberto is a case in point.

Norberto Morresi was a seventeen-year-old noncombatant member of the forbidden Union of High School Students or UES (Unión de Estudiantes Secundarios), linked to the Montoneros, who was caught by the military on 23 April 1976, together with the thirty-four-year-old Luis María Roberto, as they were distributing the illegal magazine *Evita Montonera*. They were executed on the spot, placed in their Chevrolet station wagon, and set ablaze. The police found the car with the partially torched bodies, took finger prints, and buried them as unidentified persons. Argentine forensic anthropologists exhumed and identified the two disappeared in June 1989. Their unity in death was continued into the hereafter. The skeletal remains were buried together on 7 July in one niche of a large raised tomb at the Bajo Flores cemetery (Cohen Salama 1992: 228–32).

When I interviewed Julio Morresi in 1991, he spoke of the peace of mind given by the identification and reburial of his son: "I know, unfortunately we have this little heap of bones at the Flores cemetery, no? It is like a ritual that we go there every Sunday to bring him even if it is only one flower. It is completely useless, but it helps spiritually. . . . We go there, we kiss the photo that is hanging on the niche, and it makes us feel good" (interview on 29 March 1991).

Julio Morresi's relation with Norberto had been characterized by the continued mental adjustment of his son's appearance and walks in life as time advanced. Just as he had imagined his son older, with or without long hair, and with or without a beard, when he was driving day by day through the streets of Buenos Aires to find him, so he continued to visualize Norberto after his reburial. Julio wondered in March 2010 what his fifty-two-year-old son would have been doing now, whether he would have had children and still be politically active.

Julio and his wife, Irma, still visit the Flores cemetery every Sunday, but the sentiment has changed. When I spoke with him in March 2010, he said that these visits still fill him with spiritual energy and give relief to his emotions, but his sentiments changed after a memorial wall was erected in 2007: "He [Norberto] is more present for us at the Memory Park because he is there with his comrades. Only his bones are at the cemetery and even though they are mine, they are still only bones and not really Norberto for me" (interview 22 March 2010). Norberto's name and his age at the day of his disappearance are engraved on the memorial wall. There is no mark that distinguishes him from the more than nine thousand documented disappeared who have not yet been exhumed and identified, as if to share their continued liminality in solidarity. His parents, Julio and Irma Morresi, are more attracted to the communitas experienced at the memorial than by the individuation of their son at the Flores cemetery. Likewise, the spiritual relation between the disappeared and their searching kin has also been affected by the erection of the memorial wall because their liminality is not separated from the political context that produced their status.

Argentina's national Memory Park was founded in Buenos Aires in July 1998 along the banks of the River Plata, where some disappeared had washed ashore after having been thrown alive from airplanes into the Atlantic Ocean. The park was inaugurated in August 2001, but the memorial wall remained empty because of disagreements about who counted as victims of state terrorism and how they should be listed on this Monument to the Victims of State Terrorism. The memorial wall consists of four major walls arranged along the sides of a sinuous fissure to symbolize the open wound in Argentine society, and one small separate wall at the waterside. Thirty thousand stone slabs were attached to signify the number of disappeared, even though only around ten thousand disappearances have been documented. President Néstor Kirchner finally broke the stalemate about the memorial wall by enforcing law 46/98 that stipulated the construction of a memorial with the names listed in the 1984 CONADEP truth commission report and those of other disappeared and assassinated between 1969 and 1983. Kirchner revealed the monument ceremonially on 7 November 2007. The walls contain 8,727 names, including those of guerrillas who died in combat and the disappeared who were identified through exhumations. According to an employee of the Memory Park information center, more than twenty-one thousand slabs remain empty because the military have not released any lists of the disappeared, and many people from the interior have not come forward to denounce the disappearance of loved ones. He called it "a moveable monument" because new names can be added, making the memorial wall unfinished and always under construction until all empty slabs are filled, even though the most thorough investigation of Argentine forensic anthropologists has yielded less than eleven thousand names.

Different social groups, liminal as well as nonliminal, have been represented together on the memorial wall in Memory Park because of shared hardships, suffering, struggles, ideals, and death, according to the monument's inscription: "The list of this monument comprises the victims of state terrorism, disappeared and assassinated detainees and those who died fighting for the same ideals of justice and impartiality." The nearly ten thousand names listed on the memorial wall show the magnitude of state terrorism, and the inscription emphasizes that they had been assassinated for the pursuit of a political cause.

The searching relatives have realized that most disappeared will never be found because they were thrown in the Atlantic Ocean or cremated. Most human rights, ex-disappeared, and family-based organizations have therefore emphasized the importance of memorials, monuments, museums, and name plaques to remember the disappeared. The idea behind memorialization is, according to Nora (1984) and Young (1993: 5–15), that material representations will absorb lived experiences, collective commemorations will displace individual traumatic memories, and that public memory is constructed dynamically.

Another possible effect of memorialization is the closure of liminality by reincorporating the disappeared into society as deceased members. If liminality is defined as a status of social indefinition, then the construction of a memorial wall ends this uncertainty symbolically. The material inscription of the names of the disappeared implies a presumption of death and a rebirth as victims of state terrorism and martyrs of the violent struggle for social justice. Even though the Mothers of the Plaza de Mayo Association rejects memorialization as an enclosed remembrance and wants to preserve a living memory of the disappeared through political activism, the postliminality of the disappeared is confirmed by the majority of relatives and friends through annual commemorations and informal visits to Memory Park. The disappeared have become mournable members of Argentine society because their death is making political sense and their remembrance has become integrated into a dominant historical narrative and ritualized in national life (Hallam and Hockey 2001; Horst-Warhaft 2000).

The names of the hundreds of babies and infants that were kidnapped and handed to childless military couples are conspicuously missing from the memorial wall. Unlike the disappeared who had been abducted during adulthood, most babies are believed to be alive, and over one hundred have been located since the Grandmothers of the Plaza de Mayo began their diligent investigations into their whereabouts. It is therefore justified to say that the liminality of these hundreds of disappeared continues to affect Argentine society.

## Conclusion

This chapter has shown how Argentina has struggled with the liminal statuses of ten to thirty thousand Argentines who were disappeared by the armed forces during the 1976–83 military dictatorship, and that of their searching relatives. Several attempts were made to solve this social incongruity in the bosom of Argentine society. Whereas the Argentine state pronounced the disappeared to be dead, the searching relatives and the disappeared continued to occupy liminal statuses in Argentine society, thus corroborating the classical anthropological insight that the bereaved and the deceased may nurture enduring ties through social, ritual, and spiritual means (Bloch and Parry 1982; Hertz [1907] 1960; Huntington and Metcalf 1979; van Gennep [1909] 1960). The disappeared and the searching relatives were each suspended from everyday existence in a phase of biliminality. The disappeared were neither dead nor alive as human beings, and neither participated in society as social beings nor occupied a place as deceased members. In turn, their family members were betwixt-and-between being bereaved or dispossessed relatives, and held a second liminal status through the inability to interact with their abducted loved ones when alive or bury them when dead. These compounded liminal statuses of searching kin and disappeared changed with the evolving political context. The 1984 truth commission succeeded in reducing the biliminal status by pronouncing the disappeared as deceased but could not resolve the remaining liminal status because the Argentine state was unable to locate the remains of the assassinated missing.

The dynamic liminality of Argentina's disappeared and their searching relatives shows that the interpretive use of the concept of liminality is not confined to the ritual practices analyzed by Hertz, van Gennep, and Turner but can be employed in complex political processes evolving over several decades. It also shows that these liminal statuses may be contested sociopolitical categories, as was shown by the conflictive memorialization of the disappeared listed on the memorial wall in Buenos Aires. Furthermore, the Argentine case demonstrates that liminality has cognitive, emotional, and social dimensions that are subject to different processes of change. Finally, the meaning of liminality and liminal statuses may transform under changing political circumstances.

The liminal time span of the disappeared and the searching relatives varies from person to person. Relatives who continued to search for their disappeared kin after the truth commission pronounced them dead solved liminality through exhumations or political memorialization. The members of the Mothers of the Plaza de Mayo Association instead ended liminality by embracing the revolutionary ideas of the disappeared in a process of political radicalization that caused their spiritual rebirth. The embodiment of their children's political beliefs linked them to century-old Argentine notions about the enduring spirit of human remains and the resurrection of their adversarial ideologies in political struggles.

The common Catholic belief that human remains carry a spiritual force or *virtus* that can affect the living motivated nineteenth-century commanders to mutilate enemy corpses during the Argentine civil wars. Dismemberment would disperse but not destroy the spiritual power of the deceased, however (Johnson 2004; Robben 2000b). It made José Mármol (1894: 58) cast in 1843 a curse on the Argentine dictator Juan Manuel de Rosas: "Not even the dust from your bones will America have." Rosas was cursed to never have a place to repose his tired bones and restless soul. Spirit and soul would eternally wander in liminality and could not influence the Argentine nation. The fear of such power was expressed by Domingo Sarmiento ([1845] 1986: 7–8), who wrote in 1845 about the slain ill-spirited warlord Facundo Quiroga, an ally of Rosas: "Terrible shadow of Facundo! I am going to conjure you up so that, shaking the bloodstained dust from your ashes, you will arise to explain to us the secret life and internal convulsions that tear at the entrails of a noble people! . . . Facundo has not died; he is alive in the popular traditions, in the Argentine politics and revolutions; in Rosas, his heir, his alter ego: his soul has passed to this other mold, more finished and perfect." Quiroga was believed to still be poisoning the Argentine nation ten years after his assassination in 1835. He needed to be revived to purge Argentina of its poisonous spirit.

This nineteenth-century preoccupation with the spiritual power of political figures reappears in a different form during the 1976–83 dictatorship. Disappearance replaced dismemberment as the principal means to erase political ideas and prevent the dead from becoming martyrs. The spirits of the disappeared were condemned to wander in aimless liminality between life and death. The political radicalization of the Mothers of the Plaza de Mayo Association was therefore a strategy to revoke this enforced oblivion by embodying the revolutionary ideals of their children and reinvigorate their ideological struggle. The revenge so feared by the Argentine military became a reality after decades of activism resulted in the indictment of hundreds of perpetrators.

There are again echoes of the nineteenth-century belief in a spiritual force in an obituary of Admiral Massera, written after the former junta member died of lung and heart failure on 8 November 2010 at the Naval Hospital in Buenos Aires. Massera had been condemned to life in prison in 1985, was pardoned in 1990, and placed under house arrest in 1998. In the last years of his life, he was declared unfit to stand trial on medical grounds. The Supreme Court ruled, however, a few months before his death, that the 1985 life sentence remained active, so he died a convicted man. In his scathing obituary, the former Montonero Ernesto Jauretche condemns Massera's spirit to wander in eternal liminality: "That he will never return from his decaying remains, that they will never be able to reproduce themselves; that if God exists, he will not give him shelter not even in a latrine of heaven, and that neither the devil will accept him nor in the third hell. That there will not even be for him the promised biblical resurrection" (Jauretche 2010). For Jauretche and most relatives of the disappeared, radical evil never deserves the spiritual rest so cruelly denied to others.

**Antonius C.G.M. Robben** (PhD Berkeley 1986) is professor of anthropology at Utrecht University, the Netherlands. He has been a research fellow at the Michigan Society of Fellows and the Harry Frank Guggenheim Foundation. His books include the ethnography *Political Violence and Trauma in Argentina* (University of Pennsylvania Press 2005), which won the Textor Prize from the American Anthropological Association in 2006; the edited volumes *Death, Mourning, and Burial: A Cross-Cultural Reader* (Wiley-Blackwell 2004); and (with Francisco Ferrándiz) *Necropolitics: Mass Graves and Exhumations in the Age of Human Rights* (University of Pennsylvania Press 2015).

# References

Actis, Munú, Cristina Ines Aldini, Miriam Lewin. 2001. *Ese infierno: Conversaciones de cinco mujeres sobrevivientes de la ESMA*. Buenos Aires: Editorial Sudamericana.

Anonymous. 1982. "El caso de los NN." *Somos* 319 (29 October): 11.

Bloch, Maurice, and Jonathan Parry, eds. 1982. *Death and the Regeneration of Life*. New York: Cambridge University Press.

Brysk, Alison. 1994. "The Politics of Measurement: The Contested Count of the Disappeared in Argentina." *Human Rights Quarterly* 16: 676–92.

Cohen Salama, Mauricio. 1992. *Tumbas anónimas. Informe sobre la identificación de restos de víctimas de la represión illegal*. Buenos Aires: Catálogos Editora.

CONADEP. (1984) 1986. *Nunca Más: The Report of the Argentine Commission on the Disappeared*. New York: Farrar, Straus & Giroux.

Dandan, Alejandra. 2011. "Los juicios en números." *Página/12,* 24 March.

Daleo, Graciela. 1985. "Testimonio de la señora Graciela Beatriz Daleo." 18 July 1985. *El Diario del Juicio* 22: 421-431.

Diago, Alejandro. 1988. *Hebe: memoria y esperanza. Conversando con las Madres de Plaza de Mayo*. Buenos Aires: Ediciones Dialéctica.

Douglas, Mary. 1966. *Purity and Danger: An Analysis of Concepts of Pollution and Taboo*. London: Routledge & Kegan Paul.

Durkheim, Emile. (1912, in French) 1995. *The Elementary Forms of Religious Life*. New York: Free Press.

Erikson, Erik H. 1951. *Childhood and Society*. London: Imago Publishing.

Feitlowitz, Marguerite. 1998. *A Lexicon of Terror: Argentina and the Legacies of Torture*. New York: Oxford University Press.

Fernández Meijide, Graciela. 2009. *La historia íntima de los derechos humanos en la Argentina (a Pablo)*. Buenos Aires: Editorial Sudamericana.

Francis, Doris, Leonie Kellaher, and Georgina Neophytou. 2005. *The Secret Cemetery*. Oxford: Berg.

Freud, Anna. 1969. "About Losing and Being Lost." In *Indications for Child Analysis and Other Papers, 1945–1956*, 302–16. London: Hogarth Press.

Freud, Sigmund. (1917, in German) 1968. "Mourning and Melancholia." In *The Standard Edition of the Complete Psychological Works of Sigmund Freud*, ed. J. Strachey, vol. 14, 243–58. London: Hogarth Press.

Gorini, Ulises. 2008. *La otra lucha: Historia de las Madres de Plaza de Mayo*, vol. 2: *1983–1986*. Buenos Aires: Grupo Editorial Norma.

Green, James W. 2008. *Beyond the Good Death: The Anthropology of Modern Dying*. Philadelphia: University of Pennsylvania Press.

Guembe, María José. 2006. "Economic Reparations for Grave Human Rights Violations: The Argentinean Experience." In *The Handbook of Reparations*, ed. Pablo De Greiff, 21–54. New York: Oxford University Press.

Hallam, Elizabeth, and Jenny Hockey. 2001. *Death, Memory and Material Culture*. Oxford: Berg.

Hertz, Robert. (1907) 1960. *Death and the Right Hand*. Aberdeen: Cohen & West.

Holst-Warhaft, Gail. 2000. *The Cue for Passion: Grief and Its Political Uses*. Cambridge: Harvard University Press.

Huntington, Richard, and Peter Metcalf. 1979. *Celebrations of Death: The Anthropology of Mortuary Ritual*. New York: Cambridge University Press.

Jackson, Jean E. 2005. "Stigma, Liminality, and Chronic Pain: Mind-Body Borderlands." *American Ethnologist* 32, no. 3: 332–53.

Jauretche, Ernesto. 2010. "¿El infierno es poco?" *Página/12*, 13 November.

Johnson, Lyman L., ed. 2004. *Death, Dismemberment, and Memory: Body Politics in Latin America*. Albuquerque: University of New Mexico Press.

Kertzer, David I. 1988. *Ritual, Politics, and Power*. New Haven: Yale University Press.

Klass, Dennis, Phyllis R. Silverman, and Steven L. Nickman, eds. 1996. *Continuing Bonds: New Understandings of Grief*. Washington, DC: Taylor & Francis.

Kwon, Heonik. 2006. *After the Massacre: Commemoration and Consolation in Ha My and My Lai*. Berkeley: University of California Press.

Kwilecki, Susan. 2011. "Ghosts, Meaning, and Faith: After-Death Communications in Bereavement Narratives." *Death Studies* 35: 219–43.

Lamas, Raúl. 1956. *Los Torturadores: Crímenes y tormentos en las cárceles argentinas*. Buenos Aires: Editorial Lamas.

Lewin, Miriam. 1985. "Testimonio de la señora Miriam Lewin de García." 18 July 1985. *El Diario del Juicio* 21: 412-420.

Malkki, Liisa H. 1995. *Purity and Exile: Violence, Memory, and National Cosmology among Hutu Refugees in Tanzania*. Chicago: University of Chicago Press.

Mármol, José. 1894. *Obras Poéticas y Dramáticas*. Paris: A. Bouret.

Mellibovsky, Matilde. 1990. *Círculo de amor sobre la muerte*. Buenos Aires: Ediciones de Pensamiento Nacional.

Miller, Daniel, and Fiona Parrott. 2009. "Loss and Material Culture in South London." *Journal of the Royal Anthropological Institute* 15: 502–19.

Nora, Pierre. 1984. "Entre Mémoire et Histoire: La problématique des lieux." In *Les Lieux de Mémoire I: La République*, ed. Pierre Nora, xvii–xlii. Paris: Gallimard.

Puccio Borrás, Estela. 1983. *Nunca es demasiado tarde*. Buenos Aires: El Cid Distribuidor.

Robben, Antonius C.G.M. 2000a. "The Assault on Basic Trust: Disappearance, Protest, and Reburial in Argentina." In *Cultures under Siege: Collective Violence and Trauma*, ed. Antonius C.G.M. Robben and Marcelo M. Suárez-Orozco, 70–101. Cambridge: Cambridge University Press.

———. 2000b. "State Terror in the Netherworld: Disappearance and Reburial in Argentina." In *Death Squad: The Anthropology of State Terror*, ed. Jeffrey A. Sluka, 91–113. Philadelphia: University of Pennsylvania Press.

———. 2005a. *Political Violence and Trauma in Argentina*. Philadelphia: University of Pennsylvania Press.

———. 2005b. "How Traumatized Societies Remember: The Aftermath of Argentina's Dirty War." *Cultural Critique* 59: 120–64.

———. 2011. "Silence, Denial and Confession about State Terror by the Argentine Military." In *Violence Expressed: An Anthropological Approach*, ed. Maria Six-Hohenbalken and Nerina Weiss, 169–86. Farnham: Ashgate.

Sahlins, Marshall. 1976. *Culture and Practical Reason*. Chicago: University of Chicago Press.

Sánchez, Matilde. 1985. *Historias de vida: Hebe de Bonafini*. Buenos Aires: Fraterna/ Del Nuevo Extremo.

Sarmiento, Domingo F. (1845) 1986. *Facundo o Civilización y Barbarie*. Barcelona.

Stroebe, Margaret, and Henk Schut. 2001. "Meaning Making in the Dual Process Model of Coping with Bereavement." In *Meaning Reconstruction and the Experience of Loss*, ed. Robert A. Neimeyer, 55–73. Washington, DC: American Psychological Association.

Turner, Victor W. (1967) 1970. *The Forest of Symbols: Aspects of Ndembu Ritual*. Ithaca: Cornell University Press.

———. 1974. *Dramas, Fields, and Metaphors: Symbolic Action in Human Society*. Ithaca: Cornell University Press.

———. (1968) 1995. *The Ritual Process: Structure and Anti-Structure*. New York: Aldine de Gruyter.

Ulla, Noemí, and Hugo Echave. 1986. *Después de la noche: Diálogo con Graciela Fernández Meijide*. Buenos Aires: Editorial Contrapunto.

Valentine, Christine. 2006. "Academic Constructions of Bereavement." *Mortality* 11, no.1: 57–78.

van Gennep, Arnold. (1909, in French) 1960. *The Rites of Passage*, trans. Monika B. Vizedom and Gabrielle L. Caffee. Chicago: University of Chicago Press.

Vitebsky, Piers. 1993. *Dialogues with the Dead: The Discussion of Mortality among the Sora of Eastern India*. Cambridge: Cambridge University Press.

Wagner-Pacifici, Robin E. 1986. *The Moro Morality Play: Terrorism as Social Drama*. Chicago: University of Chicago Press.

Walter, Tony. 1996. "A New Model of Grief: Bereavement and Biography." *Mortality* 1, no. 1: 7–25.

Young, James E. 1993. *The Texture of Memory: Holocaust Memorials and Meaning*. New Haven: Yale University Press.

*Figure 6.1.* Kyrgyz death memorial (*kümböz*) near Tuura Suu (Ïssïk Köl oblast, Kyrgyzstan) (photo Roland Hardenberg)

*Chapter Six*

# Three Dimensions of Liminality in the Context of Kyrgyz Death Rituals

*Roland Hardenberg*

## Dimensions of Liminality

The concept of liminality has often been applied by social and cultural anthropologists in their attempts to understand the underlying pattern of rites of initiation. In these rites, a person acquires a new social status by engaging in a double process requiring both the severance of previous relationships as well as the incorporation into new ones. Beginning with the analysis of the processual structure or "syntax" of death ceremonies by Hertz ([1907] 1960), sacrifices by Hubert and Mauss ([1898] 1964) and rites of passage by van Gennep ([1909] 1960), anthropologists have come to distinguish three typical phases when describing such rites: separation, transition and incorporation. Hertz ([1907] 1960) saw a gradual transformation of the dead body, the ghost, and the mourners from an "intermediary state" of exclusion (29–53) to a final ceremony involving admittance, liberation, and reunion (53–86); Hubert and Mauss ([1898] 1964: 95) recognized a movement between "sacralization" and "de-sacralization" in procedures of sacrifice; and van Gennep ([1909] 1960: 11) identified "preliminal," "liminal," and "postliminal rites" in rituals of transition that change the social status of an individual or that mark the passage of time (e.g., the new year).[1]

At the beginning, before it became a model for the global comparison of cultural performances, this tripartite structure was derived from an anthropological comparison of rituals and sacrifices around the world.

Its shift to a wider focus was mainly the result of the writings of Victor Turner,[2] who first dealt with the idea of liminality in an article published in 1964 and later in his book *The Ritual Process: Structure and Anti-Structure* (1969). The tripartite scheme came to be widely used in the analysis of rituals, even if critics such as Richard Werbner (1989) argue that it collapses symbolic dimensions into one central phase instead of seeing the switching between alternatives in what Werbner calls the "contrastive binary model" (113).

In later years, Turner (1985: 8, 117) searched for liminality in different historical periods and in the modern world of "complex societies," and came to coin the word "liminoid" in order to describe activities such as "leisure-time, non-religious genres of art and performance" that are "marginal, fragmentary, [and] outside the central economic and political processes."[3] With their study on monks, mendicants, and pilgrimages (Turner 1973; Turner and Turner 1978), the Turners discovered highly regulated forms of transition based on "institutionalized liminality" (Thomassen 2009: 16). The study of liminality was extended to various cultural forms including theatre plays (Turner 1982) and became synonymous with the study of cultural creativity, imaginative potentials, and social dynamics in human performances.

These generalizations stress commonalities, while differences are sometimes lost sight of. Any model, if applied too rigidly, carries the danger of misrepresenting culturally specific ideas, values, and social facts. In order to enrich general concepts such as "liminality," "communitas" or "transition," one may therefore look for variations. One way to achieve this is to discern different dimensions of liminality. This has recently been done by Thomassen (2009), who distinguishes forms of liminality not only in relation to subjects (e.g., individuals, groups, whole societies) but also to different temporal (e.g., moments, periods, epochs) and spatial (e.g., places, areas, countries) dimensions (16). With this typology he hopes to classify certain "types of liminal experiences"—that is, specific combinations of the features distinguished by him (17).

My own approach to and understanding of dimensions is different. It is not my aim to create abstract typologies of liminal experiences independent from ethnographic contexts. I intend, rather, to provide a tool that allows us to analyze degrees, processes, and fine differences within an ethnographic event. My concept of dimension does not define a type for cross-cultural comparison but a realm of investigation within a complex event. The question is this: how can we recognize and approach the multiplicity of liminal processes and the different degrees of intensiveness[4] liminality may take in a particular cultural event? For this purpose, I draw attention to the emotional, cognitive, and social dimensions of human experiences, which may be affected differently in liminal situations. When a ritual is performed, not everything must necessarily become liminal, at least not to the same degree. In this sense, liminality is not a stage or phase, but itself a process connecting emotion, conscience, and social status.

These dimensions of liminality have indirectly been addressed earlier. Depending on the concrete examples they were studying, anthropologists often put emphasis on only one of these dimensions. Thus, when dealing with death rituals, Hertz particularly stresses the social construction of emotion when explaining the different degrees of "horror" people feel for the corpse, the spirit, and the mourners (Hertz [1907] 1960: 76). Edmund Leach (1976: 33–35), in his comparative analysis of initiation rituals and sacrifices, comes to the conclusion that the liminal period both creates and connects cognitive categories of time, space and society. Gluckman (1963: 110–36), discussing fertility cults, puts emphasis on role reversal and sexuality, while Turner (1973: 129), in his analysis of pilgrimages and happenings, found a communitarian spirit at the heart of liminal events.

Discussing these examples in a more general sense, one might say that these anthropologists address different dimensions of liminality. One is the emotional aspect, which often markedly differs in liminal processes when compared to daily, so-called normal circumstances. The second, cognitive dimension is captured by Leach in his analysis of how the liminal process serves to (re-)create an overall sociocosmic order. Finally, in both Gluckman's and Turner's emphasis on people's interactions, on structure and antistructure, the social dimension of liminality—that is, the intensity and form of social interaction—comes to the fore.

In my view, ethnographic cases differ with regard to these three dimensions in two ways: first, even if all three dimensions are expressed in the rituals, their particular elaboration may differ. Thus, in some liminal phases, the emotional aspect may be of central importance; in others, the cognitive or social dimensions. Second, changes occurring within times of liminality can be quite different. Therefore, the association between liminality, antistructure, and communitas must be tested for every case and may not be a given for each of the three dimensions distinguished here. For example, it may be the case that emotions and temporal and spatial structures, as well as social interactions, become highly regulated and intensified.

To illustrate these ideas, I will use examples from my fieldwork in Kyrgyzstan, carried out from September 2007 to August 2008.[5] The main aim of my research was to document funeral and commemoration rituals from Soviet times until today and to understand the social values expressed in these (changing) ritual actions (Hardenberg 2009a, 2009b,

2010). I began my fieldwork in the capital of Bishkek and after three months moved with my family to a village located at the shore of Lake Ïssïk Köl in northern Kyrgyzstan.[6] Living in this village for almost nine months, from December 2007 to August 2008, I attended several funerals, conducted interviews (often with a biographical focus), drew detailed plans of the village and its cemeteries, and collected census data. Due to my close relationship with a family from the south of Kyrgyzstan, I was also able to collect comparative data from this region, which differs culturally from the north.[7]

Before discussing the different dimensions of liminality, I will first briefly illustrate the significance of death rituals in Kyrgyzstan by describing the relevance of memorial sites. This is followed by a general account of Kyrgyz death rituals and a detailed analysis of their emotional, cognitive, and social dimensions.

## Remember the Dead!

Death has an important role in Kyrgyz people's lives: the dead must be turned into ancestors (*arbaktar*), and for this they need a place to be remembered. As ancestors, they are considered to be a source of morality and authority, and, as such, they have an immense influence on the fate of their descendants (*tukumdar*). Not only is there no history without the memory of the ancestor's deeds, there is also no presence and future. This memory nowadays often receives a material representation, as I became aware when I first travelled to Kyrgyzstan in 2004. Driving in a car through northern Kyrgyzstan, I was struck by the impressive cemeteries (*mürzö* or *körüstön*) appearing every few kilometers on both sides of the road. Some cemeteries almost looked like villages or small towns, consisting sometimes of several hundred memorial houses and fenced by walls of stone or mud. Later, when conducting more intensive research on this topic, I learned that these elaborate cemeteries are a rather recent phenomenon. Thus, it turned out that only after the Second World War did Kyrgyz people begin to construct large memorial sites for almost all their dead, while in the past—that is, before Soviet power was established—only the rich and influential people received a monument on their own. Nowadays, when travelling on the mountain pastures, one can still see these impressive memorial houses (*korgon* or *kümböz*), some of which appear to be more than a hundred years old. They often stand in the vicinity of fields, where the common people were buried, whose graves simply consist of earthen mounds, which are sometimes marked by stones.

## Kyrgyz Death Rituals—An Overview

Giving a general account of Kyrgyz death rituals is difficult as they differ from place to place and occasion to occasion.[8] They show a number of similarities with death rituals in other Islamic communities of Central Asia, yet also clearly have a local character. In Soviet times, these rituals were altered in many ways, and what we observe today cannot be understood without some familiarity with the interventions of the state or Islamic institutions (Jacquesson 2008). The following overview provides a very brief and ideal description of what is most likely to happen nowadays in the event of a death among Kyrgyz people.[9] It does not take into account historical changes,[10] local variants, or differences deriving from personal circumstances, such as kind of death, wealth, or social status.

When a death (*kaza boluu*) occurs in a family, the women of the house will immediately begin crying (*ïjloo*) loudly. The men hurry to find a yurt (*boz üj*) and set it up in front of the house near the road. The body (*söök*[11]) is then placed inside the yurt, and a message about the death is given to relatives, friends, and neighbors of the deceased. Except for certain parts of southern Kyrgyzstan, where the corpse is buried on the same day, the bereaved family waits three days until the burial.[12] The body of the deceased is now "betwixt-and-between" (Turner 1964): it is removed from the house of the living but has not yet reached its final place, the grave in the cemetery.

In these three days, everyone who had a social relation with the deceased is expected to come to the yurt and pay last respects (*köngül ajtuu, köz körüü*[13]) to the dead. It is the responsibility of the family and the larger kin group (*uruular*) of the deceased to entertain these often numerous guests with tea and food—in particular with meat and bread. For this purpose, animals such as sheep, cows, or horses are sacrificed. Men and women mourn the deceased—the close male relatives standing outside the yurt crying loudly (*ölkürüü*), the female folk sitting inside performing laments for the dead (*košok košuu*). On the morning of the third day, the whole village, along with relatives and friends from other places, assemble at the yurt, in which the body of the deceased is washed and dressed in white linen, before men carry the corpse on a bier to the center of the road, where it is placed on carpet with the head facing towards Mecca. Following are an Islamic prayer called *janaaza* and a standard dialogue between the religious specialist (*imam* or *moldo*) and a close male relative, called "the owner of the corpse" (*sööktün eesi*), the latter formally taking over all outstanding debts of the dead.

To free the dead person from any debts so that she or he can leave this world without hindrances is of great importance on this occasion. Thus, the palms of the dead person are opened, if necessary by massage, in order to show that at the end of one's life in this "false world" (*jalgan düjnö*), one cannot take anything to the other, "real" world (*čïn düjnö*). The soul— like the body—is "betwixt-and-between," as it is still partly connected to the world of the living. People say that soul and body of the dead are experiencing thirst, hunger, and pain, something which continues even after burial.[14] The relatives come to show that they have no bad feelings towards the dead person. They prepare food and tea for the guests, but also for the dead person, and they pray in order to ease the soul's depar- ture from this world.[15]

Once *janaaza* is over, the men lift the bier and move towards the cem- etery (*sööktü kötörüü* or "carrying the bone"), while the women remain behind, first loudly wailing, then moving into the houses to share a joint meal (*kara aš*). In the cemetery, a grave (*kör*) with a special catacomb (*aj*)[16] must have been prepared into which the body is now placed by close male relatives of the deceased. Standing inside the grave, these men hold shov- els on which the other mourners place handfuls of soil, which is then put under the head of the dead person in the catacomb. This ritual is so central that the whole act of burial is referred to by a local expression meaning "put soil inside" (*topurak salgani*). When this is finished, shovels are dis- tributed among the bystanders, who are eager to help filling up the grave as this is considered to be very meritorious work. All men return to the house of the deceased, where they again enter the yurt, pray for the dead, and are then invited to different houses to share a meal called "five fin- gers" (*bešparmak*), to which I will return below.

In the following days, weeks, months, and even years, the relatives, especially the close family members, continue to mourn and commemorate (*eskerüü*) the death. Thus, in the first three days, the direct family members should not cook but instead focus their attention on the work of mourn- ing. The close female relatives of a deceased should daily mourn the dead in the yurt especially set up for this purpose, at least during the first forty days, if not for a whole year. A widow should wear dark colored clothes, not leave the house for one year, and only remarry thereafter. A widower can leave the house but should not attend any festive occasions before the lapse of the first year. Due to this separation, the family members experi- ence a liminal period of time during which they are not full members of society. They are not feared, but if they disobey these rules, they risk being considered shameful (*uyat*) by their relatives and neighbors.

While the close family members experience this liminal period, every- one who used to have a social relation with the deceased must visit the dead person's house after burial in order to jointly recite verses from the Koran (*Koran okuduu*) and share tea and food. Close female relatives will sing laments for the dead (*košok košolat*) every morning and evening, sometimes for a whole year. On the third (*üčünčü*), the seventh (*jetinči*), and the fortieth day (*kïrk*), close relatives assemble to pray for the dead (*koran okuu*), drink tea and share food, sometimes after slaughtering an animal. In the same way, the family will commemorate the deceased on the four Thursdays (*tört bejšembi*) following the person's death. The yurt where the body was kept for three days usually remains in place until the fortieth day. The mourners observe special restrictions until this day, on which most families sacrifice a sheep and cook food in order to feed the close relatives who arrive again to pray for the dead. The next occasion for commemorating the dead is either the end of Ramadan, called *orozo*[17] *ait,* or the Islamic sacrifice named *kurman ait*. The rule is that on the three *ait* following the death of a person, the relatives must come together, jointly visit the grave, prepare food, invite guests, and recite verses from the Koran.

After one or even more years, a ceremony called *jïldïk* or *aš*[18] is performed, for which more animals are sacrificed and guests invited to share the food. This event clearly shows some features of a ceremony of reintegration as described by Hertz or van Gennep. Close female relatives can now take off their mourning clothes, an act referred to as "dressing in white" (*ak kijdi*) in the south of Kyrgyzstan, and the mood changes from sorrow to joy. Especially in the north, people set up a memorial stone (*estelik*) or a monument (*kumböz*)[19] at the grave of the deceased after one year. The setting up of a memorial stone or monument marks the beginning of a new phase of commemoration. From now on, close family members will come to the grave once a year on the death day, pray to the soul of the ancestor (*arbak*), then go home, sacrifice a sheep, and jointly share a meal. This may continue for many years, even decades. On the first Sunday in April, all adult people of the village, usually divided in groups of relatives (*uruu*), move to the cemetery, where they symbolically eat something and pray to the ancestors before they return and share a meal. In general, however, people avoid going to the graveyard because they fear committing a mistake—by stepping on a gravesite, for example. They prefer to pay their respects to the ancestors from a distance by make the typical *omin* gesture: in order to receive blessings, a person holds his or her hands in front of the upper body with open palms up, utters *omin* and then wipes his or her face with both hands in a downward movement.

In summary, death rituals continue for years and exhibit a strong desire of the living to help the dead leaving this world and becoming an *arbak* or "ancestral soul," who may help the living, but also cause them harm when neglected or mistreated. The whole process, from funeral to commemoration, is intended, on the one hand, to let the soul leave its body and its former social network and, on the other, to allow the mourners to transform their grief into memory. This transition clearly involves liminality: for the mourners, who observe a number of restrictions; for the soul, which is "betwixt-and-between" the world of the living and those of the ancestors; and for the corpse, which for some days is neither in the house nor in the graveyard but in a special yurt, and thereafter slowly decomposes in the grave.

I will now turn to what I have called the "dimensions of liminality" in order to point out the specific features of the process by which a dead person turns into an ancestor and by which grief becomes memory. While I have previously given an ideal account of Kyrgyz death rituals, I will now mostly concentrate on my ethnographic experiences in Tosor at the lake Ïssïk Köl.

## The Emotional Dimension: Laments of Death

One of the most conspicuous aspects of Kyrgyz death rituals is the very intense mourning in the time between the moment the person expires and the day he or she receives a memorial stone. One evening, I was sitting in the house of an older couple when we suddenly heard loud crying and wailing coming from one of the neighboring houses. I was shocked and afraid and asked my hosts what had happened. They remained calm and answered that the neighbor, who had been sick for some time, must have died. It turned out they were right: when I passed by the house the next morning, I saw the yurt, which had been set up for the dead.

In Tosor, the dead body is placed inside the yurt, which is divided into a male and a female part. The female part is to the right of the entrance, where, in the past, the women used to keep their cooking utensils when moving on the pastures. If a woman dies, she will be placed on this side of the yurt; if a man expires, on the opposite side. In front of the corpse, people set up a wall made from sedge (*čii*) so that one cannot see the body while standing at the entrance of the yurt. This clearly differs in other regions — for example in Jalalabad, where I have been told that the body is placed in the center of a room inside the house, with the female mourners sitting down next to the deceased.

In Tosor, people avoid the sight of the dead. In the past, the female kin sat in the yurt where the corpse was lying but were separated from the body by the wall. Nowadays, the family either sets up an additional yurt for the mourners or reserves a special room for them inside the house. People argue that this is because of the bad smell of the corpse in the hot season, but when I attended a funeral in early spring, when it was still very cold, they followed the same practice. It seems, rather, that people feel horrified by the dead body. This comes to the fore when people discuss who will wash the dead. For this purpose, five people have to be selected, either women in the case of a female body or men in the case of a male body. When asked to join, many people refuse because they are too afraid of seeing and touching the corpse. An older woman, for example, told me that she declined to join the washing because of a heart problem—in other words, she was afraid to physically suffer from the shock of seeing the dead body. People often expressed the idea that only middle-aged persons should wash the corpse as either too young or too old people are emotionally incapable of accomplishing this task.

While washing the corpse requires the control of fear and horror, the laments of death require a controlled performance of sorrow and grief. As argued by Hertz, mourning is not a personal expression of emotions but a social obligation. The ritual may create emotions such as feelings of loss; these emotions are, however, not a prerequisite for someone to join the mourning. The act of mourning in Kyrgyzstan is highly regulated and based on a clear gender separation. Thus, in Tosor, men stand outside the yurt, while women sit inside the yurt or the house. The men standing outside are usually close agnates such as brothers, brothers' sons, and sons, and, if a married women died, her husband. Inside the yurt, the women assemble—usually the deceased's sisters, brothers' daughters, and daughters, and, if a married man died, his wife.

When fellow mourners approach the yurt, they go in groups of either men or women. The approaching men begin wailing by repeating standard phrases such as *ex kajgan boorum oj* ("oh, my poor beloved one") or *ex kajgan enekem oj* ("oh, my poor mother"). Hearing this, the men at the yurt join them by wailing in the same way. When the women sitting inside the yurt hear this, they start weeping loudly. In Kyrgyz language, this is called *ijlap*, which can be translated as "crying." It is distinguished from the wailing of the men, which is called *ölkürüü* in Kyrgyz. When the fellow male mourners meet the men standing at the yurt, they embrace each other or shake hands, speaking consoling words such as *artï kajrïluu bolsun* ("may it start again after the end") meaning that death should be followed by new life. The approaching women do not cry until they enter the yurt, where the close female relatives of the deceased sit. They usually take a seat next to the women they know best, embrace each other and join them in weeping. I was told that in the past, the wife of a deceased husband was expected, at the least, to scratch her face (*betin tïtuu*) on this occasion. This practice was forbidden in Soviet times, as it was considered a barbarous ritual meant to destroy the widow's beauty and prevent her from marrying again.

The close female relatives then perform the laments of death called *košok*, which are usually in the form of a rhyme.[20] The mourner takes a handkerchief in one hand, rests her head on this hand and then begins singing in a sad, melodic voice. The content of the lament differs, as it is especially composed for the deceased, sometimes on the spot but usually before the mourning starts. The intention of the *košok* is to remember the good aspects of a person by praising his or her deeds. This act of performing the lament is extremely emotional. I once asked a woman during an interview to give me an example of a *košok*. She agreed, took up the typical posture and began to sing a *košok* that she had composed for her mother. As soon as she started singing, she began to cry and could not stop weeping for a while.

The close relatives are not allowed to eat anything while mourning the dead. On the other hand, people say they should drink a lot so that they can cry more. For this reason, the daughters-in-law (*kelinder*) of the house take them from time to time to a place away from public view where they give them water to drink and soup to eat. In the past, this mourning was accompanied by extensive gift giving. Thus, the fellow mourners presented to the relatives items of clothing (*kijit*), which were hung on ropes inside the yurt. When they left, the daughters-in-law presented them with other clothing, which they took home. This practice has been stopped in Tosor in recent years, as many people argued that this exchange was a waste of financial resources.

The most intensive and collective expression of emotions occurs on the day of burial. When the close relatives bid farewell to the dead before washing the corpse, men and women alike often cry loudly and in public. At one such occasion I experienced, a Moldo—a local priest—explained to the relatives that they should not cry. In a similar way, a learned Muslim scholar explained to me that one should not cry excessively at a funeral but rather read the Koran. This demand stands in obvious contradiction to local practice, as people very openly wail and cry on this occasion.

The apex of emotional expression is reached when the men take the bier and carry away the corpse. At this moment, all women present begin crying in an unrestrained way, while the men do not show any emotions. The daughters-in-law move around and give the other women water to wash their faces. Then the women again enter the yurt, take out all clothes and mats, and clean the place thoroughly. The idea is that nothing linked to death should remain.

The mourning of the women should continue for at least forty days. Thus, after the dead person has been buried, the close female relatives should go to the yurt in the morning and the evening to sing the laments of death. This is not only a matter of personal grief, but also of social status, as people will say critical things about family members who do not take their mourning duties seriously. The performance of laments after the burial is called *joktop jatïšat*, meaning that one expresses the feeling of loss and the fact that the beloved person "is no more" (*jok*). Other occasions for joint weeping are visits by relatives and friends who come to "read the Koran" (*Koran okuu*) which implies that they share tea and food and listen to an experienced person who recites verses from the Koran.

According to one informant, some women even continue to perform laments for a whole year after death. The one-year commemoration ceremony usually marks the end of this mourning period. I experienced this ceremony in southern Kyrgyzstan, where, on the first day, the close female relatives sat in a special room where they received guests who brought sweets in a basket (*serbet*). Whenever a visitor turned up, the women began crying and sang the laments. On the second day, the female mourners sat in another room and were given new clothes in light colors. They took off the green or blue clothes they had been wearing for the last year and dressed in the new bright-colored costumes. After this ritual, the atmosphere changed visibly as people began drinking alcohol and talking with each other in a rather joyful mood.

In summary, mourning is a highly ritualized affair, mostly of women, whose duty it is to express positive memories related to the dead—the good aspects of a person—as well as the feeling of loss. Mourning is mostly collective and, even if performed individually, should be heard by others. It is highly repetitive and forces the mourners to express their liminal condition. It is often accompanied by visits of other people such as relatives, friends, or neighbors. On such visits, everyone first jointly mourns the dead and then turns to other issues. The atmosphere becomes more relaxed and the sadness of the occasion is no longer in the foreground. I once experienced how a mother, who had lost her newly married daughter in a tragic accident, changed her behavior in the process of several months of mourning. At the beginning, she was struck by grief, even needed medical attention because she could not cope with the situation. In the following weeks, her house was again and again visited by many people, often from distant places, who came to read the Koran. One room in her house was always kept ready for receiving such visitors. Even months after this event, people turned up to express their sorrow for what happened. It took a long time, but the mother slowly began to take interest in the life around her again.

I think what happens in such situations is that grief slowly turns into memory. The mourners repeat their experiences in a very formalized way and constantly confront themselves with their feelings of loss. At the end, the memory created in endless repetitions of laments becomes manifest in a stone or mausoleum. Memory is thus represented in material form, outside the person, and it becomes possible to both distance oneself from it and at the same time recollect the memory when visiting the place of its representation. Mourning is an aspect of liminality as well as a means to overcome it.

## The Cognitive Dimension: Categories of Time and Space

In his collected essays published in the book *Culture and Communication* (1976), Edmund Leach develops the idea that temporal or spatial boundaries break up a continuum into segments, thereby creating an order made up of separate categories. Rituals serve to mark these boundaries and at the same time establish a link, a form of communication, between the divided realms. The boundary between these realms is often, according to Leach, "abnormal, timeless, ambiguous, at the edge, sacred" (35).

Following Leach, one could argue that liminality establishes an order by marking boundaries but is in itself an inversion of the order it creates. Applying this idea to Kyrgyz death rituals, one can remark that normal life indeed becomes interrupted when the liminal period begins. This is particularly so for close relatives, especially spouses and agnates, who have to change their daily rhythm of life for at least forty days, if not a whole year. More distantly related people, such as members of the same descent category, affines, neighbors, or friends, will be affected in their routine for at least the first three days until burial. They pay a visit to the deceased's house even if they live in a place hundreds of kilometers away, stop working on the day of burial, and join the family members in their various mourning practices.

The normal flow of life is thus clearly interrupted. However, in contrast to Leach's argument, this period can hardly be called "timeless" and "ambiguous." It seems, rather, that time and space are more rigorously ordered and controlled following death than during normal times. In this sense, liminality does not involve inversion and ambiguity but the intensification of order. For example, the period of mourning is clearly divided into certain time segments. At first, people wait three days before burial, and during this time they follow a rather strict routine that involves slaughtering animals, cooking, mourning, washing the dead, speaking prayers, and so on. With respect to time management, the different funerals I attended did not differ significantly but rather followed a standard routine. The time following the burial is also very clearly structured because of the commemoration ceremonies on each Thursday and on the third, seventh, and fortieth day after death, as well as on the three consecutive *ait* and the one year memorial day.

If we consider spatial divisions, Leach's arguments again only partly make sense with reference to Kyrgyz death rituals. One the one hand, his generalization appears correct because the space where the yurt is set up for mourning clearly has an ambiguous character. It is set up at the border between the house and the public street. After the corpse has been taken out to be buried in the grave, the yurt is cleaned because of its association with the dead body. The yurt becomes the place where the women perform their laments of death, and when it is removed after forty days, the space where it stood is marked by a circle of stones and one is prohibited from stepping on this place. The same holds for the grave, which must be approached with respect for the dead.

On the other hand, the division of space in Kyrgyz death rituals is very ordered and far from being abnormal and ambiguous. People know exactly where to place the dead in the yurt, which direction the body has to face, and where to perform the various duties. Thus animals are sacrificed in the garden behind the house; the food is cooked in the same place but closer to the house. Inside the house, the various fellow mourners are given tea and food according to very organized seating arrangements, while the close family members remain in front of the house at the place of the yurt. Even the cemeteries are clearly ordered spaces, with walls and a chessboard pattern. Thus graves are dug in rows creating small paths in-between that can be used by the visitors. [21]

In summary, the liminal period shows certain ambiguous aspects with regard to temporal and spatial divisions. In order to characterize the cognitive dimension of Kyrgyz death rituals in times of liminality, it appears, however, more appropriate to highlight the rigid application and even intensification of norms that serve to distinguish categories. These norms provide an order to time and space and are not reversals of norms observed during everyday life. Therefore, I do not think it appropriate to speak of an antistructure, but rather of a "hyperstructure," because hierarchy and the observance of strict boundaries dominate the time of liminality. The mourners have the duty to establish a new order by giving the dead person a place among the other dead in the cemetery and by repairing the social fabric. This leads me to the last point, the social dimension of liminality.

## Social Dimension: Sacrificing, Cooking, and Feasting

What appears most striking about Kyrgyz death rituals is the important role of sacrificing, cooking, and feasting. On first observation, these activities appear to be completely secular affairs. The people present during the sacrifice of an animal will only utter a verse from the Koran, perhaps mention the name of the deceased, and make the typical prayer gesture, saying *omin* before cutting the throat of the victim. However, the Kyrgyz pay a lot of attention to dividing the animal's body into different parts, which are called *jilik*. Each *jilik* is a bone with a piece of meat. After cooking, these pieces are distributed among the guests according to their status. Men usually cut the animal and cook the meat, while women clean the bowels. Furthermore, women are responsible for preparing bread and pastry—most importantly one called *borsok,* which is deep-fried and usually spread in large numbers on the tablecloth placed on the floor.[22] Mourners who come to pay their condolences before or after burial are usually asked to sit down on the mattresses that are spread on all sides of the tablecloth. They are then served tea by a daughter-in-law and are requested by the hosts to eat *borsok*. Before soup or cooked meat is served, an old person will speak verses from the Koran and others say blessings or pray for the dead. Then everybody consumes the food, people talk with each other, and when they leave, the host will insist that the visitors take home food to distribute it to others.

On the third day of the burial, the procedure is slightly different, because full attention is given to distributing the meat of those animals that were sacrificed by the relatives in the name of the dead. On this day, first the women have a feast, and then the men, but the procedure is the same. The mourners are divided into groups of seven people, who sit on the floor, as the meat on this occasion may not be consumed while sitting at a table. Each person is first given soup, then a piece of meat according to his or her status, and finally noodles or rice. Everyone eats a little meat and gives the rest to an experienced person, who cuts the meat of all seven people into very small pieces. This meat is then mixed with the right hand with noodles and soup in a large bowl and finally distributed among those who form a commensal group. Everybody has to eat this dish called "five fingers" (*bešparmak*) with the right hand. Finally, all guests receive a plastic bag in which they put some extra meat along with whatever they have left on their plate. This bag should not be closed before an old person or a religious specialist has spoken blessings and recited verses from the Koran.

On one such occasion, my wife was beginning to close the bag with the leftovers before the prayers were spoken, when another woman stopped her, saying that the bag must be kept open so that the "good things" can touch it. The idea seems to be that the words literally touch (*tijüü*) the food and thereby transfer the contents of the prayers to it. Another informant later explained to me that on such occasions, people say *soop tijsin* when distributing the food prepared for the burial. This literally means "may the merit touch." Again, the idea seems to be that something good, in this case the merits acquired by attending the funeral, can be transferred to the food. The leftovers are taken home and distributed among the younger people, who are not allowed to attend the funeral. In this way, the merits are spread among the people. The commensality thus extends far beyond those who actually partake of the food in the house of the deceased.[23]

We may summarize this process of feeding on the day of burial as follows: the family members (*bir atadïn baldarï*), as well as the close affines (*kudalar*), give animals that are slaughtered and cooked by agnates (*uruular*) of the deceased for all those who come to accompany the dead person on his or her last journey. These people are not referred to as guests (*konoktor*) but as *batačïlar*, meaning people who make blessings (*bata*). This refers to the idea that these fellow mourners console the family members as well as the soul of the dead by saying blessings and prayers. This is done when they sit together, sharing tea and food. In return for their involvement in the mourning process, they acquire merits (*soop*). The good words spoken and the good deeds done get attached to the food and can be transferred to others by giving them the leftovers. This is, at least, how I interpret my informants' statements and actions.

Another important aspect of this commensality is the involvement of the dead person. People told me that the deceased can smell the food prepared on such occasions. The deep-fried pastry called *borsok* is of particular importance in this context, as the soul is considered to like the smell of oil. At the place where the yurt for the corpse is set up, people later sometimes burn oil, producing thick smoke as an offering to the dead. When my family and I first moved into the house in Tosor, the owner of the house immediately fried meat in the kitchen to appease the spirits of the dead because she knew that I wanted to study death rituals, which, in the eyes of most Kyrgyz, was a rather inauspicious project. In addition to heating up oil, one also slaughters and cooks at places where the souls of the dead are considered to reside. Thus, we sometimes visited a holy place (*mazar*), which contained several old graves and stood near a cemetery. Kyrgyz come to this place in order to sacrifice animals, prepare the food on the spot, and then consume it, so to speak, in the presence of the dead. One informant told me that in Tosor, a day or two before the one-year commemoration feast (he called it *čong aš* or big feast), the relatives move to the grave, slaughter a sheep, spread a table cloth, and distribute bread and sweets on it. Then everybody eats a little piece of bread, someone speaks verses from the Koran, and finally everything is packed together and carried home, where a meal is prepared. Another occasion when people spread the tablecloth in the cemetery is, again according to this informant, the day of the dead on the first Sunday in April. In other words, the feasts in memory of the dead include the living and the dead. The soul of the dead can participate in the commensality of its relatives. People say that the souls of the dead wait to see their relatives, and this is why they go to the cemetery to spread the tablecloth at their graves.

Death, then, disrupts social relations, but, in the liminal period following death, sacrificing, cooking, and feasting re-create social relations. The social dimension of liminality is marked by the enhanced activity of all participants; the closer the relationship to the dead, the more work and expenses are required. Death rituals belong to the category of bad events, *jamančĭlĭk*, but the joint feasts offer an opportunity to exchange blessings and merits. The death of an individual thus turns into a chance to renew the community morally. With regard to its social dimension, liminality is in this case not marked by antistructure but rather by intensive attempts to re-create structures.

## Conclusion: The Work of Mourning

The liminal period of Kyrgyz death rites is meant to transform the dead into ancestors by giving the body a new place, by facilitating the soul's transition to another world, and by establishing new relations. Death disrupts the social web, and this is the beginning of a liminal period during which people try to reproduce social relations both with the living and the dead. Among Kyrgyz, this is a hard work in the literal sense as people have to spend a large amount of time, energy, and resources in order to achieve this aim.

This whole ritual process may be analyzed using the classical concepts briefly mentioned in the introduction to this chapter. Thus, one may discover rites of separation, transition, or reintegration, or may point to forms of antistructure or communitas in Kyrgyz funerals. From a cross-cultural perspective, one may also classify the type of liminality created in this funeral process by applying Thomassen's analytical grid. I find, however, in order to understand this particular kind of liminality, its mechanisms, foci, and degrees of intensity, it is more useful to distinguish three analytical realms: the emotional, the cognitive, and the social. With regard to these three dimensions of liminality, the Kyrgyz work of mourning has the following special features. First, the very intense expression of sorrow and grief is strongly enforced on the close relatives. Whatever one actually feels, one has to participate in mourning rituals if one does not want to be condemned by others as shameful and bad. The closer the relationship, the stronger are the demands on showing expressions of grief. However, the need to participate in mourning rituals decreases with time: participation is intensive at the beginning and gradually lessens, until it finally stops after the great feast one or more years after death. On this day, the close relatives are reintegrated into society and the deceased finally gets a material representation in the form of a grave stone. Second, this period of liminality is highly structured. Temporal and spatial categories are rigidly marked and reproduced. One cannot discern the free spirit of a happening. Third, the liminality of death rites is characterized by the renewal of social structures through feasting and gift exchange. The sharing of food, which is collectively prepared, as well as the reciprocal exchange of gifts, offers an opportunity to reproduce social ties. The interesting aspect of this well-known effect of commensality in the Kyrgyz case is that it includes the souls of the dead.

The Kyrgyz want to keep relations with their ancestors, and, from an indigenous perspective, it would perhaps not be wrong to reverse this statement: the ancestors want to be in touch with the living. When giving a feast, they can participate and enter into a spiritual exchange with the living, who work and pray for the dead and receive their blessings in return. The medium of this exchange seems to be food, as it is said to contain the merits attained by mourning. Seen in this way, food nourishes people, both in the physical as well as in the moral or spiritual sense. Finally, some of the dead become part of the larger collective memory when their deeds are talked about in oral traditions (*sanjïra*[24]) or when special memorials or historical monuments are set up for them. This again illustrates people's attempts not to forget the past but to relate to it when coping with the challenges of the present times.

**Roland Hardenberg** (PhD Berlin 1998) is professor of social and cultural anthropology at the Faculty of Humanities of the University of Tuebingen. He is head of the Department of Social and Cultural Anthropology and vice-chairman of the Collaborative Research Center on Resource Cultures (SFB 1070). His books include *The Renewal of Jagannatha: Ritual and Society in Orissa* (Manak Publisher 2011), and he coedited *The Anthropology of Values* (Pearson 2010).

# Notes

1.  For a discussion of the "outcaste position" and the difficult intellectual relationship of van Gennep with the Durkheimians, see Thomassen 2009: 8–12.
2.  His wife, Edith Turner, provided a good overview of how the concept of liminality was developed by him over the years. See Turner 1985: 5–8.
3.  Thomassen (2009: 15) argues that in contrast to liminal, "liminoid" is not characterized by the central feature of transition.
4.  This is also an important point Thomassen makes when he writes that "it does seem meaningful to suggest *that there are degrees of liminality, and that the degree depends on the extent to which the liminal experience can be weighed against persisting structures*" (Thomassen 2009: 18, emphasis in the original).
5.  I am thankful to the German Volkswagen Foundation, which generously financed this research project.
6.  The transliteration of Kyrgyz words follows the style format of the *Central Eurasian Studies Review*. Personal names and well known places such as Kyrgyzstan or Bishkek are not transliterated.
7.  I am particularly grateful to Aziza Paisulaeva, Aigerim Dyikanbaeva, and Cholpon Dyikanbaeva for their help and inspiration.
8.  In recent years, the anthropological research on Kyrgyz funerals has intensified. Beyer (2009: 183–213) in her PhD thesis deals with the negotiation of "customs" in the context of mourning rituals and focuses particularly on gift exchanges. Jacquesson (2008) discusses the different types of critique against Kyrgyz death ceremonies brought forward by various actors in the past and present. Dealing with the impact of re-Islamization on Kyrgyz traditions, Kuchumkulova (2007) in her PhD thesis also gives an elaborate account of Kyrgyz death rituals. In an MA thesis based on three months of fieldwork, Pritchard (2009) deals extensively with the laments (*košok*) performed during death ceremonies.
9.  For a more elaborate account, see Hardenberg 2010. Jacquesson (2008: 283–86) also provides a good and short overview.
10. Information about the celebration of death ceremonies in pre-Soviet and Soviet times can be gathered from Fiel'strup (1925) 2002 and Bayalieva 1972.
11. *Söök* literally means "bone" and is here used to refer to the corpse.
12. Jacquesson (2008: 284) refers a source according to which the "length of the wake depended on the rank of the deceased: the corpses of Kyrgyz local rulers of the nineteenth century were thus kept up to nine days before being buried."
13. *Köngül* is a word with multiple meanings and here means condolences; *köz körüü* may be translated as "to see with one's eyes."
14. Thus, I have heard that on the fortieth day (*kïrk*), close relatives carefully churn a kind of porridge (*atala*). The idea seems to be that this porridge represents the corpse. By churning it very carefully, the relatives intend to alleviate the pain the dead person experiences when its body in the grave breaks open due to putrefaction.
15. I am grateful to Ildiko Béller-Hann for pointing out to me this important feature of death rituals, not only among the Kyrgyz but also other communities in Central Asia.
16. *Aj* literally means "moon" and here refers to the round opening of the inner part of the grave.
17. *Orozo* literally means "fasting."
18. *Jïldïk* derives from the word for "year," while *aš* means "feast." In the north, the *aš* is celebrated about one year after death and is usually the occasion for setting up the memorial stone and giving a feast. In the south, people first remember the dead person after one year in a feast called *jïldïk*, which marks the end of mourning. This is followed

some years later by an even larger ceremony called *aš*, which is accompanied by Kyrgyz games such as horse riding and a kind of polo (*ulak tartiš*). Jacquesson (2008: 285) mentions a similar distinction: "It can take two forms: the *may ash* 'fat feast' when just a meal is offered to the assembled guests and the *chong ash* 'great feast' at which, along with the meal, traditional games are also organized."

19. A *kumböz* is usually a stone building with a single room and a dome. A second type of monument is called *korgon* and consists of a quadrangular stone or mud wall set up around the grave, something which is usually not done anymore. Instead, metal fences are used in some places.

20. For more detailed accounts of Kyrgyz *košok*, see Kuchumkulova 2007 and Pritchard 2009. For an anthropological analysis of Azeri laments of death, see Pfluger-Schindlbeck 2000.

21. This appears to be a new development as cemeteries on the pastures were not always fenced by walls, nor did they exhibit any clear pattern. However, they used to be close to lower pastures, where the Kyrgyz assembled in larger communities in winter. In the same way, the cemeteries are nowadays often near the villages and the roads, the idea being that the living should be able to see the graves and pay their respects to the dead.

22. Some people in Kyrgyzstan told me that *borsok* should not be prepared for a funeral as this food is reserved for happy occasions.

23. A funeral feast is usually attended only by married people above forty, while the younger members of their household remain at home.

24. A *sanjïra* is an oral tradition which combines the enumeration of genealogical relations with stories about the deeds of the ancestors.

# References

Bayalieva, T.D. 1972. *Doislamskie verovaniya i ich perežitki u kirgizov*. Frunze: Tipographia Akademii Nauk.

Beyer, Judith. 2009. "According to Salt: An Ethnography of Customary Law in Talas, Kyrgyzstan." PhD diss., Martin Luther University, Halle-Wittenberg.

Fiel'strup, F.A. (1925) 2002. *Iz Obrjadovoj Zhizni Kirgisov Nachala XX veka*. Moscow: Nauka.

Gluckman, Max. 1963. *Order and Rebellion in Tribal Africa*. London: Cohen & West.

Gullette, David. 2010. "Institutionalized Instability: Factors Leading to the April 2010 Uprising in Kyrgyzstan." *Eurasian Review* 3: 89–105.

Hardenberg, Roland. 2009a. "Gabentauschtheorie und Bestattungen: Eine ethnologische Forschung in Kyrgyzstan." In *Interkulturelle wissenschaftliche Kommunikation: Probleme und Perspektiven*, ed. P. Kadyrbekova, 24–29. Bishkek: Bilim.

———. 2009b. "Reconsidering 'Tribe,' 'Clan' and 'Relatedness': A Comparison of Social Categorization in Central and South Asia." *Scrutiny: A Journal of International and Pakistan Studies* 1, no. 1: 37–62.

———. 2010. "The Efficacy of Funeral Rituals in Kyrgyzstan." *Journal of Ritual Studies* 24, no.1: 29–43.

Hertz, Robert. (1907) 1960. *Death and the Right Hand*. Aberdeen: Cohen & West.

Hubert, Henri, and Marcel Mauss. (1898) 1964. *Sacrifice: Its Nature and Function*, transl. W.D. Halls. London: Routledge.

Jacquesson, Svetlana. 2008. "The Sore Zones of Identity: Past and Present Debates on Funerals in Kyrgyzstan." *Inner Asia* 10, no. 2: 281–303.

Kuchumkulova, Elmira M. 2007. "Kyrgyz Nomadic Customs and the Impact of Re-Islamization after Independence." PhD diss., University of Washington.

Leach, Edmund. 1976. *Culture and Communication: The Logic by which Symbols Are Connected.* Cambridge: Cambridge University Press.

Lewis, David. 2008. "The Dynamics of Regime Change: Domestic and International Factors in the 'Tulip Revolution.'" *Central Asian Survey* 27, no. 3–4: 265–77.

Martin, Terry D. 2001. *The Affirmative Action Empire: Nations and Nationalism in the Soviet Union, 1923–1939.* Ithaca: Cornell University Press.

Pfluger-Schindlbeck, Ingrid. 2000. "The Power of Tropes: Laments of Death in Azerbaijan." *Journal of Social Sciences* 4: 305–12.

Pritchard, Maureen E.C. 2009. "Legends Borne by Life: Myth, Grieving and the Circulation of Knowledge within Kyrgyz Contexts." MA thesis, Ohio State University.

Thomassen, Bjorn. 2009. "The Uses and Meanings of Liminality." *International Political Anthropology* 2, no. 1: 5–27.

Turner, Victor W. 1964. "Betwixt and Between: The Liminal Period in *Rites de Passage.*" In *Symposium on New Approaches to the Study of Religion: Proceedings of the 1964 Annual Spring Meeting of the American Ethnological Society,* ed. J. Helm. Seattle: American Ethnological Society.

———. 1969. *The Ritual Process: Structure and Anti-Structure.* Chicago: Aldine.

———. 1973. "The Center Out There: Pilgrim's Goal." *History of Religions* 12, no. 3: 191–230.

———. 1984. "Liminality and Performative Genres." In *Rite, Drama, Festival, Spectacle: Rehearsals toward a Theory of Cultural Performance,* ed. John J. MacAloon, 19–41. Philadelphia: Institute for the Study of Human Issues.

———. 1985. *On the Edge of the Bush: Anthropology as Experience,* ed. Edith L. Turner. Tucson: University of Arizona Press.

Turner, Victor W., and Edith Turner. 1978. *Image and Pilgrimage in Christian Culture.* New York: Columbia University Press.

van Gennep, Arnold. (1909) 1960. *The Rites of Passage.* trans. Monika B. Vizedom and Gabrielle L. Caffee. Chicago: University of Chicago Press.

Werbner, Richard P. 1989. *Ritual Passage, Sacred Journey: The Process and Organization of Religious Movement.* Washington, DC: Smithsonian Institution Press.

*Figure 7.1.* Celebrating the departure of the dead: Gadaba men and women dancing, whistling and throwing mud as part of the last phase of death rituals (Odisha, India) (photo Peter Berger).

*Chapter Seven*

# Death, Ritual, and Effervescence

*Peter Berger*

## Death and Emotions

Death as ultimate ambiguity—"ultimate" in the double sense of the suspense concerning individual destiny, and the more general elementary political, social, and religious questions that it raises—is closely connected with emotions.[1] That death is related to emotions seems obvious enough; less so, perhaps, is why these emotions should be ambivalent. Various articulations and shades of sorrow are expected to be at the core of the emotional experience of a death. However, the affective response to a death is much more diverse, as scholars have variously noted: love turns into fear, longing into disgust, sorrow into anger (Hertz [1907] 1960; Huntington and Metcalf 1979; Malinowski [1948] 1974; Rosaldo 1984; Wolf 2001).

Are these various emotions the cause or the effect of the rituals? Malinowski ([1948] 1974: 53) argued that death rituals help the community to overcome the devastating effects and "disintegrating impulses" of death and loss, with their function being to restore the morality and solidarity of the group. Others, on the contrary, are of the opinion that the articulation of emotions, such as mourning, is not the expression of an individually felt affect but primarily a social obligation. An early description of a widespread phenomenon was provided by Radcliffe-Brown (1948: 239f) in his ethnography on the Andaman Islanders. Expressions of sorrow following a death are related to the ritual process. They are a "ceremonial custom," as Radcliffe-Brown calls it (204); mourning behavior is switched on and

Notes for this chapter begin on page 178.

off as the rite demands, and this can hardly be explained in terms of individual feelings alone. As Durkheim (1995: 405) puts it, "The dead man is not mourned because he is feared; he is feared because he is mourned." Significantly, thus, early contributions to the study of death distinguished individually experienced affective states on the one hand, and cultural conceptualizations of emotions and norms regarding their expression on the other. The important new insight for the sociologist and anthropologist was that emotions are relevant socially and signify aspects of the ethos and worldview of a community. This argument has been confirmed and refined by many later ethnographic studies—for example, with regard to the gendered structuration of emotional expressions and the reproduction of hierarchies among Brahmans in Banaras (Varanasi). Jonathan Parry (1994: 155f) has argued that standardized expressions of grief by females in the context of death rituals signify their supposedly close involvement with the physical dimensions of life (in contrast to the distanced insight that all life is transient), and hence their inferiority.

Ethnographic experience in various parts of the world has led anthropologists to question the universality of emotions. Emotions do seem to be cross-culturally recognizable; on a closer look, however, superficial similarities seem to be misleading. Emotions are part of specific cultural systems in which they make sense; they derive their meaning in relation and in contrast to each other. Joan Briggs (1970) famously described her problems among the Inuit—who conventionally laid great stress on the control of emotions—of even identifying the emotions of her hosts, and her efforts to live up to the local emotional norms. As such, the claim that ethnographers can refeel the emotions of members of the local community and even build their interpretations on this emotional participation is doubtful (Berger 2010a), and the question of universality and of the existence of basic emotions remains contested (see Beatty 2013; Leavitt 1996).

More recent contributions have strived towards a more nuanced understanding of emotions and tried to circumvent the main pitfalls in studying them. As is often the case, these pitfalls concern troublesome dichotomies. Emotions are considered as either purely natural or mainly culturally defined, and to concern the body or the mind. Accordingly, they are thought of as being either individual (because related to specific bodies) or social (because of shared meanings; Leavitt 1996: 515f). John Leavitt (1996: 531) argues that emotions are such a relevant aspect because of their transcendent nature, making it difficult to easily assign them to either side of these dichotomies: "While they are subjectively felt and interpreted, it is socialized human beings—that is, thinking human bodies—who are feeling them in specific social contexts." Building on Austin's speech act theory, William M. Reddy (1997: 331) argued that emotional expressions not only "say" something about internal affective states but also bring those emotions about as they are verbalized.[2] "Emotives," as Reddy (ibid.) calls them, thus have managerial and performative dimensions.[3] Moreover, anticipating the later discussion, not only do emotives evoke the articulated feelings in the speaker (or actor), but they are likely to have an affective impact on others too: those who join in the action — for example, the ritual. Hence they have a quality that Piers Vitebsky (1993: 255f) calls "trans-sentience."

Discussing ritual complexes in a so-called tribal community in South India, Richard K. Wolf (2001) also carefully avoids a simplified representation of the emotional expressions or, in other words, reducing his analysis to one side of the dichotomies mentioned above. Partly building on Reddy, he is concerned with the role of music and dance in the emotional setup of rituals. He developed the notions of "emotional contour" and "emotional texture" to describe the complex and interwoven emotional features that unfold in a dynamic ritual process. Contour refers to agreed-upon emotional definitions or conventional understandings of a single emotion in a particular context, such as sorrow during a certain sequence of a funeral. There is a diachronic element involved insofar as the expected intensity of the emotion may be higher or lower at certain moments. For example, among the Gadaba — a tribal community in highland Central India where I did intensive ethnographic fieldwork and to which I will repeatedly refer later — expressions of sorrow are expected from women, verbally in the forms of laments and physically in the form of bodily mutilations such as rending their hair, beating their chests, or scratching their cheeks until they bleed, with the intensity depending on kinship distance. The expressions of grief peak at particular moments throughout the ritual process, such as when the women wash the corpse in front of the house or when the procession to the cremation ground embarks from the house. Any ritual process, however, is not simply about a single emotion, and, even conventionally, several contours may be involved in a death ritual. For example, if a Brahman dies what is considered a good death in old age, after a virtuous life, joy may be a conventional element in the ritual process (Parry 1994). In addition, there will often be a tension between the expected emotional contours of a ritual and the actual experiences of the participants. The deceased may have had the reputation of being a sorcerer or a greedy person; in that case, it is feelings of relief that are actually part of the emotional situation experienced. Such tensions — moments when actors relate their actual emotional states to the normative pattern — may in turn influence the emotional scenario. This complex unfolding situation, the combinations of contours and the tensions involved, is what Wolf (2001) describes as the emotional texture of a ritual. While, as cultural categories, emotives are clearly articulated in the ritual, the "affective understanding" of the various participants in no way needs to be homogeneous (382). Their internal states are shaped by the cultural emotional forms but not determined by them. The ritual neither signifies nor produces a homogenous group feeling but helps individuals to navigate their own emotional states that are connected to the general cultural patterns and are idiosyncratic.

In sum, for the purpose of the argument concerning death and effervescence that I will develop here, it is significant that emotions have a cognitive side as well as being embodied and physical. They are individually experienced but not in isolation; on the contrary, they are experienced in close association with others as part of social processes and shared cultural conceptualizations, a shared affective culture. For example, the notion of *duk* or "sorrow" among the Gadaba is the dominant and expected emotion following a death. Relatives from other villages will bring "mourning gruel" (*duk pej*) to the house of the deceased, and during the period after death, *duk* is expressed jointly by women. Men do not have standardized means at their disposal for showing their grief. Such emotionally relevant actions signify emotions, as much as they produce or reinforce them, in the speaker/actor as well as in others who join in the action; yet a completely uniform emotional experience cannot be assumed, since the actual emotional texture is always complex and to a certain extent idiosyncratic. Moreover, emotions are context bound and unfold—in a more or less structured way—in a ritual process, with the texture being again more or less complex or elaborated, shaping but not determining individual experience.[4]

Just by looking at the examples of death-related practices in this volume, a considerable diversity becomes apparent in dealing with emotions communally, and in allowing or avoiding forms of effervescence: grief and desperation drove the mothers of abducted persons to search for their disappeared children, which ultimately led to the sharing of these experiences and to the establishment of a social movement in Argentina in the 1970s (see Robben in this volume); in extended dialogues with their dead, the Sora publicly negotiate and co-construct their emotions, and thereby also transform them (see Vitebsky in this volume); a similar transformation from sorrow to memory occurs in the long communal mourning among the Kyrgyz (see Hardenberg in this volume); playful collective violence is part of the Gadaba death rituals in highland Central India; while male Brahmans ideally display total emotional control as indicated above (see Berger in this volume).

The question thus arises of why some ritual processes of death leave room for effervescence—for trance, dance, music, violence, intoxication, play, ecstasy, excessive mourning, self-mortification, destruction, or a combination of any of these—and others do not. For several reasons, this is a problematic question. Part of the truth is that such questions probably cannot be answered. Another problem results when we attempt to answer such causal questions regardless. The history of the discipline of anthropology shows that such seemingly simple causal questions lead to equally one-dimensional answers (see Harris 1985; Sahlins 1978). In this case, an answer could run like this: cultures that generally stimulate and appreciate the public expression of emotional states tend to include some form of effervescence in their death ritual, while others do not. Therefore, because for the Javanese "evil results from unregulated passion and is resisted by detachment and self-control" (Geertz 1973: 131), "[t]he mood of a Javanese funeral is not one of hysterical bereavement, unrestrained sobbing, or even of formalized cries of grief for the deceased's departure. Rather, it is a calm, undemonstrative, almost languid letting go, a brief ritualized relinquishment of a relationship no longer possible. Tears are not approved of and certainly not encouraged. . . . For the mourner, the funeral and postfuneral ritual is said to produce a feeling of *iklas*, a kind of willed affectlessness, a detached and static state of 'not caring'" (Geertz 1973: 153). Yet, such a general correspondence between prescribed and approved emotional expressions in ritual and nonritual contexts, and hence a uniform emotional attitude for a culture as a whole, independent of context, cannot be presumed in general terms. Another example from Indonesia makes this clear. While emotional restraint is generally an ideal for the Toraja in Sulawesi as well, and conceptualized as staying "cool" (Hollan 1988), intentional deregulation of this state and "heat" is generated in particular ritual contexts, where trance and violence figure prominently (Crystal and Yamashita 1987; see also Berger 2000: 63f, 81f). Such a contextual definition of standardized emotional behavior is probably more widespread than general emotional uniformity throughout a culture.

Even though difficult and problematic, I think that an investigation into the conditions for the elaboration of effervescence and its restriction would be worthwhile—that is, a study of the various historical, social, economic, and political factors that might be relevant. Not because it would lead to straightforward answers, but rather because such an endeavor might produce new questions, and from there generate new perspectives. Apart from a few comments in the conclusion, the present contribution, however, will not be examining such causal factors but rather will aim to describe, compare, and contrast different examples of effervescence, taken from the contributions to this volume and from elsewhere, and try to distinguish different forms or types of effervescence, and in so doing hope to refine the analytical concept further.

In the following section, I will argue why it is relevant to study both dimensions of death: as a process and as an event. This will prepare the way for a relatively detailed discussion of the concept of effervescence in a later section. I will start by summarizing Durkheim's own relatively brief remarks concerning this concept, and point out those aspects I consider crucial, and then how this notion could be developed further. The section titled "Effervescence, Liminality, and Communitas" relates effervescence to Victor Turner's related notions of liminality and communitas: both terms that also figure prominently in the present volume. My discussion also entails a critical appraisal of an article by Tim Olaveson, since he discusses effervescence and communitas in detail. I later will present three types of effervescence in relation to ritual and political systems, respectively. The conclusion will summarize my argument and also touch briefly on the issue of how possible factors for the development of one or other forms of effervescence could be accounted for.

## Death as Event and Process

As a unique and contingent occurrence effecting an irretrievable change, death is probably *the* paradigmatic event. It represents a total break, a radical discontinuity manifested in an instant. Robert Hertz's ([1907] 1960: 48) major contribution to the sociological and anthropological study of death was to point out that in many societies death nevertheless tends to be perceived as a highly structured social process and as a carefully orchestrated gradual transition. Following this fruitful insight, subsequent anthropologists documented time and again the different and complex processes local cultures have designed in order to transform their dead into some kind of "ancestor" and thus take control of the process. The eventful character of death is frequently denied completely. This is, for example, true of the Brahmanic version of death, which is ideally a *"voluntary* relinquishment of life, a *controlled* evacuation of the body" (Parry 1994: 158, original emphasis), the final sacrifice after a series of ritual transformations during life. Likewise, the Toraja in Sulawesi ignore the moment of death and consider the person to be "ill" until the time it is considered appropriate to start the ritual. Eric Crystal (1985: 130) remarks in this connection, "During the weeks, months, and sometimes years that the cadaver remains in the home . . . death is neither recognized nor formally acknowledged."

Not only have anthropologists, on the basis of the numerous ethnographic examples available, argued that death is perceived as a process in most parts of the world, but some have also contrasted this perspective sharply with the Western view of death as an event. Maurice Bloch (1988:

13), one prominent voice in the anthropological study of death, wrote, for example, that Hertz rightly stressed the character of death as process, but that he did not question the notion of "biological death" as a "unique moment." Hertz thus had fallen prey to "one of the most fundamental aspects of western ideology, where death is thought of as a matter of an instant" (13). However, Bloch goes on, when dealing with other cultures, where death is imagined as transformation and journey, "the western 'punctual' notion of death is totally inappropriate" (14).

Notwithstanding the fact that, in my view, Hertz is saying something quite similar,[5] the crucial point here is the radical contrast drawn between death as event and process. Surely, the gradual, transformative nature of death in many societies cannot be denied, and I have studied such processes myself in different contexts. However, neither is the idea of process completely absent in Western societies, nor is the perception of death as event only present there. Often, those deaths—where any attempt to take control is impossible, and where the character of the event, as it were, claims center stage—are considered "bad" deaths (Bloch and Parry 1982: 15). This testifies to the fact that death as event is in some ways acknowledged, even if it is undesirable. Death as event lurks in the background of ritual processes. If unexpected things happen—for example, the ritual choreography is disturbed and death as event manifested, as in the Javanese example I will mention later—this may be perceived as an assault by chaos on the ritual order and, as such, feared. However, such an instance may also unleash creative forces that transform social relations or ideas. I would argue that, *as possibility,* the event is always acknowledged, whether feared or appreciated. Thus, I would suggest that we should consider both the aspects of death as an event and as a process, and study how they relate to each other.

There is a certain theoretical bias, however, that holds that event and structure cannot "occupy the same epistemological space" (Sahlins 2000: 294). When discussing this view, Sahlins was referring to the Annales school of historians but also argued that scholars like Saussure, Durkheim, and Radcliffe-Brown would share this assumption about the "unintelligibility of the contingent" (297). I would argue that Hertz and Bloch both oppose death as event versus death as process, because they share this theoretical habitus and, moreover, that there are some aspects in Durkheim's thinking—namely the concept of effervescence—that offer ways to reconcile structure with event, an aspect that Sahlins has overlooked. Moreover, significantly, in this view criticized by Sahlins, "process," "structure," and "ritual" are all closely linked in their conceptual antagonism to event and reinforce each other. Structure, either conceived as standardized relationships between persons or as a system of cultural ideas, unfolds and is reproduced in the ritual process, which is formalized and predictable, hence the opposite of the contingent event. For example, Radcliffe-Brown (1952: 160) conceived rituals in these structural terms as ordered expression of "sentiments" contributing to social equilibrium; as mentioned above, weeping is not an occurrence but standardized, expected behavior and "ceremonial custom." What, then, are events? How should event and structure, event and ritual process, be conceptualized? And, how can this help us in studying death?

Obviously, not every occurrence is an event. The crucial dimension that turns a happening into an event is that it is interpreted (Sahlins 1985: 153). On the one hand, there are objective forces—an earthquake, the arrival of a British captain on a Hawaiian island, or a biological death—with causes and qualities of their own, while, on the other hand, these instances are interpreted by particular human beings in concrete historical contexts and on the basis of specific cultural ideas available to them to make sense of the world, a system of cultural categories that constitute a structure (Sahlins 2000: 300f). An event, Sahlins (1985: 153) argues, is thus the relationship between an occurrence and a cultural structure, and he calls this realization of cultural categories, in connection to such specific occurrences, the "structure of the conjuncture" (1985: 139; 2000: 341). What is more, one characteristic of an event is that it dislocates structure: it is a disruption of the cultural order; it incites change. While in normal life, subjected to a standard rhythm with expected occurrences interpreted in usual ways, the cultural categories are reproduced, an event transforms structure— for example, it gives new meanings to cultural categories. Sahlins's (1985) own most famous example is the arrival and death of Captain Cook on Hawaii, which triggered a process in which local relationships and categories acquired new meaning (e.g., the notion of *tapu*). William Sewell (2005), who fruitfully discusses and modifies Sahlins's ideas, analyzes the taking of the Bastille from this perspective. In this event, the violent actions of actors, with originally rather profane motives (getting powder for their rifles), were in the process interpreted and authenticated as not "just violence" but as an expression of "popular sovereignty," and, indeed, a "revolution" (224ff). This blend of actions, occurrences, and interpretations, which may be generally accepted or rejected in favor of other meanings, is highly volatile, with their outcomes most uncertain. Had the crowd not stopped massacring the representatives of the old regime, the National Assembly would perhaps not have viewed the violence as "righteous" acts by a "sovereign people" but instead as mob frenzy, and the categories of French political culture would not have been fundamentally redefined. This, finally, reveals another crucial feature in Sahlins's theory of the event: the risk involved in processes of signification. There is the "objective risk" that cultural categories do not fit the situation, or there is the "subjective risk" when actors make interested use of the situation, when they empower or stifle certain interpretations as they arise in the particular situation (Sahlins 1985: 149f).

Death rituals have commonly been studied by anthropologists, including myself, as expressions of structure. They bring to the fore crucial social relationships in a particular community and put into play the most fundamental cultural ideas of the society concerned. Furthermore, and obviously so, the ritual process is predictable, and one function of this process is to try to gain control of a difficult and potentially disastrous situation: events are unwelcome guests during death rituals. Nevertheless, this should not lead anthropologists to ignore events in their study of death. At least in two ways, death rituals and events are significantly related. First, as mentioned above, this is because unexpected occurrences may erupt in the process of death rituals. The actors involved may manage to integrate them into the normal framework of cultural signification, or these events may more or less dramatically alter the (ritual) structure. Second, not only can events occur during ritual processes but, conversely, as Sewell (2005: 252f) points out, events may also be ritualized. Sewell argues this in connection to his French example. The situation after the taking of the Bastille, during which new political ideas were about to come into being, certain actions were ritualized, and thereby these ideas were authenticated, sanctified, and made palpable. For example, the procession from the Bastille to the city hall took on a ritualized form, as well as the parading of the severed heads of the governor of the fortress, Marquis de Launay, and of Jacques de Flesselles, in public. Sewell (2005: 252) writes regarding the latter, "By mimicking the old regime magistrates' display of body parts of executed criminals, the slaughter was solemnized and identified as an act of the sovereign—but now of the sovereign people."

Sewell's contribution to the study of events complements Sahlins's theory in important ways.[6] For the purpose of my argument, it is particularly significant that he discusses the aspects of event, ritual, and emotion, making an explicit mention of Durkheim. As transformative happenings of a collective nature, events are characterized by heightened emotion that "shapes the very course of events" (2005: 249). Furthermore, in the two-way relationship between ritual and event discussed above, emotions are an issue. While emotions are commonly triggered by ritual (as in the view of Radcliffe-Brown I cited before), Sewell argues that when events are ritualized, it is the other way around: "the emotional excitement and sense of communion—what Durkheim would call the collective effervescence—induce those present to express and concretize their feelings in ritual." Unlike Sahlins, who added Durkheim to the list of those who fail to conceptualize event and structure together, and thus miss the potential of Durkheim's ideas for his theory of the event, Sewell explicitly takes the role of emotions into account, without, however, elaborating on collective effervescence. I will now discuss this concept in greater detail in relation to death, event, and ritual.

## The Concept of Effervescence

Had Evans-Pritchard promoted Durkheim's idea of collective efferves-cence, the discussion today would probably be at a much more advanced level. Instead, the verdict of the most influential British anthropologist of his time concerning the usefulness of the concept was not very favor-able, to say the least. He dismissed the notion and argued that Durkheim was contradicting his own methodological doctrine by explaining social facts with psychological phenomena, indeed "crowd hysteria" (1965: 68). As late as 1996, Mary Douglas (in a new preface to her earlier published book *Natural Symbols*, 1996: xv), who has wrestled with Durkheimian questions throughout her career, nearly literally echoed the assessment of her teacher that "emotional effervescence, the idea that rituals rouse violent, ecstatic feelings, like crowd hysteria, which convince the worship-per of a reality of a power greater than and beyond the self," would be solely a psychological argument that, along with another psychological factor (emotional outrage as reaction to transgressions), would support Durkheim's theory of social solidarity. Through effervescence, the "crowd recognizes its unity in ritually aroused emotions" (ibid.). Another common criticism of Durkheim's notion of ritual as being merely static and mirror-ing the social has been more recently articulated by Bruce Kapferer (2008: 8), who contrasts Durkheim's approach to the dynamic view of ritual of Victor Turner: orientations such as the representational view of ritual by Durkheim would "effectively deny the ongoing creative and generative dimensions of human practice which he [Turner] shows is the potential of ritual: ritual as generation rather than reproduction."[7]

As the discussion of effervescence that follows will show, I agree with William Pickering (1984: 395f) and Brian Morris (1987: 121) that the accu-sation of psychological reductionism is misplaced. The above brief sum-mary of some of the findings of the anthropology of emotions reveals that emotions are not merely psychological and individual but have significant social and cultural, cognitive, and physical implications. Moreover, as I will further outline below, the connection between solidarity and the unity of the group through effervescence—an understanding that was certainly produced by Durkheim's own writings in the first place—seems to me to be overly one-sided and simplistic. Finally, Kapferer's criticism ignores the emergent aspects of Durkheim's theory of ritual, an aspect that is otherwise widely acknowledged, as we will see later on, while he also overlooks fundamental similarities in the work of Durkheim and Turner.

I contest these perspectives not in order to save Durkheim—who does not need that anyway—but out of the conviction that it is analytically more profitable to develop his insights and further refine his analytical notions than to dismiss his theory, or to merely point out its obvious weaknesses and deficiencies. Even though it is perhaps Durkheim's "least well-theorized concept" (Mitchell 2004: 65), the notion of effervescence offers a more nuanced application than is often realized. In this section, I want to briefly[8] summarize Durkheim's own explanation of the concept before I outline other comments on effervescence and further developments of the notion by other scholars. Given the significance of liminality in the process of death, I will in the next step critically discuss the work of Tim Olaveson, who compares the concept of effervescence to Turner's notion of communitas.

Collective effervescence refers, as Durkheim (1974) says, to "great creative moment[s]" (92) when humans assemble and "a new kind of psychic life" (91) develops that gives rise to new ideas, ideals, and behaviors. As Durkheim ([1912] 1995: 424) summarizes in the conclusion of *Elementary Forms*, "We have seen, in fact, that if collective life awakens religious thought when it rises to a certain intensity, that is so because it brings about a state of effervescence that alters the conditions of psychic activity. The vital energies become hyper-excited, the passions more intense, the sensations more powerful; there are indeed some that are produced only at this moment. Man does not recognize himself; he feels somehow transformed and in consequence transforms his surroundings." Group gatherings are a necessary condition of effervescence. They can take various forms and have all kinds of purposes, such as the seasonal assemblies of the Inuit (as discussed in the study of Mauss and Beuchat 1979), clan assemblies, initiations, or revolutions (Durkheim 1995: 215f). What is generally common to all of them is that they are extraordinary, beyond the everyday. In each case, social forces are generated through concerted action. The emotions created—a key aspect of effervescence—can vary considerably, from joy to sorrow to anger. In Durkheim's (1974: 93) view, these forces are then related in the participants' minds to certain ideas that are believed to represent these forces. Ideas therefore are dynamic, as they are related to social processes. Beyond the real, ideal worlds are thus created, and ideals emerge. The ideal world created transfigures reality. Due to contingent circumstances, contraries may be combined, hierarchies reversed, or disparities equalized (Durkheim 1974: 94f).

This creative process—reminiscent of the intellectual playfulness part of the liminal situation as described by Turner—is not necessarily smooth but often erratic. As Durkheim (1974: 91) argues, such forces "are not easily controlled, canalized and adjusted to closely determined ends. They need to overflow for the sake of overflowing, as in play without any specific objective, at one time in the form of stupid destructive violence or, at another, of heroic folly" (see also Durkheim [1912] 1995: 212). The quote below also stresses this important point: effervescence is unpredictable; it is not necessarily good, nor does it automatically lead to solidarity and a consensus of ideas and ideals. As usual, Durkheim ([1912] 1995: 425) speaks as if society is the acting, feeling, and thinking agent. This reification should not, however, distract us from the main message: "A society is not constituted simply by the mass of individuals who comprise it . . . but above all by the idea it has of itself. And there is no doubt that society sometimes hesitates over the manner in which it must conceive itself. It feels pulled in all directions. When such conflicts break out, they are not between the ideal and the reality but between different ideals, between the ideal of yesterday and that of today, between the ideal that has the authority of tradition and one that is only coming into being."

With reference to death rituals in particular, Durkheim identifies the same processes and effects. Mourning, for Durkheim ([1912] 1995: 402f), resembles other positive rites—that is, those that prescribe behavior—as it "too is made up of collective rites that bring about a state of effervescence in those who take part. The intense feelings are different [sorrow, not joy]; the wild intensity is the same." Hence, for Durkheim, assemblies in the face of death function in the same way as they do on other occasions. These "moments of collective ferment" (Durkheim 1974: 92) not only can revitalize ideas and ideals that are already present in the society under discussion but also generate emotions, "notions," and "tastes" (Durkheim [1912] 1995: 401). Real forces are produced in joint action, such as the sharing of sorrow in a group. It is the experience of the collective action and "communion of consciousness" that "increases social vitality" (ibid.: 405). As a social outcome, therefore, in the face of death "society is more alive and active than ever. In fact, when social feeling suffers a painful shock, it reacts with greater force than usual" (ibid.). Thus, the gatherings in times of such crises, in the face of violent deaths, are especially potent and unleash a force that can overthrow governments, make people want war, or sacralize a nation.

Let me draw attention to what are, in my view, the key points that can be read from this admittedly brief summary of Durkheim's view on the matter. Obviously, rituals do not just represent society or articulate meanings. In situations outside the routine of everyday life, the gathering of people and their joined actions[9] may produce social forces that have an extremely generative potential: they transform actors who, in turn, may alter their social environment. This reading is, for example, supported by Anne Warfield Rawls (1996: 434), who stresses that "enacted practices" are at the heart of Durkheim's understanding of society: "For Durkheim, society consists first and foremost of enacted practices that give rise to real social forces that participants in the assembled group experience jointly. Certain of these social forces give rise to essential ideas experienced in common, which Durkheim refers to as categories of the understanding. The purpose of religion in human history is to provide the enacted practices necessary to generate these essential ideas." The results of these communally enacted practices are in the first place diverse, and in the second place unpredictable. They are diverse in as much as they produce affective states in the participants at the same time as they include cognitive aspects, ideas, and ideals. Rawls argues that feeling not only involves a particular emotional state, but is also a recognition of the social forces, the *"feeling* is a *perception* of the efficacy of ritual" (451, emphasis in the original). Moreover, results may include various physical dimensions and affect and transform the relationships between the participants. All these features are not locked up in the individual experience but are intersubjective; they are communicated and to some extent shared.

The question of emotions or ideas being shared leads me to the second point. Effervescence is unpredictable. Too often—for example, by Mary Douglas as quoted above, and also Rawls (e.g., 1996: 448ff) is no exception here—effervescence is assumed to automatically result in social unity and intellectual consensus, in collective cohesion, and uniformly shared ideas. I do not think that this is the only possible result; perhaps in its extreme form of complete consensus and unity it is even an exception (see Baumann 1992). Ideas and emotions—as shown in the discussion on emotions—are not necessarily shared in any general, uniform, or homogeneous way; rather, as Wolf (2001) puts it, the ritual "texture" shapes individual experience without determining it, leaving room for idiosyncrasies. Durkheim's description, that such forces are not easily controlled, and his brief remark about possible conflicts over ideals seem to support this view. But to strive for the ultimate Durkheimian exegesis is not my preoccupation. Whatever support for our arguments we may find in his writings, we have to develop the concept further. In my view, then, effervescence makes as well as breaks groups. Social integration is not the inevitable outcome, or, if so, it may only be generated in a fraction of the community and thus construct one group identity in opposition to another. As is true on the social plane, consensus on the level of ideas is not an automatic result. Accordingly, Katherine Verdery's assessment regarding the usefulness of Durkheim's perspective for her analysis of "dead-body politics" (e.g., 1999: 35), to which I will return below, seems hasty. While she acknowledges his contribution to the study of political renewal, she states, "I part company with him [Durkheim] in regard to the *conscience collective*; I look not for *shared* mentalities but for *conflict* among groups over social meanings" (36, emphasis in the original). As I have argued, Durkheim's concept of effervescence encompasses both options: effervescence may produce conflicting ideals and ideas as much as it may create shared values—fission as much as fusion.

In connection to this unpredictability of effervescence, Steven Lukes's (1975) plea for a more thorough and nuanced study of ritual processes is relevant, although it does not deal with effervescence in particular. The starting point for his argument concerning the study of political rituals in "advanced industrial societies" (289) is a thorough critique of the "neo-Durkheimians" (Shils and Young, Bellah, and others). Their work on rituals in Western societies would be highly problematic, Lukes holds. For example, he criticizes Sidney Verba's analysis of the effects of the Kennedy assassination: in reaction to the violent death, nearly all Americans participated in the mourning and, consequently, in the shared emotions. With the president acting as the unifying symbol, social integration resulted (295f). This kind of analysis is too superficial, argues Lukes. The neo-Durkheimians would employ a simplistic notion of social integration, never questioning their assumption that value consensus leads inevitably to social integration. Their analyses would in turn be narrow as well, since they only deal with selected cases and would never consider variations, exceptions, or deviations, and would ignore different layers of symbolic meaning.

For my argument here, it is important that Lukes, like Baumann (1992),[10] stresses the possibility of value-heterogeneity of political rituals and the option that they may enhance conflict rather than cohesion. The processions of the Orange Order (note: Lukes's article is from the 1970s), for instance, would, in a completely Protestant environment, perhaps reinforce community solidarity; in Belfast, however, marching though Catholic neighborhoods leads to a dissent of values and social tension. Lukes (1975: 300) concludes, "In this case, collective effervescences serve not to unite the community but to strengthen the dominant groups within it. Ritual here exacerbates social conflict and works against (some aspects of) social integration." Unsurprisingly, Lukes also refers to Gluckman's view that rituals may formalize and express aspects of social conflict. Moreover, Lukes is interested in the connection between the cognitive and political sides of ritual processes. Collective representations or ideas are created, reinforced, modulated, and organized in political rituals, but selectively so, with the result that the articulation of one set of ideas distracts from the possibility of different models (this thus relates to Sahlins's notion of subjective risk). As such, ritual not only authorizes certain ideas but also "define[s] away alternatives"; it is a "mobilization of bias" (Lukes 1975: 305).[11]

Bringing me to the last two aspects I want to stress regarding Durkheim's description of effervescence that I summarized above, one of the many important questions Lukes's (1975: 302) inspiring article raises is this: "Under what conditions are political rituals most effective in getting participants and observers to internalize the political paradigms they represent?" Part of the answer is death. Because of, as Durkheim says, the particularly potent social forces that are unleashed, death is a unique chance to authorize ideas, societal models, and power structures; but death may also be the occasion where these ideas, models, and structures are challenged. I would argue that death as *process* is usually controlled by dominant groups in a society, who would prefer contributing towards reinforcing existing social and ideational forms, whereas death as *event* may also pose a threat to these. The former manages to define away alternatives, as Lukes says, while the latter actually triggers optional perspectives. The former mobilizes bias, as is desired, while the latter may evoke revolt, as is dreaded (at least by some).

Effervescence, in sum, is the consequence of collective joint action. These practices have a highly creative potential on the basis of the social forces they trigger, with effervescence being the experience of these forces. The social results of effervescence are multifaceted and unpredictable. They involve social relations as well as ideas, but they need not result in homogeneity or harmony, neither socially (solidarity) nor intellectually (value consensus). While collectively produced and intersubjectively communicated, dissent and conflict, as well as differences in ideas, may be the outcome. Individual experience is molded in the process, but not controlled. As ultimate ambiguity, death effervescence is particularly powerful, potentially conservative and reproductive as process, and possibly inventive and transformative as event. This also means that not every occasion of effervescence is part of an event as understood here (in Sahlins's and Sewell's terms), since events are necessarily transformative, while effervescence is not. What counts as effervescence cannot objectively be verified, since we are speaking of intersubjective experiences of collective processes. There is no level of excitement, or any particular action, or a certain number of actors that may turn a situation into an effervescent assembly. Whether the term can be meaningfully applied (perhaps in contrast to other analytical concepts like event or liminality—see below) depends upon the specific research context and the perceptions of the actors.

My distinction between effervescence as process and as event has been partly stimulated by the writings of William Pickering, one of the few and probably the first who extensively discussed the concept of effervescence (1984: 380–417). Not only does Pickering show that effervescence is by no means about "crowd psychology," because the effervescent assemblies, as he prefers to call them, are *intentional* gatherings, when participants are temporarily *connected* in a special way and the *outcome* of the situations is decidedly social; he also suggests an analytical distinction of two types of effervescence he considers implicit in Durkheim's writings, namely "creative" and "re-creative." Pickering (1984: 385) explains: "As an assembly of participants where the level of feeling is of a most intense kind, where the final outcome may under certain circumstances be uncertain and where it is possible that new ideas emerge. This could be called the creative function of an effervescent assembly. As an assembly of participants where the level of excitement is intense, but where those gathered together feel a bond of community and unity (as in the function above) [note the stress on unity again, PB], and where as a result the members feel at the end morally strengthened. As such this might be termed the re-creative function." This distinction indicates an original assembly — an event — actually creating something new as opposed to other gatherings that are, instead, reenactments of original events. Significantly, there is a diachronic element involved. Durkheim is not only thinking of unique events when dealing with effervescence but also of a routinized form of effervescence: "Persistence is as important as creativity" (Pickering 1984: 390). Hence, the original effervescent situations and the social outcome they generated can be recalled and collectively remembered in rituals, and in this way continue to be of influence for society. As I already indicated and as I will shortly outline in more detail, I consider the dynamic between event and process to be crucial, especially in the context of death.

However, the common development from an original event to a routinized ritualization is only one aspect of this dynamic. What interests me is how effervescence is made an integral part of ritual processes, or how it is, conversely, ritually avoided. Moreover, how does effervescence as event manifest itself: in the ritual process, adjacent to it, or unconnected to it? I suggest analytically differentiating three forms of effervescence: systemic effervescence (as integral and choreographed part of ritual), negative effervescence (avoidance of effervescence in ritual), and evenemential effervescence (as event in Sahlins's terms). As will become apparent below, I am on the one hand concerned with effervescence as part of ritual systems. On the other hand, I will discuss these forms of effervescence in a wider political field of social relations that are not part of a ritual system proper (but where actions may nevertheless be or become ritualized, as

Sewell pointed out). Before I go on to illustrate these forms of effervescence with different examples, I want to compare the concept of effervescence to Turner's notions of liminality and communitas—two concepts many authors in this volume refer to—with the intention of specifying these concepts by contrasting them.

## Effervescence, Liminality, and Communitas

While Turner did acknowledge Durkheim's influence on his work (e.g., 1974: 183), in his reflection on his most well-known concept—that is, liminality—he neither draws a connection to the work of Durkheim's student Robert Hertz and his work on the ritual process of death, nor does he discuss the obvious similarities between liminality and effervescence.[12] His standard reference point is van Gennep's ([1909] 1960) model of rites of passage. Surprisingly, no matter how obvious, not many scholars have commented on the similarity of the two concepts, let alone elaborated on this point. In the last paragraph of his discussion of effervescence, Pickering (1984: 416) notes "parallels" between both concepts; Engelke (2002: 6) mentions this briefly, and there is an implicit link in Lukes's article too (1975: 302). The only contribution I know of that compares the notions systematically is the article by Tim Olaveson (2001) on effervescence and communitas.

It is to Olaveson's credit that the similarities—or, as he calls it repeatedly, the functional equivalence (2001: 99, 115) of the two concepts—have now been clearly spelled out. However, the conclusions drawn from this observation are relatively sparse: both Durkheim and Turner, he posits, would be discussing phenomena related to altered states of consciousness, and both would be concerned with processes that can generate new ideas, values, and so forth (114). In my view, his analysis is too narrow or partial, at least on two accounts. First, he only considers parallels or correspondences between effervescence and communitas, but does not reflect on if and how they might differ. Second, Olaveson compares effervescence and communitas. But the latter is only an aspect of liminality. Why restrict the analysis to communitas? If communitas and effervescence are equivalent, how then is the latter related to other aspects of liminality, those unconnected to communitas? And, how do communitas and liminality relate to each other? In short, while the article offers many insights into the aspects that effervescence and communitas share, important questions remain unasked. Since Turner's work is well known, I will not elaborate here on the notions of liminality and communitas (see the introduction to this volume). Instead, I will only briefly mention some of the key aspects as summarized by Turner, and then point out the similarities between effervescence and communitas recognized by Olaveson, complement his comparison by pointing out where the two concepts differ, and argue, finally, that effervescence, communitas, and liminality can be regarded as a triangle of partly overlapping analytical concepts.

Liminality and communitas both belong to the sphere of what Turner calls antistructure. Although the latter term signifies the lack of a framework of social positions that commonly defines a person in society, Turner considers it something extremely positive, even necessary for human life, "a generative center" (1974: 273) or "realm of pure possibility" (1967: 97); liminality and communitas are the creative fountains of humanity, when normal structures and rules are suspended. Liminality refers to the middle period of rituals of passage as described by van Gennep ([1909] 1960), which is characterized by ambiguity of all kinds, socially and intellectually. Significantly, since this ambivalence can be regarded as dangerous by some actors in society, we may find both license and extreme control in such situations, for example, the "authority of elders over juniors" (Turner 1974: 273). In my view, Turner admits here that liminality need not be free of structure, and, indeed, as Hardenberg (in this volume) shows, the ritual process may be extremely structured. Communitas in particular describes the kind of bonds in liminal periods that are undifferentiated, where humans can meet as humans, outside of prescribed social roles, and as equals, and jointly experience their co-humanness (Turner 1969: 94–130; 1974: 274). Similar to the process indicated by Durkheim and made explicit by Pickering (from creative to re-creative effervescence), there is a development and routinization of communitas, from original "existential" or "spontaneous" to "normative" communitas, when the experience has been made part of the structure again (Turner 1969: 132).[13]

The similarities between communitas and effervescence in general will be readily apparent. Olaveson (2001: 107) provides us with a whole list, of which I will only mention some aspects. Both phenomena have an important emotional dimension that also includes cognitive aspects; they are collective, antistructural, temporary, creative, ambiguous, and they counterbalance alienating tendencies that result from the normative, sociostructural side of human life.

In what ways do they differ? The experience of effervescence is probably a necessary feature of communitas, but not the other way around. As the "strong feeling of 'humankindness'" (Turner 1969: 116), communitas seems to be generically good and benevolent, while, as I have argued above, effervescence is unpredictable; it can include such an experience, but it might just as well lead to violence, death, or destruction. While communitas seems to be the hippie's paradise, as Turner indicates (1969: 112f), effervescence can be the hooligan's heaven. Furthermore, although there are many instances to be found in Durkheim's writings that point toward effervescence as involving a loss of control and the suspension of common social norms, I do not think that is necessarily the case. As with liminality, effervescence can be—perhaps usually is—highly structured (in terms of gender, age, wealth, status, etc.) and orchestrated. When discussing the contrast between an unorganized crowd and Durkheim's effervescent assemblies, Huntington and Metcalf (1979: 32) state this point quite explicitly: "The funeral material makes it clear that emotional 'effervescence' does not replace structure but results from structure." Thus in contrast to communitas, effervescence is not typically antistructural.

Communitas and effervescence, therefore, are not merely parallel concepts but are best thought of in terms of a conceptual triangle, with liminality being the third element. Concerning their ambiguity and creative potential, the three notions certainly share significant aspects, but it may be analytically more profitable to keep them distinct and to investigate, in connection to concrete cases, how these three dimensions interact. One may envision the three concepts as three partly overlapping circles, the overlap signifying instances when the dimensions are found to be copresent. A line cross-cutting the overlapping circles contrasts structure to antistructure. The circle representing communitas would be fully on the antistructural side, while both effervescence and liminality lie mostly on the side of structure. Communitas depends on both transitional and ambivalent states (and processes), which liminality represents, and on emotional states resulting from shared enacted practices as signified by effervescence. The latter, in turn, may or may not include communitas. With liminality, effervescence has a significant feedback relationship. When phases of transition involve effervescence—as in the example of the French Revolution cited above—it may work as a catalyst for changes already underway. But effervescence may also trigger such transitions in the first place. Hence, effervescence will often be connected to transitional processes but need not necessarily be part of ritual liminality in each instance. Liminality seems to be the most independent of the three notions; it can occur both with and without communitas and effervescence. Death-related experiences and practices can combine these elements in various ways, ritually integrating effervescence or avoiding it, encompassing communitas or not, but always being necessarily liminal. Having thus, no doubt crudely, contrasted the three concepts, let me now, equally approximately I fear, illustrate with some examples the different forms of effervescence I mentioned above. Such a typology of forms of effervescence is no end in itself. It should lead to a more nuanced study of concrete cases and, in a second step, make comparisons and generalizations possible.

## Types of Effervescence in Ritual Systems

I consider effervescence as systemic when it occurs as an integral part of ritual structure. In such cases, individuals are expected to generate and express emotional states through prescribed forms of collective action. Obviously ritual effervescence can take diverse shapes, and it is relevant to investigate in ethnographic detail how such situations are given form in specific contexts, paying attention to different actors and ritual personages.

Some Gadaba rituals involve systemic effervescence. In contrast to the Javanese as described by Geertz, men and women are, in general, emotionally extrovert and expressive: joy, sorrow, or anger are articulated publicly by men, women, and children, and at times violently so, with such behavior being considered normal. The ritual process of death proceeds in four steps, with effervescent articulations of sorrow being expected from women at particular moments. The highly complex final phase of the death ritual (*go'ter*), which accomplishes the transformation of the spirits of the dead into ancestors by replacing the former in the form of living water buffaloes with the latter represented by memorial stones, shows a complex emotional texture, where systemic effervescence follows moments of (emotional) restraint, with this again being followed by effervescence. The different effervescent moments, moreover, have quite different emotional tones or "contours," which together constitute the emotional texture (Wolf 2001). Since I summarized the ritual process briefly in chapter 3 of this volume and in detail elsewhere, I will only highlight here the relevant points (see also Berger 2010b; Izikovitz 1969; Pfeffer 2001). Since the contrast between effervescence and restraint is so striking in this case, it is important to consider both features. This is probably true for other cases as well.

Among the first effervescent scenes that occur in the village of the ritual hosts are when all the buffaloes representing the "living dead" have been tied in a row at the place where there are memorial stones from former such occasions, and are then fed and mourned by women for several days. The emotional tone switches from sorrow to conquest[14] when the groups of external agnates arrive at dusk in the village in an aggressive fashion and take over the place where the buffaloes are tied and the feeding is still going on. For hours, these men, who will later take away (most of) the buffaloes, dance at this place, sing, shout, slap the buffaloes' backs, and display a gluttonous attitude. They tear the bowls with rice and beer from the hands of the females feeding the buffaloes and consume the contents themselves. This goes on for many hours until the first switch from effervescence to restraint occurs. At about 3:00 a.m., the external agnates sit down with the male heads of the hosting group and the distribution of buffaloes is formally decided. In one stroke, all the men appear to be sober, and the distribution is sealed, as usual, by the drinking of beer.

On the next main day of the ritual process, such a switch happens again. The buffaloes, now dressed according to gender, are led outside of the village to an external stone platform and tied there, where mourning is continued by (old) women. Around midday, there is a rush to this place by affinal groups from other villages and by *their* agnates, bringing their own buffaloes representing their dead. The advent contains again a display of aggression and conquest. These buffaloes are then the target of a kind of generalized predation. Except for the hosts and their affinal buffalo-bringers (the mother's brother's group, from the perspective of the deceased) everyone is free to try to slash open the bellies of the affinal buffaloes and tear out the intestines of the still living animal (only men partake in this activity). This effervescent contest is the climax of the ritual for many actors. Later that day, a quite different kind of effervescence occurs. Agnates and affines start a boisterous mud fight at the back of the hosts' houses, at the end of which they bathe together and wash each other.[15] This is immediately followed by another highly restrained situation, when all buffalo takers and bringers are honored with drink, food, and gifts, sitting on a row of bamboo mats. As with the assignment of the buffaloes to the different groups in the early morning hours, this is a moment for potential negotiation of claims related to gift giving.

Among the Sora, a community culturally and linguistically close to the Gadaba, and geographically not far removed as well, effervescence during death rituals takes shape during repeated dialogues with the dead via female shamans. While Gadaba women address the dead while feeding them, among the Sora the dead elaborately speak back. As Piers Vitebsky (1993) describes in detail in his book and in a summary in his chapter in this volume, emotions are dialogized or co-constructed in public verbal negotiations between a deceased person and his or her living kin. The social process of negotiations is based on the cultural emotional repertoire as expressed in language and gestures, as well as on the personal idiosyncrasies of those actors involved; significantly, however, the ritual process constructs "trans-sentience" (1993: 255f), a mutuality of emotions. The emotional contours and emotional intensity varies from one situation to another, and, in general, the dialogues are supposed to lead from aggression and fear to a feeling of security in the face of a nurturing, benevolent ancestor. However, emotions are constructed in these shamanic practices, and the séances often involve dramatic effervescent scenes, including crying, anger, and embraces of the dead person (via the ritual medium) by his or her living kin.

More examples of systemic effervescence could be provided, but these two brief illustrations may suffice for the present purpose, which is to distinguish the type of effervescence that is an integrated part of the ritual process. They also show that effervescence is by no means unstructured, but instead these joint actions are orchestrated; even if they leave room for more or less improvisation, they are organized along the lines of age, kinship, and gender, among other possible dimensions. The two examples presented here are surely part of a liminal process and may at certain moments also achieve what Turner calls communitas.

What is the function of systemic effervescence? Durkheim saw the function of effervescence as the sporadic regeneration of the key ideas of a society and the production of social cohesion as a result. I find it difficult to identify such functional aspects in any straightforward way. Surely, to take the Gadaba as a case in point, the social structure of their society manifests itself in collective ritual practices; social relationships would in many ways be only a theoretical possibility were they not to be concretized in ritual action (Berger 2015). Rather than only looking for utilitarian aspects, one could also argue that effervescence can be regarded as a part of the local cosmology or worldview. As the discussion concerning emotions showed, feelings are not only affective but also cognitive and cultural. Many societies value effervescence, and such phenomena may therefore also be part of their ritual practice (in specific contexts).[16] Among the Gadaba, aggression as an emotive in connection to young men, and as a behavioral attribute of them, is valued (Berger 2010a), and, through alcohol consumption, dancing, and drumming, various effervescent states are catalyzed. Systemic effervescence as a form of ritualized antagonism between social categories—thus the Gluckman argument—is, however, for the Gadaba at least, also a viable and complementary interpretation, as tension between affines is evident in several domains and finds ritual expression in the rituals of marriage as well. Yet, such arguments come close to the simple answers I sketched above: that where effervescence is valued, it is part of the ritual process; where the opposite is the case, it is absent. So this can hardly qualify as a satisfactory answer. But as I indicated earlier, the explanation of effervescence is not the aim of this contribution, even though these questions are pertinent.

Negative effervescence is the opposite of its systemic cousin, namely the deliberate ritual avoidance of effervescent situations. While low-caste death rituals might include systemic effervescence, speaking of India once more, such states tend to be avoided in the ideal north-Indian Brahmanic version of death (Parry 1994; see also Berger in this volume, ch. 3). As mentioned above, what are considered bad deaths are uncontrolled, violent deaths, and, as such, do not conform to the idea of a voluntary sacrifice—the controlled relinquishment of life according to ritual formulae.[17] While for the Gadaba—perhaps tribal Central India in general—effervescence is a value, the opposite is true from the Brahman's perspective. The biological, physical body, its fluids and expressions, with emotions being a part thereof, have to be controlled. Those associated with these processes and expressions, or who show a lack of control, are socially and spiritually regarded as low: "inferiors are to a greater extent enmeshed in the world of physicality" (Parry 1994: 157). Parry therefore argues that the grieving role prescribed for women in death rituals serves to reproduce gender hierarchies, where men are shown to be aloof towards the gross physical world—less constrained by it. Forms of effervescence in death rituals are, at least from the ideal male Brahman perspective, therefore avoided.[18] Javanese funerals, as described by Geertz, are likewise an example of negative effervescence. In this case, grieving is not even prescribed for women: "tears are not approved of" (Geertz 1973: 153).

Moreover, Geertz's (1973) famous incident also provides an example of the dimension of evenemential effervescence as an unintentional part of the ritual process. In this "unfortunate but instructive" (169) Javanese funeral, the incongruence between forms of interaction—now urbanized and structured by a variety of new criteria such as class or political allegiance—and cultural patterns of meaning and religious forms lead to a ritual limbo. Instead of solidarity constituted through the death ritual, cleavages became apparent. Death here manifested itself as an event that people were unaccustomed to and had to make sense of. In this situation, the otherwise prescribed calmness was disrupted by two women, the mother of the deceased and her sister, who burst into frenzied wailing: "In what seemed a split second, both women had dissolved into wild hysterics and the crowd had rushed in and pulled them apart, dragging them to houses at opposite sides of the kampong [neighborhood]" (159). Evenemential effervescence had briefly erupted and was immediately constrained, since emotional outbursts are considered undesirable and dangerous, and negative effervescence the institutionalized pattern.

## Types of Effervescence in Political Systems

The three dimensions of effervescence in connection to death may not only occur as part of standardized ritual processes of the life-cycle but also outside them or adjacent to them. Being fully aware that rituals in general and death rituals in particular often, if not always, involve a political dimension, I think it is nevertheless appropriate to distinguish a genuine political sphere outside of local ritual systems proper, as represented in

the cases discussed so far. Therefore, in addition to the three forms of effervescence as part of ritual systems, we can also consider them in connection
to political systems, such as national politics. Surely, the scale is different
when we consider, for example, Gadaba rituals vis-à-vis the political rituals of nation states. But this is only one aspect that differentiates them. In
particular, the status of rituals in general is quite different in the two scenarios. In the Gadaba case, the rituals form an encompassing system that
integrates economic, social, juridical, and political dimensions; in short
they are a total social fact. In the cases that follow, rituals do not (or no
longer) provide the overarching framework for the organization of society, and the religious, the political, as well as the economic are generally
recognized as distinct spheres. However, rituals are nevertheless crucial in
some contexts and are strategically employed too. Thus, while the former
cases are examples of holistic rituals, what follows are partial phenomena.
While I do not think that any strict dividing line or an absolute contrast
between the two contexts would make much sense, I also hold that they
are sufficiently distinct to be treated separately here. Among the Gadaba,
the negotiations and the exchange of buffaloes, considered as the dead,
may be regarded as "dead-body politics" (Verdery 1999), but the cases to
which I will now turn are of a different kind.

In dealing with "dead-body politics," Verdery (1999: 23–53) is concerned with processes of fundamental reconfiguration of the world in the
context of postsocialist transformations after 1989. The changes the people
in the former Soviet states experienced were politically, socially, emotionally, and intellectually fundamental, she argues. The so-called death of the
system encompassed all these dimensions, and dead bodies were a key
aspect and a site in relation to which the reconfiguration took place, since
they connect emotion, cosmology, kinship, and national identity.

A factor that contributed to the end of the Communist era in Hungary,
for instance, was the reburial of Imre Nagy in Budapest in 1989. He was a
key figure in the Hungarian revolution of 1956, when the country wanted
to break away from Soviet influence; he was executed after the Soviet invasion, and secretly buried in 1958. As István Rév (1995) shows in his article on "Parallel Autopsies," and in line with Verdery's arguments, in the
period of political transition, a whole web of buried and reburied bodies
served to shape a new understanding of history; for example, by synchro-
nizing the burial of contemporary political leaders with the reburial of
former ones, time is compressed, and the Communist era written out of
Hungarian history (32f). To mobilize bias—to return to Steven Lukes's
question about the condition under which participants internalize political paradigms—there not only needs to be powerful symbols such as dead
bodies, coffins, and monuments but also people acting jointly with respect

to these symbols. In Nagy's case, one hundred thousand people or more attended the ceremony on Heroes' Square in Budapest, so this communal action can probably be regarded as a "great creative moment" (Durkheim 1974: 92) and surely had an impact on those who participated, empowering the symbols and ideas of the political ritual, such as a continuous Hungarian (anti-Communist) history. Edward Tiryakian (1995), for one, also regards Nagy's reburial as one of several effervescent situations in the revolutionary year of 1989.[19] Certainly, neither the emotional contours nor the interpretation of the ceremony were uniform (see Verdery 1999: 31). This political ritual of reburial was not part of a series of common life-cycle rituals, as, for instance, in the Gadaba case. The reburial was no event either; it was carefully planned and choreographed as part of a political process, even though its actual results could not be predicted.

While the attacks of 9/11 were ritually embedded on the part of the suicide bombers (see Nanninga in this volume), for the victims, the American public, and the rest of the world, it certainly was an event. After the attack, as people in New York cleared away the rubble, searched for survivors, and tried to make sense of what had happened, a huge wave of solidarity swept through the city and the nation. The gatherings of people at Ground Zero, mourning the dead and sharing their grief, are what I would understand as a case of evenemential effervescence (certainly involving elements of communitas as well). And the event gave rise to a transfiguration of ideas. After the attacks of 9/11, firefighters and policemen became the new American heroes. However, the most astonishing transformation, Tiryakian (2005) observes, was that regarding George W. Bush. Before 9/11, Bush was viewed by half of the population as an illegitimate president who had defeated Al Gore not in terms of votes but on the basis of a juridical decision. Speaking on the smoking ruins of the World Trade Center to "his people," Bush, says Tiryakian (2005: 314), changed his nature: "The president of the United States, George W. Bush, became transfigured from a minority president to a wartime leader with the highest public opinion support recorded in American poll history."[20] Moreover, the motivation of bias with regard to his new goal, the "War on Terror," became an established category and received a lot of support as well.[21]

A particular kind of dead-body politics that produced evenemential effervescence with unexpected and, from the point of view of the regime, unwanted results can be observed in Argentina under military dictatorship (see Robben in this volume). In the late 1970s, parents searched in despair for their missing children, who had been abducted, tortured, and perhaps killed by the Argentine regime. They met each other while searching in state institutions such as hospitals or prisons, and gathered regularly on the Plaza de Mayo in Buenos Aires to exchange information

(Bosco 2006). When, in 1977, fourteen mothers protested in front of the presidential palace, no one could have imagined the powerful social movement that would develop out of this joint action and these shared aims, experiences, and emotions: the emotions of fear, despair, and anger they shared, and the reciprocal emotions of solidarity and empathy they came to feel for each other (see Jasper 1998: 417). The Mothers met weekly in the Plaza de Mayo (which gave them their name), expressing their grief publicly and jointly by writing poems and crying together. A routiniza-tion of the effervescent assembly as described by Pickering (and by Turner with regard to communitas) can be found in this case too, involving a transformation from evenemential to systemic effervescence. The num-bers of the women grew quickly, organizational structures developed, and their aims also shifted from demanding truth and justice for their children to a general human rights movement. For twenty-five years, between 1981 and 2006, an annual March of Resistance was organized every December, during which hundreds of Mothers walked around the central monument at the Plaza de Mayo for twenty-four hours. Hence, even after democ-racy had been reestablished, the women in this way evoked and re-created their community and communally remembered their abducted children. While the bodies of many of these children have never been found, some Mothers have decided that their own bodily remains should remain on the Plaza de Mayo and have arranged that after their death their ashes will be scattered there (Bosco 2006).

Authoritarian regimes usually appreciate systemic effervescence they control and orchestrate; with regard to the general public sphere, how-ever, they are most afraid of evenemential effervescence, knowing its gen-erative potential. Examples of this scenario are well known, and I only need to refer here briefly to the demonstrations that will most likely be repressed by the Chinese government memorializing the twenty-fifth anniversary of the Tiananmen Square Massacre in 2014.

Let me sum up the discussion of forms of effervescence illustrated by these brief examples. I suggested that, as part of ritual processes related to the life-cycle, three dimensions of effervescence in connection with death can be analytically distinguished: systemic effervescence, which is emo-tional arousal as a consequence of collective action being an integral part of the ritual process; negative effervescence, where such states are deliber-ately and systematically avoided; and evenemential effervescence, where such situations erupt unexpectedly, whatever the ritual choreography had planned. I argued that death as an event that may lead to effervescent articulations should be investigated alongside the processual aspects of death. Moreover, the three dimensions distinguished here will probably also be found in some sort of combination—for example, as systemic and negative effervescence alongside each other, organized along gendered ritual roles (as in Parry's example previously discussed).

Moreover, I argued that effervescence in relation to death is not only a feature of ritual systems, but of political systems too. What dead-body politics in the wider political arena shows is that not only can death lead to change but processes of political transition may also utilize death (Verdery 1999). On the one hand, as part of dead-body politics, death-related ceremonies can be staged for the political aim of mobilizing bias. Political regimes have, on the other hand, good reason to suppress such assemblies. Negative effervescence in this case is less concerned with the articulation of cultural values integral to ritual patterns but is instead regarded as an explicit instrument of political control. Finally, as we have come to know almost daily via news from all over the world, beyond its ritual context, evenemential effervescence is especially common as a reaction to multiple and violent deaths, potentially including forms of ritualization as described by Sewell.

As I have argued in a previous section, the results of these various forms of effervescence are unpredictable and diverse. They are diverse inasmuch as they affect the participating actors physically, emotionally, socially, and intellectually, and various outcomes on all these planes are possible. In the context of systemic effervescence, one such possible result is the expression, realization, and reinternalization of cultural categories that are not only neutral units of thought but often values or ideals that are connected to the cultural emotional repertoire and that form the basis of moral life. While such values or ideals are ritually reproduced in this way, they may actually be generated in examples of evenemential effervescence, involving the precarious processes of significations, as Sahlins and Sewell have shown. For example, the transformation of ideas into ideals — that is, ideas that are emotionally loaded, incite action, and are closely connected to people's motivations — which Rachel Weiss (2012) has argued in her interpretation of Durkheim, may occur in moments of crisis or in effervescent assemblies. Another result with respect to ideas is a shift in conceptual focus, when ideas that lead a rather latent life are dragged out into the open, so to speak.[22] How exactly cultural categories are shaped and transfigured certainly deserves more attention and research. Suffice it to say here that evenemential effervescence in connection to death has immense potential for the transformation of ideas as well as of social relationships. Regarding the latter, I have argued that, far from solidarity or even communitas being the only result of effervescence (with respect to all its dimensions), group identities can be forged that oppose others, thus inciting social conflict, destruction, violence, or resistance as a consequence.

## Conclusion

Death and effervescence have a significant relationship. In this contribution, I intended to investigate this relationship and thereby, on the one
hand, contribute to the study of ultimate ambiguities, as do the other
chapters in this volume, while, on the other, revitalizing a concept that
has led a marginal theoretical life in anthropology for more than a century.

Even though the anthropology of emotion is not concerned with the
concept of effervescence, surprisingly enough, it has contributed significant insights that are of relevance in understanding the notion. For one
thing, the criticism of psychological reductionism that had been raised
against the concept of effervescence, though refutable on other grounds
as well, seems less convincing when taking into account the fact that emotions actually transcend easy pigeonholing into cognitive, somatic, cultural, or social dimensions. Emotions, and therefore effervescence as well,
are so significant because they do involve all these aspects. Moreover,
the anthropology of emotion has highlighted the fact that emotions are
as expressive as they are performative, that they are individually experienced yet also intersubjective, that they are orchestrated in ritual contexts,
yet do not determine individual understandings, and hence completely
homogeneous group emotions are unlikely to occur.

While theses insights are important to consider when dealing with effervescence, it was one particular observation of common anthropological
representations of death that significantly inspired my argument. It was
an achievement of anthropology to point out that death in most societies
is conceived of as a process rather than a moment; in doing so, however,
the possibilities for analysis were impoverished. It is misleading to state
that people in non-Western societies experience death as a process, while
we in the West understand it as an event. Both dimensions are present in
general—even though to different degrees and in different forms—and
anthropologists should study the dynamic relationship and cultural elaborations of death as event and process in each and every case. No matter
how much death as event is culturally denied, it is always considered as a
possibility. Sahlins's insights and Sewell's additions help to conceptualize
the relationship between event and structure (ritual process). To take both
dimensions into consideration is also important, since effervescence in the
context of evenemential death and processual death takes different forms.

In my discussion of effervescence—the generative emotional arousal
as a result of jointly enacted practices—I started out with a summary of
Durkheim's view and highlighted aspects I considered crucial. First, as
William Pickering had already emphasized, with this concept Durkheim
tried to tackle the problem of social and cultural creativity, and the

question of how new social relations and collective ideas originate. Second, I stressed that the results are diverse, as indicated above, including social, cultural, political, and other dimensions. Third, I argued that the outcomes of effervescence are unpredictable. In contrast to often-voiced opinions, effervescence neither necessarily produces intellectual uniformity (that is, shared ideas, since it also does not generate homogenously experienced emotions), nor social integration (cohesion). The forces generated can result in all kinds of effects. Finally, effervescence in the context of death is particularly powerful, because it is especially charged emotionally.

I continued my argument by critically engaging with contributions by the few scholars who have been concerned with effervescence, especially the work of Tim Olaveson and William Pickering. While the former pointed out important similarities between communitas and effervescence, the latter clearly elaborated on the distinction between creative and re-creative effervescence, which was only implicit in Durkheim's writings. On the basis of their contributions, I discussed the relationship between effervescence, liminality, and communitas, pointing out similarities as well as differences between these concepts. Effervescence, I argued, is far from being always a case of antistructure, and certainly—the outcomes being unpredictable—does not always entail communitas. No doubt only in a cursory way, I then suggested that effervescence, liminality, and communitas can usefully be considered as related and partly overlapping analytical concepts, with some (like communitas) being mostly located on the side of antistructure, while others (like liminality and effervescence) being more on the side of structure.

As a development of Pickering's insights, I went on to argue that three forms of effervescence could be distinguished: systemic, negative, and evenemential effervescence. These three dimensions do not imply a process of routinization—from an original creative effervescent assembly to re-creative and commemorative effervescent occasions—but should rather be regarded as three modes that may relate to each other or even co-occur in a number of different ways. I first discussed these forms in the context of ritual systems and, in a second step, separately as part of political processes and systems.

Ritual systems integrate effervescence in many different ways and, in that sense, can also be said to reproduce key categories and relationships in a community. In many instances, however, effervescence is ritually avoided, and all forms of collective emotional excitement are stifled. While either one—or a combination of the two—may be elaborated ritually, the most unpopular version, from a ritual point of view that stresses control, evenemential effervescence may at any time manifest itself. It is this mode of effervescence that is most productive of the new. Social relationships may be questioned, authorities overthrown, peripheral ideas may become moral ideals, attention may be focused on the unexpected; ideas are "burdened with the world" (Sahlins 1985: 149) and become transfigured. While effervescence in connection to death and domesticated by ritual is probably for the most part conservative, the potential for change is always present.

While effervescence may lead to change in the context of ritual systems, actors in the context of large-scale political change also make use of death effervescence. As such, I argued that it is worthwhile to look separately at the modes of effervescence as part of political systems and processes. Dead-body politics as described by Verdery provides important examples. Because of the characteristics of effervescence in connection to death described above, such occasions may be powerful instruments to mobilize bias and make people internalize ideas, but they might likewise threaten the order that tries to control effervescence. Again, the results are unpredictable. In this way, death-related effervescence may be systemic to political orders, which elaborate it in some contexts while avoiding effervescent assemblies in others. As in ritual contexts, no matter how much control over death is desired, evenemential effervescence is a real possibility.

In this contribution, I have been concerned with the discussion of the concept of effervescence and aimed at developing it further. I have not engaged in the question of what kind of conditions may induce particular elaborations of negative or systemic effervescence, in particular with reference to ritual systems. Such questions, however difficult they may be to answer, can be nevertheless instructive. Obviously the elaboration or restriction of ritual effervescence depends on many factors. Mary Douglas ([1970] 1996: 78f) contrasted effervescence to "ritualism" in her group and grid scheme, which distinguishes different societal models on the basis of the degree to which they provide integrated and obligatory systems of classifications (grid) and exercise a high or low degree of control over its members (group), with "effervescent form[s] of religion" (88) being low on group and grid. While I do not think that her perspective on effervescence is particularly convincing—partly because she, in my view, wrongly equates effervescence with antistructure—her connection between the two bodies, the physical and the social, is certainly worthy of more reflection. Other avenues for thinking about effervescence may consider the way in which different historicities (performative or prescriptive) engage differently with effervescence (see Sahlins 1985), or how particular types of religion (soteriological, social, or instrumental; see Gellner 1999) elaborate or negate forms of effervescence. Finally, Richard Wolf (2003) pointed towards historical patterns in the ritual elaboration of emotions that are relevant here as well. He argued, with respect to the ritual emotional contours of Indian "tribal" and Muslim communities, that the historical impact of different reform movements has led to a decrease in "affective diversity" (95); a certain "class of behavior" (104)—such as ritual excitement, frenzy, passion, dancing, competitive buffalo-sacrifices, etc., all of which I would identify as aspects that may be related to systemic effervescence—has become inappropriate in terms of proper ritual expression, in connection to Christian or high-caste Hindu ideas. Such probably widespread historical developments also point to the colonial impact on the elaboration of systemic effervescence in local ritual systems. As colonial representations often defined the "primitive" in connection with exactly such allegedly wasteful, violent, and horrific practices, reform movements distanced themselves from them in order to not be so classified. On the other hand, scholars of religion and culture studying so-called primitive peoples have been particularly attracted by practices such as sacrifice or headhunting. Hence, reflecting on effervescence also involves the history of colonialism as well as a consideration of the conditions involved in the production of scientific knowledge.

This contribution has been exploratory in nature. It was based on the premise that effervescence, too, is a "vague but suggestive concept" (Gofman 1998) that deserves further theoretical interest and elaboration. This is the case, I think, especially because effervescence is crucially related to two fundamental problems of social life—namely, the problem of how social formations and religious systems may be perpetuated and continued, and, contrarily, how they may be changed and transformed. These problems are particularly evident in the face of ultimate ambiguities.

**Peter Berger** (PhD Berlin 2004) is associate professor of Indian religions and the anthropology of religion at the Faculty of Theology and Religious Studies of the University of Groningen. He was a visiting professor at the University of Zürich in 2012 and a visiting fellow at the Centre for Advanced Studies at the University of Munich in 2015. His books include *Feeding, Sharing and Devouring: Ritual and Society in Highland Odisha* (de Gruyter 2015), and he coedited *The Modern Anthropology of India* (Routledge 2013), *The Anthropology of Values* (Pearson 2010), and *Fieldwork: Social Realities in Anthropological Perspective* (Weissensee 2009).

# Notes

1.  I want to thank Bill Pickering and especially one of the anonymous reviewers for comments on an early and very different version of this chapter. Marjo Buitelaar, Justin Kroesen, and, in particular, Richard Wolf provided valuable comments on the near final version. All shortcomings are, of course, my own responsibility.
2.  Bruce Kapferer (1979: 153) has stated the same (in contrast to Durkheim, as he says) in his analysis of Sinhalese healing rituals: "When individuals or groups express anger, fear, love, sorrow, hate, and happiness in the cultural medium of ritual, they often actually feel what they express." And (154): "Performance both expresses and creates what it represents."
3.  I do not deal with Reddy's sophisticated theory here in detail. His early ideas (1997) are developed and elaborated in his book (2001; see also Plamper 2010).
4.  Let it also be noted that none of the authors mentioned — Leavitt, Reddy, Wolf, or Beatty — refers in any way to Durkheim's arguments concerning effervescence, even though his ideas touch upon many of the aspects summarized here.
5.  "In our own society," Robert Hertz writes ([1907] 1960: 28), "the generally accepted opinion is that death occurs in one instant. . . . But the facts from many societies less advanced than our own [*sic*] do not fit into this framework."
6.  In particular, Sewell's (2005) stress on a multiplicity of structures (ch. 7) and the diachronic dimension of events (ch. 8) are worth mentioning, the latter aspect of which is also present in Sahlins's writings.
7.  A similar perspective was articulated by Peacock (1981: 1001), who contrasts the "classical Durkheimian view that sees ritual as sustaining stability and solidarity in an order which is eternally stable and solidary."
8.  The discussion is not intended to be comprehensive. For a more elaborate discussion, see in particular Pickering 1984 and Olaveson 2001. A more narrow and, in my view, not satisfactory rendition of Durkheim's ideas are found in Buehler 2012 and Throop and Laughlin 2002.
9.  Sebastian Schüler (2012) stresses the aspect of synchronization in ritual behavior (especially bodily movements) in this context and also discusses contributions from neurobiological approaches that are not the focus of this contribution.
10. Even though Baumann's contribution is valuable, since he questions the common assumptions about rituals creating solidarity and value-consensus, there is also a tension running through his article. On the one hand, he claims to "unearth Durkheim's theory from the rubble of assumptions" (1992: 114) and misinterpretations, while, on the other hand, he is ascribing the same clichés to Durkheim's work (e.g., essentialism) and speaks of the classical Durkheimian view, etc.
11. Lukes here uses the term of E.E. Schattenschneider (1960: 71).
12. Turner (1974: 274) comes close to it, when he mentions Durkheim's expression of "serious life" in connection to communitas.
13. I have left out the third form, "ideological communitas," from the discussion. It refers to social ideals or utopias of communitas (Turner 1969: 132).
14. Obviously, I am simplifying the complexity of the ritual processes here (and in the other cases that follow). As Pfeffer (2001) has also described, different social categories display different forms of standardized behavior.
15. I have seen the same scene in the context of a wedding, in which it was more elaborate, first fiercer and then more boisterous dancing, in which distinctions between affines and agnates seems to temporarily disappear. This moment could have been described as an instance of (normative) communitas (Berger 2011).

16. With regard to Central India, see the work of Alfred Gell (1980), who regards states of vertigo as an essential part of Muria religion, and Lidia Guzy (e.g., Guzy 2007), who considers ecstasy to be a traditional value in highland South Odisha.

17. Surely, this ideal is not always realized in practice, and a particularly "good" death may be celebrated joyously. Moreover, while men demonstrate their emotional control, grieving is women's work (Parry 1994).

18. This is also confirmed by my personal experience of the course of death rituals among Arthavaveda Brahmans of the Odisha/Jharkhand border area. My friend and colleague Arlo Griffiths and I arrived in the household (in a village with many Arthavaveda households) three days after the old female household head had died in 2006. While I thus cannot say anything about the day of cremation and the time immediately afterwards, the events in the week that followed were highly controlled and restrained in terms of emotional expression (e.g., eating regulations; removal of the house deity; the liminal status of the elder son of the deceased and chief mourner, who did not shave and who always sat on the floor, and who was not allowed to be touched, etc.; more than twenty male Brahmans visiting the household to be served sweets and paid for the service of eating [with *dokino*]), and all without a trace of any effervescent moments.

19. Significantly, in this article he relates Durkheim's notion of effervescence to Weber's concept of charisma.

20. To be sure, Lukes would regard this as a superficial analysis as well, and his criticisms already outlined previously apply here too. Surely, the processes—also the case of the Mothers of the Plaza de Mayo that is described below—are more diverse and complex.

21. A similar transformation had occurred earlier in U.S. history, at the end of the Civil War, with Abraham Lincoln. As Barry Schwartz (1991: 343) shows, it was the funeral practices following the assassination of Abraham Lincoln in 1865 that transformed him "from a controversial president into a sacred emblem of his society." For two weeks, Lincoln's body was taken on a funeral journey from Washington, DC, to his hometown, Springfield, Illinois, with hundreds of thousands coming to pay him their respects during the many stops. The efficacy of death rituals, as described by Durkheim, can be clearly grasped by citing contemporary reactions: "The assassin's bullet that was aimed at [Lincoln] was aimed at the authority, the honor and the life of the nation, and against the authority and majesty of God" (Barr 1865, in Schwartz 1991: 355). The increased social vitality mentioned by Durkheim as a consequence of collective mourning was also clearly formulated after the assassination: "Never was the government so strong— never was our country so secure" (Howlett 1865, in Schwartz 1991: 355).

22. This process of the shifting of focus in effervescent assemblies, leading to new outcomes, resembles in significant ways the model of radical change Joel Robbins (2010) puts forward on the basis of the work of the philosopher Alain Badiou. Every context ("situation") contains countless elements that exist but that are relatively insignificant, and not within the focus of attention. They lead a kind of latent life; they are "present . . . but not represented" (Robbins 2010: 639). The myriad dormant elements that are contained in every situation are the reservoir for potential change. The irruption of an event triggers the process in which previously unrepresented aspects become represented; they mount the stage, so to speak. The subjects involved in the event connect old and newly represented elements in novel ways in a process Badiou calls "forcing," which actually leads to the transformation of the situation.

# References

Baumann, Gerd. 1992. "Ritual Implicates 'Others': Rereading Durkheim in
    a Plural Society." In *Understanding Rituals*, ed. Daniel de Coppet, 97–116.
    London: Routledge.
Beatty, Andrew. 2013. "Current Emotion Research in Anthropology: Reporting
    the Field." *Emotion Review* 5, no. 4: 414–22.
Berger, Peter. 2000. "Von Häusern und Gräbern: Die Bestattungsrituale der Toraja
    auf Sulawesi, Indonesien." In *Die lange Reise der Toten. Zwei Studien zu Ideologie
    und Praxis des Todes in Süd- und Südostasien*, ed. P. Berger and R. Kottmann,
    1–162. Hamburg: Kovac.
————. 2010a. "Assessing the Relevance and Effects of 'Key Emotional Episodes'
    for the Fieldwork Process." In *Anthropological Fieldwork: A Relational Process*,
    ed. Dimitrina Spencer and James Davies, 119–43. Newcastle upon Tyne:
    Cambridge Scholars Publishing.
————. 2010b. "'Who Are You, Brother and Sister?' The Theme of 'Own' and
    'Other' in the *Go'ter* Ritual of the Gadaba." In *The Anthropology of Values: Essays
    in Honour of Georg Pfeffer*, ed. Peter Berger, Roland Hardenberg, Ellen Kattner,
    and Michael Prager, 260–87. New Delhi: Pearson Education.
————. 2011. "Feeding Gods, Feeding Guests: Sacrifice and Hospitality among
    the Gadaba of Highland Orissa (India)." *Anthropos* 106, no. 1: 31–47.
————.2015. *Feeding, Sharing, and Devouring: Ritual and Society in Highland Odisha,
    India*. Boston: De Gruyter.
Bloch, Maurice. 1988. "Introduction: Death and the Concept of the Person." In *On
    the Meaning of Death: Essays on Mortuary Rituals and Eschatological Beliefs*, ed.
    Sven Cederroth, Claes Corlin, and Jan Lindström, 11–29. Stockholm: Almquist
    & Wiksell International.
Bloch, Maurice, and Jonathan Parry. 1982. "Introduction: Death and the
    Regeneration of Life." In *Death and the Regeneration of Life*, ed. Maurice Bloch
    and Jonathan Parry, 1–44. Cambridge: Cambridge University Press.
Bosco, Fernando J. 2006. "The Madres de Plaza de Mayo and Three Decades of
    Human Rights' Activism: Embeddedness, Emotions, and Social Movements."
    *Annals of the Association of American Geographers* 96, no. 2: 342–65.
Briggs, Jean L. 1970. *Never in Anger: Portrait of an Eskimo Family*. Cambridge:
    Harvard University Press.
Buehler, Arthur. 2012. "The Twenty-first-century Study of Collective
    Effervescence: Expanding the Context of Fieldwork." *Fieldwork in Religion* 7,
    no. 1: 70–97.
Crystal, Eric. 1985. "The Soul That Is Seen: The Tau Tau as Shadow of Death.
    Reflection of Life in Toraja Tradition." In *The Eloquent Dead: Ancestral Sculpture
    of Indonesia and Southeast Asia*, ed. Jerome Feldman, 129–46. Los Angeles:
    University of California.
Crystal, Eric, and S. Yamashita. 1987. "Power of Gods: Ma'bugi' Ritual of the
    Sa'dan Toraja." In *Indonesian Religions in Transition*, ed. Rita S. Kipp and Susan
    Rodgers, 48–70. Tucson: University of Arizona Press.
Douglas, Mary. (1970) 1996. *Natural Symbols: Explorations in Cosmology*. London:
    Routledge.

Durkheim, Emile. 1974. *Sociology and Philosophy*. New York: Free Press.

———. (1912, in French) 1995. *The Elementary Forms of Religious Life,* trans. Karen E. Fields. New York: Free Press.

Engelke, Matthew. 2002. "The Problem of Belief: Evans-Pritchard and Victor Turner on 'The Inner Life.'" *Anthropology Today* 18, no. 6: 3–8.

Evans-Pritchard, Edward E. 1965. *Theories of Primitive Religion*. Oxford: Clarendon Press.

Gell, Alfred. 1980. "The Gods at Play: Vertigo and Possession in Muria Religion." *Man* 15, no. 2: 219–48.

Geertz, C. 1973 *The Interpretation of Cultures: Selected Essays* New York: Basic Books.

Gellner, David N. 1999. "Religion, Politics, and Ritual. Remarks on Geertz and Bloch." *Social Anthropology* 7, no. 2: 135–53.

Gofman, Alexander. 1998. "A Vague but Suggestive Concept: The 'Total Social Fact.'" In *Marcel Mauss: A Centenary Tribute*, ed. Wendy James and Nicholas J. Allen, 63–70. New York: Berghahn Books.

Guzy, Lidia. 2007. "'Negative Ecstasy or the Singers of the Divine': Voices from the Periphery of Mahima Dharma." In *Periphery and Centre: Studies in Orissan History, Religion and Anthropology*, ed. G. Pfeffer, 105–30. New Delhi: Manohar.

Harris, Marvin. 1985. *Good to Eat: Riddles of Food and Culture*. New York: Simon & Schuster.

Hertz, Robert. (1907) 1960. *Death and the Right Hand*. Aberdeen: Cohen & West.

Hollan, Douglas. 1988. "Staying 'Cool' in Toraja: Informal Strategies for the Management of Anger and Hostility in a Non-Violent Society." *Ethos* 16, no. 1: 52–72.

Huntington, Richard, and Peter Metcalf. 1979. *Celebrations of Death: The Anthropology of Mortuary Ritual*. Cambridge: Cambridge University Press.

Izikowitz, Karl G. 1969. "The Gotr Ceremony of the Boro Gadaba." In *Primitive Views of the World*, ed. Stanley Diamond, 129–50. New York: Columbia University Press.

Jasper, James M. 1998. "The Emotions of Protest: Affective and Reactive Emotions in and around Social Movements." *Sociological Forum* 13, no. 3: 397–424.

Kapferer, Bruce. 1979. "Emotion and Feeling in Sinhalese Healing Rites." *Social Analysis* 1: 153–76.

———. 2008. "Beyond Symbolic Representation: Victor Turner and Variations on the Themes of Ritual Process and Liminality." *Journal of the Finnish Anthropological Society* 33, no. 4: 5–25.

Leavitt, John. 1996. "Meaning and Feeling in the Anthropology of Emotions." *American Ethnologist* 23, no. 3: 514–39.

Lukes, Steven. 1975. "Political Ritual and Social Integration." *Sociology* 9: 289–308.

Malinowski, Bronislaw. (1948) 1974. "Magic, Science and Religion." In *Magic, Science and Religion and Other Essays,* 17–92. London: Souvenir Press.

Mauss, Marcel, and Henri Beuchat. 1979. *Seasonal Variations of the Eskimo: A Study in Social Morphology*. London: Routledge.

Mitchell, Jon P. 2004. "Ritual Structure and Ritual Agency: 'Rebounding Violence' and Maltese *Festa*." *Social Anthropology* 12, no. 1: 57–75.

Morris, Brian. 1987. *Anthropological Studies of Religion: An Introductory Text*. Cambridge. Cambridge University Press.

Olaveson, Tim. 2001. "Collective Effervescence and Communitas: Processual Models of Ritual and Society in Emile Durkheim and Victor Turner." *Dialectical Anthropology* 26: 89–124.

Parry, Jonathan P. 1994. *Death in Banaras*. Cambridge: Cambridge University Press.

Peacock, James L. 1981. "Durkheim and the Social Anthropology of Culture." *Social Forces* 59, no. 4: 996–1008.

Pickering, William S.F. 1984. *Durkheim's Sociology of Religion: Themes and Theories*. London: Routledge & Kegan Paul.

Pfeffer, Georg. 2001. "A Ritual of Revival among the Gadaba of Koraput." In *Jagannath Revisited: Studying Society, Religion and the State in Orissa*, ed. Hermann Kulke and Burkhard Schnepel, 99–123. New Delhi: Manohar.

Plamper, Jan. 2010. "The History of Emotions: An Interview with William Reddy, Barbara Rosenwein, and Peter Stearns." *History and Theory* 49, no. 2: 237–65.

Radcliffe-Brown, Alfred R. 1948. *The Andaman Islanders*. Glencoe: Free Press.

———. 1952. *Structure and Function in Primitive Society*. Glencoe: Free Press.

Rawls, Anne W.1996. "Durkheim's Epistemology: The Neglected Argument." *American Journal of Sociology* 102, no. 2: 430–82.

Reddy, William M. 1997. "Against Constructionism: The Historical Ethnography of Emotions." *Current Anthropology* 38, no. 3: 327–51.

———. 2001. *The Navigation of Feeling: A Framework for the History of Emotions*. Cambridge: Cambridge University Press.

Rév, Istvan. 1995. "Parallel Autopsies." *Representations* 49: 15–39.

Robbins, Joel. 2010. "Anthropology, Pentecostalism, and the New Paul: Conversion, Event, and Social Transformation." *South Atlantic Quarterly* 109, no. 4: 633–52.

Rosaldo, Renato. 1984. "Grief and a Headhunter's Rage: On the Cultural Force of Emotions." In *Text, Play, and Story: The Construction and Reconstruction of Self and Society*, ed. Edward M. Bruner, 178–95. Washington, DC: American Ethnological Society.

Sahlins, Marshall D. 1978. "Culture as Protein and Profit." *New York Review of Books* 25, no. 18: 45–53.

———. 1985. *Islands of History*. Chicago: University of Chicago Press.

———. 2000. "The Return of the Event, Again." In *Culture in Practice: Selected Essays*, Marshall D. Sahlins, 293–351. New York: Zone Books.

Schattenschneider, E.E. 1960. *The Semi-Sovereign People*. New York: Holt, Rinehart and Winston.

Schüler, Sebastian. 2012. "Synchronized Ritual Behavior: Religion, Cognition and the Dynamics of Embodiment." In *The Body and Religion: Modern Science and the Construction of Religious Meaning*, ed. David Cave and Rebecca Sachs Norris, 81–101. Leiden: Brill.

Schwartz, Barry. 1991. "Mourning and the Making of a Sacred Symbol: Durkheim and the Lincoln Assassination." *Social Forces* 70, no. 2: 343–64.

Sewell, William H. 2005. *Logics of History: Social Theory and Social Transformation*. Chicago: University of Chicago Press.

Tiryakian, Edward A. 1995. "Collective Effervescence, Social Change and Charisma: Durkheim, Weber and 1989." *International Sociology* 10, no. 3: 269–81.

————. 2005. "Durkheim, Solidarity, and September 11." In *The Cambridge Companion to Durkheim,* ed. Jeffrey C. Alexander and Philip Smith, 305–21. Cambridge: Cambridge University Press.

Throop, C. Jason, and Charles C.D. Laughlin. 2002. "Ritual, Collective Effervescence and the Categories: Toward a Neo-Durkheimian Model of the Nature of Human Consciousness, Feeling and Understanding." *Journal of Ritual Studies* 16, no. 1: 40–63.

Turner, Victor W. 1967. "Betwixt and Between: The Liminal Period in *Rites de Passage.*" In *The Forest of Symbols,* 93–111. Ithaca: Cornell University Press.

————. 1969. *The Ritual Process: Structure and Anti-Structure.* Chicago: Aldine.

————. 1974. *Dramas, Fields and Metaphors: Symbolic Action in Human Society.* Ithaca: Cornell University Press.

————. 1982. *From Ritual to Theatre: The Human Seriousness of Play.* New York: PAJ.

van Gennep, Arnold. (1909, in French) 1960. *The Rites of Passage,* trans. Monika B. Vizedon and Gabrielle L. Caffee. Chicago: University of Chicago Press.

Verdery, Katherine. 1999. *The Political Lives of Dead Bodies: Reburial and Postsocialist Change.* New York: Columbia University Press.

Vitebsky, Piers. 1993. *Dialogues with the Dead: The Discussion of Mortality among the Sora of Eastern India.* Cambridge: Cambridge University Press.

Weiss, Raquel. 2012. "From Ideas to Ideal: Effervescence as the Key to Understanding Morality." *Durkheimian Studies* 18: 81–97.

Wolf, Richard K. 2001. "Emotional Dimensions of Ritual Music among the Kotas, a South Indian Tribe." *Ethnomusicology* 45, no. 3: 379–422.

————. 2003. "Return to Tears: Musical Mourning, Emotion, and Religious Reform in Two South Asian Minority Communities." In *The Living and the Dead: Social Dimensions of Death in South Asian Religions,* ed. Liz Wilson, 95–112. Albany: SUNY Press.

*Part III*

# Imageries

***Figure 8.1.*** A Hindu priest (right) performs the Shraddha ceremony on the banks of Nepal's holy river Bagmati, which flows past the National Hindu shrine Pashupatinath, dedicated to the local manifestation of the god Shiva. The rice/flour balls (*pinda*) represent the ancestral generations of the *yajamana*, i.e. the person commissioning the ceremony (left) (photo Nina Mirnig).

*Chapter Eight*

# Hungry Ghost or Divine Soul?
## Postmortem Initiation in Medieval Shaiva Tantric Death Rites

*Nina Mirnig[1]*

The study of rituals of premodern India faces the general predicament that there is an array of prescriptive texts that tell us how the rituals are supposed to look, but little descriptive material that allows us to reconstruct the reality of their practice, thus leaving crucial questions unanswered, such as how often, by how many, by whom, and for what reason a rite was performed. Therefore, analyses are necessarily often limited to either examining the ritual structure for its own sake or taking recourse to a more meaningful interpretation of the rites by means of substantiating the analysis with the theological notions that are supposed to be enacted in the rituals according to exegetical literature. Such approaches are also commonly applied to the surviving textual materials on premodern death rites, since little material evidence or descriptive literature has survived (Hinüber 1992: 36). In order to uncover aspects of the socioreligious context largely hidden from us in the prescriptive literature, a different conceptual lens can help to formulate significant questions about the text which have remained unasked. For this volume, centered on the notion of the liminal in the context of death rites, I will attempt to pose questions arising from the concept of liminality to the surviving premodern textual materials on tantric funeral rituals of the Shaiva religion, an Indian religious tradition emerging in the early medieval period (starting from ca. the 5th century c.e.), centered around the worship of the Hindu god Shiva as the highest deity and constituting the essence of everything contained in the universe.

Notes for this chapter begin on page 202.

Tantric ritual practices are characterized by accompanying meditative visualizations used to identify oneself with the deity while worshipping it at the same time (Davis 1991). Grounded in this ritual language of self-identification with the supreme god, the surviving medieval textual materials for Shaiva funerary rites prescribe a ritual cycle that is permeated with paradoxical notions of the ontological status of the deceased's soul. The material suggests that it is simultaneously regarded as a liberated entity that has lost its individuality and realized its godhood, as well as a spirit that has to be separated from the corpse and subsequently enters a state of ghosthood in which it needs to be fed by the living and is ritually transformed into an ancestor. The latter view carries on ancient conceptions of afterlife generated in the Vedic period (ca. 1500–500 B.C.E.), which remain manifest in Hindu death rites today.

As we will see, such doctrinal inconsistencies arise from the Shaiva initiation practice, which challenges the notion of the liminal period as defined by van Gennep in his cross-cultural model of *Rites de Passage* ([1909] 1960) since the practitioners receive their initiation ritual, which bestows ultimate godhood, twice, once during their lifetime and once after their death. Thus, moments marking the beginning, middle, and end of the transformative processes overlap and are further convoluted with Vedic beliefs of ghosthood during death rites. In turning our attention to the community of mourners, however, Turner's (1991) further theorization of liminality and "communitas" draws our attention to the essential feature of antistructure as it emerges during the liminal period caused by critical life crises. In the analysis of Shaiva funerary rites, this allows us to bring into focus the communal context, where we find antistructure associated with Hindu social rules of impurity, and therewith make sense of the organizational scheme of the rituals.

In the first part of the chapter, I will give a short overview of the core elements of Shaiva soteriology, followed by a descriptive account of tantric funeral rites according to the Shaiva Siddhanta (i.e., the earliest tantric Shaiva school of which we have material on funerary rites) and of their Brahmanical precursors, highlighting the doctrinal inconsistencies that are generated about the status of the deceased from a theological point of view. The second part of the chapter will explore aspects of liminality in the context of these premodern textual sources on Shaiva funerals, with an aim to reveal some of the socioreligious dynamics underlying the performance of the ritual.

## Early Tantric Shaivism and the Doctrine of Liberation

In the early medieval period, the Shaiva religion rose to become a major player in the religiopolitical landscape of India and Indianized South-East Asia, reaching as far as Cambodia and Indonesia (Sanderson 2011).[2] It is this tradition that was instrumental in the formation of tantric ritual and philosophy, which were to impact most religious traditions throughout Asia. The core doctrine of the Shaiva Siddhanta tradition professes that, by his grace, Shiva grants liberation to an individual[3] through the ritual of initiation (*diksha*) (Davis 1991, Sanderson 1995). Liberation, in this system, means to realize one's true identity as being equal to Shiva[4] and not confined by worldly bonds. During the initiation ritual, Shiva is believed to act through the Shaiva officiant, who, through the power of potent syllables and sounds—collectively referred to as mantras—destroys in the ritual fire all the karmic fetters that would keep the candidate's soul bound to the cycle of rebirth (*samsara*). The only fetter that is not destroyed is that which already determines the candidate's current life (*prarabdha karma*), and thus the initiate continues to live to the end of his present existence, at which point liberation manifests itself, the soul realizing its true divine identity at the time of death. Thus, the *Kiranatantra* (6.20–21a), one of the pre-ninth-century Shaiva scriptures—that is to say, works that are believed to have been revealed by Shiva himself and constitute the authoritative body of religious scriptures—teaches the following: "The action of many existences has its seeds burnt, so to speak, by mantras [in initiation]. Future [action] too is blocked; [but] that by which this body is sustained can be destroyed only by experience. [Only] when the body collapses (*dehapate*), [does the soul attain] liberation" (Edition and translation Goodall 1998: 152-53 and 383–84). In order to gradually reduce this experience or *karma* that has been left intact, the initiate is required to follow certain postinitiatory rules (*samaya*), such as performing daily Shaiva worship, which will gradually consume all the *karma* until none is left by the end of the individual's present existence. Once this is achieved, liberation manifests itself at the time of death and the transition of the soul to its final destination is considered completed.

## Shaiva Death Rites: Upgrading Existing Practices

Shaivism's success in attaining a dominant position in medieval India is partly visible through the influence the tantric ritual repertoire exerted on the practices of the Brahmanical mainstream, as well as on those of religious competitors such as Buddhism (Sanderson 2009). But the Shaiva ritual specialists also took inspiration from and strategically designed their ritual repertoire in such a way as to conform to the Brahmanical mainstream, their main clientele. Thus, even though Shaiva tantric rites are mostly concerned with matters of Shaiva doctrine and soteriology, much of their ritual repertoire can be analyzed as adoptions and modifications of existing Brahmanical rituals (Sanderson 1995: 27 and 2009: 301–3). It is in this ritual sphere that notions of Shaiva soteriology meet with deeply embedded values of Brahmanical or Hindu society, a phenomenon most poignantly manifesting in the sphere of rituals that deal with death. The standard sequence of the Hindu funerary ritual, which constituted the structural basis for Shaiva funerals, is arranged around rites to separate the individual soul or life force from its physical body, rites to ritually process the corpse by cremation, ritual food offerings for the deceased to build a new body, and rites to integrate the deceased into the world of ancestors. Thus, the fundamental paradox that the Shaiva ritual specialists and theologians faced when legitimating their own set of funerary rites was that the claim that the soul is liberated at the time of death should theoretically render any postmortuary rites superfluous, given that their function in the original Brahmanical setting is to appease and guard the soul through the various postmortem stages, none of which should be applicable to the liberated soul.

In order to illustrate this, we shall trace the soul's path as enacted by the Brahmanical sequence of funerary rites.[5] At first, the locus of the soul is more closely associated with the corpse, from which it is released only during its incineration on the funeral pyre lit by the chief mourner. Up to this point, the rites evolve largely around the preparation of the corpse and the funeral procession. Any offerings made along the way are not addressed to the deceased but are rather measures to appease demons and other ill-favored creatures that are believed to be present at such an inauspicious time of transition from the living to the dead. Only when the corpse is burning up—and sometimes, more specifically, in the moment when the skull bursts (or is crushed by the chief mourner)—is the life force believed to leave the corpse and become a kind of ghost or *preta*, literally "someone who has gone." This moment is also the point at which death impurity is believed to affect those left behind. The common belief is that during this time, the ghost lingers about the cremation ground and gradually builds up a body through the offerings of rice balls and water made by the living. Thus, the individual turns into a dangerous disembodied entity that needs to be appeased and fed and has not yet reached the peaceful plane of ancestors. After some days, ritual offerings are made in honor of the deceased (*ekoddishta shraddha*) and finally the

Sapindikarana is performed, which is the procedure through which the deceased's soul is incorporated into the ancestral line. From this point onwards, the deceased is worshipped consecutively as one of the three ancestral generations, namely the father (*pitr*), grandfather (*pitamaha*), and great-grandfather (*prapitamaha*), and eventually as part of the group of undifferentiated ancestral deities (*vishvedevas*). He ascends along this hierarchy whenever the next person in line has died.

When the Shaiva ritual specialists developed their own funerary rituals, it was the basic structure, timing and socioreligious function of this cycle of rites that was adapted by them, despite the fact that they are based on a belief system which presupposes that the deceased's soul retains his individual identity and takes up his place in the ancestral heavens. Their strategy in transforming the Brahmanical cycle of funerary rites was twofold: Vedic mantras, deities, and substances offered during worship were substituted by their Shaiva equivalents (Sanderson 1995), and a funerary initiation of the deceased's soul inserted, which upgraded the ritual into a powerful rite of liberation (Davis 1988; Mirnig 2010; Sanderson 1995: 31–33). This funerary initiation was inserted before the incineration of the corpse and was essentially a compressed version of the initial initiation ritual performed during the individual's lifetime, thus climaxing in the union of the deceased's soul with its divine consciousness. Throughout this chapter, I shall refer to the initiation rite proper performed during the initiate's lifetime simply as "initiation," and to that performed during the funeral ceremonies as "funerary initiation."

The implications about the ontological state of the soul thus enacted through the funeral ceremonies are downright paradoxical, a fact best elucidated by a brief outline of the sequence of rites. I will proceed with such an account, based on the famous eleventh-century Saiddhantika ritual manual *Somashambhupaddhati*[6] (or *Kriyakandakramavali*), by Somashambhu, which greatly impacted many of the later manuals. The account will be supplemented with one of the manuals influenced by this work, namely the twelfth-century *Jnanaratnavali,* by the South Indian Jnanashiva.[7] Both manuals contain the basic structure as it was also propounded in other works prior and following.

## Shaiva Death Rites

The instructions of the *Somashambhupaddhati* start with the funeral procession to the cremation ground. There, the corpse is lifted on to a platform that was prepared for Shaiva worship. Next, the Shaiva officiant, the Acarya, transforms the corpse into a suitable receptacle for the Shaiva

ritual by installing the so-called mantra body on it—that is to say, transforming the different parts of the body with certain Shaiva mantras. For
this procedure, he employs practices based on visualizations and meditation. The initiand was prepared in a similar manner in the initiation ritual
during his lifetime, only that the actual locus of the ritual destruction of
the bonds took place not on the initiand himself but on a thread representing his body.

Next, the deceased's soul is captured by the officiant using an elaborate procedure called the Great Net method (*mahajalaprayoga*), in which
the Great Net mantra is employed to draw in the soul. These manipula-
tions of the soul are accompanied with ritual hand gestures called *mudras*,
which constitute an essential part of Shaiva ritual (Saraogi 2010). Here, the
Acarya fuses his hand with the end sound of the letter "Om" (the *nada*),
through which it is believed that the soul can be grasped.[8] Once he has prepared the trap, he visualizes the soul as a point of light wandering about
in accordance with its past actions (*karma*) and catches it with this net. He
then gets hold of the soul with a special *mudra* called the Joining Gesture
(*samyojanamudra*). Next, he uses the Gesture of the Hook (*ankusamudra*)
in order to pull the soul into his own heart, where he separates it from
the net, grasps it again, and leaves his body with it in order to cast the
deceased's soul on to the corpse.

In order to secure the soul's presence in the corpse, the guru places
Shiva's body of mantras on the corpse again, emplacing the appropriate
mantras on the respective body parts. After that, he installs all the levels
of the universe on it, thus all the possible spheres of existence into which
the soul could be reborn in accordance with its past actions. In the philosophical system employed in the *Somashambhupaddhati*, the universe is
conceived as divided into five parts (*kala*), which are installed on the head,
face, heart, navel, and the lower body respectively. This procedure of
installing the reality levels is also carried out in the initiation rite proper;
then, however, these segments are installed on a thread called the *pasha-
sutra*, which substitutes the initiand's body, equaling it in its length. After
this, further installations of mantras on the corpse take place, such as the
Circle of Shiva's Powers (*shakticakra*), as well as Shiva himself. The presence of the consciousness in the corpse is then sealed by the act of offering
a hundred oblations into the fire.

Now the destruction of all the soul's bonds can begin. For this, the
Acarya takes each of the segments of the universe (*kala*) and unites them
with the fire. He worships them and summons Shiva and the other deities that preside over the respective *kala,* and then ritually invokes and
performs all the actions and rites of passage that the soul would have

experienced on the respective cosmic level and eventually burns them in the consecrated Shiva fire. During the initiation rite that was performed in the individual's lifetime, the ritual destruction of these actions was achieved by burning the thread on which they had been installed earlier. As we have seen, here no thread was employed as the locus of all actions; instead it is the corpse itself, which is later on destroyed by burning it on the cremation pyre. Another difference to the initiation rite proper is that the Acarya not only destroys the soul's past and future actions, but also the present ones, therewith leaving nothing behind that would keep the soul bound to the cycle of rebirth.

After this total destruction of all the soul's bonds, the Acarya finally extracts the now purified soul and unites it with Shiva, therewith marking the moment of liberation. The procedure of burning the corpse in the cremation fire, which in the Brahmanical tradition serves for the ritual processing and the disposal of the sacrificer's body and implements he used during his lifetime, is rendered more meaningful and effective by completing the initiatory destruction of the soul's bonds in the consecrated Shiva-fire. The regular sequence of the cremation rite is continued and the corpse incinerated, while reciting a mantra that preserves the Brahmanical notion that the corpse is a sacred offering to the fire god Agni, while also stressing that it has just been purified by mantras and all the actions have been consumed: "Om, O Agni, you are the Southern One, you are Time, accept this great oblation of the corpse which is accomplished through time alone and has been purified by Mantras" (for Sanskrit text, see *Somashambhupaddhati*, Antyeshtiprakarana 33 in Brunner-Lachaux 1977:605).

After this point, the procedure, paradoxically, returns to the Brahmanical sequence of rites revolving around feeding the hungry ghost, purification, and observation of impurity restrictions by the affected mourners, such as the interruption of the study of the Veda. The continuation of the conventional rites at this point implies a return to the belief that the soul is still somehow lingering around and needs to be looked after by offerings of water and rice balls, regardless of the fact that its liberation had just been enacted—for a second time. Witness to such beliefs are statements such as the following in the twelfth-century Shaiva Siddhanta ritual manual of the South Indian Jnanashiva: "He should perform [this rite of offering postmortuary worship to the recently deceased] with the same procedure in the subsequent months, O Skanda. When a year is completed in this way and the thirteenth month has arrived, he should perform the ritual worship of the ancestors (*pitrshraddha*) for the deceased, in order to put an end to his being a ghost (*preta*)" (*Jnanaratnavali*, Shraddhaprakarana 79–80b; see Mirnig 2010: 284, 295).

Once the deceased's soul is believed to have ended its ghostlike existence, the whole sequence of postmortuary offerings to the recently deceased follows. We have seen that in their original Brahmanical context, these rites are addressed to the deceased father, grandfather, and great-grandfather, a notion that is insupportable in the light of Shaiva doctrine concerning the liberated soul. Thus, these rites were reinterpreted not as rites of worship to the ancestral line, but as acts of worship to Shiva manifestations. Hence, during the rite, which originally signifies the deceased's incorporation into the ancestral line (the Sapindikarana), the deceased's soul is instead incorporated and identified with a line of increasingly potent forms of Shiva, namely successively Isha, Sadashiva, and Shanta. In this way, the rites symbolize the soul's gradual ascent to ultimate Shivahood. This poses yet another doctrinal awkwardness that undermines the notion of ultimate liberation by introducing a concept of differentiated stages of liberation in which the deceased ascends depending on the lifespan of his descendants (Sanderson 1995: 34–36).

*Table 8.1.* Sequence of Brahmanical death rites and the Shaiva additions and conceptual modifications.

| Brahmanical Cycle of Funeral and Postmortuary Rituals | Shaiva Additions (+) and Conceptual Changes (→) |
| --- | --- |
| – Rites at the place of death | |
| – Funerary procession | |
| – Preparation of the cremation ground and the pyre | |
| | + Funerary initiations: |
| |     Preparation of the corpse for initiation |
| |     Capturing the deceased's soul |
| |     Fixing the consciousness in the corpse |
| |     Destruction of all the soul's bonds |
| |     Liberation of the deceased's soul |
| – Preparation of the corpse for incineration | |
| – Lighting of the funeral pyre | |
| – (Skull cracking and/or pot-breaking) | |
| – Funeral party leaves the cremation ground | |
| – Mourners' bath and water offerings to the deceased | |
| – Return home, rite of purification | |
| – Start of the series of postmortuary offerings to the deceased (Navashraddha and Ekoddishtashraddha) | |
| – Integration of the deceased into the ancestral line (Sapindikarana) | → Integration of the deceased into a line of increasingly potent Shiva manifestations |
| – Postmortuary food offerings to the group of ancestors (Shraddha) | → Postmortuary offerings to the group of increasingly potent Shiva manifestations |

## Funerary Initiation: Bridging Two Liminal Phases

From the account, we see that Shaiva funerary rites combine two functions: (1) the initiation of the deceased's soul and (2) the Brahmanical-
based ritual processing of the corpse which initiates the procedure of
ritually guiding the deceased to a postmortuary sphere that resembles
the Brahmanical ancestral heavens. This two-fold purpose poses diffi-
culties in detecting a clear structure of the rituals, especially in regard to
determining the beginning and end of the liminal period in relation to the
deceased as the ritual subject. On several occasions between the moment
of death and the incorporation into a stable environment during the rites
of Shraddha the soul could be considered as having transformed, reaching
the state of ultimate liberation: first, at the demise of the body (*dehapate*);
second, at the guru's enactment of liberation during the initiation before
cremation; and, third, in the period in which the soul gradually ascents to
Shivahood during the rites of postmortuary ancestor worship. At the same
time, the ritual gestures after cremation imply that the soul is believed
to remain a ghostlike entity that needs to be appeased and sustained by
feeding, a state certainly not befitting of a liberated soul. Thus, there are de
facto two transitional periods towards a single destination for the initiate:
one that ends with death and one that begins with death, both bridged by
the funerary initiation.

The former is itself structurally ambiguous. We have seen that the initiate has undergone an initiation during his lifetime, culminating in the
guru's ritual gesture, which symbolically leads the soul to realize its divine
state. However, after the rite, the initiate remains bound to his present
life until death in order to ritually work away the *karma* that is determining his current existence (*prarabdha karman*)—the unattractive alternative
being that he would die immediately after the initiation rite is completed.
Thus, though the fruit of the ritual—*moksha*—is already activated, the soul
remains bound to worldly life and enters a transitional period in which
the performance of postinitiatory rites gradually strip the individual of
residual bonds that obscure the soul's divine nature. As a consequence,
the event of death becomes an important moment in the transition from
the mundane to the divine, as was made explicit in the quotation of the
*Kiranatantra* earlier (6.20–21; for text and translation see Goodall 1998:
152–53 and 383–84). If we apply van Gennep's cross-cultural model of
transformative rites to the case of the liberating initiation ritual, we see
how the procedure is structurally flawed: of the tripartite framework consisting of rites of separation, transition, and reintegration during the initiation rite, it is the last stage that is potentially ambiguous. On the one
hand, the concluding rites of the initiation enact the individual's liberating

godly nature, and on the other hand, the transformation is only fully completed at the moment of death. As such, the end of this transitional period would be marked by an unpredictable natural event rather than an organized ritual, which would defy the ritual dynamics that van Gennep postulated underlie life-cycle rites. Thus, as far as van Gennep's first liminal phase is concerned, the funerary initiation, essentially a repetition of the initiation rite that was performed on the living person, can be seen as the ritual marking the completion of the transformative process.

That this remains nevertheless paradoxical is highlighted even from an emic point of view. If we turn to some Shaiva textual material, we find that theoretical expositions accounting for this funerary initiation are sparse, regardless of the fact that such a central claim as liberation is at stake. In order not to fundamentally undermine the efficaciousness of the original initiation rite, or to pass off the funerary initiation as a mere formality, some sources establish the notion that the rite acts as some sort of expiatory ritual (*prayashcitta*). The *locus classicus* for this is the *Sardhatrishatikalottara* 26.6c–8b (for Sanskrit text, see Bhatt 1979: 163): "The funerary ritual has been ordained, O Skanda, to remove the sin of anyone who transgresses the rules to be observed during the period after initiation, for [one who] is guilty of major sins against Shiva and the Gurus, those who have not lost their doubts [concerning their liberation at death through initiation], and for any others who have some impurity."

However, we do not find that this explanation is ever pressed too far. One reason for this could be that, from a doctrinal point of view, it would seem surprising that the religion's core ritual of bestowing liberation through initiation during lifetime can be threatened by comparatively trivial errors that can be taken care of by common expiatory rites, and that an individual that has already been initiated into such a sanctified state is capable of falling from his status. It appears to be these kinds of criticism that Nirmalamani, one Shaiva commentator, had in mind when he postulated that the stumbling blocks on the way to liberation concern only transgressions that the individual performed *without* being aware of them (for Sanskrit text, see Brunner 1977: 569–71):

> [The objection is] that the purification of all *karma*s is [supposed to be] achieved through [their ritual] experiencing and consummation etc. [which is accomplished by pouring offerings into the ritual fire at the time of] the Nirvanadiksha (i.e., the initiation ritual that bestows liberation). And the *karma*s that are already intact are destroyed through experiencing [them during this lifetime]. Every day some part of this impurity that comes about as a result of this [process] is destroyed through [the performance of postinitiatory] rites such as bathing, visualizations, worship, and oblations. [Any impurities that may result from] forbidden practices or impious conduct and which occur knowingly are

destroyed by the performance of expiatory rites. What, then, is the purpose of cremation? [This objection is] true. [But] cremation is performed for the purification of [impurities resulting from] forbidden practices and impious conduct that had been performed unknowingly.

This implies that there must also be initiates that are not in need of such ritual rectification. And, in fact, we do find that the option to perform the Shaiva cremation without initiation is given in the ritual manuals, in accordance with the deceased's spiritual state (Mirnig 2010). However, in this case, the ritual is reduced to its Brahmanical-inspired core structure again, which defies the claimed function of Shaiva funerary rites just postulated and leads us to the next question: what, then, is the purpose of cremation and postmortuary worship that take place during the second liminal phase, starting with the death of the individual?

In order to address this question, we may now shift the analytical focus from the deceased to the community of living mourners. Given that the last rite of passage, as it were, is classified as the last of the deceased individual, the community of mourners is rarely the subject of the analysis in the context of the liminal. However, already Hertz ([1907] 1960), in his seminal essay "A Contribution to the Study of the Collective Representation of Death," emphasizes the parallelism of the transformative processes that are undergone not only by the soul and corpse, but also by the mourners. Van Gennep ([1909] 2004: 213–14) further includes the case of the mourners within his theoretical framework of the *Rites de Passage* as a special group that collectively experiences a transitional phase, which is marked by a certain set of features the community shares during this period, such as wearing a special dress. Here too, he identifies rites of separation that mark the beginning of the liminal phase and rites of reintegration into society that mark its end, often defined by the moment the deceased is believed to be incorporated into the world of the dead (van Gennep [1909] 2004: 213). The community of living mourners thus join the deceased in being "situated between the world of the living and the world of the dead" (van Gennep [1909] 2004: 214). This results in an awkward analytical position of funeral rites, since the main ritual subject is no longer a living agent, which may explain why Turner does not engage with the sphere of death rites when developing his theory of communitas (Turner 1969), despite the fact that it is built on van Gennep's notion of the liminal during transitional rites. However, the defining features Turner (1995) identifies for this communitas are also applicable when analyzing the community of mourners, in which structures and norms are suspended in order to create space to accommodate changes in its organization during this liminal phase of the mourning period. In those terms, I argue that the

Brahmanical cycle of death rites can be analyzed as facilitating precisely such processes of restructuring, and thus conceive of the community of mourners as the communitas for the present analysis.

In the context of Hindu funerary rites, the nature of the communitas spirit finds expression in the concept of death impurity (*ashauca*), which affects all those related to the deceased person and creates a sense of community that separates itself from active society and follows certain rules that underline their social isolation and exclusion from regular activity, including ritual obligations. The length of this period for those closely related to the deceased is interlinked with the timing of the ritual cycle accompanying the visualized after-death journey of the deceased. Thus, impurity comes about at the moment in which the skull bursts during cremation and the soul is believed to exit its old shell, turning into a hungry disembodied ghost, and ends with the Sapindikarana ritual, during which the deceased's soul is transformed into an ancestor and ceases to be a ghost. From that point onwards, the community of mourners reemerges as a healed whole and takes up its social and ritual obligations in a newly organized form. Thus, this period of antistructure is arranged around the sequence of postmortuary offerings (*shraddha*). These, in turn, are deeply embedded in the socioreligious structure of Brahmanical society, dating back to the early Vedic period, ritually securing the patrilineal structures which regulate inheritance,[9] since it is the chief mourner who is defined as the person who will inherit the deceased's property (Olivelle 2009).[10]

The period in which the community of mourners may experience this sense of togetherness without the pressure of ordinary structures and norms is thus facilitated under the umbrella "impurity" (*ashauca*), dictated in length by the ritual structure of postmortuary offerings. As the propagators of Shaivism adopted this whole package accommodating communal needs, these rites came to account for what appears to us as the second liminal phase, in which we find the contradictory notion of the deceased as the hungry ghost still reflected in the implied beliefs that govern the rites after cremation, despite the fact that, technically, the individual has realized his otherworldly divine identity, a state diametrically opposed to ghosthood. However, this quandary does not end there: we have seen that the Brahmanical ritual ending this state of ghosthood was centered on transforming the deceased into an ancestor quite literally by merging the rice ball representing the deceased with those representing the ancestral generations. In the Shaiva case, the ritual gestures remained the same, but the transformation into an ancestor became the transformation into a Shiva manifestation, and the feeding of the ancestors turned into offerings for increasingly potent manifestations of Shiva instead of the three ancestral generations. In this way, a sense of traceable identity of the deceased and his ancestors was retained while bridged with the act of worshipping Shiva in his various forms.[11]

Despite these efforts to inflect this ritual cycle with the Shaiva ritual language of liberation and deification, the underlying paradoxes are too pronounced to be ignored by some authors of the prescriptive literature, where a certain sense of acknowledging pragmatism can be detected. Thus, Jnanashiva, the author of one of the major twelfth-century Shaiva Siddhanta ritual manuals, declares that the rituals performed in the period in which the deceased is treated as a ghost are to be carried out merely for the sake of conformity (*Shraddhaprakarana* 5c–6; see Mirnig 2010: 277, 288): "Up to the *sapindikarana* (i.e., the rite of incorporating the deceased into the ancestral line), the rites are taught to be Vaidika (i.e., according to the traditional Brahmanical ritual system) for the purpose of worldly interaction. After this [point], the Shivashraddha (i.e., the postmortuary offerings given to Shiva manifestations rather than ancestors) is to be performed for Putrakas (i.e., full initiates) and the like who adhere to the Shaiva teaching." This suggests that also from an emic point of view, the need to provide the space for the communitas experience determined by orthodox Brahmanical householder values was a compelling requirement that could not be ignored even in the light of doctrinal claims of Shaiva superiority. An even stronger statement to this effect is found in the section giving instructions for the days of death impurity to be observed. From a Shaiva doctrinal point of view, impurity cannot be an issue, as the elevated spiritual state induced by Shaiva initiation should preclude any production or effect of impurity, given that ultimate godhood is at stake. Thus, Jnanashiva stresses that the period of impurity is merely determined by the individual's social position in society, rather than relating it to some Shaiva hierarchy (*Jnanaratnavali*, Antyeshtiprakarana 114; see Mirnig 2010: 253, 274): "A householder must not transgress the mundane religion (*lokamargam*) even in his thoughts [and therefore] the period of impurity arising from one's caste is in accordance with the practice of the mundane religion (*laukikacararupena*)."

## Conclusion: Ascetic Values in a Householder Context

The last quotation from the *Jnanaratnavali* provides us with one of the key concepts that relates to a central issues at stake here, namely the "mundane path" (*lokamarga*), or the "practice pertaining to worldly life," as a more literal rendering of the Sanskrit term *laukikacara* would suggest. This notion is opposed to the sphere of renouncers or ascetics, who have rejected all aspects of worldly life and society. It is this opposition that is

at the core of underlying structural dynamics and our reading of communitas in the sphere of death rites, and that accounts for the conflicting
representations of the deceased's soul as a hungry ghost and a liberated
soul at the same time.

The socioreligious functions of classical Shaiva funerary rites, as we
have seen, are structured around the communal needs of Brahmanical
mainstream society, but the asserted outcome of the rituals is ultimate liberation, a claim that originally represents the result of ascetic practices
based on the rejection of worldly life. This notion of liberation—*moksha*—
was in its beginnings developed among renouncer movements (*shramana*)
in the late Vedic period and is defined by the transcendence of constrain-
ing worldly desires for life, reproduction, and material pursuits, as well
as the attainment of mystic knowledge about the true state of things. Also,
Shaivism has its origin in a purely ascetic milieu on the fringes of society, where Shaiva practitioners pursued (partly eccentric) practices such
as living on the cremation ground and smearing the body with ashes, as
well as meditative and yogic procedures that were believed to spiritually
advance the individual towards liberation. In tantric Shaivism, subsequently, the importance of mystic knowledge and ascetic lifestyles were
substituted by the power of mantras and ritual, a move that made it possible to offer these ascetic-based values and spiritual benefits to the householder active in society. In this way, even though the ascetic remained at
the higher end of the spiritual hierarchy, the ritual repertoire increasingly
reflected the communal needs of the householder active in society, a point
we saw poignantly manifested in the sphere of death rites.

In order to substantiate that point, we can move a little further back in
history to surviving prescriptive sources for Shaiva funerary rites in tantric scriptures predating these manuals, where we find that very little information is given concerning the behavior of the community of mourners,
thus obscuring the communitas from us at an earlier stage of the development. In most of the surviving pre-tenth-century tantras, the instructions
are confined to the funerary initiation and the burning of the corpse and
remain silent on postmortuary offerings for the dead, a fact echoing the
failure to come up with a doctrinally sound explanation justifying their
performance and perhaps indicative of a different social position of the
tradition at an earlier phase. Given Shaivism's origin in the ascetic milieu,
it is not surprising that the tension resulting from ascetic-based values
meeting with worldly communal needs for mourning and regeneration
were not immediately openly resolved. Apart from the doctrinal inconsistencies generated by a ritual cycle that would treat the liberated soul as
a hungry ghost subject to the mercy of his descendants, there is also the
pragmatic aspect that renouncers and ascetics were considered socially

dead,[12] having renounced all familial ties and claims to property, factors that we saw constitute the main motivation underlying the Brahmanical strategy of dealing with the liminal period surrounding the event of death in form of rituals structured around postmortuary offerings. In fact, in one early scriptural source, the *Svayambhuvasutrasangraha*, we have an explicit example of a nonworldly context, namely the death of a guru in a monastic institution. Here, the degree of impurity, which we saw to be an indicator of a communitas moment, is defined by the relationship to the Acarya—e.g., his disciples—and prescribed to result in a prohibition to study and perform daily rituals. Incidentally, this early source also gives an example of Shaiva funerary rites in its embryonic stage, depicting a cremation without funerary initiation.[13]

In the other early tantric sources, the funerary initiation is prescribed, but without specifying the context and referring to the deceased as merely "the initiate," which leaves us in the dark about the socioreligious context in which the funeral rituals were performed once the householder entered the scene as the beneficiary of the funeral rites. If we accept the premise that cross-culturally similar communal patterns arise in a liminal period initiated by life-crisis moments, and that in Brahmanical mainstream society the liminal period after the event of death was regulated by a ritual routine revolving around social impurity restrictions and feeding the hungry ghost, we may speculate that the Shaiva officiant was only responsible for that part of the ritual which concerned the actual cremation and initiation of the deceased's soul, the rest being carried out by Brahmanical funerary priests. In any case, we know that by the time the ritual repertoire was standardized in ritual manuals as we find them from the late tenth century onwards, the instructions for Shaiva tantric priests already aimed at giving guidelines that would enable them to officiate throughout the whole cycle of funerary and postmortuary rituals for the Brahmanical mainstream, a process which can be tallied with an increasing presence of tantric Shaivism in the medieval Indianized world.

The project to capture the reality of ritual practice from these prescriptive texts, which was voiced in the beginning of this chapter, remains a problematic quest. Even though questions such as "how often?" "by how many?" and "by whom?" continue to be elusive, we are now in a better position to answer the question "for what reason?" Thus, we have seen how the liminal period in the cycle of Shaiva funerary rituals presents a symbolic arena in which newly emerging values of ultimate liberation are negotiated in a religious environment with deeply embedded ritual structures revolving around regeneration, which are central to the clientele of the Brahmanical householder society. Furthermore, the consideration of how Turner's notion of communitas may be applied to the community of mourners, whose sense of antistructure and togetherness finds expression in the rules for impurity, opens up conceptual angles in our reading of these premodern texts, which attune us to indicators of the historical socioreligious context in which these prescriptions were composed.

**Nina Mirnig** (DPhil Oxford 2010) is a researcher at the Institute for the Cultural and Intellectual History of Asia (IKGA) of the Austrian Academy of Sciences in Vienna. Until 2013 she held a postdoctoral research fellowship at the Institute of Indian Studies, University of Groningen, and was subsequently awarded a Jan Gonda Fellowship (Leiden) by the Dutch Royal Academy of Arts and Sciences. Her upcoming monograph is on early Shaiva tantric death rituals and she coedited *Pushpika: Tracing Ancient India through Texts and Traditions*, Volume I (Oxbow Books 2013) and the special issue "Epigraphical Evidence for the Formation and Rise of Early Shaivism" (*Indo-Iranian Journal* 56, 3/4, 2013).

## Notes

1.    I woud like to express my sincere gratitude to the editors of this volume, Peter Berger and Justin E.A. Kroesen, both from the University of Groningen, for organizing the conference in 2010 on which this outcome is based, and their careful feedback and hard work throughout putting together this volume. Further, I would like to thank Hans Bakker for his valuable comments and suggestions as the respondent to my paper, as well as Adheesh Sathaye for reading and commenting on an earlier draft. Much of the material that provides the basis for the theoretical considerations in the second half of the chapter are drawn from my doctoral thesis, written under the supervision of Alexis Sanderson, to whom I would also like to express my deepest gratitude. Due to the format of the book and the intended audience reaching beyond that of the philological specialist of Indology, it was not possible to use diacritics or quote the original Sanskrit sources in footnotes. Where possible, I have tried to use published sources that the reader can consult; where not, text and translations are taken from my doctoral thesis, which is in preparation for publication in 2016 (see Mirnig 2010). For transcription of Sanskrit terms, the diacritic marks are simply lost; palatal and retroflex sibilants are transcribed as "sh". In the translations, square brackets indicate added text that is understood in the Sanskrit original but not directly expressed; round brackets indicate additional explanatory remarks. All translations are my own unless otherwise stated.
2.    The prevailing material presence of Shaivism is now visible to us in the context of the Sanskrit literary culture associated with elite circles and royalty. However, that tantric Shaivism was not only confined to this social strata is suggested by the fact that much of what are considered mainstream ritual practices also betray tantric influence from a certain point onwards. Further, it is difficult but crucial to keep in mind the distinction between the religion of Shaiva initiates and that of lay Shaivas, the latter of which encompasses a wide range of practitioners. In this chapter, it is strictly the former that is at the center of the analysis. At this point one can only hypothesize about the exact social scope: most likely such rituals as discussed here were confined to the sphere of twice-born males, presumably with enough means to finance the elaborate Shaiva rituals.

3.  The initiates here are all men and thus the entire discussion on Shaiva funerary rites is in reference to these male initiates in this chapter. The role and presence of women at this early point of tantric Shaivism is still an enigma and not visible in the early prescriptive Saiddhantika literature. That women should be given a passive position and are not much visible in the prescriptive texts is not surprising in the Indian context, where it is a commonplace that women may never be autonomous at any stage of their lives. See, for instance, the important treatise on dharma, the *Yajnavalkyasmriti*, Acaryadhyaya 85d: "Women are never autonomous."

4.  Shaivism is divided into different philosophical schools, the main distinction being made between the dualistic system of the Shaiva Siddhanta and a number of nondualistic systems. The former propagates the doctrine that the soul can attain equality (rather than unity) to Shiva, the premise being that Shiva, the souls, and the material cause out of which the universe is fashioned are all eternally distinct but equally divine entities. This is in contrast to the nondualistic non-Saiddhantika systems, such as the Trika and Krama, which teach that each soul is in reality a part of Shiva's consciousness rather than a separate entity.

5.  Accounts of Hindu funeral rites in translation can be found, for example, in Evison 1990, Kane 1968, and Michaels 1998: 148–175.

6.  The *Somashambupaddhati* was translated and annotated by Brunner-Lachaux in 1977 and still remains one of the main references for Shaiva ritual.

7.  For a discussion on evidence for Jnanashiva's date and South Indian origin see Goodall 2000: 209.

8.  The account of capturing the soul is supplemented with details from the *Mudralakshana*.

9.  Much of Indian mythology is also concerned with the paradigm that a person needs offspring—ideally male—in order to be saved from the tortures of hell, since only their own descendants can perform the necessary rites to avert such misery. See, for instance, the story in the *Mahabharata* (e.g., 1.13.9–22) of a Brahmin who has taken up a vow of chastity. One day he finds his ancestors hanging upside down from a tree, dangling over the hole that is the entrance to hell. In distress, they appeal to him to take a wife and produce offspring, so that they can be saved from hell.

10. In the case of the absence of any relatives, this principle results in the practice that all property goes to the king, who, in turn, has to pay and arrange for the deceased's shraddha rites.

11. In a way, a similar process is visible in the adaptation of Shraddha rites into the ritual cycle of classical Hinduism, in which the concept of rebirth already replaced a linear conception of afterlife based on ancestorhood. Olivelle argues that the original feeding of the ancestors was extended to feeding the gods, which came to constitute the principle behind Hindu worship (*puja*) (Olivelle 2009: 68).

12. The renouncer's status as socially dead could even go so far that the option emerged to perform his postmortuary offerings at the time of renunciation, as if he had already physically died.

13. Incidentally, it is also in this early source that we find that no specific instructions for the funerary initiation are given, but only a cremation of the corpse in Shiva-fire takes place, indicating that no ritual marking of liberation and death was considered necessary and that householder concerns did not apply (Mirnig 2010: 24–30).

# References

Bakker, Hans. 2011. "Origin and Spread of the Pashupata Movement: About Heracles, Lakulisha and Symbols of Masculinity." *Studia Orientalica* 110: 21–37.

Bhatt, Niddodi R., ed. 1979. *Sardhatrishatikalottara*. Pondicherry: Institut français d'indologie.

Bisschop, Peter, and Arlo Griffiths. 2003. "The Pashupata Observance (*Atharvavedaparishishta* 40)." *Indo-Iranian Journal* 46: 315–48.

Brunner-Lachaux, Hélène, ed. 1977. *Somashambhupaddhati. Troisieme Partie. Rituels Occasionnels dans la tradition shivaïte de l'Inde du Sud selon Somashambhu. III: diksha, abhisheka, vratoddhara, antyeshti, Shraddha*. Pondicherry: Institut français d'indologie.

Davis, Richard H. 1988. "Cremation and Liberation: The Revision of a Hindu Ritual." *History of Religion: An International Journal for Comparative Historical Studies* 28, no. 1: 37–53.

———, ed. 1991. *Ritual in an Oscillating Universe. Worshipping Shiva in Medieval India*. Princeton, NJ: Princeton University Press.

Evison, Gillian. 1989. "Indian Death Rituals: The Enactment of Ambivalence." PhD diss., University of Oxford.

Goodall, Dominic, ed. 1998. *Bhatta Ramakantha's Commentary on the Kiranatantra*. Volume I, *Chapters 1–6: Critical Edition and Annotated Translation*. Pondicherry: Institut français d'indologie.

———. 2000. "Problems of Name and Lineage: Relationships between South Indian Authors of the Shaiva Siddhanta." *Journal of the Royal Asiatic Society* 3, No. 10/2: 206–16.

Hertz, Robert. (1907) 1960. *Death and the Right Hand*. Aberdeen: Cohen & West.

Hinüber, Oskar von. 2009. "Cremated like a King: The Funeral of the Buddha within the Ancient Indian Cultural Context." *Journal of the International College for Postgraduate Buddhist Studies* 8: 33–66.

Jnanashivacarya. [ca. twelfth century]. *Jnanaratnavali*. (1) ORI, Mysore, Ms. No. P. 3801 [obtained by D. Goodall]; (2) Transcript of Re. 1025/52 (57) copied by V. Rangasvami [photographed by D. Goodall]; (3) Institut Français, Pondicherry, Transcript No. T. 231.

Kane, Pandurang V., ed. 1953. *History of Dharmashastra*. Vol. IV. Poona: Bhandarkar Oriental Research Institute.

Michaels, Axel, ed. 2006. *Der Hinduismus. Geschichte und Gegenwart*. Munich: C.H. Beck.

Mirnig, Nina. 2010. "Liberating the Liberated: A History of the Development of Cremation and Ancestor Worship in the Early Shaiva Siddhanta. Analysis, Texts, and Translations." PhD diss., University of Oxford.

Olivelle, Patrick. 2009. "The Living and the Dead: Ideology and Social Dynamics of Ancestral Commemoration in India." In *The Anthropologist and the Native: Essays for Gananath Obeyesekere*, ed. H.L. Seneviratne, 65–73. Florence: Società editrice fiorentina.

Panshikar, W.L.S. 1926. *Yajnavalkyasmrti with the Commentary (Mitakshara) of Vijnaneshvara*. Bombay: J.R. Gharpure.

Parry, John, ed. 1994. *Death in Banaras*. Cambridge: Cambridge University Press.

Pathak, Vishwambhar S., ed. 1960. *History of Shaiva Cults in Northern India from Inscriptions (700 A.D. to 1200 A.D.)*. Varanasi: Ram Naresh Varma.

Sanderson, Alexis. 1995. "Meaning in Tantric Ritual." In *Essais sur le rituel III: Colloque du centenaire de la section des sciences religieuses de l'Ecole Pratique des Hautes Etudes,* ed. Anne-Marie Blondeau and Kristofer Schipper, 15–95. Louvain: Peeters.

———. 2009. "The Shaiva Age: An Explanation of the Rise and Dominance of Shaivism during the Early Medieval Period." In *Genesis and Development of Tantrism,* ed. Shingo Einoo, 41–349. Tokyo: University of Tokyo, Institute of Oriental Culture.

Saraogi, Olga S. 2010. "When to Kill Means to Liberate: Two Types of Rituals in Vidyapitha Texts." In *Grammars and Morphologies of Ritual Practices in Asia,* ed. Axel Michaels and Lucia Dolce, 65–84. Wiesbaden: Harrassowitz.

Turner, Victor W. 1995. *The Ritual Process: Structure and Anti-Structure.* New York: Aldine de Gruyter.

van Gennep, Arnold. (1909, in French) 1960. *The Rites of Passage,* trans. Monika B. Vizedom and Gabrielle L. Caffee. Chicago: University of Chicago Press.

———. (1909) 2004. "Funerals." In *Death, Mourning, and Burial: A Cross–Cultural Reader,* ed. Antonius C.G.M. Robben, 197-212. Malden, MA: Blackwell Publishers.

***Figure 9.1.*** Midwolde (the Netherlands), reformed church, tomb of Carel Hieronymus van In- en Kniphuizen and Anna van Ewsum; detail of Anna lovingly looking down on her deceased husband, who appears to be asleep (photo Regnerus Steensma, used with permission).

*Chapter Nine*

# Between Death and Judgment
Sleep as the Image of Death in Early Modern Protestantism

*Justin E.A. Kroesen and Jan R. Luth*

According to Christian doctrine, afterlife in its final state of heaven and hell will only materialize at the Second Coming of Christ, when the Last Judgment will be inflicted upon mankind. Conspicuously, theologians have never reached consensus over the whereabouts of the deceased's body and soul between his or her death and the Last Judgment. Ideas about this intermediate phase—when temporary earthly life has ended, but eternal life has not yet taken shape—have remained quite vague and disputed over the centuries. This ambiguous stage "betwixt and between," which in anthropology is generally known as "liminal" after van Gennep (1909) and Turner (1969), has traditionally received relatively little attention in Christian theology. In writings, iconography, and ritual, most attention has rather been focused on the preparations for death on the one hand (such as the long tradition of *Ars moriendi*) and the Last Judgment at the end of time on the other (see the many, often violent, representations of the Judgment in European art, from the Ste-Foy abbey in Conques to the Sistine Chapel, and music, such as the hymn *Dies irae*) (Jezler 1994).

With regard to the period between death and judgment, a series of ideas and visions have developed over the course of time. In his treatise *De Anima*, written somewhere between 203 and 213, Tertullian alludes to an underground space where the human soul would await the end of time, referring to the *Passio Perpetuae* as the primary proof for his doctrine (Bremmer and Formisano 2012). Some believed that an individual judgment would be carried out "in the hour of our death," an idea first

---

Notes for this chapter begin on page 222.

expressed by Pope Gregory the Great (590–604). He believed that the "not very good ones" (*non valde boni*) among the souls — in practice, this would amount to almost all of them — would have to do penance for their sins in a place of purification (Angenendt 1997: 700).

Belief in purgatory, which was officially recognized by the church only in 1336,[1] had an enormous resonance in late medieval Europe (Le Goff 1989). The stay of the souls of the deceased in this realm could be short-ened by means of intercessions, which usually consisted of the reading of prayers and Masses. The success of purgatory in medieval Christianity is easily understood in the light of the human condition: nobody is perfect and the idea of an empty heaven is hard to accept. Next to the sharp dis-tinctions between heaven and hell, good and bad, and reward and punish-ment, purgatory offered a welcome intermediate category that not only soothed the living when they thought of the deceased, but also provided consolation with regard to their own afterlife.

The origins of purgatory must certainly not be sought in Jewish tra-dition, and the concept of purification has been traced back to Gnostic thought (Bremmer 2002: 65). Although purgatory was terrifying as such, it also included sections where the stay was pleasant, such as paradise, which was also called "Abraham's lap" or *refrigerium*, a nice, cool wait-ing room before the gates of heaven. Dante considered this top level of purgatory to be the Garden of Eden from which Adam and Eve had been expelled. Augustine had already stated that the *valde boni* ("the very good ones") among the souls would stay in a lovely place full of light and with a lush landscape. The thought that this paradise could be reached immedi-ately after death was based on the words which Christ himself had spoken to the remorseful villain on his right-hand side while hanging on the cross: "Verily I say unto thee, today shalt thou be with me in paradise" (Luke 23:43, King James Version). In popular belief, the distinction between tem-porary paradise and eternal heaven often became blurred. For obvious reasons, the image of a deceased loved one walking in heavenly spheres provides much more consolation to the bereaved than the image of a soul doing penance in purgatory.

Another question that has continuously stirred up theological debate concerns the relationship between body and soul: is only the soul lifted into the afterlife, while the body remains in the grave, or are they both assumed? Some representations showed both body and soul (the *homo totus*) being carried upward by angels. Most widespread, however, was the image of a body that was put to rest in the earthly grave, while the much lighter soul — the immortal *anima* or *spiritus* — departed for the here-after, to be reunited with the body only at the end of time. Conspicuously, in many medieval works of art, the soul was depicted as a small person (a *homunculus*) with no sexual characteristics who escapes from the mouth of the dying, fleeing the body with the last breath.

The Middle Ages produced a rich visionary literature and imagery around the transition from earthly life to the hereafter (Dinzelbacher 2002). This transition is often depicted as a perilous journey in which different elements play a role, such as the narrow and dangerous bridge or the ferry across the River of Death, untrustworthy guides, and the support of saints and angels (Dinzelbacher 1973). In these ideas and images, elements from Jewish belief and concepts from classical antiquity often intertwined.

In the age of the Reformation, belief in purgatory became an important bone of contention. In 1530, Martin Luther published his *Revocation of Purgatory* (*Ein Widerruf vom Fegefeuer*). He denied its existence as nonbiblical, contrary to the Last Judgment, which is described in detail in the book of Revelation (20:11–15). Intercessions were abolished and the practice of *Ars moriendi* was curtailed because the individual believer could no longer influence his own fate or that of his loved ones. Dying was no longer conceived of as an art and salvation of the soul became a matter of pure faith. On the contrary, belief in purgatory continued to reign supreme in Catholic tradition, as is clear from seventeenth- and eighteenth-century artworks that often portray the souls doing penance. In Catholic liturgy, Requiem Masses and *Commendatio Animae* practices became (or remained) very common.

Most Protestants regarded death as a nondescript sleep, from which one would be awakened only when the Last Judgment was imminent. Biblical grounds for the view of death as sleep were found in the resurrection of Jairus's daughter, of whom Jesus said, "The damsel is not dead, but sleepeth" (Mark 5:39, KJV) and Lazarus, of whom Jesus said: "Our friend Lazarus sleepeth; but I go, that I may awake him out of sleep" (John 11:11, KJV).[2] The image of death as sleep had a long tradition and was already known in the classical world—in Greek mythology, *Hypnos* (Sleep) reveled in imitating his twin brother *Thanatos* (Death). In the Roman era, dead persons were for the first time conceived of as sleeping, in accordance with the words of Cicero: *Somnus est imago mortis*.[3] This idea had a continuing influence in the European Middle Ages: the moment of death was often described as a *dormitio*, and the souls of the blessed "rested" in Abraham's lap (consider also *r.i.p.*—*requiescat in pace*) (Einig 1987).

Examples of the sleeping dead became increasingly common in late medieval tomb sculpture (Scholten 1996: 334–43). The idea of death as sleep was theologically founded by important late medieval thinkers, including Pietro Pomponazzi (1462–1525), a professor in Padua and Bologna (Wonde 1994), and is also suggested by some sculpted reposing figures or *gisants*, for example in the tomb of Pedro Hernández de Velasco (d. 1492), constable of Castile, in the cathedral of Burgos (Ariès 1985: 58).

With the disappearance of purgatory, this old conception of death as sleep became the dominant Protestant view on the state of human beings after death. Martin Luther described death as a deep, strong, and sweet dreamless sleep, exempt from time and space, without consciousness and without feeling (Pesch 1987). When the dead are raised by Christ on the Last Day, they will neither know where they are nor how long they have slept. According to Luther, we shall rise "suddenly" and shall not know how we came to die or how we have passed through death (Moltmann 2000: 248–49). From 1535 to 1545, Luther further elaborated his thoughts about the soul's sleep in his *Commentary on Genesis* (*Enarrationes in Genesin*), in which he stated, "Soul after death enters its chamber and peace, and sleeping does not feel its sleep." In his introduction to the funeral hymns from 1542, Luther described the grave as "Our Lord's lap or paradise, and the grave is no other than a soft, lazy resting bed,"[4] and he continued to refer to the raising of Lazarus in John 11 and Jairus's daughter in Mark 5 as awakenings from sleep. For Luther, therefore, a funeral should not be an occasion for lamentations and suffering songs, but rather for consoling songs about forgiveness of sin, sleep, life, and resurrection. The idea of the death-sleep would become widespread in other branches of Protestantism as well, especially among the Anabaptists or Mennonites (Zimmerli 1932: 19).

John Calvin followed Luther in vehemently rejecting purgatory (see *Institutio Christianae Religionis* III, 5,6–10 and 25,6), but he held quite a different view on the relationship between death and sleep. He taught that the soul would not be deeply asleep after death, but rather remain awake in full consciousness until the Last Judgment. This view was termed "psychopannychism," literally meaning "soul-vigil," after the title of one of Calvin's treatises. The subtitle to the first edition, published in Strasbourg in 1542, reads, "They live to Christ and do not sleep those souls of the saints who die in faith of Christ. Assertion." The subtitle to the second edition in 1545 reflects the controversy that had arisen around the question of sleep or vigil: "A refutation of the error entertained by some unskillful persons, who ignorantly imagine that in the interval between death and the judgment the soul sleeps" (Zimmerli 1932).[5] The French translation of this treatise was called *Psychopannychie—La nuit ou le sommeil de l'âme* (the night or the sleep of the soul), which certainly did not help to clarify the subtle differences between Luther's and Calvin's views on the state of the souls of the deceased (Oberman 1993; Schwendemann 1996). Conspicuously, contrary to Calvin's own teachings, the Second Helvetic Confession from 1566 stated that the soul of the deceased Christian would migrate to Christ immediately after death.[6]

This chapter analyses how the liminal period between death and the Last Judgment was imagined in Protestant culture during the seventeenth and eighteenth centuries by looking at a number of artistic and musical expressions. In contrast to doctrinal treatises, works of art and music may provide more direct insights into the beliefs held by societies at large and by people on the ground. Compared to the often theatrical images found in the baroque art of Catholic Europe, where open graves showing emaciated skeletons were no exception, Protestant imagery remained rather comfortable.

The first section focuses on the tombs sculpted by Rombout Verhulst in a number of Dutch churches. Subsequently, attention will turn to some of the texts accompanying cantatas, motets, and passions composed by Johann Sebastian Bach. In spite of the distance in time (seventeenth versus eighteenth centuries), space (the Dutch Republic versus central Germany) and confessional tradition (Calvinism versus Lutheranism), both the Verhulst sculptures and the Bach compositions express the dominant Protestant idea of death as sleep. Both artists sought, each in their own way, to create a vivid image of how the inevitable future after earthly death might look. It will become clear that doctrine and belief did not necessarily always coincide.

## Death as Sleep in Tombs Sculpted by Rombout Verhulst

The fact that Calvin firmly opposed the idea of the soul-sleep could not prevent it from becoming a widespread belief among seventeenth-century Calvinists in the northern Netherlands (see Den Boer 1976). Its popularity may have resulted from an influential book by Cornelis van Hille, titled *Ziekentroost* (Consolation for the Sick), from 1567, which can be regarded as a Calvinist continuation of the medieval *Ars moriendi* tradition. The end of this treatise reads, "Like Isaiah has said, that the earth and the sea will give up the dead, *who have slept in them*. Because Christ is the resurrection, the first one of those who have been raised" (italics ours).[7] The writer and playwright Joost van den Vondel wrote a funeral poem for Susanne van Baerle (wife of Constantijn Huygens) in 1637, in which he said that she lies "asleep, waiting for eternity." A deathbed poem for Lord Joan Banning Wuyttiers, written by the same author in 1660, reads, "Yet [he] is not dead: he rests, appears to sleep" (Smits-Veld and Spies 1986: 882, 889).

The spread of the image of death as sleep is also visible in the oeuvre of Rombout Verhulst (b. Mechelen 1624, d. The Hague 1698), who became one of the leading sculptors in the northern Netherlands during the Dutch golden age (Scholten, 1996). Verhulst settled in Leiden as an independent master around 1658. Between 1650 and 1672, he created several monumental tombs and mausolea in honor of the "heroes at sea" (*zeehelden*) in the young Dutch Republic.

In 1658, Verhulst completed a splendid tomb for Admiral Maarten Harpertszoon Tromp in the Old Church of Delft. The deceased is portrayed as a gisant in full military attire, lying on a sarcophagus, which also functions as a pedestal. On the wall behind the figure in repose, two putti are depicted carrying the arms of the states-general of the republic, who commissioned the tomb. The representation of Tromp is remarkably heroic and militaristic in comparison to that of William of Orange (alias William the Silent) in the New Church at Delft, created by Hendrick and Pieter de Keyser between 1614 and 1621. Here, the prince is represented on his deathbed shortly after breathing his last breath as a postmortem portrait. His bedclothes, which consisted of a house tabard, an embroidered hat, and slippers, had not yet been replaced by the stately armor in which princes were traditionally buried (Scholten 1996: 342).

In his early Leiden years, Verhulst also worked on commission for individual clients. In these projects, he much more closely connected to the domestic thrust of William of Orange's tomb. In 1662–63, he erected a tomb for Baron Willem van Liere (d. 1654), Lord of Katwijk, on behalf of his wife, Maria van Reygersberg, in the parish church at Katwijk aan den Rijn. Conspicuously, in this case, Verhulst portrayed the couple together in a much cozier atmosphere than he had done in Delft. In the foreground lies the armored baron; Willem is being gazed upon by his wife, who wears a nightgown and rests on her right elbow. In this way, client and sculptor reached a double goal: Maria could simultaneously represent herself as a grieving widow and as an affluent noblewoman (Scholten 2003).

The design of the Katwijk tomb may have been daring, but it was also highly esteemed. A year after its completion, Anna van Ewsum asked Verhulst to come to Midwolde in the northern province of Groningen. Anna was the widow of Carel Hieronymus van In- en Kniphuizen, who was descended from distinguished East Frisian nobility. The monument in Katwijk was copied to a great extent with the sleeping metaphor carried even further: Verhulst no longer portrayed the deceased, who is lying in the foreground, as a knight in armor, but rather in domestic dress with a nightcap, a nightshirt, and a pair of slippers; his mouth is half-open as if he is snoring [Fig. 9.1]. The idea that the onlooker is standing at Carel Hieronymus's deathbed is reinforced by the fact that he is lying on a mattress, as if he is lying in state. Behind the deceased, his wife Anna looks upon him, lying half-raised, her elbow resting on the Bible and her hand on a winged hourglass (*Memento Mori*). Furthermore, her placement on a pedestal renders the widow more prominent than had been the case in Katwijk.

The richly plaited nightgown that Anna is wearing is even more of a *négligé* (a piece of underclothing consisting of whalebone corsets and petticoats) than that of Maria in Katwijk (Scholten 1996: 346). Here, the metaphor of the sleeping deceased was visually combined with that of the bereaved "going to sleep." Thus, the figure of Anna can be interpreted as an image of preparing before death. In this context, death is obviously seen in a positive light, since it would bring husband and wife together again (Scholten 1998: 22). In 1709, a statue of Carel Hieronymus's cousin, Georg Wilhelm van In- en Kniphuizen, to whom Anna was then married, was added to the left of her feet. Strikingly, he is portrayed as a valiant knight, standing erect and wearing his armor with a shield in his hand. This was one of the appropriate ways of portraying a nobleman, even those without a military career (Alma 2008: 129–30). Surrounded by her two spouses, Anna van Ewsum showed herself to be a dignified widow, averse to any exaggerated mourning, with whom the memory and legacy of the families Van In- en Kniphuizen and Van Ewsum were in good hands. Scholten went so far as to conclude that "It is not the deceased who are the focal points of the composition, as one would expect, but their living consorts" (Scholten 1996: 334).

The image of death as sleep is also encountered in the tomb Verhulst created for Johannes Polyander van Kerckhoven in St. Peter's Church in Leiden in 1663. On the sarcophagus-cum-pedestal lies a mattress with cross seams and a cushion with elegant tassels at the corners. The lying figure represents Van Kerckhoven, Lord of Heenvliet, who is wearing a robe, nightcap, and slippers. The monument was completed one year before the one in Midwolde, so this was the first time a dead person was represented in his domestic attire. His dress and posture suggest that the deceased is taking a nap, from which he may awaken at any moment. A striking and innovative detail is the deceased's left hand supporting his head, which is slightly turned towards the side; may we interpret this posture as a disguised reference to Calvin's view of a vigil or *psychopannychia* rather than as an unconscious sleep? It may seem almost unworthy to represent somebody in his night dress, as if one stood in the private dormitory of the deceased rather that in the public space of the church interior. In connection to the metaphor of death as a vigilant sleep, however, this obviously reinforced the persuasiveness of the representation (Scholten 2001: 390).

The style of Johannes van Kerckhoven's tomb was followed ten years later, in 1672, by Adriaan Clant's, which was erected by his son Johan in the church at Stedum in Groningen, not far from Midwolde (Scholten 1983:

47–53). The Clant family possessed Nittersum Manor and belonged to the Groningen nobility, like the Van Ewsums. Clant had undoubtedly seen the tomb in Midwolde and must have felt inspired by it.[8] The posture of the gisant follows the Leiden model in great detail: like Van Kerckhoven, Clant is depicted in everyday dress, lying on a mattress, with his head resting on a tasseled pillow. His left hand supports his head, while his right arm is draped across his body, where his hand rests. Clant is wearing loose slippers on his feet, a nightshirt over another shirt, and a small skullcap on his head. Clant's face and hands are very realistic and feature many naturalistic details. Next to the red marble sarcophagus are two putti above a coat of arms sculpted in white marble, standard elements at the tombs of military leaders. Interplaying with the domestic dress, these objects depict the two varieties of noble death, namely in battle and on the deathbed (Alma 2008: 128).

In spite of its very poetic and powerful imagery, the model that Rombout Verhulst developed in the 1660s was hardly ever adopted by later artists. It may have been felt that the informal domestic atmosphere was, after all, too different from the decorum that clients desired. Outside the Netherlands, comparable representations of the deceased can hardly be found in funerary art.[9] Verhulst's striking iconography is reflected in contemporary spiritual literature, however, in which death and sleep were often compared. An analysis of surviving funerary inscriptions from the seventeenth century in the province of Groningen shows that the image of death as sleep was widespread among large strata of society (see Kroesen 2014; Pathuis 1977). Terms referring to sleeping and waking dominate, including "passed away in the Lord," "rested in the Lord," "resting place of . . . ," and "awaiting a blessed (or a merry) resurrection in Christ" (Pathuis 1977).[10] The sleeping deceased is explicitly mentioned on the 1634 gravestone of Judge Henricus Addens in Bellingwolde: "He who for forty-four years in Bellingwolde with glory separated good and bad, sleeps here with his wife in the dust" (Pathuis 1977: 210, no. 920).[11] In 1651, the grave of Rickert Mennes in Baflo was inscribed, "My time is over, I am at rest" (Pathuis 1977: 177, no. 723).[12] The inscription on the 1697 tomb of Focko Olgers, a merchant in Zuidbroek, reads, "He who lies here is not dead but lives! In Abra[ha]m's lap his body is asleep and works no more. His soul lives gloriously with the Lord. He now possesses the salvation of the earth's soil prepared for him until his body will be raised without a stain by Christ" (Pathuis 1977: 817, no. 4521a).[13] Inscriptions such as these provoke the question of how the precise relationship between body and soul was imagined. The sleeping state seems to be ascribed to the body rather than to the soul, as is the case in Verhulst's tomb monuments.

Although, as we have seen, death portrayed as sleep was hardly represented in tomb sculpture after the seventeenth century, it lived on in grave inscriptions. The gravestone of the Reverend Adolphus Molanus from 1729 in Beerta reads, "Molaan shows his weapon in his heart, an anchor firmly rooted in Jesus' dear wound. His body lies down here and is asleep, the soul rests with its hope after its course was finished" (Pathuis 1977: 201, no. 864).[14] The aforementioned popularity of the image of death as sleep among Mennonites is reflected by Groningen gravestones from the last decade of the century. The gravestone of Ammo Jochums from 't Zandt, created in 1792, reads, "Here sleeps a scion of Menno's doctrine sprung from a famous stem," an inscription paraphrased four years later on the grave of Tamme Egges Huisinga in the same cemetery.[15] As late as 1813, the grave for Martjen Wibes Brommersma in Stitswerd was inscribed with the following words: "My body sleeps here with no sorrow until the world's youngest day" (Pathuis 1977: 652, no. 3593).[16] The grave of Tamme Lues Huizinga in Huizinge from the same year even refers to the classic theme of the fraternity between death and sleep: "How well does sleep resemble you, precarious death; his beginning dawns at the end of our restless life" (Pathuis 1977: 392, no. 2054).[17]

This anthology of grave poetry in a predominantly rural province in the north of the Netherlands during the seventeenth and eighteenth centuries may serve as an illustration of the wide currency that the idea of death as sleep had gained among Dutch Calvinists in the early modern period. Seen in this light, it may even seem surprising that Rombout Verhulst would remain virtually the only artist to give this idea material form in his sculpted tombs. Verhulst developed new visual formulas with innovative iconography and complex structures in order to convey layered, multiple messages. The deceased and the bereaved are portrayed together, making these images refer to death (faithful portraits of the deceased) and memory (the loving and caring posture of the mourners). Thus, attention is paid to both the natural and the social bodies of the persons involved (see Llewellyn 1991).

## Body, Soul, and Sleep in Compositions by Johann Sebastian Bach

In his magisterial study *Bach among the Theologians*, Jaroslav Pelikan highlighted a "preoccupation with death that, in the opinion of some historians of literature and art, was almost an obsession" in the works of Johann Sebastian Bach (b. Eisenach 1685, d. Leipzig 1750) (Pelikan 1986: 68). Death became a very central theme in seventeenth-century art and literature, especially during the decades following the Thirty Years' War (1618–48). The population of the Holy Roman Empire had been decimated, dropping from some sixteen million to less than six million; some regions of Germany, such as the Palatinate and Württemberg, had lost between 80 and 90 percent of their populations (Pelikan 1986: 69). The war was followed by several epidemics, which even led to a revival of the medieval *danse macabre* and *Ars moriendi* traditions. During the second half of the seventeenth century in Germany, the Christian "art of dying" (*christliche Sterbekunst*) became hugely popular; in many German hymnbooks of the period, we find divisions on such topics such as "About dying and burial" (*Vom Sterben und Begräbnis*).

Bach's cantatas provide us with a large corpus of texts used in Lutheran orthodox circles around the middle of the eighteenth century in Thuringia and Saxony. Most cantatas were sung within the cycle of the church year and were connected to the Bible texts which were read on specific Sundays and feast days. In many of the texts accompanying Bach's compositions, death is a central topic. A strong desire to die is often expressed: death is described as the moment when the body finds rest and the soul is liberated from sin. This view is very powerfully expressed in the cantata *Bach-Werke-Verzeichnis* (Bach Works Catalogue, hereafter BWV) 8, "Dearest God, when will I die?" (*Liebster Gott, wenn werd ich sterben?*) (Neumann 1974: 134). Death brings rest to the body and liberates the soul from its "yoke of sin" (*Sündenjoch*). This view departs from the notion of the separation of body and soul: while the body, which is considered "the dress of mortality," is given back to its origin, namely the earth, the soul is lifted upwards into heaven. This moment is described as a joyful liberation and a joining of Christ in heaven (see no. 5, soprano recitative, and no. 6, choir). Therefore, death is strongly welcomed as a moment in which all necessities disappear, although the texts do not deny the pains which sometimes accompany death.

Death is also connected to the divine judgment which, in most instances, is presented as something which takes place immediately after the believer has died, implying an immediate arrival in heaven. As was shown earlier, this idea had a long tradition in medieval Christianity and a Biblical foundation was considered to have been found in Christ's own words on the cross. The cantata "I am content with the fortune" (*Ich bin vergnügt mit meinem Glücke*), BWV 84, describes how the believer immediately enters heaven at the moment of death (Neumann 61, no. 4, recitative). In BWV 125, "With peace and joy I depart" (*Mit Fried und Freud ich fahr dahin*), heavenly life also starts right after the death of the believer.[18] Other examples in the same vein include BWV 83, "Joyful time in the new covenant" (*Erfreute Zeit im neuen Bunde*); BWV 35, "Spirit and soul become confused" (*Geist und Seele sind verwirret*); and BWV 106, "God's time is the very best of times" (*Gottes Zeit ist die allerbeste Zeit*).[19]

The cantata BWV 60, "O eternity, you word of thunder" (*O Ewigkeit, du Donnerwort*), describes how the pangs of death are soothed by the confidence that Christ will assist the believer in his last struggle. This trust makes the grave not only terrifying but also turns it into "a house of peace" (*Friedenshaus*). In this cantata, attention is continuously focused on the two faces of death: those who die as believers in the Lord are blessed — so the bass sings as a symbol of trust in recitative no. 4. At the same time, the alto represents fear and uncertainty by singing that dying may as well mean eternal destruction. The end of this cantata states that the believer is assumed into heaven and leaves "my great lamentation" (*Mein grosser Jammer*) behind on earth (Neumann 1974: 150–51).

A cantata that describes divine judgment without any eschatological notion is BWV 27, "Who knows how near my end is?" (*Wer weiss, wie nahe mir mein Ende*) (Neumann 1974: 134–35). Recitative no. 1 describes some pangs of death, but welcomes them at the same time as heralds of the glory which is about to come because all other misery will then disappear. The final choir describes how the believer attains eternal rest in heaven. The same idea is found in cantata BWV 56, "I will gladly carry the cross" (*Ich will den Kreuzstab gerne tragen*), where pain and the desire for death are combined (Neumann 1974: 140–41). Death can therefore be glorified, as in cantata BWV 95, "Christ is my life" (*Christus, der ist mein Leben*) (Neumann 1974: 133).

A cantata illustrating the strong desire to die is BWV 161, "Come, o sweet hour of death" (*Komm du süsse Todesstunde*), which was composed for the sixteenth Sunday after Trinity. It is based on that Sunday's readings, namely Ephesians 3:31–21 and Luke 7:11–17, which narrate the resurrection of the young man of Nain. At the end of the first hymn is the line "I wish to depart from this evil world, I long for heavenly joys, O Jesus, come quickly!" (*Ich hab Lust abzuscheiden Von dieser bösen Welt Sehn mich nach himml'schen Freuden O Jesu, komm nur bald!*) (Neumann 1974: 132). Here, the believer desires the joys of heaven and asks Jesus to come soon, which reflects the eschatological maranatha formula at the end of the book of Revelation (22:20): "Amen! Yes come, Lord Jesus." However, this cantata does not refer to Christ's Second Coming at the end of time, but to his presence at the death of the believer, who is taken up with him into heaven; here, "Come soon" means "Come take me soon." The same idea is present in part 5 of the same cantata, where it is sung that glory starts immediately when the believer dies. The end of the cantata is the fourth stanza of *Herzlich tut mich verlangen*, with the thought that the body will eventually also be awakened and glorified.

Eschatological passages, referring to the Last Judgment at the end of time, are much less often found but they are not entirely absent.[20] They usually focus on the body of the deceased, which will have to wait in the cold and dark grave until it is resurrected at the moment of Christ's Second Coming. The intermediate period is often described in terms of sleep until the Resurrection at the end of time. As we have seen before, the image of death as sleep was propagated by Martin Luther himself and it became common in Lutheran hymns written from the seventeenth century on. It features prominently in the works of Heinrich Müller (1631–75), a professor of theology at the University of Rostock, whose writings Bach possessed almost all and which he is known to have greatly appreciated (Leaver 1983).[21] In a sermon about Matthew 9:18–26 on the fourth Sunday after Trinity, Müller wrote, "Because death is a sleep, do not be afraid of him, but fix your eye upon God and sigh: I will sleep and have a fine rest, nobody can wake me up except the Son of God, He will open the door of heaven! And will lead me into eternal life" (*Weil der Tod ein Schlaf ist, so lass dir nicht für ihm grauen, sondern befehle dich Gott und seufze: So schlaf ich ein und ruhe fein, Kein Mensch kan mich aufwecken, Denn Jesu Christ, Gottes Sohn, Der wird die Himmels-Thür aufthun! Und führen zum ewgen Leben*) (Müller 1741, no. 1382),

Examples of death portrayed as sleep in Bach's cantatas include BWV 106, "As God has promised me: Death has become my sleep" (*Wie Gott mir verheißen hat: Der Tod ist mein Schlaf geworden*), and BWV 145 (recitative no. 4), "I live, my heart, for your pleasure" (*Ich lebe, mein Herze, zu deinem ergötzen*) (Neumann 1974: 74), as well as the hymns in the rubric "On death and funeral" (*Vom Sterben und Begräbnis*) in the songbook *Schuldiges Lob Gottes* (Weimar 1713). In the last choir of BWV 56, the final verse of the song *Du, o schönes Weltgebäude*, written by Johann Franck in 1653, expresses the classical view of death and sleep as brothers: "Come, o death, brother of sleep, come and lead me away" (*Komm, o Tod, du Schlafes Bruder, Komm und führe mich nur fort*). These hymns describe death as a state of deep sleep until the moment of resurrection on the Final Day. This is even more explicitly expressed by the final chorale of Bach's Johannes Passion (BWV 245), which reads, "Let my body, in its little sleeping chamber, absolutely softly, without any anguish or pain, rest until the last day" (*Den Leib in seim Schlafkämmerlein Gar sanft ohn einge Qual und Pein Ruhn bis am jüngsten Tage*).

The same ideas are widespread in death hymns in the *Musicalisches Gesang-Buch* (hymn book) of Georg Christian Schemelli ([1736] 1975), which was used during Bach's time in Leipzig and to which he contributed many melodies. Here, death is described as a state of sleep from which the deceased will only be awakened by Christ: "My tired body sleeps in the mold, he sleeps till Jesus wakes him up" (*Mein matter leib schläft in der Erden, er schläft bis ihn mein Jesus weckt;* 864/3); "My body sleeps easy, till he wakes up again" (*mein leib schläft sanft, bis das er wiederum erwacht;* 867/5); and "He has his sleep and wakes up again at the last day" (*da schläft er aus und wachet drauf am jüngsten tage wieder auf;* 882/3). The following lines are also illustrative: "When I finish my sleep in my grave, I will rise up" (*Wenn ich in meinem grabe nun ausgeschlafen habe, so werd ich auferstehn;* 895/8).

Some of Bach's cantatas directly refer to the separation of body and soul at the moment of death, such as BWV 127/3: "The soul rests in Jesus' hands, when earth covers this body. Ah, call me soon, you death-knell, because my Jesus will awaken me again" (*Die Seele ruht in Jesu Händen, wenn Erde diesen Leib bedeckt. Ach ruft' mich bald ihr Sterbeglocken, Ich bin zum Sterben unerschrocken, Weil mich mein Jesus wieder weckt;* Neumann 1974: 65). The same situation is expressed in the cantata for the seventeenth Sunday after Trinity, BWV 114, "Ah, dear Christians, be comforted" (*Ach, lieben Christen, seid getrost*). Here, death is portrayed as a sleep until the end of time, but this mainly concerns the body, since the soul is called to actively let go of it. Recitative 6 reads, "Therefore consider your soul and open it up to the Savior; give your body and your limbs back to God, who gave them first to you" (*Indes bedenke deine Seele, Und stelle sie dem Heiland dar; Gib deinen Leib und deine Glieder Gott, der sie dir gegeben, wieder;* Neumann 1974: 136).

The cantata "Come, o sweet hour of death" (*Komm du süsse Todesstunde*) focuses entirely on the soul when it describes death as "the sun of glory and heavenly delight" (*die Sonne der Herrlichkeit und Himmelswonne;* no. 2, tenor recitative). While the soul is united with Christ, the body is laid down to rest in the grave and decays into ash and mold (no. 3, tenor aria). When attention focuses on the body, then the believer is thought to be sleeping in his grave until Jesus will wake him up: "By dying soon in Jesus' arms: He is my gentle sleep. My cool grave shall be covered with roses until Jesus shall reawaken me, until His sheep shall be guided to the sweet pasture of life" (*In Jesu Armen bald zu sterben: Er ist mein sanfter Schlaf. Das kühle Grab mit Rosen decken, Bis Jesus mich wird auferwecken, Bis er sein Schaf führt auf die süsse Lebensweide*). Here, death is glorified as a situation that anticipates reaching the heavenly pasture at the end of time. At the same time, however, the soul has already reached immortality: "If it is my God's will, I wish that the weight of my body might even today occupy the earth, and that the spirit, the body's guest, clothe itself in immortality in the sweet joy of heaven. Jesus, come and take me away! May this be my last word" (*Wenn es meines Gottes Wille, Wünsch ich, dass des Leibes Last Heute noch die Erde fülle, Und der Geist, des Leibes Gast, Mit Unsterblichkeit sich kleide, In der süssen Himmelsfreude. Jesu, komm und nimm mich fort! Dieses sei mein letztes Wort;* no. 5, choir recitative, Neumann 1974:

132). The promise of eternal life for the soul upon relinquishing the body induces the believer to develop a strong desire for death. The lifting up of the soul brings about a *unio mystica* that cannot be attained during one's lifetime. BWV 162 describes how the deceased participates in the Lord's Supper: "Ah! I see, now, as I go to the wedding" (*Ach! Ich sehe, itzt, da ich zur Hochzeit gehe*; Neumann 1974: 141–42). Astonishment is expressed at the sinners who are also allowed to participate in this feast (no. 2, tenor recitative), and then Christ is invoked to invite the believers to his Supper, ending in the exclamation: "Come, be united with me!" (*Komm, vereine dich mit mir!* no. 3, soprano aria). At this moment, the believer receives a white robe and reaches his desired union with Christ in the consumption of the heavenly meal. The desire to be a guest at the heavenly table is found in cantatas BWV 180, "Adorn yourself, O dear soul" (*Schmücke dich, o liebe Seele*), and BWV 49, "I go forth and seek with longing" (*Ich geh und suche mit Verlangen*), which were both composed for the twentieth Sunday after Trinity (Neumann 1974: 142–43).

In conclusion, Bach's cantatas imbue the idea of rest (*Ruh*) with several meanings. It is used to designate the heavenly rest of the soul that is found in heaven right after death. In this sense, it becomes a synonym for heavenly joy and eternal life. This rest is closely connected to the believer's self-surrender to Christ at the moment of death. With regard to the body, however, the rest is temporary, a state of sleep until the Day of Judgment at the end of time. Bach's renderings of rest and sleep after death are therefore somewhat ambiguous and sometimes even contradictory, since "I" may mean both body and soul, or either one of both. The basic theological obscurity resides in the double conception of judgment that was widespread in Lutheran thought during the seventeenth and eighteenth centuries: while the soul was thought to be tried right after death, the body was laid down in the grave to await the Last Judgment. Bach usually adopted the Lutheran image of death-sleep to describe the state of the body in the intermediate period.

## Conclusion

Christian thought generally assumed a threefold life structure, consisting of (1) earthly life, (2) an intermediate phase between the death of a person and the end of time, and (3) the final destination of eternal afterlife after the Second Coming of Christ, who will carry out the Last Judgment.

One of the topics that was never fully clarified in Christian theology concerns the whereabouts of body and soul during the liminal intermediate phase between death and judgment. The idea that the deceased would have to wait in a cold and dark tomb until the end of time obviously provided little comfort for the bereaved. This is one of the explanations for the evolution of the widespread belief that the soul would escape from the body and immediately reach the afterlife, in accordance with the dominant view in classical antiquity. Thus, people could imagine deceased relatives and friends enjoying paradise, in accordance with Christ's words on the cross: "Today shalt thou be with me in paradise." However, this automatically implied a double judgment: a personal trial right after death and a universal one on the Day of Judgment. In the Middle Ages, souls were thought to migrate to purgatory, where they would be purified from sin. To the comfort of the survivors, purgatory only had one exit: the door of heaven.

After the refutation of purgatory by sixteenth-century Reformers, the idea of the soul's sleep became widespread among most Protestants. While the body is laid down to rest in the grave, the soul of the deceased enters a state of sleep until it is awakened by Christ for the Last Judgment. The nature of this sleep remained disputed: while Luther imagined death as an unconscious, deep state of sleep, when "a thousand years would be like one day," Calvin propagated the idea of a vigilant sleep, in anxious anticipation of the Second Coming.

This chapter has discussed the ways in which these views were expressed in art and music by taking a close look at Rombout Verhulst's sculpted tombs from the Calvinist northern Netherlands in the seventeenth century and the texts accompanying Johann Sebastian Bach's cantatas in Lutheran Germany during the eighteenth century. In their own ways, both artists adopted the consoling image of the sleeping dead. Significantly, these artworks did not follow official doctrine in all aspects: the sleeping gisants in Verhulst's tombs hardly show any traces of the vigil that John Calvin had defended so vehemently and references to the Biblical Last Judgment in Bach's cantatas are far outnumbered by instances of an immediate journey into heaven.

**Justin E.A. Kroesen** (PhD Groningen 2003) is associate professor in the art history of Christianity at the Faculty of Theology and Religious Studies of the University of Groningen, the Netherlands. In 2007 he was a visiting scholar at the Getty Research Institute in Los Angeles. Studies on ecclesiastical art and religious culture of the late Middle Ages and early modern period, particularly in Spain, the Low Countries, Germany, and Scandinavia. His books include *Staging the Liturgy: The Medieval Altarpiece in the Iberian Peninsula* (Peeters 2009), and (as coauthor) *The Interior of the Medieval Village Church* (Peeters 2012).

**Jan R. Luth** (Phd Groningen 1986) is associate professor of hymnology and church music at the Faculty of Theology and Religious Studies of the University of Groningen, the Netherlands. His studies concern congregational singing and organ accompaniment in the Netherlands and Germany, and the field of theological Bach research. His books include *E. Haein, Le problème du Chant Choral dans les Eglises Réformées et le Trésor liturgique de la Cantilène huguenote* (Gooi & Sticht 1995) and *Het kerklied. Een geschiedenis* (Boekencentrum 2001).

## Notes

1. It was subsequently raised to the status of a dogma at the Councils of Florence (1439) and Trent (1562).
2. Furthermore, Matthew 27:52 reads, "[A]nd the graves were opened. And many bodies of the saints which slept arose."
3. See *Tusculanae disputationes* I, 38.
4. "Unser Herrn Schoss oder Paradies. Das Grab nicht anders, denn als ein sanfft faul oder Rugebette zu halten."
5. *Psychopannychia. Qua refellitur quorundam imperitorum error, qui animas post mortem ad ultimum dormire putant.*
6. "Credimus enim fideles recta a morte corporea migrare ad Christum."
7. Cornelis van Hille, *Ziekentroost*: "Insgelijks zegt Jesaja, dat de aarde en de zee hun doden geven zullen, die in haar geslapen hebben; want Christus is de opstanding, de eersteling dergenen, die ontslapen zijn."
8. Although it was not signed, the strong resemblance between the supine figure of Adriaan Clant and that of Johan van Kerckhoven in Leiden strongly suggests that the Groningen monument was also created by Rombout Verhulst and his workshop. The position of this tomb, at right angles to the wall on the axis of the chancel, is wholly different from those in Katwijk, Midwolde, and Leiden.
9. "Dutch funerary sculpture offers a few other instances of the deceased wearing domestic attire, but it is virtually unknown elsewhere. Only in England are there one or two examples, but they are far less significant" (Scholten 1996: 342). A striking example is found in Westminster Abbey, namely an effigy of Elisabeth Russell (d. 1601), a godchild of Queen Elisabeth. The deceased is represented in a seated position, with her head resting on her hand (as a *reverie*) and is accompanied by the inscription *Dormit, non est mortua*, a reference to Jairus's daughter (Ariès 1985: 56).
10. In Dutch: "ontslapen in den Here," "gerust in den Here," "rustplaats van . . . ," and "verwachtende een zalige (or vrolicke) opstandinge in Christo."
11. "Die vier en veertigh jaer tot bellingwold met loff / 't reght scheyd van 't onreght, slaept hier met syn vrouw int stof."
12. "Myn tyd is uit / ick ben in rust."
13. "Die hier nu leyt en is niet doot / maar leeft eirus! in abrams schoot / zyn lichaem slaept en werckt niet meer/ zyn ziel leeft! heerlyck by den heer / hy nu besit de saelicheyt voor 's werelts gront hem toebereyt / totdat syn lichaem onbevleckt / door christum werde opgeweckt."
14. "Molaan vertoond in 't hart zyn wapen / een anker vast gegrond / in jesus dyrb're wondt / zyn lichaam leit hyr neer te slapen / de ziel rust by haar hoop / na zyn voleinde loop."

15. The inscription of Ammo Jochums reads, "Hier slaapt een telg van Mennoo's leer / uit een vermaard geslacht gesproten" (Pathuis 1977: 800 [no. 4427]), and that of Tamme Egges Huisinga reads, "Hier slaapt een mennonyt uit een vermaarde stam gesproten" (Pathuis 1977: 561 [no. 3085]).
16. "Myn ligchaam slaapt hier zonder zorgen / tot aan des werelds jongsten dag."
17. "Hoe wel gelykt de slaap u broeder vege dood / zyn aanvang zweemt na 't eind van ons onrustig leven."
18. "Who even at the deathbed delights the spirit with the sweetness of Heaven" (*Der auf dem Sterbebette schon Mit Himmelssüßigkeit den Geist ergötzet*).
19. Verse no. 3b reads: "Today you will be with me in paradise" (*Heute wirst du bei mir im Paradies sein*).
20. See Cantatas BWV 20 and 60, "O eternity, you word of thunder" 1 and 2 (*O Ewigkeit, du Donnerwort I und II*), and 90 "A terrible end shall sweep you away (*Es reißet euch ein schrecklich Ende*).
21. After Martin Luther, Müller was the second most represented author in Bach's library.

# References

Alma, Redmer. 2008. "Rouwborden en monumenten. De adellijke dood ver-beeld." In *De Groninger cultuurschat. Kerken van 1000 tot 1800*, ed. Justin Kroesen and Regnerus Steensma, 124–34. Assen: Van Gorcum.

Angenendt, Arnold. 1997. *Geschichte der Religiosität im Mittelalter*. Darmstadt: Primus.

Ariès, Philippe. 1985. *Images of Man and Death*, trans. Janet Lloyd. Cambridge, MA: Harvard University Press.

Becker, Hansjakob, Dominik Fugger, Katja Süß, and Joachim Pritzkat, eds. 2004. *Liturgie im Angesicht des Todes*. Teil 1, *Reformatorische und katholische Traditionen der Neuzeit*. Pietas Liturgica 13. Tübingen: A. Francke.

Bremmer, Jan N. 2002. *The Rise and Fall of the Afterlife*. London: Routledge.

Bremmer, Jan N., and Marco Formisano, eds. 2012. *Perpetua's Passions: Multi-Disciplinary Approaches to the Passio Sanctarum Perpetuae et Felicitatis*. Oxford: Oxford University Press.

Den Boer, Pim. 1976. "Naar een geschiedenis van de dood. Mogelijkheden tot onderzoek naar de houding ten opzichte van de dode en de dood ten tijde van de Republiek." *Tijdschrift voor Geschiedenis* 89: 161–201.

Dinzelbacher, Peter. 1973. "Die Jenseitsbrücke im Mittelalter." PhD diss., University of Vienna.

———. 2002. *Himmel, Hölle, Heilige. Visionen und Kunst im Mittelalter*. Darmstadt: Primus.

Einig, Bernhard. 1987. "Somnus est imago mortis. Die Komplet als allabendliches Memento Mori." In *Im Angesicht des Todes. Ein interdisziplinäres Kompendium*, Band 2. Pietas Liturgica 4, ed. Hansjakob Becker, Bernhard Einig, and Peter-Otto-Ullrich, 1299–1320. St. Ottilien: EOS.

Hille, Cornelis van. 1567. *Ziekentroost*.

Jezler, Peter, ed. 1994. *Himmel, Hölle, Fegefeuer. Das Jenseits im Mittelalter*, Zurich: Neue Zürcher Zeitung.

Jordahn, Ottfried. 2004. "Sterbebegleitung und Begräbnis bei Martin Luther." In *Liturgie im Angesicht des Todes*. Vol. 1, *Reformatorische und katholische Traditionen der Neuzeit*. Pietas Liturgica 13, ed. Hansjakob Becker, Dominik Fugger, Katja Süß, and Joachim Pritzkat, 2–22. Tübingen: A. Francke.

Kroesen, Justin. E. A. 2014. "De doodsslaapmetafoor in de Groninger grafkunst." *Nederlands theologisch tijdschrift* 68, no. 1–2: 52–66.

Leaver, Robin. A. 1983. *Bachs theologische Bibliothek. Eine kritische Bibliographie.* Neuhausen and Stuttgart: Hänssler Verlag.

Le Goff, Jacques. 1989. *La naissance du purgatoire.* Paris: Gallimard.

Llewellyn, Nigel. 1991. *The Art of Death: Visual Culture in the English Death Ritual, c. 1500–c. 1800.* London: Reaktion Books.

Luth, Jan R. 1989. "De liturgische context van Dietrich Buxtehude's orgel-werken." *Jaarboek voor Liturgie-onderzoek* 5: 255–74.

Moltmann, Jürgen. 2000. "Is There Life after Death?" In *The End of the World and the Ends of God: Science and Theology on Eschatology*, ed. John C. Polkinghorne and Michael Welker, 238–55. Harrisburg: Trinity Press International.

Müller, Heinrich. 1741. *Evangelisches Präservativ.* Library of the Kirchengemeinde Altstadt Bielefeld.

Neumann, Werner. 1974. *Sämtliche von Johann Sebastian Bach vertonte Texte.* Leipzig: VEB.

Oberman, Heiko A. 1993. "The Pursuit of Happiness: Calvin between Humanism and Reformation." In *Humanity and Divinity in Renaissance and Reformation: Essays in Honor of Charles Trinkaus*, ed. John W. O'Malley, Thomas M. Izbicki, Gerald Christianson, and Charles Edward Trinkaus, 251–83. Leiden: E.J. Brill.

Pathuis, Adolf. 1977. *Groninger gedenkwaardigheden. Teksten, wapens en huismerken van 1298–1814.* Assen: Van Gorcum.

Pelikan, Jaroslav. 1986. *Bach among the Theologians.* Philadelphia: Fortress Press.

Pesch, Otto H. 1987. "Theologie des Todes bei Martin Luther." In *Im Angesicht des Todes. Ein interdisziplinäres Kompendium.* Pietas Liturgica 4, ed. Hansjakob Becker, Bernhard Einig, and Peter-Otto Ullrich, 709–89. St. Ottilien: EOS.

Schemelli, Georg Christian, ed. (1736) 1975. *Musicalisches Gesang-Buch, Darinnen 954 geistreiche, sowohl alte als neue Lieder und Arien, mit wohlgesetzten Melodien, in Discant und Bass, befindlich sind.* Hildesheim: Georg Olms.

Scholten, Frits. 1983. *Rombout Verhulst in Groningen. Zeventiende-eeuwse praalgraven in Midwolde en Stedum.* Stad en Lande historische reeks, 1–2. Utrecht: Matrijs.

———. 1996. "Good Widows and the Sleeping Dead: Rombout Verhulst and Tombs for the Dutch Aristocracy." *Simiolus: Netherlands Quarterly for the History of Art* 24, no. 4: 328–49.

———. 1998. "De dood als slaap verbeeld. Grafmonumenten door Rombout Verhulst in Katwijk en Leiden en andere zeventiende-eeuwse grafsculptuur in Zuidhollandse kerken." *Bulletin van de Stichting Oude Hollandse Kerken* 46: 11–23.

———. 2003. *Sumptuous Memories: Studies in Seventeenth-Century Dutch Tomb Sculpture.* Zwolle: Waanders.

———. 2011. "Een praalgraf voor een *schoolmeesters soon*, het grafmonument voor Johannes Polyander van Kerckhoven door Rombout Verhulst." In *De Pieterskerk in Leiden. Bouwgeschiedenis, inrichting en gedenktekens*, ed. Elizabeth den Hartog and John Veerman, 386–94. Zwolle: WBooks.

*Schuldiges Lob Gottes: oder, geistreiches Gesang-Buch / ausgebreitet durch D.M. Luther und andere vornehme Evangelische Lehrer*. 1713. Weimar.

Schwendemann, Wilhelm. 1996. *Leib und Seele bei Calvin. Die erkenntnistheoretische und anthropologische Funktion des platonischen Leib-Seele-Dualismus in Calvins Theologie*. Stuttgart: Calwer.

Smits-Veld, Mieke B., and Marijke Spies, eds. 1986. *Vondel: volledige dichtwerken en oorspronkelijk proza, verzorgd door Albert Verwey*. Amsterdam: Becht.

Turner, Victor W. 1969. *The Ritual Process: Structure and Anti-Structure*. Chicago: Aldine.

van Gennep, Arnold. 1909. *Les rites de passage: étude systematique des rites de la porte et du seuil; de l'hospitalité; de l'adoption, etc*. Paris: Emile Nourry.

Wonde, Jürgen. 1994. *Subjekt und Unsterblichkeit bei Pietro Pomponazzi*. Stuttgart: Teubner.

Zimmerli, Walther, ed. 1932. *Psychopannychia von Jean Calvin*. Quellenschriften zur Geschichte des Protestantismus, 13. Leipzig: Deichert.

*Figure 10.1.* Attic black-figure hydria: Achilles dragging the body of
Hector, with the psychê of Patroclus hovering over his tomb to the right.
Attributed to the Antiope Group. Museum of Fine Arts, Boston, 63.473
(drawing Valerie Woelfel).

*Chapter Ten*

# Body and Soul between Death and Funeral in Archaic Greece

*Jan N. Bremmer*

When discussing the postmortem state of the person, students of ancient cultures are at a considerable disadvantage.[1] Unlike modern anthropologists, we cannot observe how the "natives" dispose of their dead nor interrogate them about the ideas they hold regarding their eventual fate. In our investigations we are wholly limited to literary texts and visual representations. Moreover, not all texts are suitable sources. If we look at Archaic Greece, the period of about 800–500 B.C.E., there are many literary compositions that mention neither the soul nor the funeral nor the afterlife. We need only think of Hesiod's *Theogony* or *Works and Days*, poems traditionally dated to the seventh century B.C.E., to realize that not all texts are helpful in this respect. Even iconographic representations rarely give a full picture of the funeral but concentrate on particular moments, such as the *prothesis*, "the laying out of the corpse." Consequently, we have to mine our early Greek texts and representations carefully in order to find passages that will enable us to give a rough sketch of the liminal period of the body and the soul between life and death. This sketch cannot be well anchored in time and place either, given the uncertainty about the date and place of origin of many early Greek texts and, to a lesser degree, images. Our results, then, will only be a kind of ideal picture, which may not be the exact reflection of any specific historical community. Yet if we think of the Wittgensteinian notion of "family resemblances" (Ginzburg 2004), we may safely assume that most Greek communities would recognize themselves in the sketch presented here, as none of our evidence seems to fundamentally contradict our results.

---

Notes for this chapter begin on page 243.

My interest here is in the fate of the soul in the immediate postmortem period. However, as its fate cannot be separated from that of the body, we will not neglect the latter either. The Archaic Greeks may have supplied the basis for the key terms of modern terminology regarding our soul—*psych*ology and *psych*iatry—but this terminology wrongly suggests that Greeks shared with us the concept of a unitary soul that is the main seat of consciousness and emotions and that also represents man after death. In fact, in our oldest Greek literature, Homer's *Iliad* and *Odyssey*, the word *psychê*, which is the basis of the modern terminology and is often translated as "soul," has no connection with the psychological side of a person, which is in fact represented by a multitude of terms. We will therefore look first at the anthropological aspect of the soul, then turn to the eschatological side of the soul and complete our investigation by inquiring to what extent the immediate rituals after death were important for the eventual fate of the soul.

## The Anthropological Aspect

Our oldest sources for a study of the earliest Greek concept of the soul are the epics of Homer, the *Iliad* and the *Odyssey*,[2] traditionally dated to about 700 B.C.E. and probably composed on the west coast of modern Turkey or one of the adjacent islands. In Homer we find a surprising terminological plurality for what we moderns normally call "soul." It falls outside the scope of our book to discuss all these terms, and instead I will concentrate particularly on *psychê*,[3] the Greek term that, as we just saw, is associated in particular with modern ideas about the soul. To start with, *psychê* is evidently a highly prized possession. This characteristic is well illustrated by Achilles' complaint, when the embassy of the Greek army beseeches him to suppress his anger and resume fighting, that he has been continually "staking" (*paraballomenos*) his *psychê* (*Iliad* IX.322).[4] The metaphor derives from gambling and implies that Achilles is putting a valued possession at risk. It seems that Homer represented the *psychê* as an entity that was worth fighting for, and that is why Achilles and Hector can run a race in which Hector's *psychê* is the main prize.[5] That is also why the more-or-less contemporary Hesiod (*Works and Days* 686) observes that men take risks because they equate money with the *psychê*.[6]

*Psychê* is also the basis for consciousness. This becomes clear from Homer's description of swoons, which are all described in an approximately similar manner (Nehring 1947; Schnaufer 1970). For example, when a spear was pulled from the thigh of Sarpedon, one of the allies of the Trojans, "his *psychê* left him and a mist came upon his eyes" (*Iliad*

V.696). The leaving of the *psychê* clearly coincides with the loss of consciousness. Once the latter has been recovered, *psychê* is no longer mentioned. This can hardly mean that its departure was permanent. People have only one *psychê* (see below), and they clearly cannot live without it. Evidently, its existence is no longer worth mentioning once its owner is again alive and well, as *psychê* is only mentioned as part of the living person at times of crisis, but never when its owner is functioning normally. It is now the *thymos* (see below) that is important and, unlike the *psychê*, often mentioned in living persons.[7] In other words, *psychê* is the basis of life and consciousness, and without it these are no longer possible, an aspect sometimes stressed by the combination of *psychê* with *aiôn*, the source of vitality in man.[8] And because it is this basis, people consider it to be a most valuable possession.

*Psychê* is etymologically connected with *psychein* ("to blow, to breathe"); indeed, in many Indo-European cultures, the term for soul is connected with the breath.[9] The association also appears from the fact that the *psychê* leaves the body at the beginning of a swoon, as in Andromache's swoon where she "breathed forth" (*ekapusse*) her *psychê* (*Iliad* XXII.467), a verb that is most likely connected with Greek *kapnos*, "smoke." In Greece, the connection between *psychê* and breathing or blowing was already made by the philosopher Anaximenes (*ca.* 550–500 B.C.E.), who seems to have stated that the *psychê* held our body together and controlled it just as the wind controls the earth (fragment B 2 Diels/Kranz); in fact, a number of pre-Socratic philosophers, such as Anaximander, Anaxagoras, and Archelaos, connected the *psychê* with *aêr*, "air" (Aëtius IV.3.2; Kalogerakos 1996). The Orphics, members of a kind of Greek New Age movement, connected the soul with the winds (*Orphicorum Fragmenta* 421 Bernabé), and the connection with the breath occurs as a *figura etymologica* in an Orphic gold tablet of *ca.* 400 B.C.E.: "(the Underworld), where the *psychai* of the dead *psychontai*, 'breathe.'"[10]

Yet the metaphor of gambling also means that *psychê* has been "reified as an entity that one can pick up and put down, and thus expose to danger."[11] In the *Iliad*, this is illustrated also by the words of Hector that he will take away the *psychê* of Achilles (XXII.257) and the words of Agenor that Achilles' "flesh too, I suspect, is vulnerable to sharp bronze, and there is only one *psychê* in him, for men say that he is mortal" (XXI.568–70). Apparently, Homer imagines Achilles' body as a container that somewhere contains the *psychê*. Such ontological metaphors are a cross-cultural phenomenon and should be recognized too for Archaic Greece (Kövecses 2000; Lakoff and Johnson 1980). The recognition of *psychê* as a concrete entity also conforms to the fact that early Greece did not yet know the concepts of incorporeality and immateriality (Renehan 1980). It is only with

Plato that the soul becomes represented as incorporeal, but Democritus (in Aristotle, *De anima* 405a8–13) still thought of it as a small, round, firelike atom.[12] The reification probably stimulated people to speculate about its precise place in the body, since *psychê* is described as flying away through the mouth (IX.409), the chest (XVI.505), a wound in the flank (XIV.5–18), or from the limbs[13] (XVI.856, XXII.362). Moreover, it may well have facilitated the notion of the *psychostasia*, the idea that Zeus could weigh the souls of two opponents in order to decide which was to die. This idea seems to precede Homer, as small scales have often been found in Mycenaean graves (Gallou 2005).[14] In no Homeric passage does *psychê* have any psychological connection. We can only say that when it has left the body forever, its owner dies.

If *psychê* did not have any connection with the psychological side of the person, what, then, constituted the psychological makeup of the early Greeks? Reading Homer, one finds that there is no single seat of the psychological attributes of man, but an enormously varied vocabulary.[15] The most important word for the seat of emotions such as friendship, anger, joy, and grief, but also denoting emotion itself, is *thymos* (see most recently Caswell 1990; Koziak 1999; Sullivan 1993, 1994; Van der Mije 2011), a word still used today to denote a kind of gland. But there are other words as well, such as one for fury (*menos*), one for the act of the mind (*noos*; Sullivan 1989), and the words for heart (Biraud 1989; Cheyns 1985; Sullivan 1996b), lungs (*phrên/phrenes*; Balles 2002; Van der Mije 2011), and gallbladder (*cholos;* Cairns 2003: 68–74)—all of which are used to indicate the seat of emotions or the emotions themselves; moreover, these terms are often used in a semantically indistinguishable and redundant way (see also Van der Mije 1991). It thus seems that there is in Homer not one center of consciousness, not a firm idea of an "I" that decides what we are doing. Whereas we have one word, "soul," to denote the dimension of human life that is distinguishable from the body and that to a large extent determines the nature of the human being, the early Greeks had a variety of words to denote this dimension.

How can we explain this situation? It is the great merit of Scandinavian anthropologists, especially Ernst Arbman (1891–1959) and Åke Hultkrantz (1920–2006), to have collected large amounts of data to show that according to many so-called primitive peoples, humans have two kinds of soul. On the one hand, there is what these scholars call the *free soul*, a soul that represents the individual personality. This soul is inactive when the body is active; it only manifests itself during swoons, dreams, or at death (the experiences of the "I" during the swoons or dreams are ascribed to this soul), but it has no clear connections to the physical or psychological aspects of the body. On the other hand, there are a number of *body-souls*, which endow the body with life and consciousness, but of which none stands for that part of a person that survives after death.[16] The Homeric concept of the soul of the living is clearly close to these ideas. Here, too, we find on the one hand the *psychê*, a kind of free-soul, and on the other the body-souls, of which the *thymos* is the most prominent. The free soul was often associated with the breath, and this seems to have happened in Greece as well, given the etymological connection already mentioned between *psychê* and *psychein* (to blow, to breathe).

## The Eschatological Aspect

The fate of the soul at death has not received the same systematic attention from scholars as the soul of the living: only a few comparative studies exist to guide our way in a systematic approach to this subject (Bremmer 1983: 70–124; Cairns 2003: 54–64). Not surprisingly, these studies have looked at the elements of the souls that survive death. In Greece, we would expect it to be the *psychê* that survived the person, as in many cultures it is the free-soul that survives into the afterlife. This is exactly what we find in the *Iliad*, as in a number of cases it is said of warriors that their *psychê* leaves them at the moment they are killed: after Hyperenor had been fatally hit, his *psychê* quickly left him (XIV.518–19), and when the Trojan Pandarus had been fatally struck by Diomedes with the help of Athena, "his *psychê* and *menos* (see above) were loosed" (V.296).[17] Regarding others, such as Patroclus (XVI.856), Hector (XXII.362), and Odysseus' comrade Elpenor (*Odyssey* 10.560 and 11.65), it is added that the *psychê* went to Hades.[18] The *thymos*, on the other hand, never goes to Hades: it is so closely connected to the body that it disintegrates and disappears with it. It is interesting to see that Homer felt the need to explain this anthropology to his audience: it seems that there was some discussion going on about the eventual fate of mankind after death. When Odysseus meets his mother, Antikleia, in the underworld, she tells him

> Persephone, Zeus' daughter is not deceiving you,
> but this is the law of mankind, when somebody dies:
> the sinews no longer hold flesh and bones together,
> but the strong force of blazing fire subdues them,
> as soon as the *thymos* leaves the white bones,
> and the *psychê*, flying away like a dream, has flown off.
> (*Odyssey* 11.217–22)

The terminology of flying fits the appearance of winged souls in contemporary Greek art. In fact, the idea of the flying soul may well go back to the Mycenaean era of the second millennium B.C.E., as golden butter-flies—*psychê* is also the Greek term for "butterfly"—have been found in Mycenaean graves, and depictions of soul-birds appear on sarcophagi of that period (Gallou 2005; Vermeule 1979).

It is important to note, though, that we do not find a Cartesian dualism of body and soul in Homer. No opposition is set up between the *psychê* and the body it has left. On the contrary, it is remarkable that, in Homer, *sôma*, "body," is almost certainly used only for corpses of people and animals,[19] as was already noted by the ancient literary scholar Aristarchus.[20] A good example is found in the description of Odysseus' visit to the underworld:

> The first to come was the *psychê* of my comrade Elpenor.
> for he had not yet been buried beneath the broad-wayed earth,
> as we had left his *sôma* in the hall of Circe,
> unwept and unburied, since another task urged us on.
>
> (*Odyssey* 11.51–55)

Yet a poem of Homer's younger contemporary Archilochus (fragment 196a.51 West[2]) shows that the early Greeks could very well use *sôma* as a term for the body of a living person, as the "I" of the poem says, "and caressing all of her beautiful *sôma*, I let go my (white?) force [probably semen], touching her blond hair." Theognis (*ca.* 550 B.C.E.), too, can say: "Ah wretched Poverty, why do you lie upon my shoulders and disfigure my *sôma* and *noos*" (649–50). Apparently, we have here an idiosyncratic usage of *sôma* by Homer.[21] However this may be, it is clear that the dead no longer feel a connection to their bodies, as it is twice said explicitly of those in the underworld that their *sôma*, "corpse," was left on earth (*Odyssey* 11.52–53, 24.186–87). These expressions clearly stress the difference between the living bodies they once were and their present wraithlike state. It fits the latter way of picturing the dead that the *psychê* of the dead cannot be touched (*Iliad* XXIII.100), that they lack *phrenes* (*Iliad* XXIII.104), and that only the dead seer Teiresias possesses a *noos*: the others are mere *skiai*, "shadows" (*Odyssey* 11.493–95). With the latter term, which in this connection appears only in the plural in Homer, we meet another characterization of the souls of the dead as a group in the underworld, which stresses their wraithlike state, but which is not used in connection with the soul of the living, unlike, for example, in India (O'Sullivan 2010).

Instead of contrasting the *psychê* with the body (Bremmer 2010), Homer uses the demonstrative pronoun *autos*, "self," to denote that which we would call "body" in similar circumstances and to contrast in this way the actual body with something of somewhat lesser importance (Bonifazi 2009; Brown 2005; Rohde 1898: 5). This is well illustrated by the beginning of the *Iliad*, where it is said that the wrath of Achilles

> sent down to Hades many strong *psychas*, "souls,"
> of heroes, but made *autous*, "themselves," into a spoil for dogs
> and a banquet for birds.
>
> (Iliad I.3–5)

A similar case is found in the description of a dream of Achilles:

> Then there came to him the *psychê* of unhappy Patroclus,
> in every respect like *autôi*, "himself," in stature, fair eyes
> and voice, and like were the clothes that he bore about his body.
>
> (Iliad XXIII.65–67)

It is striking that at this moment, when he is not yet buried (see section 3), Patroclus still very much looks like the person he was when he was alive (Note also *Iliad* XXIII.105–07). This seems to be an elementary characteristic of recently dead persons in Archaic Greece during the liminal period between death and entry into the underworld, which was only possible after a proper burial. This clearly appears from the description just cited of Odysseus' meeting with Elpenor, where the latter's *psychê* comes forward, "for he [no change of subject] had not yet been buried": evidently Homer makes no distinction between the individual Elpenor and his *psychê*; the properties of the one are the properties of the other (Cairns 2003: 62).

The identity of the deceased and his soul could also be expressed by the term *eidôlon*, "image," a word that suggests that, for the ancient Greeks, the dead looked like the living. Sometimes *psychê* is connected with *eidôlon*, as in the case of Patroclus. As soon as he leaves in the dream just cited, Achilles notes that his *eidôlon* looked like him but lacked *phrenes* (*Iliad* XXIII.104). In other words, Homer stresses that the *psychai* look like their owners when they were alive, but can no longer function like them. Evidently, the Archaic Greeks believed that recently dead souls moved and spoke like the living, and the image of the deceased in the memory of the living must have played a major part in this way of imagining them. In Odysseus' visit to the underworld in book 11 (541–43) of the *Odyssey*, Orion and Heracles are even depicted as continuing their earthly activities, and Ajax's *psychê* stands "angrily" aside whereas others are "grieving."[22] On the other hand, the souls of the dead are also depicted as being unable to move or speak properly: when the soul of Patroclus leaves Achilles, he disappears squeaking like a bat (*Iliad* XXIII.100–1).

At death, then, it was the *psychê* that left the body of the dying person. Certainly during the liminal period between death and the funeral, the notion of the *psyche* was influenced by the image of the deceased in the memory of the living, by the circumstances of the death, and by the brute fact of the actual dead body. In the end, we cannot imagine the recently deceased other than as normal human beings. We have to translate from the known to the unknown, but we do this via the known. These ideas were never completely systematized and could occur together in a single description, as we have seen with Achilles and Patroclus. Given that we are talking about the area of the unknown, a certain lack of consistency should not surprise us. After all, there is no established authority to inform humankind reliably about the hereafter.

## The Ritual Aspect

What happened after death at the ritual level? It is not as easy to answer that question. Whereas with Homer we have a relatively homogeneous corpus of texts that inform us about the soul, his epics are less helpful for a substantial description of the immediate aftermath of death. This means that we have to add details from other texts to acquire a better picture. Fortunately, we can also add iconographic evidence (Haug 2012: 45–118; Huber 2001) because, from the eighth century onwards, the Athenians put funeral scenes on vases in order to glorify their aristocratic families (Boschung 2003). Moreover, we have several stipulations about funeral rites that were ascribed to the Athenian politician Solon who lived at the beginning of the sixth century b.c.e. (Blok 2006). Even where we cannot be certain about the reliability of this ascription, there can be little doubt that most of them belong to the Archaic period. We know that the Homeric text was written in an Ionian dialect (Wachter 2007), and, as the Athenians were Ionians too, we may at least suppose that they probably had related rites, the more so as they shared several festivals, even though there will have been local developments and variations. At the same time, the vases illustrate some limitations of our investigation. Virtually all our evidence derives from Homer and the upper class of Attica and, moreover, its male members: there is no literary description of a female funeral in the Archaic Age, although iconographic representations of the *prothesis* of women are also attested.[23] This evidence may well point to a fact of Greek life: the funeral rites of passage as described here were limited to the more well-to-do inhabitants, even though the rest of the population, too, will have buried its dead, as burial was normative (see below). It is doubtful, however, that the elite thought of the underworld as also a place for the poor and slaves, who are never mentioned in our evidence. One final but important point: anyone who studies the literature about Greek funeral rites will soon notice that the evidence from Archaic and Classical times is usually combined in the descriptions (Garland 1985; Kurtz and Boardman 1971). I intend to avoid that mistake and therefore concentrate on the Archaic period only.

Let us start by observing that a proper disposal of the body of the deceased was of paramount importance to the Archaic and Classical Greeks, as Sophocles' famous tragedy *Antigone* so poignantly demonstrates.[24] The right to burial was seen as a Panhellenic custom (Euripides, *Supplices* 526), to which even enemies were entitled, and only traitors and temple robbers could expect their bodies to be thrown out unburied (Bremmer 1983: 90–92; Parker 1983: 43–48). This is twice stressed by a soul of the dead in Homer. Patroclus' *psychê* says to Achilles,

> You sleep, but you have proved forgetful of me, Achilles.
> You were not unmindful of me when you were alive, but you are now I am dead.
> Bury me as fast as possible, let me pass inside the gates of Hades.
> The *psychai*, the *eidôla* of the worn out, keep me far away,
> and they do not yet allow me to mingle with them beyond the river,
> but vainly I wander through the wide-gated house of Hades.
> And give me your hand, I beg you, for never more again
> will I return from Hades, when once you have given me my share of fire.
>
> (*Iliad* XXIII.69–76)

And Elpenor beseeches Odysseus:

> Do not, when you depart, leave me behind unwept and unburied
> and turn away, lest I become a cause of the gods' wrath against you,
> but burn me with my weapons, such as they are,
> and heap up a mound for me on the shore of the grey sea,
> in memory of an unlucky man for future generations.
>
> (*Odyssey* 11.72–76)

It has been argued that these passages do not indicate a belief that the souls of the dead could not enter Hades unless their bodies had been properly cremated and the remains buried, on the grounds that, in a number of passages, the dead pass straight to Hades (section 2; Cairns 2003: 55; Clarke 1999: 187–89; Rohde 1898: 26f.). This seems to me a misjudgment of the literary character of these passages. First, it is not necessary for the poet to add that these slain warriors had to have a funeral before entering Hades. That was perfectly familiar to his audience. Second, although not yet buried, Patroclus can say that he wanders through the "wide-gated house of Hades," an expression which must be very old as it has Hittite, Indian, Latin, and Irish parallels;[25] Elpenor, too, states that his *"psychê* had gone down to the house of Hades" (*Odyssey* 10.65), but he still requests a proper funeral (see above) as he had been left unburied. Apparently, it was possible to use the expression "Hades" to denote both the whole of the underworld, including the area before the Styx, and the underworld in the strict sense. Last, but not least, according to an old myth, the trickster Sisyphus had ordered his wife to omit the final rites. This meant that he could not be properly admitted by the god Hades, who sent him back to order his wife to complete the rites. Understandably, Sisyphus did not return and in retribution received the famous penalty of having to roll a boulder uphill and then watch it roll back down again.[26]

But what did these rites entail? (For general surveys, see Alexiou 2002; Garland 1985; Kurtz and Boardman 1971: 142–61; Rohde 1898: 22–32). Taking descriptions by Homer as our point of departure and following an emic Greek division,[27] we may divide the final rites into three parts: the *prothesis*, "the laying out of the body," the *ekphora*, "the carrying to the place of the cremation," and the cremation with its concomitant rites. Let us start with the *prothesis*, which was by far the most frequently depicted of the three parts of the Archaic funeral.[28] We get a good idea of the beginning of the funeral rites from the events following the death of Patroclus. Achilles ordered his comrades to heat water in a cauldron:

> And then they washed him [Patroclus] and anointed him richly with oil,
> filling his wounds with ointment nine years old,
> and they laid him on his bed and covered him with a soft linen cloth
> from head to foot, and on top of it a white robe.
>
> (*Iliad* XVIII.350–53)

Similarly, Agamemnon's *psychê* tells the *psychê* of Achilles that, after the latter had been killed, they carried his body out of the battle and

> We laid you on a bed, and cleansed your beautiful flesh
> with warm water and with ointment, and many
> hot tears the Danaans shed around you, and they cut locks from their hair.
>
> (*Odyssey* 24.44–46)

In these two cases, we have warriors killed in action, but there must also have been male Greeks who died quietly in their beds, as Andromache's words of mourning to Hector illustrate: "when dying you did not stretch your hands out to me from your bed and you did not speak a word of wisdom for me to remember forever, crying night and day" (*Iliad* XXIV.742–45). Apparently, and interestingly, a man could expect his wife to be at his side and to support him in his last moments. Similarly, Agamemnon (*Odyssey* 11.424–26) reproaches his wife and murderess Clytaemnestra that "she did not close my eyes nor did she close my mouth with her hands" — a pathetic detail as Clytaemnestra's hands did rather different things to him. It is needless to add, but let it be mentioned in passing, that we never hear of Greek husbands performing the same service for their wives.[29]

The rites continued with the washing of the body, an act that is still as important today as it was in Classical times (Andronikos 1968: 2–4; Ginouvès 1962). However, what is noticeable in these passages is the absence of any sense of pollution, which is well attested in the Classical period in connection with corpses. It seems not unlikely that later times were less free in this respect than the Archaic Age: in the *Iliad* Achilles touches the breast (XVIII.317; XXIII.18) and head (XXIII.136) of Patroclus, and Hecuba together with Andromache touch the head of Hector (XXIV.712, 724). Such touching can be regularly seen on Archaic representations of the *prothesis*.[30] Lack of data makes it difficult for us to decide whether this lack of a sense of pollution in Homer is due to an artistic choice or if the notion first developed later.[31] Ointment with perfumed oil may have helped to suppress the smell of the body—at least that was the emic interpretation in Roman times (Lucian, *De luctu* 11); at the least, there were special containers for this oil, the so-called *phormiskoi*, whose clay copies seem to have been exclusively funerary (Hatzivassiliou 2001: 123–33; Kefalidou 2003; Shapiro 1991: 637). Given the combat situation in Homer, it is not surprising that men performed all these tasks in the preparation of the body, whereas in the Classical period, it was always women who did these rather dirty tasks, as may well have been the case, too, in Archaic Greece in peaceful circumstances.[32]

After being cleansed, the body was laid out on a bed on top of a cloth (Ahlberg 1971: 55–63), the feet towards the door (Eustathius on *Iliad* XIX.212) and the head supported by a kind of pillow (Ahlberg 1971: figs. 24, 25, 29, etc.). Patroclus is covered by a white robe and a cloth from head to foot. Although this is the case on only half of the Geometric vases, the trend was towards being covered, with females always covered (Ahlberg 1971: 40–45). The cloth that Penelope was spinning to keep the suitors at bay was, as she says (*Odyssey* 2.96–102), meant to be the shroud for Odysseus' father Laertes. Yet it must have been normal to have more than one cloth, as Achilles keeps "two robes and a fair-woven tunic" from Priam's ransom to wrap Hector's body in (*Iliad* XXIV.580–81). In later times, more garments may have even been the norm, as Solon ordered that there should be no more than three.[33] The white robe has been found again in the tomb precinct of Hipparete, the daughter of Alcibiades (Barber 1991; Kübler 1976: 83–84), and is regularly mentioned in later literary sources;[34] in the second century C.E., it was still a bad omen for a sick person to dream of a white robe (Artemidorus 2.3). But archaeological finds show that there were also fabrics with purple stripes and linen cloths embroidered with a gold and silver thread: the laying out of the body must have also been the occasion for a conspicuous display of wealth (Closterman 2007: 53f).

There were probably two more parts to the preparation of the body. In Classical times, the dead, but not the mourners (Aristotle, fragment 101 Rose3), were adorned with a wreath consisting of seasonal plants, which were also strewn on the bed. Yet this is not mentioned by Homer and is absent from the vases, although it is often mentioned in later literature.[35] The wreath made the deceased stand out among the living, but is hardly a sign of purity (*contra* Parker 1983: 35). At the end of the Archaic period, we start to find mention of the ferryman Charon, a traditional feature of many underworlds, who is found first in the late Archaic epic *Minyas* (F 1 Davies/Bernabé).[36] The growing monetization of Athens also affected belief in the ferryman, and the custom of burying a deceased person with an obol, a small coin, for Charon becomes visible on Athenian vases in the late fifth century, just as it is mentioned first in literature in Aristophanes' *Frogs* (137–42, 269–70) of 405 B.C.E., although it never became a practice accepted by everybody.[37] This development will have been too late for the Archaic period, but we also hear of the gift of a honey cake to the dead in order to calm Cerberus (Aristophanes, *Lysistrata* 601 and scholion ad loc), which may well have preceded the gift of an obol, as Cerberus is well attested in the Archaic period (Woodford and Spier 1992).

Yet the *prothesis* concerned not only the deceased, but also their relatives and friends. When mourning Patroclus, Achilles put dust and ashes on his head and face and even wallowed in the dung (*Iliad* XVIII.23–27, XX.414, XXIV.163–65, 640), and both Priam (*Iliad* XXII.414; XXIV.163–64) and Laertes (*Odyssey* 24.315–17) behaved in a similar manner. Achilles also tears out his hair (*Iliad* XVIII.27), and the shade of Agamemnon mentions that the Greek warriors cut locks from their hair (*Odyssey* 24.46), and that is what Achilles, too, did to mourn Patroclus (*Iliad* XXIII.46). They demeaned themselves—but in moderation. Mourners could refrain from food and washing, like Achilles (*Iliad* XIX.304–8, XXIII.42), or Demeter when grieving the loss of her daughter (*Homeric Hymn to Demeter* 47–50). Women expressed their grief in a more intense manner: they beat their chests (*Iliad* XVIII.31, 51, XIX.285), struck their heads with two hands (Ahlberg 1971: 118–20; Coldstream 1996–97: 7; Haug 2012: 110), scratched their neck and cheeks (*Iliad* II.700, XI.393, XIX.284; Hesiod, *Aspis* 242–3;),[38] tore out their hair, and ripped up their clothes (*Iliad* XVIII.30–31, XXII.405–6; *Homeric Hymn to Demeter* 40–1; Aeschylus, *Choephoroi* 21–28, 423–28; Euripides, *Hecuba* 650–56, *Helen* 374 and 1089, *Suppliants* 51, *Troades* 279–80, 789–95 and 1235).[39] This greater female emotional intensity was also expressed in another manner. On most vases, we see women and youths standing closest to the deceased, whereas the males keep some distance. The Sappho Painter, who worked around 500 B.C.E., has even written the kinship relationships as captions near the mourners on one of his images. Not surprisingly, perhaps, it is the mother who embraces the deceased youth of this black-figure funerary plaque, but we also see his younger sisters, grandmother, aunts, and even his nurse, all close to the deceased, whereas the father is greeting the guests (Garland 1985: 29;

Shapiro 1991: 638–39 [captions]. In general, Dillon 2002; Haug 2012: 96f; Havelock 1982).

The difference between the roles of men and women appears not only in the mourning gestures they make, but also in their verbal roles, and in particular in their respective lamentations (On lamentation, see especially Alexiou 2002; De Martino 1958; Holst-Warhaft 1992; Loraux 1990; Reiner 1938; Richer 1994; Schauer 2002; Stevanovic 2009. Cross-cultural: Meuli 1975: 1.325–31). The contrast can be well seen in the description of the laying out of the corpse of Hector. After it has been brought home, they

> laid him on a corded bed, and by his side set singers,
> leaders of the dirge, who led the song of lamentation,
> they chanted the dirge, and to it the women added their laments.
> And among these white-armed Andromache led the *goos*, "wailing,"
> holding in her hands the head of man-slaying Hector.
> (*Iliad* XXIV.720–24)

Subsequently, we hear the laments of Hector's mother, Hecuba, and of Helen. This is a unique case, as normally our sources stress the fact that the women's wailing was shrill and immoderate. It is only in this literary text, seemingly, that they were controlled and articulate. Of course, the mourners mourned the dead, but they also lamented their own fate.[40] One final aspect: lamentation was obligatory and considered to be an honor for the dead (*Iliad* XXIII.9; 4.197; *Odyssey* 24.190), and we hear that even slaves and subjected peoples had to lament the death of Greek grandees (Tyrtaeus, fragment 7 West[2]; Meuli 1975: 1.365). It was clearly a matter of the highest reproach that Clytaemnestra had buried her murdered husband Agamemnon without lamenting him (Aeschylus, *Choephoroi* 429).

With these observations we have come to the end of the *prothesis*. There is only one problem left. Where did all this take place? A war is of course not a normal situation, and Homer cannot be the norm in this respect. Regarding less spectacular funerals, earlier discussions had always taken the view that this part of the funerary ritual occurred in the home of the deceased. Yet a careful study of the iconographic representations on the vase paintings has now established that, normally, the laying out of the corpse took place in a kind of tent in front of the house. This must have been the case in Athens until Solon, who ordered in his laws that the *prothesis* should take place inside the house.[41] Given that other Archaic cities also tried to limit ostentatious display by the aristocracy, we may surmise that this development took place in most communities in the Greek world.[42] There must have been other developments as well. During the period under discussion, there seems to have been a certain trend towards a more egalitarian society regarding the males, even though we should not push this development too much (Duplouy 2010: 295). On the other hand, differences in gender became more stressed and were put on public display by letting the women do the most emotional work as well as the actual preparations of the body; at the same time, though, the social position of women in general seems to have become increasingly restricted, as rich female graves disappeared in the course of the Geometric period (Houby-Nielsen 1995; Whitley 1996).

Yet we should not end by stressing the developmental aspect of the ritual. It is rather amazing that on visual representations the same scheme occurs from Mycenaean to Late Archaic times. Apparently, Greek funeral ritual, or at least its representation, remained conservative over many centuries (Boschung 2003: 31–32; see also Cavanagh and Mee 1995; Haug 2012: 63; Panagiotopoulos 2007).

After some days—we do not know how many exactly—the body was transported in daylight to the place of the funeral, the so-called *ekphora*. The noun itself is attested first only in the fifth century,[43] but the corresponding verb already occurs in the description quoted below. It is rather striking that this part of the funeral is rarely represented on the surviving vases: only three examples are known.[44] Our texts are also not very informative. Regarding Hector, Homer tells us only that, after Priam addressed the Trojans,

> They yoked oxen and mules to wagons, and
> quickly then gathered together before the city.
> For nine days they brought in abundant wood,
> but when the tenth dawn arose, giving light to mortals,
> then they carried bold Hector out (*exepheron*), shedding tears,
> and on the topmost pyre they laid the corpse and cast fire on it.
>
> (*Iliad* XXIV.782–87)

In this description, all attention is focused on the making of the pyre, as is the case with the cremation of Patroclus (*Iliad* XXIII.110–27). When the pyre is ready, Achilles orders his Myrmidons to arm themselves and prepare the horses:

> They rose and put on their armour,
> and mounted their chariots, warriors and charioteers alike.
> In front were the men in chariots, and after them followed a cloud of foot soldiers,
> men past counting, and in their midst his comrades carried Patroclus.
> And they wholly clothed the corpse with their hair that they cast on it,
> cutting it off. And behind them noble Achilles clasped the head,
> sorrowing, for he was sending his incomparable comrade to Hades.
>
> (*Iliad* XXIII.131–37)

It is clear that the description focuses on the essentials of the ritual. Yet in reality, things will have happened less speedily. There must have been preparations for collecting the wood, but also the food and drink for the meal afterwards. Solon's (Plutarch, *Solon* 21.5) laws limited the size of funerary baskets to no longer than a cubit in length, which suggests that, in his time, people used quite sizable baskets to bring the funerary paraphernalia to the place of cremation or the crypt afterwards. But even the description of Patroclus' *ekphora* suggests that the funeral of a mighty warrior must have been an impressive occasion. From an Attic early seventh-century clay model of the *ekphora* and the few other available visual representations, we can see that the bed with the deceased was usually lifted on a cart drawn by horses or mules, to be followed by chariots and horses as well as by lamenting women (e.g., see Duplouy 2010: 285). The fact that Solon ordered that the bier should be followed first by the men and only then by the women suggests that, in his time, this order was still not the rule. Patroclus' *ekphora* indicates that in exceptional circumstances, the bed with the body was carried by hand, and in later times, this still happened sometimes with famous dead, such as during the funerals of Timoleon (Plutarch, *Timoleon* 39), Demonax (Lucian, *Demonax* 67), and Herodes Atticus (Philostratus, *Life of the Sophists* 2.1.15; see also Kavoulaki 2005).

The final disposal of the bodies, the *thêkê*, of Patroclus and Hector took place in Homer by means of impressive pyres, and, in real life, these pyres would probably have been somewhat smaller. When the pyre was extinguished, the bones, covered with robes, were collected in an urn (*Iliad* XXIII.236–54 [Patroclus]; XXIV.795–96 (Hector); Euripides, *Suppliants* 1126; Petropoulou 1988). In the period under discussion, cremation was not always the norm, but cremation and inhumation regularly alternated in Athens, although children were always inhumed—cremation was perhaps too costly an affair for them.[45] Earlier generations of scholars often postulated changes in beliefs as the background to these alternations, but contemporary scholars are much more skeptical about this, and there is no reason to suspect volatility in the Athenian belief system in this respect (Polignac 2005; Zurbach 2005).

After the disposal of the body, came the reassertion of the values of life. In the heroic era this happened most conspicuously with funerary games, which allowed the warriors to show off their strength and vitality (Meuli 1968; Roller 1981a, b). When the aristocracy started to lose ground in the course of the sixth century B.C.E., such games became a thing of the past. But there was also the meal after the funeral, the *perideipnon*, which was so obligatory that not even Orestes could skip one after the murder of his mother, Clytaemnestra, and her lover, Aegisthus (*Odyssey* 3.309; *Iliad* XXIV.801–3; Aeschylus, *Choephoroi* 483ff; Hegesippus, fragment 1.12–13

Kassel/Austin).[46] In the Archaic period, this meal was originally held near the pyre or the grave, as numerous archaeological finds of food and bones demonstrate (Kistler 1998), but after Solon, the meal in Athens had to be celebrated at the home of the deceased. An official end of mourning is not recorded in our period, but in later sources, we hear of ceremonies on the third, ninth, and thirtieth day, as well as annual celebrations (Bremmer 1987; Garland 1985: 39–41; Johnston 1999). In contrast to modern times, the ancients clearly structured the mourning periods, which must have made it easier to take leave of the dead.

But where was the soul all this time? Our Homeric material, as quoted above, suggests that after death the so-called body-souls were no longer mentioned, but that only the *psychê* was thought to linger at the entrance to Hades. Yet that was perhaps not the only possibility, and both literary influences and compositional necessities may well have determined this picture. Black-figured vases of the end of the sixth century show Patroclus' soul in the shape of an armed *homunculus* hovering over his dead body.[47] Such representations had a long life, and on the fifth-century Athenian white lekythoi, these winged souls are often pictured near the bier or the tomb (Oakley 2004: 81, 211–13). On a well-known lekythos by the Sabouroff Painter of about 440 B.C.E., Hermes guides the deceased to Charon, who is surrounded by a swarm of small souls (Oakley 2004: 115 fig. 72). Their plurality fits the description of the dead in Homer, who are called "the outworn ones" (*Iliad* III.278, XXIII.72; *Odyssey* 11.476, 24.14) or "the feeble heads of the dead" (*Odyssey* 10.521, 11.29): after the funeral, the deceased gradually seems to have joined the other dead, who were not represented as individuals but as an enormous, undifferentiated group: we never find the Homeric vocabulary of *nekyes/nekroi*, "the dead," in the singular.[48] This lack of individuality is well illustrated by a fragment of Sophocles, where the dead are compared to a swarm of bees: "Up (from the underworld) comes the swarm of the souls, loudly humming" (fragment 879 Radt).[49] With so many visitors, it is not hard to understand that Aeschylus called the Lord of the Underworld "the most hospitable Zeus of the dead" (Aeschylus, *Supplices* 157 and fragment 228 Radt; Henrichs 1991: 194f). Evidently, as time went on, the deceased lost their individuality, the last step in their transition from life to death.

Finally, it is not difficult to see in the Greek notions of *prothesis, ekphora,* and *thêkê* also a reflection of van Gennep's famous *rites de séparation, de marge,* and *d'agrégation* ([1909] 1960). The former living person is first treated as a dead person, then transported out of the world of the living to the grave and, finally, is left in the grave and joins the society of the dead. From this triad, the initial stage, the *prothesis,* was clearly the most important phase of the funeral ritual. Although van Gennep himself noted that not all of his three stages were always equally important in rituals, it has recently been observed that ritual beginnings in particular have long been underconceptualized (Lambek 2007), and our sources indeed leave us uncertain about who actually started the funerary proceedings and who supervised them. This is not really surprising, as the Greeks themselves called the funeral rites *ta nomizomena*, "the customary acts" (Lysias 32.8; Isaeus 2.4, 4.19, 9.4, and 32; Aeschines 3.77). The term shows that they did not feel the need to give many details of what was clearly considered to be familiar to everyone. What was important for the Archaic Greeks, it seems, was the actual separation of the deceased from the world of the living, with relatively little attention to the actual disposal of the body or the survival of the soul. It was this life, not the life everlasting, which was of significance to the Greeks. It was therefore the separation from this life that concerned them most and made the liminal period between death and funeral such a striking ritual event.[50]

**Jan N. Bremmer** (PhD Amsterdam 1979) is Professor Emeritus of Religious Studies at the Faculty of Theology and Religious Studies of the University of Groningen, the Netherlands. He was visiting scholar in Princeton, Christ Church (NZ), Los Angeles, Edinburgh, Cologne, Munich, New York, Erfurt and Freiburg. His main areas of research are Greek and Roman religion and Early Christianity. His most recent books include *Greek Religion and Culture, the Bible and the Ancient Near East* (2008), *The Rise of Christianity through the Eyes of Gibbon, Harnack and Rodney Stark* (2010) and *Initiation into the Mysteries of the Ancient World* (2014).

## Notes

1. In this chapter, I make generous use of my studies of the soul since Bremmer 1983, where I also give the previous bibliography. I mention especially Bremmer 2002a; 2002b; 2009; 2010.
2. In my translations, I have happily, but not slavishly, followed those of Wyatt (*Iliad*) and Dimock (*Odyssey*) in the Loeb Classical Library (published by Harvard University Press).
3. For close analyses of the Homeric material, see more recently Chadwick 1996; Clarke 1999 (to be read with the important review article by Cairns 2003); Meyer 2008; Nordheider 2010; Padel 1992; Sullivan 1988; 1995.
4. Note also Tyrtaeus 10.14, 10.18, 11.5, and 12.18 West[2] for risking one's *psychê* in battle; Pisander fragment 8.1 West and Bernabé for lying and risking one's *psychê*; the *varia lectio* in Archilochus 5.3 West[2].
5. Similarly, *Iliad* V.654, IX.406–09, XI.445, XVI.625, XX.159–61; *Odyssey* 1.5; note also the connection between *psychê* and a race in Hesiod, fragment 76.7 Merkelbach/West.
6. Note also Solon, fragment 13.46 West[2] for risking the *psychê* in the context of making money
7. Cf. *Iliad* XXII.475; *Odyssey* 24.349, *contra* Cairns 2003: 50, note 23.

8.    *Iliad* XVI.453; *Odyssey* 9.523–24 (cf. Bremmer 1983: 15–16); Cairns 2003: 49, note 21.

9.    Greece: Jouanna 1987. Indo-European: Adams 1999; Eichner 2002.

10.   The quotation is from Gold Leaf no. 1 (*Orphicorum Fragmenta* 476 Bernabé) in the standard edition of Graf and Johnston 2013²; note also Euripides, *Orestes* 1163; Plato, *Cratylus* 399de.

11.   As is stressed by Cairns 2003: 47–49 (quote at 47).

12.   For this development, see the very learned analysis of Frede 2001; Mansfeld 1990: 3065–85.

13.   The meaning of *rhetea*, the term interpreted here as limbs, is debated. See Cairns 2003: 53, note 31; Markwald 2010.

14.   In *Iliad* XXII.208 Zeus weighs the *kêres*, "fates," of Achilles and Hector, but in Aeschylus (F 279–80a Radt) we find the weighing of souls; in the iconographic evidence, it is often difficult to decide if souls or fates are represented; cf. Vollkommer 1992. Note also Archilochus, fragments 91.30 and 144 West² (unfortunately, these fragments are too fragmentary to help us any further).

15.   For a thorough survey of the various discussions of this phenomenon in the course of the nineteenth and twentieth centuries, see Jahn 1987; note also Barra-Salzédo 2007; Gelzer et al. 1988; Sullivan 1996a; see also the various lemmata in the *Lexikon des frühgriechischen Epos* (see bibliography s.v. Nordheider).

16.   For a review of the Scandinavian approach, see Bremmer 1983: 9–12; Wernhart 2002: 53–57.

17.   See also *Iliad* V.696; VIII.123, 315; XI.333–34, 762–63; XVI.453, 505; XXII.256–57; XXIV.167–68, 754–56; *Odyssey* 11.217–22; 19.90–92; 21.153–54, 170–71.

18.   See also *Iliad* I.3–4; V.654; VII.328–30; XI.445; XVI.625; *Odyssey* 24.1–4.

19.   *Iliad* III.23, VII.79, XXII.342, XI.53, XII.67, XVIII.161, XXIII.169, XXIV.187; 11.53; cf. Clarke 1999: 116–19, 163–65, 315–19; Holmes 2010.

20.   Aristarchus in Apollonius Sophistes, *Lexicon Homericum* 148.23 Bekker; H. Erbse on scholion *Iliad* III.23–27.

21.   Note also Hesiod, *Works and Days*, 540; *Meropis*, fragment 6.3 Bernabé.

22.   This idea will long remain popular; see Verdière 1991.

23.   Ahlberg 1971: 39 notes forty-one male scenes to five female and seven uncertain examples; Shapiro 1991: 639; see also Hürzmüzlü 2010: 122–46.

24.   This aspect of the *Antigone* has often been discussed: see most recently Patterson 2006; Shapiro 2006.

25.   *Iliad* VII.131, XI.263, XIV.457, XX.366; Empedocles B 142 Diels/Kranz; Graf and Johnston 2013²: no. 1.2 (*Orphicorum Fragmenta* 474.2 Bernabé); Vergil, *Aeneid* 6.269; Janda 2000; West 2007: 388.

26.   Alcaeus, fragment 38 Voigt; Theognis 711fff. West²; Pherecydes *FGrH* 3 F 119 (F 119 Fowler); Eustathius on *Odyssey* 11.592; Fabiano 2008; Oakley 1994.

27.   Plato, *Laws* XII.947.

28.   For numbers, see Closterman 2007: 57. All previous discussions of the *prothesis* have now been superseded by Brigger and Giovannini 2004; add: Hiller 2006; Sheedy 1990. Note that the term *prothesis* occurs first in Plato, *Laws* XII.947, 959.

29.   Closing eyes: *Iliad* XI.452–53; 24.296; Euripides, *Hecuba* 430, *Phoenissae* 1451. Closing mouth: Andronikos 1968; Kurtz and Boardman 1971: pl. 33.

30.   See also Ahlberg 1971: 89; a *pinax* of about 500 B.C.E. (New York MMA 54.11.15); Boardman 1955: 56f.

31.   See the nuanced discussion by Parker 1983: 66–73. Perhaps, we should not talk of Achilles "polluting" himself when he is actually making himself dirty, *contra* Parker 1983: 68.

32.   Euripides, *Phoenissae* 1667; Plato, *Phaedo* 115; Isaeus 6.41, 8.22; Hame 2008.

33. Funeral garments: *Odyssey* 24.293; Plutarch, *Solon* 21.5; similar legislation can be found elsewhere in Greece, cf. Toher 1991.
34. Archilochus, fragment 9 West²; Lysias 12.18; Plato, *Laws* XII.947; Plutarch, *Questiones Romanae* 26; Lucian, *De luctu* 11; Pausanias 4.13.1.
35. Twigs on the bed: Ahlberg 1971: 293; Blech 1982 (dead without wreaths); Boardman 1955: 60–63. Literature: Aristophanes, *Lysistrata* 602, *Ecclesiasuzae* 538, 1032; Lucian, *De luctu* 11.
36. For Charon, see most recently Diez de Velasco 1995; Mugione 1995; Oakley 2004: 108–25; Sourvinou-Inwood 1995.
37. Oakley 2004: 123–25, 242 note 49 with bibliography; add Gorecki 1995; Schmitt 1991; Stefanakis 2002; Thüry 1999.
38. Blok 2006: 216 unpersuasively suggests a possible connection with a blood-sacrifice for the dead.
39. For a wide cross-cultural perspective, see Meuli 1975: 1.333–51. On youths, see Haug 2012: 77f.
40. *Iliad* XIX.301–2, 338–9, XXIV.166–68.
41. This is the persuasive conclusion, it seems to me, of Brigger and Giovannini 2004; Plutarch, *Solon* 21; scholion on Aristophanes, *Lysistrata* 611; Photius s.v. *prothesis*.
42. For the gradual "domestication" of the mourning gestures, see Huber 2001: 118f.
43. Aeschylus, *Choephoroi* 9 and 430, *Seven against Thebes* 1024.
44. Moore 2007: 11 note 7 compares Athens NM 803, Athens NM 990 and Bonn inv. 16 and mentions a still unpublished fourth example.
45. For a very clear chronological survey, see Étienne 2005.
46. Cf. Aristotle, fragment 611.60 Rose³; Menander, *Aspis* 232–33; Cicero, *De legibus* 2.59; Valerius Maximus 2.6 ext. 7; Plutarch, *Moralia* 296f.
47. See most recently Sourvinou-Inwood 1995: 325 n. 99, 328, 336–37, 340–41; Vollkommer 1997.
48. In the Archaic epic *Nostoi* (fragment 2 Bernabé), the souls of the dead are called *nekades*, again a plural.
49. Add now the Derveni Papyrus Col. VI.6, 8 Kouremenos, cf. Henrichs, 1984: 261–66.
50. This contribution was written in the stimulating environment of the Internationales Kolleg Morphomata in Cologne and completed in the equally stimulating environment of the Münchner Zentrum für Antike Welten. I profited from comments by Peter Berger, Justin Kroesen, and Bas van der Mije. Johannes Isépy helped with the bibliography. Orla Mulholland kindly and skillfully corrected my English.

# References

Adams, Douglas Q. 1999. *A Dictionary of Tocharian B*. Amsterdam: Rodopi.

Ahlberg, Gudrun. 1971. *Prothesis and Ekphora in Greek Geometric Art*. Göteborg: P. Åström.

Alexiou, Margaret. 2002. *The Ritual Lament in Greek Tradition*. Lanham, MD: Rowman & Littlefield.

Andronikos, Manoles. 1968. *Totenkult*. Archaeologica Homerica III W. Göttingen: Vandenhoeck & Ruprecht.

Balles, Irene. 2002. "Air. barae, gr. phrenes, gr. paprides und die Vertretung von idg. *-ku im Griechischen." In *Novalis indogermanica: Festschrift für Günter Neumann zum 80. Geburtstag*, ed. Matthias Fritz and Susanne Zeilfelder, 1–23. Graz: Leykam.

Barber, Elizabeth J.W. 1991. _Prehistoric Textiles_. Princeton, NJ: Princeton University Press, 204.

Barra-Salzédo, Edoarda. 2007. _En soufflant la grâce. Âmes, souffles et humeurs en Grèce ancienne_. Grenoble: J. Millon.

Biraud, Michèle. 1989. "Signification et histoire du mot êtor." _Les cahiers du LAMA_ 10: 1–32.

Blech, Michael. 1982. _Studien zum Kranz bei den Griechen_. Berlin: De Gruyter.

Blok, Josine H. 2006. "Solon's Funerary Laws: Questions of Authenticity and Function." In _Solon of Athens_, ed. Josine H. Blok and André P.M.H. Lardinois, 197–247. Leiden: Brill.

Boardman, John. 1955. "Painted Funerary Plaques and Some Remarks on Prothesis." _Annual British School Athens_ 50: 51–66.

Bonifazi, Anna. 2009. "Discourse Cohesion through Third Person Pronouns: The Case of _keinos_ and _autos_ in Homer." In _Discourse Cohesion in Ancient Greek_, ed. Stéphanie Bakker and Gerry Wakker, 1–19. Leiden: Brill.

Boschung, Dietrich. 2003. "Wie das Bild entstand: Kunstfertigkeit, Ruhmsucht und die Entwicklung der attischen Vasenmalerei im 8. Jahrhundert v. Chr." In _Medien in der Antike: kommunikative Qualität und normative Wirkung_, ed. Henner von Hesberg and Wolfgang Thiel, 17–49. Cologne: Lehr- und Forschungszentrum für die antiken Kulturen des Mittelmeerraumes der Universität zu Köln.

Bremmer, Jan N. 1983. _The Early Greek Concept of the Soul_. Princeton, NJ: Princeton University Press.

———. 1987. "Genesia." In _The Encyclopedia of Religion_, Vol. 5, ed. Mircea Eliade, 506–7. New York: Macmillan.

———. 2002a. _The Rise and Fall of the Afterlife_. London: Routledge.

———. 2002b. "The Soul in Early and Classical Greece." In _Der Begriff der Seele in der Religionswissenschaft_, ed. Johann Figl and Hans-Dieter Klein, 159–69. Würzburg: Königshausen & Neumann.

———. 2009. "Die Karriere der Seele: Vom antiken Griechenland ins moderne Europa." In _Europäische Religionsgeschichte_, Vol. 1, ed. Hans G. Kippenberg, Jörg Rüpke, and Kocku von Stuckrad, 497–524. Göttingen: Vandenhoek & Ruprecht.

———. 2010. "The Rise of the Unitary Soul and Its Opposition to the Body: From Homer to Socrates." In _Philosophische Anthropologie in der Antike_, ed. Ludger Jansen and Christoph Jedan, 11–29. Frankfurt am Main: Ontos Verlag.

Brigger, Eliane, and Adalberto Giovannini. 2004. "Prothésis: étude sur les rites funéraires chez les Grecs et les Étrusques." _Mélanges de l'École française de Rome_ 116: 179–224.

Brown, Christopher G. 2005. "The Stele of Mnesagora and Nikochares (CEG 84)." _Zeitschrift für Papyrologie und Epigraphik_ 152: 1–5.

Cairns, Douglas. 2003 "Myths and Metaphors of Mind and Mortality." _Hermathena_ 175: 41–75.

Caswell, Caroline P. 1990. _A Study of Thumos in Early Greek Epic_. Leiden: E.J. Brill.

Cavanagh, William, and Christopher Mee. 1995. "Mourning before and after the Dark Age." In _Klados: Essays in Honour of J.N. Coldstream_, ed. Christine Morris, 45–61. London: University of London, Institute of Classical Studies.

Chadwick, John. 1996. *Lexicographica Graeca*. Oxford: Clarendon Press, 307–20.

Cheyns, André. 1985. "Recherche sur l'emploi des synonymes êtor, kêr et kradiê dans l'Iliade et l'Odyssée." *Revue Belge de Philologie et d'Histoire* 63: 15–73.

Clarke, Michael J. 1999. *Flesh and Spirit in the Songs of Homer*. Oxford: Clarendon Press.

Closterman, Wendy E. 2007. "The Sappho Painter's Loutrophoros Amphora (Athens, NM 450) and Athenian Burial Ritual." *Classical Bulletin* 83: 49–64.

Coldstream, Nichola. 1996–97. "The Dipylon Krater Sydney 46.41: Context, Style and Iconography." *Mediterranean Archaeology* 9–10: 1–11.

De Martino, Ernesto. 1958. *Morte e pianto rituale nel mondo antico*. Turin: Edizioni scientifiche Einaudi.

Diez de Velasco, Francisco P. 1995. *Los caminos de la muerte*. Madrid: Trotta.

Dillon, Matthew. 2002. *Girls and Women in Classical Greek Religion*. London: Routledge.

Duplouy Alain, Olivier Mariaud, and François de Polignac. 2010. "Sociétés grecques de VIIe siècle av. J.-C." In *La Mediterranée au VIIe siècle avant Jésus-Christ*, ed. Roland Étienne, 275–309. Paris: De Boccard.

Eichner, Heiner. 2002. "Indogermanische Seelenbegriffe." In *Der Begriff der Seele in der Religionswissenschaft*, ed. Johann Figl and Hans-Dieter Klein, 131–41. Würzburg: Königshausen & Neumann.

Étienne, Roland. 2005. "L'incinération: l'exemple Athénien." *Ktèma* 30: 183–88.

Fabiano, Doralice. 2008. "La fatica di Sisifo e le astuzie di Hades." *I Quaderni del Ramo d'Oro on-line* 1: 238–57.

Frede, Michael. 2001. "Seelenlehre." In *Der Neue Pauly*, Vol. 11, 326f. Stuttgart: J.B. Metzler.

Gallou, Chrysanthi. 2005. *The Mycenaean Cult of the Dead*. Oxford: Archaeopress.

Garland, Robert. 1985. *The Greek Way of Death*. London: Duckworth.

Gelzer, Thomas and William Scovil Anderson. 1988. *How to Express Emotions of the Soul and Operations of the Mind in a Language That Has No Words for Them*. Proceedings of the Center for Hermeneutical Studies in Hellenistic and Modern Culture 55. Berkeley: Center for Hermeneutical Studies in Hellenistic and Modern Culture.

Ginouvès, René. 1962. *Balaneutiké, recherches sur le bain dans l'antiquité grecque*. Paris: De Boccard.

Ginzburg, Carlo. 2004. "Family Resemblances and Family Trees: Two Cognitive Metaphors." *Critical Inquiry* 30: 537–56.

Gorecki, Joachim. 1995. "Die Münzbeigabe, eine mediterrane Grabsitte. Nur Fahrlohn für Charon?" In *Des Lichtes beraubt. Totenehrung in der römischen Gräberstrasse von Mainz-Weisenau*, ed. Marion Witteyer and Peter Fasold, 93–103. Wiesbaden: Reichert.

Graf, Fritz, and Sarah I. Johnston. 2013². *Ritual Texts for the Afterlife: Orpheus and the Bacchic Gold Tablets*. London: Routledge.

Hame, Kerri J. 2008. "Female Control of Funeral Rites in Greek Tragedy: Klytaimestra, Medea, and Antigone." *Classical Philology* 103: 1–15.

Haug, Annette. 2012. *Die Entdeckung des Körpers*. Berlin: De Gruyter.

Hatzivassiliou, Eleni. 2001. "The Attic Phormiskos: Problems of Origin and Function." *Bulletin of the Institute of Classical Studies* 45: 113–48.

Havelock, Christine M. 1982. "Mourners on Greek Vases: Remarks on the Social History of Women." In *Feminism and Art History: Questioning the Litany*, ed. Norma Broude and Mary D. Garrard, 44–61. New York: Harper & Row.

Henrichs, Albert. 1984. "The Eumenides and Wineless Libations in the Derveni Papyrus." In *Atti del XVII Congresso Internazionale di Papirologia* II, 255–68. Naples: Centro internazionale dello studio dei papiri ercolanesi.

———. 1991. "Namenlosigkeit und Euphemismus." In *Fragmenta dramatica*, ed. Heinz Hofmann and Annette Harder, 161–201. Göttingen: Vandenhoeck & Ruprecht.

Hiller, Stefan. 2006. "The Prothesis Scene: Bronze Age–Dark Age Relations." In *Pictorial Pursuits. Figurative Painting on Mycenaean and Geometric Pottery*, ed. Eva Rystedt and Berit Wells, 183–90. Stockholm: Svenska Institutet i Athen.

Holmes, Brooke. 2010. *The Symptom and the Subject: The Emergence of the Physical Body in Ancient Greece*. Princeton: Princeton University Press.

Holst-Warhaft, Gail. 1992. *Dangerous Voices: Women's Lament in Greek Literature*. London: Routledge.

Houby-Nielsen, Sanne. 1995. "'Burial Language' in Archaic and Classical Kerameikos." *Proceedings of the Danish Institute at Athens* 1: 129–91.

Huber, Ingeborg. 2001. *Die Ikonographie der Trauer in der Griechischen Kunst*. Mannheim: Bibliopolis.

Hürmüzlü, Bilge. 2010. "Gruppe Klazomenischer Sarkophage aus Klazomenai." *Jahrbuch des Deutschen Archäologischen Instituts* 125: 89-153.

Jahn, Thomas. 1987. *Zum Wortfeld 'Seele-Geist' in der Sprache Homers*. Munich: C.H. Beck.

Janda, Michael. 2000. *Eleusis. Das indogermanische Erbe der Mysterien*. Innsbruck: Institut für Sprachwissenschaft der Universität Innsbruck.

Johnston, Sarah I. 1999. *Restless Dead*. Berkeley: University of California Press.

Jouanna, Jacques. 1987. "Le souffle, la vie et le froid: remarques sur la famille de psychô d'Homère à Hippocrate." *Revue des Etudes Grecques* 100: 203–24.

Kalogerakos, Ioannis G. 1996. *Seele und Unsterblichkeit. Untersuchungen zur Vorsokratik bis Empedokles*. Stuttgart: B.G. Teubner, 75–89 ("Anaximenes") and 96–97 ("Archelaos").

Kavoulaki, Athina. 2005. "Crossing Communal Space: The Classical Ekphora, 'Public' and 'Private.'" In *Idia kai demosia: Les cadres "privés" et "publics" de la religion grecque antique*. Kernos, Suppléments 15, ed. Véronique Dasen and Marcel Piérart, 129–45. Liège: Centre international d'étude de la religion grècque antique.

Kefalidou, Eurydice. 2003. "Vases for the Dead: Local Workshops of White-Ground Polychrome 'Phormiskoi.'" In *Griechische Keramik im kulturellen Kontext*, ed. Bernhard Schmaltz and Magdalene Söldner, 185–87. Münster: Scriptorum.

Kistler, Erich. 1998. *Die "Opferrinne-Zeremonie." Bankettideologie am Grab, Orientalisierung und Formierung einer Adelsgesellschaft in Athen*. Stuttgart: F. Steiner.

Kövecses, Zoltán. 2000. *Metaphor and Emotion: Language, Culture, and Body in Human Feeling*. Cambridge: Cambridge University Press.

Koziak, Barbara. 1999. "Homeric Thumos: The Early History of Gender, Emotion and Politics." *Journal of Politics* 61: 1068–91.

Kübler, Karl. 1976. *Die Nekropole der Mitte des 6. bis Ende des 5. Jahrhunderts*. Kerameikos, vol. 7.1. Berlin: W. de Gruyter.

Kurtz, Donna C., and John Boardman. 1971. *Greek Burial Customs*. London: Thames & Hudson.

Lakoff, George, and Mark Johnson. 1980. *Metaphors We Live By*. Chicago: Chicago University Press.

Lambek, Michael. 2007. "Sacrifice and the Problem of Beginning: Meditations from Sakalava Mythopraxis." *Journal of the Royal Anthropological Institute* 13: 19–38.

Loraux, Nicole. 1990. *Les mères en deuil*. Paris: Seuil.

Mansfeld, Jaap. 1990. "Doxography and Dialectic: The Sitz im Leben of the 'Placita.'" In *Aufstieg und Niedergang der Römischen Welt* II.36.4, ed. Wolfgang Haase, 3056–229. Berlin: W. de Gruyter.

Markwald, Georg. 2010. "Rhetos." In *Lexikon des frühgriechischen Epos*, vol. 4, 13. Göttingen: Vandenhoeck & Ruprecht.

Meuli, Karl. 1968. *Der griechische Agon*. Cologne: Historisches Seminar der deutschen Sporthochschule.

———. 1975. *Gesammelte Schriften*, 2 vols. Basel: Schwabe.

Meyer, Martin F. 2008. "Der Wandel des Psyche-Begriffs im frühgriechischen Denken. Von Homer bis Heraklit." *Archiv für Begriffsgeschichte* 50: 9–28.

Moore, Mary B. 2007. "Athens 803 and the Ekphora." *Antike Kunst* 50: 9–23.

Mugione Eliana, 1995. "La raffigurazione di Caronte in età greca." *Parola del Passato* 50: 357–75.

Nehring, Alfons. 1947. "Homer's Descriptions of Syncopes." *Classical Philology* 42: 106–21.

Nordheider, Hans W. 2010. "Psychê." In *Lexikon des frühgriechischen Epos*, vol. 4, 1310–18. Göttingen: Vandenhoeck & Ruprecht.

Oakley, John H. 1994. "Sisyphos I." In *Lexicon Iconographicum Mythologiae Classicae* 8.1, 781–87. Zurich: Artemis.

———. 2004. *Picturing Death in Classical Athens: The Evidence of the White Lekythoi*. Cambridge: Cambridge University Press.

O'Sullivan, John N. 2010. "Skiê." In *Lexikon des frühgriechischen Epos*, vol. 4, 149. Göttingen: Vandenhoeck & Ruprecht.

Padel, Ruth. 1992. *In and Out of the Mind: Greek Images of the Tragic Self*. Princeton, NJ: Princeton University Press.

Panagiotopoulos, Diamantis. 2007. "Mykenische Trauerbilder. Zu den Anfängen der griechischen funerären Ikonographie." In *Stephanos Aristeios. Archäologische Forschungen zwischen Nil und Istros. Festschrift für Stefan Hiller zum 65. Geburtstag*, ed. Felix Lang, Claus Reinholdt, and Jörg Weilhartner, 205–14. Vienna: Phoibos.

Parker, Robert. 1983. *Miasma: Pollution and Purification in Early Greek Religion*. Oxford: Clarendon Press.

Patterson, Cynthia B. 2006. "The Place and Practice of Burial in Sophocles' Athens." *Helios* 33, Supplement: 9–48.

Petropoulou, Angeliki. 1988. "The Internment of Patroklos (Iliad 23.252–57)." *American Journal of Philology* 109: 482–95.

Polignac, François de. 2005. "Perspectives et limites de l'analyse de l'incinération dans le monde grec." *Ktèma* 30: 173–81.

Reiner, Eugen. 1938. *Die rituelle Totenklage bei den Griechen*. Stuttgart: W. Kohlhammer.

Renehan, Robert. 1980. "On the Greek Origins of the Concepts Incorporeality and Immateriality." *Greek, Roman, and Byzantine Studies* 21: 105–38.

Richer, Nicolas. 1994. "Aspect des funérailles à Sparte." *Cahiers du Centre Gustave Glotz* 5: 51–96.

Rohde, Erwin. 1898. *Psyche*, 2 vols. Tübingen: J.C.B. Mohr.

Roller, Lynn E. 1981a. "Funeral Games for Historical Persons." *Stadion* 7: 1–18.

———. 1981b. "Funeral Games in Greek Art." *American Journal of Archaeology* 85: 107–19.

Schauer, Markus. 2002. *Tragisches Klagen: Form und Funktion der Klagedarstellung bei Aischylos, Sophokles und Euripides*. Tübingen: Narr.

Schmitt, Rüdiger. 1991. "Eine kleine persische Münze als Charonsgeld." In *Palaeograeca et Mycenaea Antonino Bartoněk quinque et sexagenario oblata*, 149–62. Brno: Universitas Masarykiana Brunensis.

Schnaufer, Albrecht. 1970. *Frühgriechischer Totenglaube*. Hildesheim: G. Olms.

Shapiro, Harvey A. 1991. "The Iconography of Mourning in Athenian Art." *American Journal of Archaeology* 95: 629–56.

———. 2006. "The Wrath of Creon: Withholding Burial in Homer and Sophocles." *Helios* 33, Supplement: 119–34.

Sheedy, Kenneth A. 1990. "A Prothesis Scene from the Analatos Painter." *Athenische Mitteilungen* 105: 117–51.

Sourvinou-Inwood, Christiane. 1995. *"Reading" Greek Death to the End of the Classical Period*. Oxford: Clarendon Press.

Stefanakis, Manolis I. 2002. "An Inexpensive Ride? A Contribution to Death-Coin Rites in Hellenistic Greece." *Numismatica e Antichità Classiche* 31: 171–89.

Stevanovic, Lada. 2009. "Funeral Ritual and Power: Farewelling the Dead in the Ancient Greek Funerary Ritual." *Bulletin of the Institute of Ethnography SASA* 57: 37–52.

Sullivan, Shirley D. 1988. "A Multi-Faceted Term: Psychê in Homer, the Homeric Hymns and Hesiod." *Studi Italiani di Filologia Classica* NS 6: 151–80.

———. 1989. "The Psychic Term Noos in Homer and the Homeric Hymns." *Studi Italiani di Filologia Classica* NS 7: 152–95.

———. 1993. "Person and Thymos in the Poetry of Hesiod." *Emerita* 61: 15–40.

———. 1994. "'Self' and Psychic Entities in Early Greek Epic." *Eos* 82: 5–16.

———. 1995. *Psychological and Ethical Ideas: What Early Greeks Say*. Leiden: E.J. Brill.

———. 1996a. "Metaphorical Uses of Psychological Terminology in Early Poetry: Evidence for Distinctive Meanings of the Terms." *Studi Italiani di Filologia Classica* NS 14: 129–51.

———. 1996b. "The Psychic Term Êtor: Its Nature and Relation to Person in Homer and the Homeric Hymns." *Emerita* 64: 11–29.

Thüry, Günther E. 1999. "Charon und die Funktionen der Münzen in römischen Gräbern der Kaiserzeit." In *Fundmünzen aus Gräbern*, ed. Olivier F. Dubuis and Suzanne Frey-Kupper, 17–30. Lausanne: Editions du Zèbre.

Toher, Mark. 1991. "Greek Funerary Legislation and the Two Spartan Funerals." In *GEORGICA: Studies in Honor of George Cawkwell*, ed. Michael A. Flower and Mark Toher, 159–75. London: University of London, Institute of Classical Studies.

Van der Mije, Sebastiaan R. 1991. Review of Jahn 1987. *Mnemosyne* IV 44: 440–45

———. 2011. "Peithein Phrena(s), Peithein Thymon: A Note on Homeric Psychology." *Mnemosyne* IV 64: 447–54

van Gennep, Arnold. (1909, in French) 1960. *The Rites of Passage*, trans. Monika B. Vizedom and Gabrielle L. Caffee. Chicago: University of Chicago Press.

Verdière, Raoul. 1991. "Le concept de la sensibilité après la mort chez les anciens." *Latomus* 50: 56–63.

Vermeule, Emily. 1979. *Aspects of Death in Early Greek Art and Poetry*. Berkeley: University of California Press.

Vollkommer, Rainer. 1992. "Ker." In *Lexicon Iconographicum Mythologiae Classicae* 6.1, 14–23. Zurich: Artemis

———. 1997. "*Eidola.*" In *Lexicon Iconographicum Mythologiae Classicae* 8.1, 566–70. Zurich: Artemis.

Wachter, Rudolf. 2007. "Greek Dialects and Epic Poetry: Did Homer Have to Be an Ionian?" In *Phônês charaktêr ethnikos*, ed. Miltiades B. Hatzopoulos, 317–28. Athens: Ethnikon hidryma Ereunon.

Wernhart, Karl R. 2002. "Ethnische Seelenkonzepte." In *Der Begriff der Seele in der Religionswissenschaft*, ed. Johann Figl and Hans-Dieter Klein, 45–60. Würzburg: Königshausen & Neumann.

West, Martin L. 2007. *Indo-European Poetry and Myth*. Oxford: Oxford University Press.

Whitley, James. 1996. "Gender and Hierarchy in Early Athens: The Strange Case of the Disappearance of the Rich Female Grave." *Mètis* 11: 209–32.

Woodford, Susan, and Jeffrey Spier. 1992. "Kerberos." In *Lexicon Iconographicum Mythologiae Classicae* 6.1, 24–32. Zurich: Artemis.

Zurbach, Julien. 2005. "Pratique et signification de l'incinération dans les poèmes homériques." *Ktèma* 30: 160–71.

*Figure 11.1.* A portrait of Giuseppe Tomasi di Lampedusa (Palermo 1896–Rome 1957).

# Chapter Eleven

# Death, Memory, and Liminality
Rethinking Lampedusa's Later Life as Author and Aristocrat

*Yme B. Kuiper*

> "Historical facts are, in essence, psychological facts."
> —Marc Bloch, *The Historian's Craft*

P alermo, the summer of 1956. In a room filled with cigarette smoke, a young man in his twenties is sitting behind a typewriter, facing a tall, plump, sixtyish chain-smoking gentleman in short shirtsleeves, who is dictating a text from a scrapbook. This late afternoon, the city is covered in a blanket of heat. Days and weeks are spent on these sessions. On 23 August 1956, the older gentleman notes in his diary that the typescript of his novel has been finished. In the course of this work, the title *Histoire sans nom* (Unnamed Story), has changed into *Il Gattopardo* (The Leopard). The young man's name is Francesco Orlando. The older gentleman is the novelist Giuseppe Tomasi di Lampedusa (1896–1957), who died one year later. As early as 1962, Orlando wrote his *Ricordo di Lampedusa* (published in Milan: All'Insegna del Pesce d'Oro, 1963). This slender volume of memoirs is still a good read (Orlando 1996).[1]

## A Sicilian Prince and a Baltic Baroness

When Orlando made the acquaintance of the eccentric Prince of Lampedusa in late 1953, he was a nineteen-year-old law student (Orlando 1996: 9). The Prince was at that time living with his wife Alessandra ("Licy") Wolff (1894–1982), a German Baltic baroness, in a large mansion near Palermo's

---

harbor. The couple had married in Riga in 1932—quite suddenly, to the horror of Giuseppe's mother Beatrice (1870–1946), to whom he was much closer than to his father Giulio (1868–1934) (Gilmour 1996: 67–68). From the latter, Giuseppe inherited two titles: Duke of Palma and Prince of Lampedusa (in 1934). His wife, Licy Wolff, was an erudite woman as well as a practicing psychoanalyst. During the Second World War, she was forced to abandon her large castle near Riga. The well-read couple spent many delightful evenings reading Marcel Proust's *A la recherche du temps perdu* to each other (Gilmour 1996: 61). Orlando was one of the small group of young men to whom Lampedusa would lecture on English literature during the summer of 1954 at his home on Via Butera, as he had in previous seasons on English language and grammar. During the 1920s, Lampedusa had traveled extensively in England. But his Britain was very much that of his own social class: he spent his time visiting famous historic sites, castles, stately homes, and society parties (Tomasi di Lampedusa 2010: 227). His uncle was then Italian ambassador to the Court of St. James, where Lampedusa met his future wife Licy. He also developed a fondness for England, its literature, humor, and long-standing parliamentary tradition (Gilmour 1996: 53–56).

It was his contact with Lampedusa that made Orlando change studies after a few years, from law to literature. In 1984, Orlando would become the first Italian professor of literary theory at the University of Pisa. In addition to his recollections on Lampedusa, Orlando published *L'intimità e la storia. Lettura del "Gattopardo"* (1998) as well as many other works on literary theory, especially from a Freudian perspective. "Life and works of an author can, without any doubt, illuminate each other," Orlando (1996: 90) writes in *A distances multiples*, but "never presuppose a simple homogeneity between those two incommensurable phenomena."

Lampedusa probably started writing *The Leopard* in late 1954. His nephew Gioacchino ("Giò") Lanza, whom he would adopt shortly before his death and who was attending the same literature class as Orlando, says that the last Prince of Lampedusa's final years were entirely dedicated to writing—not only *The Leopard*, but also the first part of his autobiography, a fragment of a new novel, and a short story (Lanza Tomasi 2000: 13). In Orlando's words, "literature was the great occupation and consolation of this nobleman from whom various patrimonial misfortunes had removed all worldliness and practical usefulness" (quoted in Gilmour 1996: 106). In his earlier life, this silent and socially isolated gentleman of Sicilian dynastic extraction had merely read the best English, French, and German literary authors, such as Shakespeare, Joyce, Stendhal, Proust, Goethe, and Mann, each in their own language. He also read the great Russian novelists, but then in translation. Although he was also well read in Italian literature, he was less fascinated by it.

## The Problem: Late Writership

The enigma of Lampedusa's transformation into a writer is related to what the late Edward Said (1935–2003) wrote in his posthumously published book *On Late Style* (2006). Said wondered how the approaching death of a writer or composer eventually allows him to cope with anachronisms, anomalies, and exile in his work. Said's analysis of "late style" in terms of the evolution of a creative life is strongly inspired by Adorno's analysis of Beethoven's late works. In this context, "lateness" refers to creative performances rife with deep conflict and dazzling complexity. Another fascinating trait of "late style" is that it contradicts what is *en vogue* at the time of its manifestation. In Said's (2006: 24) own words, "late style is *in*, but oddly *apart* from, the present." When Lampedusa's novel appeared in print, it caused consternation among the surviving noble families of Palermo, but, as these met each other in closed circles, their indignation seldom reached the press (Gilmour 1996: 190). Outside Sicily, his Italian critics, themselves also famous writers and historians, at first found it unsatisfying as a literary experiment, while its political vision—which was identified as the author's own—of the history of Sicily and Italy, especially of the unification movement (the *Risorgimento*), was judged as cynical, pessimistic, fatalistic, conservative, and even reactionary (Gilmour 1996: 186–87).

The questions central to this chapter are the following: why did Lampedusa start writing his novel at this mature age? How was this exceptional reader able to transform himself in such a short time into a major writer? Was his earlier lethargy broken by a turning point or crisis in his later life, or by some sudden conversion to authorship? Recent literature on conversion rejects the traditional view of sudden shifts, instead highlighting it as a more gradual and time-consuming process (see, e.g., Bremmer 2006). And in *The Language of Autobiography*, John Sturrock (1993) argues that the autobiographer himself is eager to construct turning points in his life in order to stress its unique aspects. On the other hand, the anthropologist Victor Turner (1920–1983) has pointed out that the coming out of a new identity is often preceded by a liminal phase (Turner 1969 and 1974). Although Turner's view on liminality primarily refers to the processual structure of rituals, it can also be construed as a state of mind evoked by the crossing of temporal thresholds such as old age, incurable illness, or approaching death. Do we reach a deeper insight into Lampedusa's late call to authorship if we interpret his explosion of literary creativity as a liminal phase? I hope to show that in the writer-ship of Lampedusa, this liminal state of mind had been deeply affected by his wrestling with "ultimate ambiguities" — such as finding, at last, a literary vocation in his dull and calm life (but without *le plaisir de se voir imprimé*) — and his fear of death.[2] This kind of liminality also led to the typical fusion of tragic and playful elements so characteristic of his mas-terpiece, *The Leopard*.

## Death, Manuscripts, and a Movie

Lampedusa did not live to enjoy his fame. In January 1955, his phy-sician told him that he had emphysema. He knew that his energy was diminishing. His difficulty breathing reminded him constantly that he was not well. In May 1957, a leading pulmonologist in Palermo exam-ined the Prince; the diagnosis was lung cancer, and "Lampedusa's morale collapsed" (Gilmour 1996: 155). Shortly before he passed away in Rome in July 1957, following unsuccessful treatment of the diagnosed tumor, another major Italian book publishing firm had turned down his manu-script. On his deathbed, he had his spouse and his adopted son promise never to have it published at their own expense. And that is what hap-pened. After the author Giorgio Bassani had been given the typescript, the novel was published by Feltrinelli in 1958. The posthumously published novel *Il Gattopardo* won The Strega Award, Italy's highest literary prize, in 1959; the English translation *The Leopard* followed the year after, and, ever since, the book has had the reputation of a masterpiece.

However, when it was about to go to press, Bassani found a second ver-sion in manuscript at the widow's home in Palermo. Under the pressure of the moment, it was decided that the new manuscript was to be followed, with two additional chapters that Lampedusa had read to Francesco Orlando in April 1957, but which the latter had been unable to type out. Until 1968, the Bassani edition would remain the undisputed basis of all reprints and translations. In that year, experts began to challenge the authority of the second manuscript. The title page of the first manuscript, after all, carried Lampedusa's own handwritten note: *completo*. In 1968, a Sicilian professor claimed to have found "hundreds of variations" between the two versions (Gilmour 1996: 152). In spite of Lampedusa's adopted son Giò Lanza Tomasi's laconic reaction that there was no question of an "essentially different novel," the second manuscript has formed the basis for all subsequent editions (Lanza Tomasi 2000: 13).[3] In 1963, the fame of *The Leopard* received a boost when Luchino Visconti (1906–1976), who like Lampedusa was of Italian noble descent, turned it into a spectacular film.

Visconti's cinematic version of *The Leopard* figures prominently in Said's analysis. *The Leopard* marked the beginning of Visconti's fascination with degeneration in all its manifestations, often closely related to the decline of an old aristocratic world (Said 2006: 94–95). After *The Leopard*, Visconti directed the historical films *Death in Venice, The Damned, Ludwig, The Stranger*, and *The Innocent*. His death in 1976 prevented Visconti from completing the film he would have loved to make of Marcel Proust's *A la recherche du temps perdu*. Said is right to note that there is already a lot of Proust in Visconti's *The Leopard*. I would like to add that the Proust imagined by this Marxist film director was essentially the hilarious Proust who at the end of his novel ripped the old and new aristocracies of the Parisian *salons* into shreds (Kuiper 2010: 43). It is significant that Visconti's *Leopard* ends with a grand society ball, situated in Palermo in 1862, but with a strong whiff of *fin de siècle* Paris. "Unlike Proust, Lampedusa is neither a snob nor a gossip," Said (2006: 98) writes, but a "real aristocrat." His intention was not to "retrieve time" or to record each and every snub which the aristocratic world had dealt to him. Orlando (1996: 53) noted in his recollections that Lampedusa was a great admirer of Proust, but that he could also typify him as "a *chroniqueur mondain*, effeminate and snobbish."

In the definitive printed edition of *The Leopard*, the detailed description of the 1862 ball in chapter 6 is followed by the key chapter 7, in which the protagonist Don Fabrizio, Prince of Salina, dies about twenty years later, in the summer of 1883. Seated in an armchair on the sea view balcony of a hotel in Palermo (some researchers claim that this hotel is on the street where the author himself spent the last twelve years of his life), his health undermined by an exhausting trip to Naples, he reflects on his life as the last Prince of Salina (Cainen 1998: 71). Looking back in resignation he considers: "It was useless to try to avoid the thought, but the last of the Salinas was really himself. . . . For the significance of a noble family lies entirely in its traditions, that is its vital memories; and he was the last to have any unusual memories, anything different from those of other families." (Lampedusa 1991: 285–86)

On his deathbed, Don Fabrizio draws up the balance of his life. When all is said and done, he had only been living life to the full for two or three years. Among his assets he counts his honeymoon, the joy of the birth of his first son, several conversations with his other son, and the hours spent studying the stars in his observatory. But were these hours really the assets of life or an advance on the beatitude of death? He remembers his hounds and his horses (the latter already more distant than his hounds), his country seat Donnafugata ("tradition and eternity expressed in stone and water, time solidified"), his hunts, his medal of honor from the Sorbonne, the beauty and the character of his daughter Concetta ("a real Salina"), some instants of amorous passion, and, finally, a young, sensuous woman he had seen the day before at Catania railway station, in her brown traveling dress with deerskin gloves (Lampedusa 1961: 258–59). Hours later, when the end is near and the entire family is gathered around his bed, suddenly the young lady from Catania station appears, coming to fetch the Prince. Lampedusa (1961: 260) writes, "She looked lovelier than she ever had when glimpsed in stellar space." Visconti's *Leopard* does not include this scene. While Lampedusa is delicately painting how an elderly aristocrat experiences his final hours, Visconti's Hollywood spectacle transposes this private story into the history of Italy around the struggle for national unification in the early 1860s.

## Autobiography or Historical Novel?

When Francesco Orlando first visited Lampedusa on the Via Butera, he noticed that this bibliophile kept two separate libraries, one literary and one historical, each in separate rooms on different floors (Orlando 1996: 17). Orlando describes both libraries in great detail. When the Prince was lecturing on his literary heroes, he would often bore his young audience with long digressions on the political constellations of these authors' lifetimes. A major plus point of the *The Last Leopard*, the magnificent biography published by David Gilmour in 1988, is that it confronts the question of whether *Il Gattopardo* is a historical novel or an autobiography. Until her death, the Princess of Lampedusa denied that it was the latter. Her late husband was nothing like Don Fabrizio, and *Il Gattopardo* was therefore definitely not a *roman à clef*. In his letters to some old friends, including one Baron di Tagliavia, Lampedusa says something different. Don Fabrizio was of course his own great-grandfather, although some intimate friends felt he was indeed much like the author himself. Yet everything Lampedusa writes about the Prince of Salina is consistent with the biography of this great-grandfather Giulio, Prince of Lampedusa (1815–1885): his houses, his astronomy, his skeptical *habitus*, his German mother, his refusal to become a senator (Colquhoun 1960: xii). To a friend in Brazil, Lampedusa wrote, "Don Fabrizio expresses my ideas completely, and his nephew Tancredi is, so far as appearance and habits are concerned, a portrait of Giò; as for his morals, however, Giò is fortunately very much better than him" (Gilmour 1996: 163).

Gilmour feels that both Lampedusa and his widow were exaggerating the point, as were those critics who opted for either autobiography or historical novel. Gilmour's conclusion that it actually is both follows Lampedusa's English translator Archibald Colquhoun. In a biographical appendix to his translations of the 1960s, Colquhoun (1962: 25) writes, "Don Fabrizio is neither historical symbol, family memoir, self-portrait, nor wish-fulfilment, and yet something of all four." He also relates how Prince Niscèmi, Lampedusa's cousin, told him how Lampedusa had considered adding a final chapter on the Allied invasion of Sicily in 1943. Could he also have intertwined his description of Garibaldi's landing on Sicily in 1860 with his own memories of the arrival of the American troops in Palermo? Yet the strength of the novel, as Colquhoun concludes, is not in the verisimilitude of persons or events, let alone of political positions, but in "its poetry about the human condition" (25). This vision closely follows that of E.M. Forster (1960), who interpreted *The Leopard* not as a historical novel but rather as "a novel which happens to take place in history."

It would indeed be foolish to peruse *The Leopard* with the aim of studying the history of Sicily. It is nevertheless obvious that Lampedusa's novel was written to reclaim some part of [Sicilian] history through the resources in the author's own historical library. For example, in order to obtain an adequate image of Garibaldi's triumph on Sicily and of the emotions this stirred up in aristocratic circles, he read the printed diaries of young aristocrats who had joined the battle. Not surprisingly, Gilmour reveals Lampedusa's great interest in historians of the French *Annales* school, particularly Marc Bloch.

In this context, it is clear why Lampedusa, along the lines of Joyce's *Ulysses*, initially intended to describe a single day of the events on Sicily during the national unification of Italy, which he saw as a watershed heralding the decline of the Sicilian nobility in the following five decades. In the process of writing, he soon parted from the Joyce formula. In its final cut, the novel includes scenes from the early 1860s (chapters 1–6), 1883 (chapter 7), and 1910 (chapter 8). Historical novel or autobiography? A third possibility: the novel is also a family history. The change in its title from *Histoire sans nom* into *Il Gattopardo*, although only mentioned by Gilmour in a single footnote, is quite telling. Firstly, as Gilmour also noticed, in standard Italian a *gattopardo* is not exactly a leopard. It refers to the serval, a feline predator living in sub-Saharan Africa. According to Lampedusa's Italian biographer Andrea Vitello, however, the leopard in Lampedusa's coat of arms is called *gattupardu* in the local dialect of Torretta, the Sicilian village where his family had a country estate (Vitello 1963: 22). The new title of the novel is indeed an obvious reference to family history and heraldry and, on a more subjective note, to the family's aristocratic self-perception.

Reading *Il Gattopardo* as a family history clarifies, among other aspects, the ambiguous, complex, and multi-interpretable ways that family members cling together in this aristocratic setting. By focusing on the enigmatic character of Don Fabrizio, who is described from several angles, the author is able to come much closer to his family and eventually to himself. His many references to animals and to the ways they are treated also shed new light on this family. Don Fabrizio's favorite dog, Bendicò, Lampedusa once wrote, is "a vitally important character and practically the key to the novel" (Colquhoun 1962: xii). At first sight, his mention of a bomb made in Pittsburgh, Pennsylvania, in the chapter on the Palermo ball in 1862, appears somewhat anachronistic. It is in fact an intentional anachronism, referring to the Allied carpet bombing of Palermo in 1943, when the Palazzo Lampedusa was reduced to ruins, sealing the fate of an old aristocratic family whose pedigree could be traced back to a sixth-century Byzantine emperor.

## History and Memory

The events in the first six chapters of *The Leopard* cover the period from 1860 to 1862. The main themes are the political vicissitudes of Sicily and the betrothal of the impetuous Tancredi, Don Fabrizio's nephew and protégé, to the beautiful Angelica, the daughter of the mayor and major landowner Calogero Sedàro. The latter represents a rising class of nouveaux riches and also, as Lampedusa discreetly hints, a relatively new defining element in Sicilian history: the rise and activity of Mafiosi during the second half of the nineteenth century (see Blok 1974: 11). Chapter 1 introduces Don Fabrizio's extended family in the wake of Garibaldi's invasion of Sicily in May 1860. Soon after that, Tancredi, who is from the prestigious but impoverished house of Falconeri, tells his uncle in what has become the most-quoted line of the entire novel, "If we want things to stay as they are, things will have to change" (Lampedusa 1961: 35). This paradox has been explained in many different ways, usually as the author's own view of Sicily's long domination by foreign powers. None of these political usurpations ever led to essential change. Apparently, the Prince would have preferred Tancredi to join the incumbent Bourbon king, Francis II, than Garibaldi's self-styled freedom fighters—as far as he was concerned, a mere bunch of Mafiosi intriguers. Tancredi counters that he is actually fighting for another king, namely Victor Emmanuel II, of the House of Savoy, and that his support for the *Garibaldini* or Redshirts is meant to prevent them from turning Italy into a republic. With the one-liner quoted above, Tancredi then leaves his uncle in distress. The Prince foresees a dreadful death for his nephew, as miserable as the dead Neapolitan soldier whose putrid corpse he had once found in the garden of his villa outside Palermo.

It must have come as a relief to Lampedusa when the Savoyards eventually marginalized Garibaldi. In August 1862, a colonel in the Royal Army shot the charismatic revolutionary in the foot. In chapter 6, Lampedusa depicts this officer as a proud guest of honor at the Palermo ball.

After Tancredi's departure, the Prince and his dog Bendicò move to his study in the Villa Salina. His eyes are wandering along the rows of antique paintings of the Salina land holdings when his steward and a tenant visit him with the reassuring words that the national unification will not spill a single drop of blood and no harm whatsoever will be done to the nobility. Father Pirrone, the chaplain with whom the Prince often observes the stars, has different feelings. When he predicts that the revolution will eradicate both the Church and the nobility, the Prince in turn quotes Tancredi's advice that neither of them should cling to their respective authority and status.

In November 1860, a senior government envoy visits the Prince at Donnafugata to invite him to become a member of the National Senate, bearing in mind his influential position as a representative of the high aristocracy. Don Fabrizio declines the offer for two reasons. First, he confronts his guest, who is himself a Knight, with Sicily's long tradition of colonial and absentee government. Second, he expresses his disdain of the new class of powerful landowners and their political accomplices: "We were the Leopards, the Lions; those who'll take our place will be little jackals, hyenas" (Lampedusa 1961: 191). The Prince takes his time to convince his guest that he has good reasons to refuse his offer: "Sleep, my dear Chevalley, sleep, that is what Sicilians want, and they will always hate anyone who tries to wake them, even in order to bring them the most wonderful of gifts; and I must say, between ourselves, I have strong doubts whether the new Kingdom will have many gifts for us in its luggage. . . . That is my answer to you too, my dear Chevalley: the Sicilians never want to improve for the simple reason that they think themselves perfect; their vanity is stronger than their misery" (183). The Prince finishes his exuberant argumentation by referring to the inciting ideas of Proudhon and Marx ("some German Jew whose name I can't remember"): "[It] is all due to feudalism; that, my fault, as it were. Maybe. But there's been feudalism everywhere, and foreign invasions too" (189). It will turn out, in chapter 7, that Tancredi succeeds in joining the new ruling class. In 1883, when the Prince dies, Tancredi has become a successful politician and diplomat of the new kingdom. His mésalliance with Angelica has supposedly earned him this position.

In this couple, two worlds meet: the old nobility and the new bourgeoisie, which has earned its fortune through speculation and blackmail. Lampedusa describes this from the Prince's perspective. Don Fabrizio despises Don Calogero, Angelica's father, a calculating man without erudition or manners, but is captivated by the charm and beauty of Angelica herself. Although his own daughter Concetta is madly in love with Tancredi, the Prince asks for Angelica's hand on Tancredi's behalf. In chapter 4 (November 1860), Tancredi and Angelica wander through all the rooms of the impressive country estate. Lampedusa turns this into a subtle description of a titillating tour, rife with lust and curiosity. Two years later, at the Palermo ball, Angelica, now Tancredi's fiancée, meets Don Fabrizio in the library, where he has retired for a brief meditation on his own death, inspired by a macabre painting. Tancredi, arm in arm with Angelica, ironically guesses his mood: "Uncle, you are courting death" (234). After the Prince has accepted Angelica's invitation for a dance, he feels more rejuvenated with every turn of the waltz they are dancing. "For a second, that night, death seemed to him once more 'something that happens to others'" (236). At dawn, when the Prince is walking home alone after the ball and routinely looking at the sky, he notices Venus, familiar to the astronomer he is. Yet he wonders when she will receive him in her residence of eternal security.

Throughout the entire novel, religion is closely associated with death. The very first line is telling: *Nunc et in hora mortis nostrae. Amen* ("Now and in the hour of our death. Amen") (Lampedusa 1961: 13). In the following lines we meet the whole Salina family reciting their daily rosary in the drawing room of the Villa Salina. And in the final paragraph of the last chapter of the book ("Relics"), the skeleton of the Prince's favorite dog, Bendicò, which has been treated by his children as a relic for many decades, is thrown away by his favorite daughter, Concetta, now a pious old lady: "A few minutes later what remained of Bendicò was flung into a corner of the courtyard visited every day by the dustman. During the flight from the window, its form recomposed itself for an instant; in the air one could have seen dancing a quadruped with long whiskers. . . . Then all found peace in a heap of livid dust" (285). In the book, religion usually refers to the Roman Catholic Church, to its officials and rituals. In a later addition to the manuscript, Father Pirrone, the rustic priest mentioned above, is explaining to his audience in his native village that it is the primary task of the clergy to reassure the elite about the afterlife. But his old friends, most of them petty landowners, are more concerned with the old elite's view of the revolution. The local abbey has lost much of its land holdings to one major speculator. Pirrone then takes his time to answer these concerns. He tells them that it is not easy to understand these *signori*. They are living in a different world with a very strong collective memory, which explains their concern with quite different matters than we care for. The peasants fail to understand their former fellow townsman when he pontificates that the splendor of the *palazzi* and *ville* of the *signori* is something impersonal, like the luster and the liturgy of the Church. The aristocracy has great tenacity as it is constantly innovating. Not feudal titles nor large land holdings make a gentleman, but the feeling of being different from commoners.

In his *Les cadres sociaux de la mémoire* (1925), the French sociologist Maurice Halbwachs characterized the existence of the nobility (or, as we would say today, the idea of "nobleness") as *un phenomène du croyance*, a matter of belief. This concept of belief (if not faith) has inspired recent research in the tradition of Pierre Bourdieu on nobility in a denobled society such as modern France (see Saint Martin 1993: 10–11). Halbwachs (1992: 134) attached this "fiction of noble blood" to the world view and mentality of the nobles themselves: "The essential thing is the fiction of the continuity of titles. What counts is the belief that titles are transmitted from generation to generation together with personal qualities that they represent, so that those who possess them today can lay claim to the valor of those who attained them in the first place." But the part played by Pirrone in the plot of *The Leopard* shows perfectly how important brokers like this family chaplain were in spreading the belief of the nobility's otherness among other groups in society.

According to Orlando, Lampedusa himself was not a religious person. "Everything ends here on earth," he once said "sharply and slowly" in a serious conversation with his pupil (Orlando 1996: 64). In *The Leopard,* the term "religion" is only once explicitly used by the author to switch Don Fabrizio's description of the young women at the society ball from a "zoologic vision" ("the group of crinolined monkeys") to "religion," referring to girls who were perpetually exclaiming to each other "Maria! Maria! The name of the Virgin, invoked by that virginal choir, filled the gallery and changed the monkeys back into women, since the *wistiti* of the Brazilian forests had not yet, so far as he knew, been converted to Catholicism" (Lampedusa 1961: 228–29).

Death and memory are both central themes in *The Leopard*. Stars and houses are intimately connected with them. During his final weeks at the clinic in Rome—when he knew that the treatment was now only palliative—Lampedusa was still changing scenes in the chapter "The Ball," in which the protagonist considers his own death. Smells, melancholic sentiments, changing moods, ambiguous feelings, repressed desires, and wishes misunderstood are all as much part and parcel of this novel as the political, social, and economic changes to Sicily and the Sicilian aristocracy after 1860. In past decades, historians have written and debated much about macro and microhistory, and about the complementarity or antagonism between the two. Lampedusa's complex, multi-layered novel can be interpreted as a kind of commentary on such a debate on historical method, or even as an experiment to combine a grand narrative of Sicilian political and economic history with the *microstoria* (or personal narrative) of a Sicilian nobleman. The grand narrative has a chronological, linear structure; the personal narrative is more discontinuous, as it is built up in a series of episodes, organized around an event. Said (2006) recognizes in *The Leopard* Antonio Gramsci's vision of the impact of the process of unification on Sicilian society. In Said's view, Gramsci does not interpret the *Risorgimento* as a revolutionary movement, but as *transformismo*, that is "the formation of an ever more extensive ruling class" (102). Said does not know whether Lampedusa ever read Gramsci's *La questione meridionale* (The Southern Question). Nevertheless, in his opinion the views of Lampedusa and Gramsci are close on this subject. The characters of Tancredi and his father-in-law, Don Calogero, in particular can act as evidence here. Is this all there is? No. In his political philosophy, Lampedusa shows himself as "totally anti-Gramsci," Said (2006: 104) states firmly. But one could also argue here that we find in the novel echoes of some of Gramsci's analyses, or even of Gaetano Mosca's (1939) *The Ruling Class*.

In a rich essay on microhistory, Carlo Ginzburg argues that two crucial aspects of *his* kind of *microstoria* are reduced scale and the explicit use of narrative strategies. Thus microhistory does not restrict itself to the reconstruction of the life of an individual, a family, or a village, or to the narration of individual events. Ginzburgian microhistory shows affinities with modern literature; it skips over the figure of the omniscient historian-narrator and embraces the idea of discontinuity of reality and identity, as shown by authors such as Woolf, Musil, Joyce, and Proust. "Hypotheses, the doubts, the uncertainties became part of the narration; the search for truth became part of the exposition of the (necessarily incomplete) truth attained" (Ginzburg 2013: 233–34). Are we far removed from Lampedusa's *The Leopard* now? Not at all. In the narration of the elderly Prince of Salina, the reader is confronted with a kind of intersecting macro- and microhistory. For example, the theme of all-pervading mortality in this novel refers to the decay of a whole society, to the vanishing world of a former ruling class, to the degeneration of an old, noble family, and to the death of a protagonist, portrayed by the author as a family giant, a landlord with mercy, and a respected astronomer. This Prince also represents a strong pessimism and shows a permanent lack of initiative to rescue his family from loss of power and prestige. His habitus is a key symbol of the decay of his class (Ortner 1973: 1340). *The Leopard* appears to be a conventional historical novel, but it is not, and it resists simple generalizations. After more than half a century it is still unclear how important the autobiographical drive behind this text was.

## Transformation and Identification

Let us return to the central question of this chapter—the how and why of Lampedusa's late authorship. All his biographers—Orlando, Colquhoun, Gilmour, and Lanza Tomasi—consider the Prince's coping with the destruction of Lampedusa Palace in Palermo in 1943, together with his visit to a literary congress at San Pellegrino Terme in Lombardy in the summer of 1954, as the decisive factors. Some furniture and the bulk of the library of the ruined palace were later installed in Lampedusa's new house on the Via Butera. His wife had allegedly encouraged Lampedusa to write down his memories of his destroyed native house (Colquhoun 1962: 21). Gilmour (1996: 83) writes, "The destruction of his home weighed on him oppressively and continuously, and he thought about little else; ten years later [1953], according to a close friend, he still had not recovered from the loss." When his eccentric cousin Lucio Piccolo was awarded a poetry prize at the 1954 congress, a certain competitive drive was stirred up in him. In March 1956, Lampedusa wrote to his friend in Brazil that he saw himself as "no more foolish" than Lucio and that he had written a novel (Gilmour 1996: 127). The realization that he was not merely the last of his family but also the only one to intimately know the lost world of the Sicilian nobility, both as an insider and as a distant critic, may also have mattered to him. Although still unaware of the tumor that was growing inside him, he had noticed that he was experiencing increasing difficulty breathing.

In the summer of 1955, Lampedusa interrupted his work on *The Leopard* to write his childhood memoirs, with strongly poetic descriptions of his earliest reminiscences of his father's and mother's family estates. He also started rereading Stendhal's autobiography and wrote, "I should like to try and do the same. . . . Indeed it seems obligatory. When one reaches the decline of life it is imperative to try and gather together as many as possible of the sensations which have passed through our particular organism. Few can succeed in thus creating a masterpiece (Rousseau, Stendhal, Proust) but all should find it possible to reserve in some such way things which without this slight effort would be lost forever" (Lampedusa 1966: 33–34). Even more telling is Orlando's (1996: 54–56) observation that after mid-1955, his teacher suddenly began to treat him in a totally different way: haughtier, less patient, and more sarcastic. Orlando is almost too embarrassed to describe this change of attitude which, with hindsight, he attributes to Lampedusa's discovery of his true vocation of being an author. In front of the young commoner Orlando, Lampedusa was no longer the congenial connoisseur of things literary, but rather an aristocrat taking offence at his unfamiliarity with aristocratic mores and manners. On the other hand, Orlando observes, the Prince was developing a growing fondness for his well-mannered nephew Gioacchino, whom he eventually adopted as his son. This was suggested to him by Licy during the winter of 1956. Before the summer, the application was finalized. His newly acquired father gave Giò a box of visiting cards bearing the title "Duke of Palma" (Gilmour 1996: 144).

Orlando's revelation that Lampedusa's two dormant coidentities were reinforcing one another as he was writing *The Leopard* also sheds new light on some aspects of the novel and their potential relationship to the final years of the author himself. Gilmour (1996: 165) feels Don Fabrizio shares many traits with his creator. In his character, autobiography rules over fiction. Don Fabrizio is the person Lampedusa would have loved to be. He himself was rather milder and more indolent than his ancestor, but they shared world views of political abstention and religious conformism. They were no outspoken defenders of the old order, but their attitude towards their own family remained complex, ambiguous, and indeed—as their attitude to the lost houses reveals—not entirely devoid of nostalgia. The Prince's ambiguity is revealed when he is coldly watching his peers during the ball: "And then these people filling the rooms, all these faded women, all these stupid men, these two vainglorious sexes were part of his blood, part of himself; only they could really understand him, only with them he could be at ease. 'I may be more intelligent, I'm certainly more cultivated than they are, but I come from the same stock, with them I must make common cause'" (Lampedusa 1961: 232). Without doubt, these words illustrate the paradox initially identified by Orlando. The recording of his vital memories not only transformed Lampedusa into a novelist, it also strengthened his identification with his aristocratic background. The adoption of "a son" is also a striking aspect of his spurt in identification with an aristocratic worldview.

The last years of Lampedusa's life show several crucial aspects of the models of interpretation of Turnerian liminality and Said's "late style." More than before, Lampedusa felt himself standing outside society (with no significant role for the nobility in it), but, at the same time, he identified himself strongly with his noble ancestors (see also Blok 2013: 274, 277). Writing against the grain, as Said would have it, Lampedusa saw that the great time of the Sicilian nobility was definitely over, so he dived into his family history to rescue the vital memories in which, in his view, the true meaning of a noble dynasty lies. He really knew that he was the last Lampedusa who could tell and show this truth.[4]

## Conclusion: Lampedusa's Liminality

From the very moment that Lampedusa started writing fiction, he crossed a threshold and entered a liminal phase in his later life. In this liminal phase, a new significant other came to life: the Prince of Salina. Lampedusa ritualized and intensified his daily routines a little more by writing nearly every day in his own library or at a table in his habitual pub. Memories inspired his writing, and he started to trigger them by visiting the former villas, palaces, and estates of his family in the small towns in the countryside. Was he courting death? We will never know. After finishing the manuscript of *The Leopard*, Lampedusa continued writing. He did not change his major themes: decay and death. His most productive period was right before the dramatic discovery of his illness. It was an explosion of productivity and creativity, and as such an aspect of liminality: he added two new chapters to his novel, wrote two stories (one short story and a longer one), and even started a new novel. In April 1957, lung cancer was diagnosed, and, on 23 July 1957, Lampedusa died in his sleep in Rome. He was buried in the family tomb at the Capuchin monastery near Palermo (Gilmour 1996: 159). His liminal phase as an active but unknown writer had now ended, but soon his late creation *The Leopard* began on its road to world fame.

**Yme B. Kuiper** (PhD Groningen 1993) is emeritus professor of anthropology of religion and historical anthropology at the Faculty of Theology and Religious Studies of the University of Groningen and holds an endowed chair on country houses and landed estates at the same university since 2012. Recent publications include "Tolstoyans on a Mountain: From New Practices of Asceticism to the Deconstruction of the Myths of Monte Verità" (*Journal of Religion in Europe*, 2013), "Mennonites and Politics in Late Eighteenth-Century Friesland," in *Religious Minorities and Cultural Diversity in the Dutch Republic* (Brill 2014), and *Nobilities in Europe in the Twentieth Century* (Peeters 2015).

## Notes

I would like to express my gratitude to Carlo Ginzburg for his stimulating comments on an earlier version of this chapter and for his invaluable advice to read Francesco Orlando's rich biographical sketch of Lampedusa's writership. For many helpful suggestions I am also grateful to Peter Berger, Anton Blok, Jan Bremmer, Justin Kroesen, and Kees Kuiken.

The epigraph is from page 194 of Marc Bloc's *The Historian's Craft* (1953).

1.  For this chapter, I used the French edition, Orlando 1996. The Italian film *The Prince's Manuscript* (*Il manoscritto del Principe*) from 2000, directed by Roberto Andò, is freely based on Orlando's book. In this movie, Jeanne Moreau plays the role of Lampedusa's wife, Alessandra (Licy) Wolff.
2.  There are some striking similarities (and differences!) between the emergence of the authorship of Marcel Proust and Giuseppe Tomasi di Lampedusa. I cannot go into detail here; however, a literary calling and "le plaisir d'observer" are important resemblances, while ridiculing aristocratic mentality against strongly identifying with it represents a striking opposition.
3.  This preface to the Dutch edition is an updated version of the preface to the Italian edition of 1969.
4.  According to Said (2006: 107), "The last Salina is in effect the last Lampedusa, whose own cultivated melancholy, totally without self-pity, stands at the center of the novel, exiled from the continuing history of the twentieth century, enacting a state of anachronistic lateness with a compelling authenticity and an unyielding ascetic principle that rules out sentimentality and nostalgia." I suspect that in Said's phrasing we also meet his own attitude towards death; when he wrote down these words, Said knew that he had only a short life expectancy.

## References

Bloch, Marc. 1953. *The Historian's Craft*. New York: Vintage Books.

Blok, Anton. 1974. *The Mafia of a Sicilian Village: A Study of Violent Peasant Entrepreneurs*. Oxford: Blackwell.

———. 2013. *De vernieuwers. De zegeningen van tegenslag in wetenschap en kunst 1500–2000*. Amsterdam: Prometheus-Bert Bakker. [*The Innovators: The Blessings of Adversity in Science and Art, 1500–2000*, Polity Press, forthcoming]

Bremmer, Jan N., Wouter J. van Bekkum, and Arie L. Molendijk. 2000. eds. *Cultures of Conversion*. Louvain: Peeters.

Cainen, Brian. 1998. *Study Guide to Tomasi di Lampedusa's Il Gattopardo*. Market Harborough: Troubadour.

Colquhoun, Archibald. 1966. "Giuseppe di Lampedusa: A Note by the Translator." In *Two Stories and a Memory*, by Giuseppe [Tomasi] di Lampedusa, 13–26. Harmondsworth: Penguin.

Forster, Edward M. *Spectator*, 13 May 1960.

Gilmour, David. 1996. *The Last Leopard: A Life of Giuseppe Tomasi di Lampedusa*. London: Quartet Books.

Ginzburg, Carlo. 2012. *Threads and Traces: True, False, Fictive*. Berkeley: University of California Press.

———. 2013. "Microhistory: Two or Three Things That I Know about It." In *Theoretical Discussions of Biography: Approaches from History, Microhistory, and Life Writing*, ed. Hans Renders and Binne de Haan, 211–50. Lewiston: Edwin Mellen Press.

Halbwachs, Maurice. 1992. *On Collective Memory*. Chicago: University of Chicago Press.

Kuiper, Yme B. 2010. "Aristocracy, Roman Fleuve, and Culture History: Louis Couperus' *Books of the Small Souls* and Dutch High Society around 1900." *Virtus: Yearbook of the History of the Nobility* 17: 43–58.

Lanza Tomasi, Gioacchino. 2000. "Voorwoord." In *De tijgerkat*, by Giuseppe Tomasi di Lampedusa, 7–27. Amsterdam: Athenaeum-Polak & Van Gennep.

Mosca, Gaetano. 1939. *The Ruling Class*. New York: McGraw-Hill.

Orlando, Francesco.1996. *Un souvenir de Lampedusa, suivi de A distances multiples*. Paris: L'Inventaire.

———. 1998. *L'intimità e la storia. Lettura del "Gattopardo."* Turin: Einaudi.

Ortner, Sherry B. 1973. "On Key Symbols." *American Anthropologist* 75, no. 5: 1338–46.

Said, Edward W. 2006. *On Late Style: Music and Literature Against the Grain*. New York: Pantheon Books.

Saint Martin, Monique de. 1993. *L'espace de la noblesse*. Paris: Éditions Métailié.

St. John, Graham, ed. 2008. *Victor Turner and Contemporary Cultural Performance*. New York: Berghahn Books.

Sturrock, John. 1993. *The Language of Autobiography: Studies in the First Person Singular*. Cambridge: Cambridge University Press.

[Tomasi di] Lampedusa, Giuseppe. 1961. *The Leopard*. London: Collins & Harvill.

———. 1966. "Places of My Infancy." In Giuseppe [Tomasi] di Lampedusa, *Two Stories and a Memory*, 27–70. Harmondsworth: Penguin.

Tomasi di Lampedusa, Giuseppe. 2010. *Letters from London and Europe, 1925–30*. Reading: Alma Books.

Turner, Victor W. 1969. *The Ritual Process: Structure and Anti-Structure*. Chicago: Aldine.

———. 1974. "Liminal to Liminoid in Play, Flow, and Ritual: An Essay in Comparative Symbology." *Rice University Studies* 60: 53–92.

Vitello, Andrea. 1963. *I Gattopardi di Donnafugata*. Palermo: S.F. Flaccovio.

# Index